After Effects 5.0/5.5 │ H·O·T
Hands-On Training

lynda.com/books

By Lynda Weinman and Craig Newman

Design: Ali Karp

After Effects 5.0/5.5 | H•O•T
Hands-On Training

By Lynda Weinman and Craig Newman

lynda.com/books | Peachpit Press
1249 Eighth Street • Berkeley, CA • 94710
800.283.9444 • 510.524.2178 •
510.524.2221 (fax)
http://www.lynda.com/books
http://www.peachpit.com

lynda.com/books is published
in association with Peachpit Press,
a division of Pearson Education
Copyright ©2003 by lynda.com

ISBN: 0-201-75469-X

0 9 8 7 6 5 4 3 2 1

Printed and bound in the
United States of America

H•O•T | Credits

Original Design: Ali Karp, Alink Newmedia *(alink@earthlink.net)*

Peachpit Editor: Cary Norsworthy

Peachpit Project Coordinator: Suzie Lowey

Copyeditor: Rebecca Pepper

Peachpit Production: Myrna Vladic

Peachpit Compositors: Rick Gordon, Emerald Valley Graphics; Deborah Roberti, Espresso Graphics

Beta Testers: Dina Pielaet, Jan Kabili, Leila Toplic

Cover Illustration: Bruce Heavin *(bruce@stink.com)*

Indexer: Steve Rath

H•O•T | Colophon

The original design for *After Effects 5.0/5.5 H•O•T* was sketched on paper. The layout was heavily influenced by online communication— merging a traditional book format with a modern Web aesthetic.

The text in *After Effects 5.0/5.5 H•O•T* was set in Akzidenz Grotesk from Adobe and Triplex from Emigré. The cover illustration was painted in Adobe Photoshop 6.0 and Adobe Illustrator 10.

This book was created using QuarkXPress 4.1, Adobe Photoshop 6.0, Microsoft Office 2001, and After Effects 5.0/5.5 on a Macintosh G4, running MacOS 9. It was printed on 50 lb. Lynx Opaque at Commercial Documentation Services, Medford, Oregon.

Introduction

H•O•T
_____

After Effects 5.0 / 5.5

A Note from Lynda Weinman

It's been a great pleasure to dig back into my After Effects roots. While many people know me as a Web graphics specialist, I started my creative life in filmmaking—specifically by creating special effects and motion graphics for television, music videos, industrial films, commercials, and motion pictures. My professional life in animation began around 1980, when my then-boyfriend owned an animation camera service. He introduced me to a world that I have never wanted to leave. I hate to sound old, but I remember the days before personal computers, when people actually made physical artwork and shot it with analog cameras. While it might seem like a life-time ago, the truth is that within the past 22 years a lot has changed. I don't think I could have fathomed that one little computer program named After Effects would one day replace an ani-mation camera, optical printer, Moviola, and light box.

I started teaching After Effects with CoSa version 1.0, and the first place I taught it was at Art Center College of Design in 1991. It's quite possible that you've never heard of ACCD, but it is among the top art colleges in the world. It was amazing to see students from different disciplines create wonderful projects set to sound with moving graphics. I've been hooked on After Effects ever since, and the good news is that the program keeps getting better and better. To write a book on this software has been a dream of mine since those early days when I was first captivated by the magic and power of this product.

The Hands-On Training series of books is my brainchild, because I believe there is a need for this type of training in the computer book field. In my opinion, most people buy computer books in order to learn, yet it is amazing how few of these books are actually written by teachers. In this book, you will find carefully developed lessons and exercises to help you learn After Effects 5.0/5.5. There are many excellent books out on After Effects, but most if not all are for intermediate to advanced users. This book will help you build the strong foundation you need to approach the more difficult projects that you'll find in those books (many are listed in the Resource Appendix, at the end).

This book is written for beginning After Effects learners who are looking for a great tool to make motion graphics for the Web, CD-ROM, DVD, video, or film. The premise of the hands-on exercise approach is to get you up to speed quickly in After Effects while actively working through the book's lessons. It's one thing to read about a product and another experience entirely to try the product and get measurable results. Our motto is, "Read the book, follow the exercises, and you will know the product." We have received countless testimonials to this fact, and it is our goal to make sure it remains true for all of our hands-on training books.

Many exercise-based books take a paint-by-numbers approach to teaching. While this approach works, it's often difficult to figure out how to apply those lessons to a real-world situation, or to understand why or when you would use the technique again. What sets this book apart is that the lessons contain lots of background information, advice, and insights into each given subject, designed to help you understand the process as well as the exercise.

At times, pictures are worth a lot more than words, and moving pictures are even better! When necessary, we have also included short QuickTime movies to show any process that's difficult to explain with words. These files are located on the **H•O•T CD-ROM** inside a folder called **movies**. It's our style to approach teaching from many different angles, since we know that some people are visual learners, others like to read, and still others like to get out there and try things. This book combines a lot of teaching approaches so you can learn After Effects 5.0/5.5 as thoroughly as you want to.

In this book, we didn't set out to cover every single aspect of After Effects. The manual and many other reference books are great for that! What we saw missing from the bookshelves was a process-oriented tutorial that taught readers core principles, techniques, and tips in a hands-on training format.

We welcome your comments at ae5hot@lynda.com. Please visit our Web site at **http://www.lynda.com**. The support URL for this book is **http://www.lynda.com/products/books/ae5hot/**.

It's Craig's and my hope that this book will increase your skills in After Effects and motion graphics. If it does, we will have accomplished the job we set out to do!

−Lynda Weinman

NOTE | About lynda.com/books and lynda.com

lynda.com/books is dedicated to helping creative professionals understand tools and design principles. **lynda.com** offers hands-on conferences, on-site training, training CDs, and an online movie training library. To learn more about our training programs, books, and products, be sure to give our site a visit at http://www.lynda.com.

About the Author, Lynda Weinman

Lynda Weinman graduated from Evergreen State College in Olympia, Washington, in 1976. She owned two retail stores named Vertigo until 1982, when she left retail to pursue a career in special effects and animation. She has worked on many animation projects, from *Return of the Jedi* to Dodge commercials to Howard Jones videos and industrial films for Apple and Momenta computers. She purchased the first model of the Macintosh computer in 1984, and her life forever changed.

In 1987, Lynda created animatics on a Macintosh FX for the motion picture *Star Trek V*, using Macromind VideoWorks (the predecessor to Macromedia Director) and Super 3D. From that point on, she has never left the computer graphics medium. After having her daughter in 1989, she left film and video production and began teaching full time.

Lynda has written for numerous magazines, including *MacUser, MacWeek, MacWorld, DV, Diem, Step-by-Step Graphics*, and *HOW Design*. She wrote her first book, *Designing Web Graphics*, in 1995 (published in 1996) and has been writing books and teaching ever since. A teacher at Art Center College of Design for seven years, she also taught at UCLA Extension, American Film Institute, and San Francisco Multimedia Studies Program.

lynda.com began as a Web site for her Art Center students and has grown into a business that supports a full-time staff, and multiple locations in Ojai, California. The focus of lynda.com is to provide education for creative professionals. lynda.com produces training materials in the form of books, CD-ROMs, an online movie library, on-site training, and events such as FlashForward2000–2002, and After Effects West.

About the Author, Craig Newman

After graduating from California Institute of the Arts in 1978, Craig Newman began his career in visual effects as an assistant art director on commercials at Robert Abel and Associates, the most well-respected commercial visual effects facility of the day. While there, he worked as technical director on his first feature film, *Star Trek: The Motion Picture*. He also had the opportunity to work on an early Evans & Sutherland computer graphics workstation.

In 1979, at Midocean Motion Pictures, he continued working as art director and learned the techniques of visual effects editing and optical compositing supervision. He oversaw numerous commercial projects for two years. From 1981 to 1986, Craig worked on numerous feature films, commercials, and theme park projects, using his talents in animation, art direction, editorial, and optical supervision. He was also exposed to the first use of computer graphics in the feature film *Tron*.

Craig joined DreamQuest in 1986, where he made major contributions to the development of the company. He started as Animation Department supervisor and quickly moved into the role of production supervisor. At the same time, he worked on numerous feature films in both organizational and creative roles. He was promoted to production manager and finally line producer.

In 1989, seeing a major change in the visual effects industry with the advent of computer-generated imagery, Craig accepted the position of producer at Degraf/Wahrman, one of the industry's first computer graphics boutiques. He produced computer graphics effects for one feature and one theme park ride for Universal.

For the next three years, he freelanced as a visual effects producer for a number of projects that utilized traditional and computer-generated imagery. During this time he expanded his knowledge and contacts in the computer graphics industry.

In 1992 Craig accepted a position at the Walt Disney Company as manager of the Digital Department for Buena Vista Visual Effects. He was responsible for building the department from the ground up. He also continued to creatively supervise a number of feature film projects while serving as administrator of the department.

During the summer of 1996, Craig joined VIFX as the head of digital production. Responsible for management of the 2D and 3D departments, he hired approximately 40 artists for the company, doubling the size of the Digital Department to 80 artists. He also oversaw the training manager and the development of the Training Department.

In 1998, Craig joined Industrial Light + Magic to manage the digital postproduction. He was responsible for approximately 140 artists working in six areas: digital compositing, digital matte painting, matchmove, Rebel Unit, roto/paint, and Sabre compositing.

While Craig's professional focus has been visual effects, he has also written fiction and optioned one screenplay. Craig is currently enjoying the opportunity to act as a consultant.

Our Team

Craig and Lynda enjoy a moment away from their computers.

Craig's family: Robin, Jack, Craig and Nicola (left to right).

Craig's Acknowledgments

Books are wonderful encapsulations of ideas and experiences from many people. This book represents a lifelong desire to reflect what I've learned from others and to carry on a tradition of knowledge that, I believe, enriches all. I am indebted to a number of talented people.

My deepest appreciation to:

Lynda Weinman, my co-author and longtime friend. Thank you for giving me the opportunity to work with you on a subject that has special significance. It's has been one of my dreams to write about visual effects, and this opportunity brought the dream to fruition.

Bruce Heavin, who created the cover art, as well as all the artwork used for the exercises in this book. Thanks for your tireless commitment to visual arts and the inspiration produced by your formidable talent.

Cary Norsworthy, our editor at Peachpit Press, whose thoughtfulness and attention to detail are unsurpassed. Thank you for doing the hard work of making this book exactly what it needs to be.

Ali Karp, our book designer, whose talent and dedication are evident on every page of the book. I am most appreciative.

The Adobe After Effects team, headed up by Steve Kilisky, and all of the After Effects engineers, who have created a great product! Thank you for supporting our efforts. Working with you has been terrific.

Garo Green, who contributed valuable and insightful feedback on the book and exercises, and who himself is a master educator. Thank you for lending your expertise.

The beta test team, Dina Pialet, Leila Toplic, and Jan Kabili. Thank you for working through each exercise and providing the comments that helped to keep us all moving in the right direction. Much appreciation.

The lynda.com staff, Tony Winecoff, Ramey McCullough, and Heather Rowe, who get things done. You made it easy!

My wife, Nicola, and two sons, Jack and Robin, who supply constant support and encouragement.

Lynda's Acknowledgments

This book is the culmination of the work of many! Sincerest gratitude to:

Craig Newman, co-author, friend, and master of visual effects. Who would ever have guessed that we'd end up on these pages together after knowing each other and working together for over 20 years? Kinda scary, but good scary. Thanks for all your hard work—can you believe it's finally done???

To my husband, Bruce Heavin. Thank you for insisting that I get back to my After Effects roots after a long detour. Thank you for loving me, even when I'm a stress-bunny and no fun to be with. I feel very lucky to have found you, and to share my life with you.

To my daughter, Jamie. Rawr! You sick-minded freak! Elm Dancing! Twinsies. Banana Suits. Only you know what I mean, but our private jokes keep me laughing and smiling, even when I'm a stress-bunny! I love you and am very proud to be your mom.

To Garo Green, my partner in crime. It's such a pleasure to work together—thanks for sharing my vision for this book series and making stuff happen 'round da clock!

To Ramey McCullough, my exercise buddy and co-worker at lynda.com. Thank you for kicking my butt up those hills! We'll be riding our first century by the time this book hits the stores. Imagine two computer potatoes doing such a thing ;-).

To the team at lynda.com. Thank you for all your contributions to our company and making me proud to have my name at the helm.

To Leila Toplic of Adobe. Thanks for taking the time out of your busy schedule to read some of the chapters. Your comments were very appreciated!

To the team at Peachpit. It's a joy to work with a company that really cares. We feel right at home with you! Nancy and Cary—you are two of my favorite people. Thanks so much for working with us!

Extra Special with Sugar on Top Acknowledgement to Suzie Lowey at Peachpit. Thanks for going the extra mile—Garo and I really appreciate it!

To Chris and Trish Meyer. Thanks for your moral support and your friendship over the years. It's been great to reconnect, and I respect what you have done for the After Effects community enormously. You guys go!

To the team at Adobe—Erica, Steve, Dave H., Dave S., Dan—and everyone else. You rock so many people's worlds—thank you for making this amazing product.

To David Rogelberg. Thank you for making this book series dream come true. Your support and contributions are appreciated beyond measure.

> **NOTE | The Formatting in This Book**
>
> This book has several components, including step-by-step exercises, commentaries, notes, tips, warnings, and movies. Step-by-step exercises are numbered, and file names and command keys are shown in bold so they pop out more easily. Captions and commentary are in italicized text: *This is a caption*. File names/folders, command keys, and menu commands are bolded: **images** folder, **Control+click**, and **File > Open**. Code is in a monospace font: `<html></html>`. And URLs are in bold: **http://www.lynda.com**.

Opening Files in After Effects 5.5 vs. 5.0

When you open a project file created in After Effects 5.0 (and that's the version we used to create all the project files for this book), you will encounter a warning.

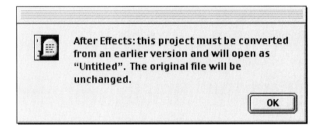

Click OK, and the project will open as originally intended, except that it will appear as an Untitled project until you save it. We chose to leave all the projects as 5.0 projects so readers who had either After Effects 5.0 or 5.5 could use this book.

The After Effects 5.0 Upgrade

If you have worked with past versions of After Effects, the 5.0 upgrade is a must-have! Of most significance is the introduction of 3D layers, parenting, and expressions. Here's a short list of 5.0 feature enhancements:

- 3D compositing—manipulate layers in 3D space and animate lights and cameras

- Parenting—animate layers hierarchically

- Vector paint tools (Production Bundle only)—paint nondestructively on layers over time

- Expressions—create live relationships between layer properties

- New visual effects—Shatter, Radio Waves, Vegas, and Fractal Noise (Production Bundle only)

- Enhanced masking—draw masks in the Composition window, expand masks, and add motion blur to masks

- Enhanced productivity features—improved interactivity, enhanced RAM previews, and changes to the user interface

- Tighter integration with Photoshop, Illustrator, and Premiere

- Output to Macromedia Flash (SWF)—create animations for Web sites

- 16 bit per channel color support (Production Bundle only)—use high-fidelity color support

The After Effects 5.5 Upgrade

While we were in the midst of writing this book for After Effects 5.0, Adobe released an update called After Effects 5.5. The differences between 5.0 and 5.5 are minimal and are noted throughout the book. If you don't use Macintosh OS X, there may not be that many reasons to upgrade to this newer version, since the main reason for this upgrade was to support Macintosh OS X. Here is a short list of other new features distinct to After Effects 5.5:

- Colored shadows and projection layers

- Adjustment lights

- High-quality layer intersections with the Advanced 3D Renderer

- Multiple composition views

- New masking enhancements

- Enhancements to expressions

- Eight powerful new effects, including Color Stabilizer (Production Bundle only), Advanced Lightning (Production Bundle only), Grid, 4-Color Gradient, and Roughen Edges

What Is the Production Bundle?

There are two versions of After Effects 5.0 and 5.5—one that ships with the Production Bundle and one that ships without it. Both versions have a full-featured version of After Effects 5.0 or 5.5; the only difference is that the Production Bundle version includes a lot more advanced and sophisticated effects and is therefore more expensive. As you'll learn in the hands-on exercises in this book, effects offer ways to add extra features to your After Effects movies, such as drop shadows, blurs, lighting, or warping effects. An effect is also called a plug-in and is similar to filter effects in programs like Photoshop or Premiere.

Once you learn After Effects by reading this book and following its step-by-step tutorials, you'll learn the process of working with effects. Some of the Production Bundle effects have settings that are unique to those specific plug-ins. Since this is a beginning-level book, we chose not to cover the Production Bundle effects packages. At the end of this book, in the Resource Appendix, you'll find a lot of other books and resources that will help you advance your After Effects skills beyond this book. We highly recommend that you purchase the Production Bundle if you are serious about working as an After Effects professional. If you can't afford it just yet, however, don't fear! The standard version of After Effects has the same core product as the Production Bundle version.

Macintosh and Windows Interface Screen Captures

Most of the screen captures in this book were taken on a Macintosh using OS 9. We started writing the book using After Effects 5.0, before an OS X version of After Effects 5.5 was available. The only time we used Windows shots was when the interface differed from that of the Macintosh. We made this decision because we do most of our design work and writing on a Macintosh. We also own and use a Windows system, so we noted important differences when they occurred, and took screen captures accordingly.

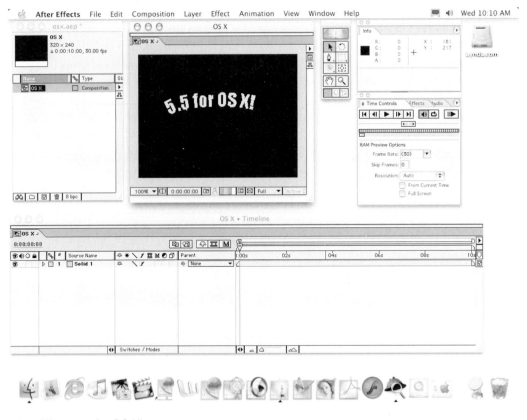

After Effects 5.5 for OS X!

Mac and Windows System Differences

Adobe has done a great job of ensuring that After Effects looks and works the same between the Macintosh and Windows operating systems. However, there are still some differences that should be noted. If you are using this book with one of the Windows operating systems, please be sure to read the following section, "Making Exercise Files Editable on Windows Systems," carefully.

WARNING | "Open" for Mac and "Select" for Windows

Throughout this book, you will be instructed to click the **Open** button. This is the correct way to do it on the Macintosh with OS 9. On a PC running Windows, you will instead see a **Select** button. The two buttons are interchangeable and do the same thing.

WARNING | "Open" in Mac OS 9 and OS X Is "Choose" in OS 8.6

Since some of you will be using OS 8 and others OS 9, it is necessary to be aware of the following difference. When you **Browse for Files**, OS 8 displays a **Choose** button, whereas OS 9 and OS X both display an **Open** button. Both buttons perform the same function, even though they have different names.

Making Exercise Files Editable on Windows Systems

By default, when you copy files from a CD-ROM to your Windows 95/98/2000/NT/XP hard drive, they are set to read-only (write protected). This will cause a problem with the exercise files, because you will need to write over some of them. You will notice that the files have a small lock next to them, which means they have been set to read-only. To remove this setting and make them editable, follow the short procedure below:

1. Control+click on each of the files that has a lock next to it.

2. Once you have all of the files selected, choose **File > Turn Off Read Only**.

After Effects 5.0/5.5 System Requirements

Macintosh

- PowerPC® processor (multiprocessor G4 recommended)

- Mac OS software version 9.1, 9.2.1, or Mac OS X version 10.1 (Note, After Effects 5.0 does not work on Mac OS X)

- 128 MB of RAM installed (256 MB or more recommended)

- 120 MB of available hard-disk space for installation (500 MB or larger hard disk or disk array recommended for ongoing work)

- CD-ROM drive

- 24-bit color display adapter

- Apple QuickTime™ software (recommended)

Windows

- Intel® Pentium® II, III, or 4 (multiprocessor recommended)

- Microsoft® Windows® 98, Windows Millennium Edition, Windows 2000, or Windows XP

- 128 MB of RAM installed (256 MB or more recommended)

- 120 MB of available hard-disk space for installation (500 MB or larger hard disk or disk array recommended for ongoing work)

- CD-ROM drive

- 24-bit color display adapter

- Apple QuickTime™ 5.0 software (recommended)

- Microsoft DirectX 8.1 software (recommended)

WARNING | **Windows XP and QuickTime**

Unfortunately, Windows XP may disable QuickTime. If this happens, try going to the Apple site and downloading the latest QuickTime plug-in. Make sure that After Effects is not open while you do this. If you are using Windows XP, make sure you have installed the latest updates. This is accomplished by choosing **Start > All Programs > Windows Update**. There have definitely been some updates that have affected QuickTime compatibility, so don't neglect to try this!

What's on the CD-ROM?

Exercise Files and the H•O•T CD-ROM

Your course files are located inside a folder called **exercise_files** on the **H•O•T CD-ROM**. These files are divided into chapter folders, and you will be instructed to copy the chapter folders to your hard drive during many of the exercises. Unfortunately, when files originate from a CD-ROM, the Windows operating system defaults to making them write-protected, meaning that you cannot alter them. You will need to alter them to follow the exercises, so please read the preceding section, "Making Exercise Files Editable on Windows Systems," for instructions on how to convert them.

Demo Files on the CD-ROM

In addition to the exercise files, the **H•O•T CD-ROM** also contains free 30-day trial versions of After Effects 5.5 and QuickTime 5.0 software applications for the Mac or Windows. All software is located inside the software folder on the **H•O•T CD-ROM**.

I.

Background

What is After Effects?	Animation	File Formats
AE & Photoshop	Compositing	Video	Video into AE
Digital Images	Other Tools	Learning More

chap_01

After Effects 5.0/5.5
H•O•T CD-ROM

What is After Effects?

After Effects is a program that allows you to compose moving images in the same way an artist might compose a drawing or a painting. It gives you the ability to create relationships between images, sounds, and moving footage. You can compose an animation by positioning images in locations on the screen and moving them or changing their characteristics over time (such as opacity, scale, and rotation). As well, After Effects includes the capability of synchronizing audio to playback with your moving images.

You've already seen footage developed in After Effects, in movies such as "The Matrix," though you might not be aware of it at the time. After Effects is used professionally throughout the motion picture and video industry for title sequences, identity campaigns for television stations, TV commercials, industrial videos, CD-ROMs and DVDs, Web animations and much, much more.

One of the coolest things about After Effects is that you can make a single project, yet publish it to a variety of formats that support video, film, and CD-ROM, DVD, or Web content.

What is Animation?

The word "animation" comes from the Latin word *anima*, which means "life" or "soul." As an artist working with images, you bring them to life when you make them move. Still images can appear to move by arranging them in a specific order and changing from one image to the next in a fairly rapid sequence.

A flipbook is a simple form of animation, but live-action filmmaking and video also bring still images to life. Although not all films and video are classified as being "animated," they all share the same principal of animation.

Animation could be defined as making images move, but that would be an inaccurate definition. In animation, you choose to move an image, or not move an image, as a creative decision. Creatively speaking, animation is an **art process.** Art processes are "open ended," meaning there is no right way or wrong way to do something. Many great works of art have been successful because they broke the rules. An art process is without limits or bounds.

It's easy to understand animation as an art process by this example. Watch a live-action film and notice when a "freeze frame" is used. A freeze frame stops moving a sequence of images in time and holds on a single image for a specific duration. Animation can be defined as "choosing when and how to make images move." A freeze frame is a creative example of animation without motion.

An art process can include **art technique.** There are certain ways of getting things done that work better than other ways. Technique deals with creation from the point of view of making an art process efficient. After Effects is a great tool for efficiently producing animated images, while giving you an extremely broad range of creative possibilities.

In order for you to learn After Effects, we will be teaching both art processes and techniques. It's our hope that, once you learn the specific techniques taught in this book, you will personalize them so they are an expression of your own artistic intentions.

NOTE | Why Does Animation Appear to Make Still Images Move?

Our eyes have sensors that retain an image for a moment. Stare at a high contrast image for a while, then close your eyes. You'll see a ghost image although your eyes are closed. This is called "persistence of vision" or an "after effect" of vision. The name of the computer program, After Effects, comes from this sensory phenomenon.

The whole trick in animation is to have a series of related images and move them quickly enough that our eyes do not perceive the difference between separate images. It takes about 24 individual images per second to overcome the tendency for images to appear to separate and gain an illusion of fluid motion.

What Formats Does After Effects Produce?

As we said earlier, After Effects (also referred to as AE) can be used for film, video, digital video, CD-ROMs, Web and print output. It produces a wide variety of file formats that are specifically tailored for each medium. AE provides ample options to meet the demands of artists and media professionals.

```
    Amiga IFF Sequence
    Animated GIF
    BMP Sequence
    Cineon Sequence
    ElectricImage IMAGE
    FLC/FLI
    Filmstrip
    JPEG Sequence
    MP3
    PCX Sequence
    PICT Sequence
    PNG Sequence
    Photoshop Sequence
    Pixar Sequence
 ✓  QuickTime Movie
    SGI Sequence
    TIFF Sequence
    Targa Sequence
```

The most common format to output from After Effects is QuickTime, which can be published at a variety of resolutions that support everything from Web content to feature film quality. In addition to QuickTime however, it supports all the other formats listed above.

How Does AE Differ From Photoshop?

Photoshop is designed to work with still images. If your project demands high-quality still images, Photoshop is probably the best tool for the job.

After Effects is designed to work with a series of images in motion. It provides specific tools to aid you with making images move. As a tool, it can manage thousands of files, provide composition and animation capabilities, and give you a wide variety of options for media output. After Effects, in our opinion, is the best off-the-shelf package available for the money to perform **compositing** of animation, visual effects and motion graphics.

How is After Effects Different From Avid, Final Cut Pro, and Premiere?

The tools Avid, Final Cut Pro, and Premiere are used for non-linear editing. They are geared towards putting finished video shots together as a single short-form or long-form movie. They don't focus on creating frame-by-frame animation, sophisticated title effects, or the manipulation of special effects. You can do some similar work in these programs, but After Effects has far more features for creating professional animation and motion graphics. You wouldn't want to cut a movie in After Effects, and you wouldn't want to do a title sequence in a non-linear editing program.

How is After Effects Different From Macromedia Flash?

Flash is a tool that combines still images, video, and sound, just like After Effects. As well, through Actions, it is possible to create interactive presentations. Macromedia Flash writes files with vectors and bitmaps, while After Effects writes movie files that are converted entirely to bitmaps, even if the movie contained vector artwork to begin with.

The key difference is that After Effects can render at any resolution—all the way up to IMAX! It has much more sophisticated effects and keyframe manipulation than Flash. You could bring an After Effects sequence into Flash, but After Effects does not offer any interactive features like Flash does.

What is Compositing?

Just as artists compose drawings, paintings and photographs, compositing is a specific form of composing images. In this form, you compose either still images, or moving images, by using image processing techniques. Image processing is a term for specific technical processes that affect images, such as adding a filter like a blur or color, or modifying an image's color or contrast. After Effects allows you to use image-processing techniques without getting bogged down in technical details. It frees you to focus on composition.

Compositing is an art process where you choose to compose images by using image processing. There is no right way or wrong way to composite, but there are techniques and tools that you can employ to make your work efficient and powerful. With After Effects, you can spread a single image across time, smear it like paint, or make it echo like sound. How you use the tool is up to you as an artist.

What is Video?

Video is an electronic system for recording, storing, and displaying moving images. There are different types of video systems that are used throughout the world. For example, North America and Europe have different standards for their video systems. In addition, there are two basic types of video technologies, **analog** and **digital**. As part of the tutorials in this book, we will provide specific information about video systems where they apply to the use of After Effects.

How Do I Get Video Content Into AE?

There are basically three ways to do it. The first method uses Digital Video. You need four things:

- a camera or playback deck with a FireWire port

- a computer with a FireWire port

- a cable to connect the camera with your computer

- software that controls the transfer of digital video into your computer (Premiere is an Adobe tool that enables this type of transfer)

Most computers that have FireWire ports also include the software to transfer digital video. A short list of software products that supports this process is Adobe Premiere, Apple iMovie, Apple FinalCut Pro and Sony MovieShaker, Transferring the footage from camera or video deck to computer is usually a simple process using this method.

In the second method, using analog video, you must convert analog video into digital format as part of the process. This is also accomplished with four components:

- an analog video camera or playback deck

- a computer that has video digitizing hardware

- an appropriate cable to connect the camera with the digitizing hardware

- software that allows you to control the digitizing process.

Digitizing analog video is generally not a simple process and can require a fair amount of time and technical knowledge to ensure success. In general, we recommend using digital video (DV) rather than analog video as source footage for your video projects. The image quality is usually higher with DV and today's technologies make it easy to bring DV directly into your computer.

In the third method, video that has already been transferred to a computer may be available to you on CD-ROM, portable hard disks, or other computer storage media. This video can be copied directly into your computer system and used by After Effects.

Ultimately, all of the images that After Effects uses are digital images.

What is a Digital Image?

Digital images are stored as numbers and can be viewed on electronic devices. Your computer is one type of electronic device that can read numbers, interpret them, and display them as images, just as a digital camera is another type of device that can do the same.

Digital Image

Pixel Values

1	1	1	1	1	1	1	1	1	1	1
1	1	1	1	1	1	1	1	1	1	1
1	1	0	0	0	0	0	0	0	1	1
1	1	0	1	1	0	1	1	0	1	1
1	1	1	1	1	0	1	1	1	1	1
1	1	1	1	1	0	1	1	1	1	1
1	1	1	1	1	0	1	1	1	1	1
1	1	1	1	1	0	1	1	1	1	1
1	1	1	1	0	0	0	1	1	1	1
1	1	1	1	1	1	1	1	1	1	1
1	1	1	1	1	1	1	1	1	1	1

Digital images are formed by picture elements, also called **pixels**. Pixels are the rectangular building blocks that make up an image. The left portion of image above shows a group of pixels that comprise a very simple image. The right side diagrams the numbers, or values, that are associated with each pixel. The number 0 displays as black, and number 1 displays as white in this image.

Digital Image

Pixel Values

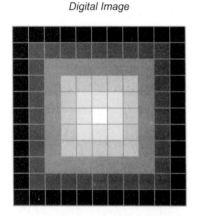

0	0	0	0	0	0	0	0	0	0	0
0	64	64	64	64	64	64	64	64	64	0
0	64	128	128	128	128	128	128	128	64	0
0	64	128	192	192	192	192	192	128	64	0
0	64	128	192	224	224	224	192	128	64	0
0	64	128	192	224	255	224	192	128	64	0
0	64	128	192	224	224	224	192	128	64	0
0	64	128	192	192	192	192	192	128	64	0
0	64	128	128	128	128	128	128	128	64	0
0	64	64	64	64	64	64	64	64	64	0
0	0	0	0	0	0	0	0	0	0	0

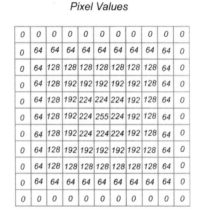

If you want gray tones in the image, rather than just black and white, a broader range of numbers must be specified for each pixel value. A grayscale image is shown on the left, with the associated pixel values on the right. Here the number 0 still displays as black, but the white pixel in the center is defined as the number 255. All the values in-between are grayscale values.

```
Red = 104

Green = 30

Blue = 214
```

What about a color image? A color pixel has three values associated with it—red, green, and blue. This representation of a single pixel shows how red, green, and blue values, or color *channels*, are associated with a color pixel.

What Tools Do I Need Besides AE?

If you are using After Effects to produce animation for the Web, you may only need an image scanner and your computer. For a video project, you'll need access to appropriate hardware for your chosen video system. A motion picture film project might require that you utilize an outside service to scan your film images into digital form and provide the recording of your finished output onto film.

The extra software tools, if you need any, depend mostly on the type of media that plan to create. After Effects can import a wide variety of file formats, allowing you to work with many types of computer art, such as bitmaps (from programs like Photoshop), vectors (from programs like Illustrator), or 3D content (from programs like 3D Studio Max). You don't need extra programs, but it's great to know that if you create artwork in them, you can use these images easily in After Effects.

How Do I Learn More About Animation, Video and Compositing?

This book provides a good introduction to all of these subjects. We'll make sure that you get a strong foundation that will make the process clear. In the back of the book, we've included a reference section of books, videos and CD-ROMs that you can use to further your knowledge.

2.

Interface

First View	Project Window	Composition Window
Timeline	Time Controls Palette	Audio Palette
Info & Toolbox Palettes	Shortcut Keys
Using the Interface

chap_02

After Effects 5.0/5.5
H•O•T CD-ROM

Adobe provides a consistent interface throughout its products. If you've used Photoshop or Illustrator, many of the tools in After Effects will be familiar to you. On the other hand, After Effects is based on some concepts and features that might be new to you too.

Because the program can combine multiple files (unlike Photoshop or Illustrator), it has a Project window that holds all the footage you'll work with. It also has a Timeline window for setting up the motion for your moving images and a Composition window that acts as a stage where you can build, preview, and edit your projects. When working in After Effects, you'll primarily use these three windows. This chapter gives you a quick overview of these windows and walks you through a simple project so you can see how the interface changes in relation to your content. Other chapters will go into much more detail. As you'll see later, the After Effects interface gets a lot deeper when you start to build projects and moving pictures.

First View of After Effects

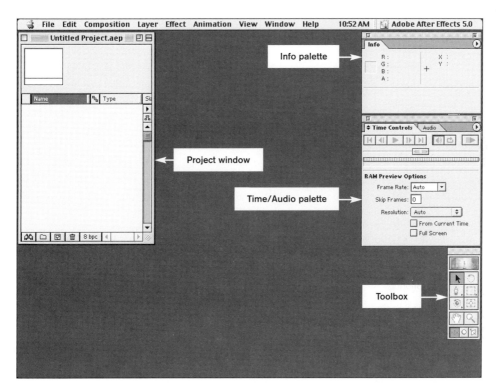

This is what you'll see the first time you open After Effects. The default windows and palettes are the Project window, the Info palette, the Time Controls/Audio palette, and the Toolbox. None of these windows and palettes do anything until you bring content into the program, such as movie footage, Photoshop files, Illustrator files, or other supported document types. You'll learn how to bring in footage very soon!

The Project Window

After Effects is different from many other programs that you might be familiar with, because it uses something called the **Project** to organize content and store the settings you create to produce animation and audio. When you bring artwork into Photoshop, for example, that artwork is saved with the Photoshop document. The project file in After Effects is quite different because the project file only maintains pointers to whatever artwork you import. For this reason, After Effects project files are quite small in file size.

The **Project window** is one of the three primary windows you use in After Effects. Think of it is where you store all the media you'll be working with—from still images to video footage to sounds. The word **footage** is an umbrella term for most media, even still images or audio. Importing or adding footage into your project creates references in the Project window. This means that the footage isn't actually copied into After Effects; instead, the project maintains pointers to where the footage resides on your hard drive.

Whenever you open a new After Effects document, a new empty Project window appears. When you import footage, it appears in the Project window. When you save your work, you save a project file, hence the file extension .aep (After Effects Project). The project file memorizes all kinds of things, including but not limited to the footage references of content you've imported. This will become much clearer as you work through the book.

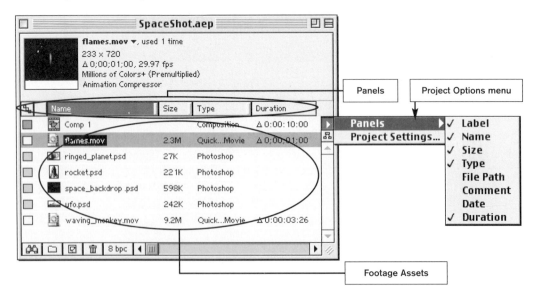

Here's an example of a Project window that is filled with content. Footage references and compositions show up as a list in the Project window.

Panels in the Project window allow you to view details about your footage or composition. They form columns of information showing the name, label, size, type, file path, comments, date, and duration of each item. You can make a panel wider or narrower, and you can rearrange the order of panels simply by clicking and dragging the panel you want to move. You'll learn how to do this in later chapters.

The Composition Window

The **Composition window** is the second of the three primary windows in After Effects. While the Project window contains a list of files and folders, the Composition window is where the visual preview or playback of your project appears. It's the equivalent of a screen area in a movie theater. The Composition window does not appear until you create a composition and open that file. You create and open a composition file from the Project window. You will see how to open a composition later in this chapter.

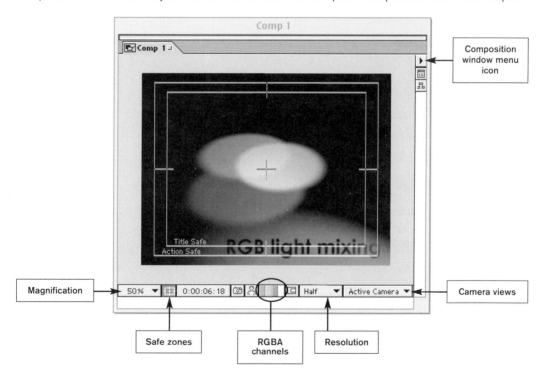

The Composition window is the equivalent of a stage or movie screen. It is where the visual preview of your project appears. You cannot view the Composition window until you create and open a composition. You'll learn how to do this later in this chapter.

The Timeline Window

The **Timeline window** is the third primary window you use in After Effects. Like the Composition window, the Timeline window does not appear until you have opened a composition. It will be missing from your screen until you do this in Exercise 1, later in this chapter.

The main function of the Timeline window is to give you the ability to control time relationships between the various visual elements in your composition. However, it also gives you many other options too, such as the ability to change the position, opacity, scale, rotation, or mask in the Composition window.

The Timeline window also allows you to synchronize audio elements with your moving images. The rich options of the Timeline window will be covered fully in later chapters.

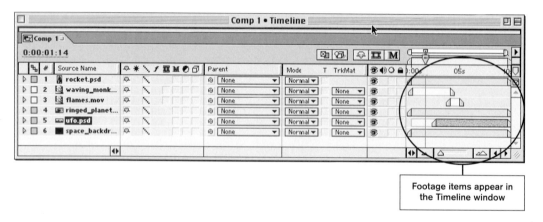

Footage items appear in the Timeline window

Footage elements are arranged in layers in the Timeline window. The length of each layer represents its duration in time. You can cause each layer to start or stop at any point in the composition by adjusting it in the Timeline.

Time Controls Palette

The **Time Controls palette** allows you to preview the compositions you create as moving images. You can play back the entire piece or select a specific frame.

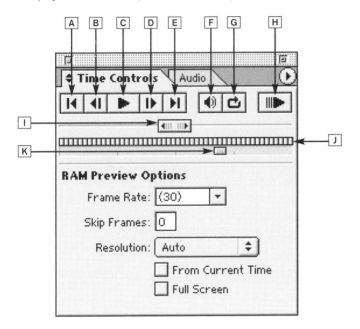

The Time Controls palette: **A.** First Frame; **B.** Previous Frame; **C.** Play/Pause; **D.** Next Frame;
E. Last Frame; **F.** Audio; **G.** Loop; **H.** Ram Preview; **I.** Shuttle; **J.** Jog; **K.** Time Indicator.
These terms are defined in Chapter 5, "Timeline, Keyframes and Animation".

Audio Palette

By default, the **Audio palette** is located in the same window as the Time Controls palette. You can separate the Audio palette into its own window by clicking and dragging the Audio tab.

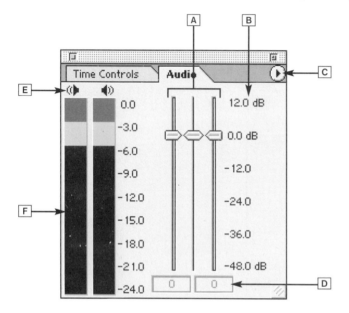

The Audio palette: **A.** *Level controls;* **B.** *Level units;* **C.** *Audio Options menu;* **D.** *Level values;* **E.** *Audio Clipping warning icons;* **F.** *VU meter. The audio level controls allow you to set the volume for each audio layer. The VU (**V**olume **U**nit) meter displays audio levels during playback. You will learn about these terms in Chapter 15, "Audio."*

Info and Toolbox Palettes

The **Info palette** gives you information about images in the Composition window.

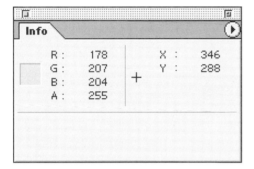

The Info palette.

The **Toolbox palette** provides a number of tools for drawing in the Composition window or for selecting elements and objects.

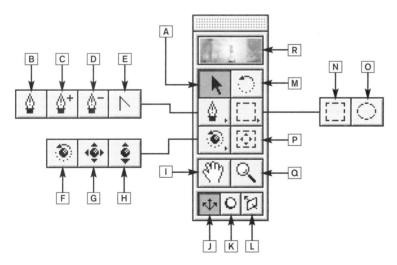

The Toolbox palette: **A.** *Selection;* **B.** *Pen;* **C.** *Add Point;* **D.** *Delete Point;* **E.** *Convert Point;* **F.** *Orbit Camera;* **G.** *Track XY Camera;* **H.** *Track Z Camera;* **I.** *Hand;* **J.** *Local Axis mode;* **K.** *World Axis mode;* **L.** *View Axis mode;* **M.** *Rotation;* **N.** *Rectangle Mask;* **O.** *Oval Mask;* **P.** *Pan Behind;* **Q.** *Zoom;* **R.** *Adobe Online. You will learn about these different tools in future chapters.*

Shortcut Keys

There are many shortcut keys in After Effects, and all of them are listed in your program manual. The following chart lists the ones we find most useful. We will refer to specific shortcut keys throughout the book as you encounter reasons to use them, so don't spend too much time memorizing them here. This list will prove more useful after you have learned the program.

Shortcuts in After Effects		
Command	**Mac**	**Windows**
Open last project	Command+Alt+Shift+P	Control+Alt+Shift+P
Import file	Command+I	Control+I
Set interpret footage options	Command+F	Control+F
Project settings	Command+Alt+Shift+K	Control+Alt+Shift+K
Suspend window updates	Caps Lock	Caps Lock
Display/hide palettes	Tab	Tab
Go to previous visible keyframe	J	J
Go to next visible keyframe	K	K
Scroll current time to center of window	D	D
Scroll selected layer to top of window	X	X
Step forward 1 frame	Command+right arrow	Control+right arrow
Step backward 1 frame	Command+left arrow	Control+left arrow
Start/pause playback	Spacebar	Spacebar
RAM preview	0 on numeric keypad	0 on numeric keypad
Wireframe preview	Alt+0 on numeric keypad	Alt+0 on numeric keypad
Nudge keyframe 1 frame forward	Alt+right arrow	Alt+right arrow
Nudge keyframe 1 frame backward	Alt+left arrow	Alt+left arrow
Nudge layer 1 pixel in specific direction	Arrow key	Arrow key

continues on next page

Shortcuts in After Effects *continued*

Command	Mac	Windows
Nudge layer rotation +1 degree	+ (plus) on numeric keypad	+ (plus) on numeric | keypad
Nudge layer rotation −1 degree	− (minus) on numeric keypad	− (minus) on numeric keypad
Select next layer back	Command+down arrow	Control+down arrow
Select next layer forward	Command+up arrow	Control+up arrow
Zoom in	. (period)	. (period)
Zoom out	, (comma)	, (comma)
Zoom in and resize window	Alt +. (period)	Alt +. (period)
Zoom out and resize window	Alt + ; (comma)	Alt + ; (comma)
Position	P	P
Scale	S	S
Expand/collapse effect controls	` (grave accent)	` (grave accent)
Switch from Selection tool to Pen tool	Hold down Command	Hold down Control
Switch from Pen tool to Selection tool	Hold down Command	Hold down Control

I. —————————**Using the After Effects Interface**

This exercise introduces you to the three primary windows in After Effects and lets you explore the basic functionality of each.

To see the Composition and Timeline windows, you must first open a composition. Compositions are described in full in Chapter 4, "*Compositions*." All you need to know for now is that a composition holds your design.

We have prepared an After Effects project file that you will open in this exercise. The files are located in the **chap_02** folder of the **exercise files** folder that you should have transferred to your hard drive from the **H•O•T CD-ROM**. If you haven't transferred these files yet, please do so now. Make sure that you read the Introduction if you are using a Windows system. It contains important information for Windows users. You will need to unlock the files before you can edit them. This is also described in detail in the Introduction.

1. Launch After Effects and select **File > Open Project**.

As an alternative you can use Command+O (Mac) or Control+O (Win). However, while you're learning After Effects, we suggest using the menus so you see the available options and get to know the interface.

2. In the **Open** dialog box, navigate to the **exercise_files** folder and open the **chap_02** folder. Select **Interface.aep** and click **Open**.

NOTE | After Effects 5.5 Untitled Project

When you open a project file created in After Effects 5.0 (as all the project files for this book were created), you will encounter a warning.

 After Effects: this project must be converted from an earlier version and will open as "Untitled". The original file will be unchanged.

OK

Click OK, and the project will open as originally intended, except that it will appear as an Untitled project until you save it. We chose to leave all the projects as 5.0 projects so readers who had either After Effects 5.0 or 5.5 could use this book.

> ## WARNING | AE 5.5 Users
>
> If you are using After Effects 5.5, the interface.aep project file will open in an Untitled window.
> Everything will still work properly, just don't be alarmed! See the Introduction Chapter for more details.

3. In the **Project** window, locate the item named **Comp 1** and double-click on it to open it.

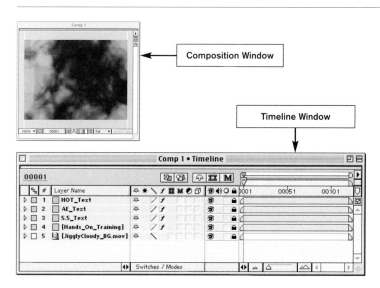

Notice that the Composition window and the Timeline window are open. Inside the Composition window, you'll see a preview of some artwork. Inside the Timeline window you'll see a number of layers with a lot of settings. These settings will be described in detail in later chapters.

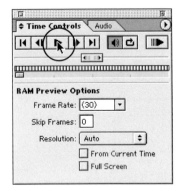

4. In the **Time Controls** palette, locate the **Play** button and click it.

5. Watch the animation play as a preview in the **Composition window**. Click the **Play** button again to pause the animation.

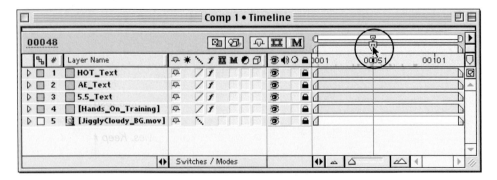

6. In the **Timeline** window, locate the **Time Marker**. Drag the Time Marker left and right, and observe how its position affects the preview in the Composition window.

7. Click the **close window** icon to close the Composition window. ***Note:*** The close button for Windows users is in the upper-right corner of the Composition window.

Observe that the Timeline window also closes. Without an open composition, the Timeline will not appear. To get the Timeline and the Composition windows back, you would double-click Comp 1 in the Project window again.

8. Select **File > Close** to close the **Interface.aep** project.

9. Choose **File > Quit** to quit After Effects.

Congratulations! You've completed your first exercise, and you've gotten a good look at the After Effects interface. Best of all, you've been able to interact with After Effects and see results firsthand. In the next chapter, you'll learn more of the details involved in creating After Effect projects. Soon you'll be making your own compositions, making them move, and saving movies. Keep reading on!

3.

The Project

| What Is a Project? | Setting Up a Project |
| Importing Assets | Organizing Your Project |

chap_03

After Effects 5.0/5.5
H•O•T CD-ROM

Animation, motion graphics, and visual effects often require a large number of individual images that make up a finished piece. Programs like Photoshop and Illustrator store all the artwork for a picture on layers or flattened inside a single layer. After Effects is different in that it keeps art, video, and audio elements separate, allowing you to combine different kinds of documents in unrestricted ways. That is why an After Effects document is called a project instead of a file.

The **Project window** is where you store references to all the footage and image elements for your project. You were introduced to the Project window in the previous chapter. This window helps you organize the images, audio tracks, and compositions used by your project.

In this chapter you'll learn exactly what a project is and you'll see how to set up a project, import images, and organize items using the tools provided in After Effects.

What Is a Project?

An After Effects **project** is a single file that holds references to all of the images, video, and audio files that you'll need for your work. A **reference** is a pointer to the location of a file on your hard drive. After Effects uses references instead of copying the images, video, and audio files into the project file. Your project knows where to find the files it needs because After Effects automatically creates a reference to each file as part of the process of setting up your project.

In After Effects, all images, video, and audio elements—any media that After Effects uses inside a project—are called **footage** items.

In addition to holding references to footage, the project holds one or more **compositions** that you create in After Effects. You'll learn about compositions in detail in the next chapter. For now, think of compositions as your instructions to After Effects regarding the specifics of your design. Compositions hold all the details of exactly what your final product will look like. As the name implies, compositions are what you compose in an After Effects project.

The project is a container for all the footage and compositions that go into the final product that you create. Inside a project you can create a single **shot** or series of shots. In live-action filmmaking, a shot is the viewpoint from a single camera that is edited into film. In After Effects, you can think of a shot in the same way. It is a viewpoint from a single camera.

You can create many versions, or **takes**, of the same shot, and keep all the takes in one project file. This is valuable, for instance, when working with clients. You can automatically maintain a record of exactly what you did in each take during the course of the project.

It's also important to understand that when you save an After Effects document, that you are saving the project, not the individual footage items or compositions. The only way you can save a composition or compositions is to save the project file. Since an After Effects project file can contain multiple compositions, this is important to understand. Each time you save in After Effects, it is saving the reference to where all your footage items reside on your hard drive, and it is saving updated composition file or files. For this reason, project files are very small in file size, while the footage items that they reference might be huge.

Only one project can be open at a time. Closing a project will close all windows associated to it and leave only the palettes open.

I. _____Creating and Setting Up a Project

Setting up a project in After Effects is quite simple. In this exercise, you'll create your first project, set basic project options, and learn to save the project.

When you open After Effects, you will notice that an untitled.aep window appears in the upper left corner of your screen. This is the project window that holds your footage items and compositions. Right now it is empty and untitled because you haven't saved it yet, and you haven't imported any footage or created any compositions.

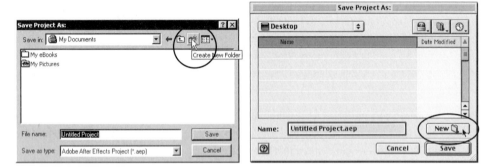

1. Choose **File > Save As**. In the **Save Project As** dialog box, click the **New** button on your Mac or the Create New Folder icon Windows computer to create a new folder with the name "**HOT AE Projects.**"

This will be the place that you store all the exercises that you work on in this book. It's important to save your exercises in a different folder, so that you don't write over the originals.

2. Navigate inside the new **HOT AE Projects** folder that you just created.

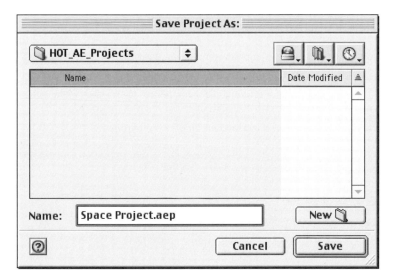

3. Name the file "**Space Project.aep.**"

4. Click **Save**.

You've now successfully created a project and saved it. It's time to import footage into your project. You'll learn how to do this next.

Importing Assets

As we stated earlier, images, video, and audio tracks that are used in a project are called footage items. All footage items are considered to be **assets** for your project. Think of assets as valuable items necessary to create new compositions. Given how long it can take to create images, video, or sounds, they are truly assets!

Remember, when you import assets into After Effects, you don't actually copy the files into your project. With the import process, you are creating references inside your project to files that reside on your hard drive. In the following exercises, you will learn to import several different types of footage assets into your new After Effects project. Each type of footage asset has its own characteristics, and After Effects offers many options to take advantage of various file formats.

2. _____Importing Photoshop Documents

We have prepared a series of Photoshop files that you will learn to import in this exercise. The files are located in the **chap_03** folder of the **exercise files** folder that you should have transferred to your hard drive from the **H•O•T CD-ROM**. If you haven't transferred these files yet, please do so now. Make sure that you read the Introduction if you are using a Windows system. You will need to unlock the CD-ROM files before you can edit them. This is also described in detail in the Introduction.

1. Choose **File > Import > File**, and navigate to the folder called **01_space scene** inside the **chap_03** folder on your hard drive.

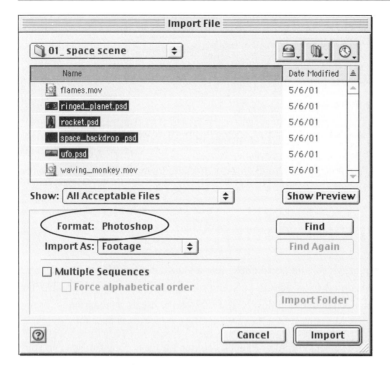

2. Select all the items that end in **.psd** by holding down the **Shift** key as you click on each file. The **Import As: Footage** option should be selected. Click **Import** (Mac) or **Open** (Windows). *Note:* Using the Shift key allows you to select multiple files.

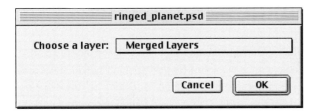

3. For each item, you'll see a prompt box like this. Click **OK** for each item.

Photoshop files can have multiple layers. This import process ensures that all layers are flattened or "merged" for this particular project. You will learn to work with more complex layered Photoshop files in future chapters.

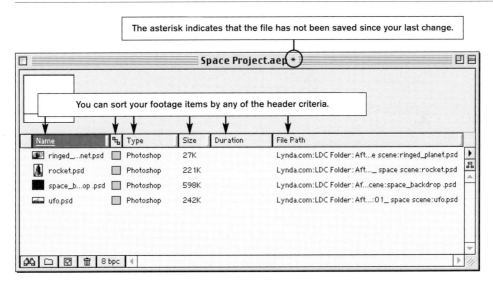

4. Widen your Project window and observe the additional information available. You can click on any of the Panel headings, Name, Label, Type, Size, Duration or File Path to sort the project by those criteria. Narrow the Project window to return it to a smaller view, and make sure that the **Name** header is selected.

In the Project window title bar, an asterisk appears at the end of the file name. This means that you've made changes to your After Effects project that have not been saved.

5. Save your project now, either by choosing **File > Save**, or by pressing **Command+S** (Mac) or **Control+S** (Windows). Leave the file open; you will continue to work with it in the next exercise. Notice that the asterisk goes away as soon as you save the file. The asterisk is a handy message from After Effects to remind you to save your work.

3. ——————————Importing Illustrator Documents

Illustrator files are great to work with in After Effects. That's because they are resolution independent, unlike Photoshop files. This means that if you zoom into an Illustrator file during an animation, it will stay crisp and in perfect focus. A Photoshop file would get progressively blurry, depending on how high the magnification of your zoom into the artwork was. For this reason, After Effects and Illustrator work really well together. Importing Illustrator files is quite simple, as you'll soon learn.

1. Choose **File > Import > File**, or as a shortcut, press **Command+I** (Mac) or **Control+I** (Windows).

2. Navigate to the **chap_03 > illustrator files** folder.

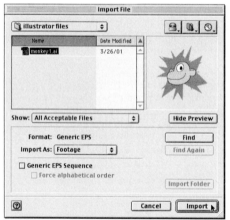
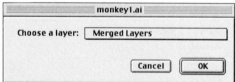

3. Select **monkey1.ai** and click **Import** (Mac) or **Open** (Windows). In the prompt window, click **OK** to accept merged layers.

Notice that the Illustrator file is added to the Project window, and the asterisk in the title bar indicates that you have changed your project.

4. Save your project. Leave the file open; you will continue to work with it in the next exercise.

4. ————————Importing QuickTime Movies

QuickTime movies are easy to import into an After Effects project. The efficiency and portability of QuickTime is truly a timesaver when working with moving images because QuickTime movies contain a sequence of images in a neat package. In this exercise you'll learn how to import QuickTime movies.

1. Choose **File > Import > File**, or as a shortcut, press **Command+I** (Mac) or **Control+I** (Windows).

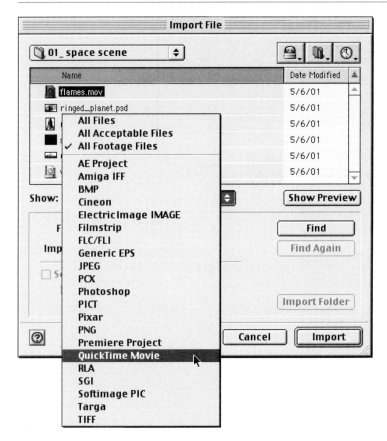

2. Browse to the **01_space scene** folder inside the **chap_03** folder and, from the **Show** (Mac) or **Files of Type** (Windows) menu, choose **QuickTime Movie**.

This step isn't mandatory; it's shown here to illustrate how the interface can help you select exactly what you need from a long list of files.

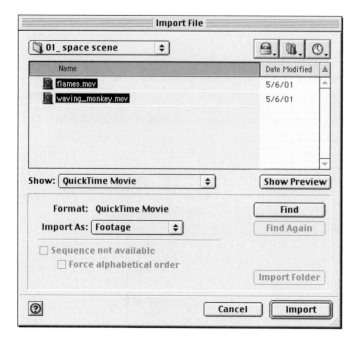

3. Select both QuickTime movies by holding down the **Shift** key while you click on the files. Click **Import** (Mac) or **Open** (Windows).

4. The QuickTime footage has been added to your Project window, and the title bar shows an asterisk after the file name. Save your project, using **Command+S** (Mac) or **Control+S** (Win). Leave the file open; you will continue to work with it in future exercises.

Get in the habit of using shortcut keys; they will save time when you start working on compositions.

NOTE | What Is a QuickTime Movie?

Think of a QuickTime movie as an extremely handy container. Rather than having many different image files and a separate audio file, a QuickTime movie allows you to place all of the frames and synchronized audio into one neat package. With the QuickTime player installed on your computer, a single QuickTime file will play back hundreds or thousands of images with synchronous sound. Many other settings are available as well. We'll cover many of QuickTime's options as they relate to After Effects when we talk about rendering your project in Chapter 16, "*Rendering Final Movies.*"

Organizing Your Project

In the next set of exercises, you'll learn about organizing the footage assets in the Project window. These are quick and simple techniques, easily mastered and very valuable to making your work process more efficient.

By organizing project assets, you can access footage in a way that makes the most sense to you. This can be a real aid when you have a deadline and you're desperately looking for something that you need right away.

NOTE | You Can Import Multiple File Types At Once

In the past few exercises, you imported Photoshop, Illustrator and QuickTime files separately. You don't have to work this way, as you could have chosen to import all the different file types at once, and After Effects would have figured out what type of file they were automatically. We chose to have you learn to open the different types of files in separate exercises to have an opportunity to focus on each file type. In reality, it is much faster to import all the footage at once!

---

5. ——————————**Creating Folders**

After Effects allows you to create folders in the Project window. This is a great way to organize footage items. There are two ways to create folders. You'll see both methods covered below.

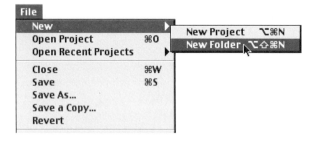

1. Choose **File > New > New Folder**.

This creates a new folder inside the Project window. The folder name will be highlighted and ready to accept a new name.

2. In the Project window, name the new folder "**Movies**," and press **Return** (Mac) or **Enter** (Windows).

3. Drag the two QuickTime movies into the **Movies** folder.

4. Click the **arrow** to the left of the **Movies** folder to see your movie footage inside the folder.

5. Click in the **empty gray area** anywhere below the files in the Project window to make sure that your **Movies** folder is not selected.

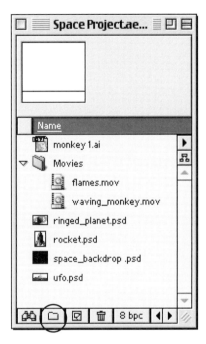

6. At the bottom of the Project window, click the **folder** icon.

This is an alternative way to create a new folder.

---

7. Name your new folder "**Stills**."

---

8. Drag all of the Photoshop documents (**.psd** files) into the **Stills** folder.

You can select multiple files by dragging across them in the window or by holding down the Shift key as you click on the files.

---

9. Click the **arrow** to the left of the **Stills** folder to see the footage contained inside.

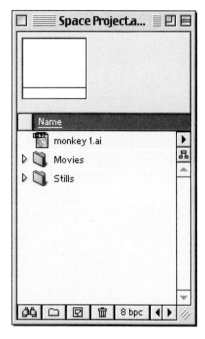

10. Click the **arrows** to the left of both folders to close them.

11. Save the file, and leave it open for the next exercise.

6. ——————————Renaming Folders

After you've created a folder, you might want to change its name at a later time. In this exercise you'll learn how.

1. Click the **Stills** folder to select it.

2. Press **Return** (Mac) or **Enter** (Windows).

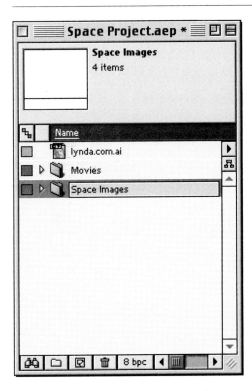

3. Rename the folder "**Space Images**."

You can use several words and spaces when naming folders.

4. Save your project file, and leave it open for the next exercise.

7.——————————**Deleting Footage**

Deleting footage from your Project window is very easy and very safe. In this exercise, you'll learn two methods for deleting footage from your Project window.

Note: Remember that an After Effects project maintains only references to the files on your hard disk. When you delete footage from the project list, you delete only a reference. The actual file is still on your hard disk in the same place, completely untouched by reference changes inside your After Effects project.

1. Select the **monkey1.ai** footage from the Project window.

2. Press **Delete** (Mac) or **Backspace** (Windows) on your keyboard, and note that the footage reference is deleted.

3. Press **Command+Z** (Mac) or **Control+Z** (Windows) to undo the deletion.

4. With the **monkey1.ai** footage selected, choose **Edit > Clear**.

Note that you can undo the deletion from the Edit menu, but don't do so at this point.

5. Save your project.

6. Go to the Edit menu again and notice that you cannot undo the deletion now that you've used the Save command.

Although the reference is gone, you can import the footage again as you did earlier in this chapter. The Illustrator file is still on your hard disk! Check it out.

NOTE | Project Window Panels and Menus

The Project window is organized in rows and columns that offer information about your footage, such as the name, size, label, type, file path, comments, date, and duration. These organizational structures are called **panels** in After Effects.

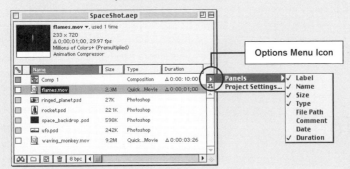

By clicking the **Options Menu** icon, you will see the options for which panels to display. Here you can make different panels visible by selecting or deselecting the list of choices.

To make the panels wider or narrower, drag the divider lines between the columns.

To rearrange the order of the panels, click and drag the panel headings.

Test Yourself on This Chapter!

You might not realize that you learned a lot of new procedures in this chapter. See if you can remember how to do the following on your own, without looking at the book.

A. Create a new project by choosing **File > New Project**

B. Save and name a new project

C. Import Photoshop, Illustrator and QuickTime footage. You can use the footage from the **chap_03** exercise files, or try your own files if you have some!

D. Create folders to organize your footage and place your footage inside those folders.

E. Save the project.

If you don't remember how to do some of these procedures, re-read the exercises and then try again on your own.

You've now successfully completed everything you need to do to set up, organize and import footage assets into your first project! There are deeper nuances to working in the Project window that you'll learn about as you work though other exercises later in this book.

If you feel ready, move on to the next chapter, or feel free to pick the book up again after taking a break.

4.

The Composition

| What Is a Composition? | Starting a New Composition |
| Getting Footage into the Composition |
| Importing a Photoshop File as a Composition |

chap_04

After Effects 5.0/5.5
H•O•T CD-ROM

If you were a musician, you might use a piano to work out your musical ideas while you wrote your score on sheets of paper. Ultimately, your music might be performed using a variety of instruments. However, the process of deciding exactly what your music should be is called composition, and the paper with the musical notations is the plan of how your music will be performed.

Just like a musician composing music on a piano, you can compose moving images using After Effects. Instead of writing down your ideas on sheets of paper, you document your work in After Effects until it's ready to be performed. The document that holds your plan in After Effects is called a **composition**. Like a musical score, the composition holds the notation that will be interpreted to create your finished piece.

Up until now, you have learned only to create a project file. The project file holds references to all your footage, but the composition is where you put this footage to use. Without a composition, you cannot create animation, video, graphics, or audio. Think of the composition as the instructions that tell After Effects what to do with your footage and as the preview that shows you how those instructions are being executed.

In this chapter you'll get to know exactly what a composition is, and you'll see how to work with the Composition window. It is your main visual window and provides many options for working with the images that you compose.

What Is a Composition?

A composition defines your creative intentions for your project. It does this by acting as a container for your design plan. It holds the images and the settings together in a relationship that you create.

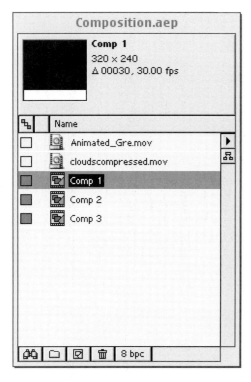

You open a composition by double-clicking it in the Project window. This project contains three compositions. Projects can hold an unlimited number of composition files. Later in this chapter, you'll learn how to make your own composition.

When you open the composition, you'll see two windows . The first is called, appropriately enough, the **Composition window**.

In the **Composition window**, you can graphically interact with the images in your composition. You can think of this window as being similar to a painter's canvas, because you visualize your design in it. You can also preview animation in the Composition window to see your animation move.

The second window associated with a composition is the **Timeline window**. Your composition settings are visible in this window.

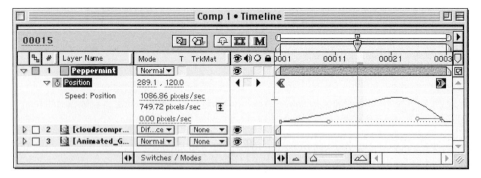

Think of the Timeline window as the equivalent of a musical score that will be interpreted to create your finished piece. The settings you make here are like musical notations, and your finished piece will be your final animation. Note that the Composition and Timeline windows are separate, but one will not open or close without the other. If you are working and you lose your Timeline or Composition window, you need to reopen it from your Project window.

Compositions are your frame-by-frame instructions to After Effects. Ultimately, After Effects will read your instructions, interpret them for each frame, and perform an output of your final product based on the settings you specify in your composition.

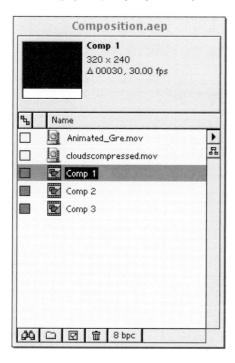

Compositions appear within your Project window along with other footage items.

Unlike footage items that are created outside After Effects in programs like Photoshop, Illustrator, or Premiere, compositions can be made only from within your After Effects project. Compositions reside inside the project file and cannot be stored separately on your hard drive, as other footage items can.

Your project can have as many different compositions as you wish. You can try out multiple versions of an idea and keep all of them in the project file, or you can choose to delete compositions that you no longer need.

I. _____Composition Settings

Starting a composition requires that you define a few settings. In the following exercises, you will learn to define settings using the Composition Settings window. When you set up a new composition, you'll automatically see the **Composition Settings** window. It's best to decide on all the options in the Composition Settings window early in your composition. Most of the options are obvious, and we'll explain any terms that may be new to you.

1. Create a new project by choosing **File > New > New Project**.

2. Choose **File > Save As**, and navigate to the **HOT AE Projects** folder you created in the previous chapter. Save this new empty file there as **Space Project 2.aep**. You'll be filling it soon with footage and a composition.

3. Choose **Composition > New Composition**.

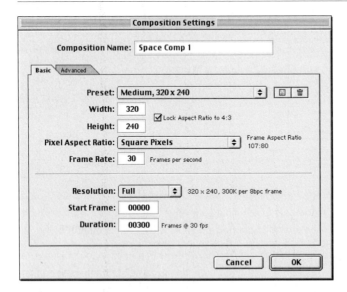

4. In the **Composition Settings** window, set the **Composition Name** to **Space Comp 1**.

Naming your composition appropriately is important. Because most projects go through several versions, it's a good idea to give each version a number. If you should have to output to two different media types (like video and film), you'll want different names for each set of compositions to delineate the two output types. Another reason to name composition versions carefully is that your client may make changes as the project moves along. Giving each composition its own name and number will allow you to keep track of version changes.

Frame Rate: 30 | Frames per second

5. Make sure the **Frame Rate** is set to **30** frames per second for this composition.

A frame rate of 30 frames per second will produce smooth animation.

Width: 320
Height: 240
☑ Lock Aspect Ratio to 4:3

6. Make sure that **Lock Aspect Ratio** is checked.

The aspect ratio is the ratio of your movie's image width to image height. Selecting this option makes it easy to adjust your composition to a different resolution while maintaining the proper relative proportions. Aspect ratio is a common term in professional film and video circles that signifies keeping the size relationship if you change the dimensions of a movie.

Resolution indicates the number of pixels used in the width and height of an image. Increasing the number of pixels will produce a clearer and sharper image. Increasing clarity and sharpness means increasing resolution.

7. Set the **Width** to **640**. Notice that the Height value automatically adjusts to 480 to preserve the aspect ratio.

8. Set the **Width** to **320**. The Height adjusts to 240. Leave this setting at **Width: 320, Height: 240**.

This automatic height adjustment is the direct result of setting the Lock Aspect Ratio option in step 6.

9. Set the **Start Frame** to **00001**, if it is not already set that way. **Note:** If you do not see a Start Frame option, click **Cancel** and then select **File > Project Settings**. Click the **Frames** check box and click **OK**, and then choose **Composition > New Composition** again. You will now see a Start Frame option, which you can set to 00001.

The start frame is the number at which your composition starts identifying its frames. Although you could start numbering with any five-digit number, for this exercise you will use 00001 because it is the most straightforward numbering scheme.

10. Set **Duration** to **240**.

Duration is the overall length of the movie you are creating in your composition. You can safely lengthen the duration after setting it here. However, shortening the duration might cut off work that you've already completed, so you will want to carefully consider whether you really do want to shorten or lengthen a composition. In this case, with a duration of 240 frames at 30 frames per second, the movie will be 8 seconds long.

NOTE | Determining Time

Frames per second refers to the number of frames changed sequentially before your eyes each second to create the illusion of moving pictures. To compute the length of time for your composition, divide the duration by the number of frames per second.

For example, you might be using a standard video frame rate of 30 frames per second. If you have 300 frames in your composition, the calculation would be 300 / 30 = 10. Thus, your composition would be 10 seconds long.

Or you might be using a standard motion picture frame rate of 24 frames per second. If you have 240 frames in your composition, the calculation would be 240 / 24 = 10. Here too, the length of time for your composition would be 10 seconds.

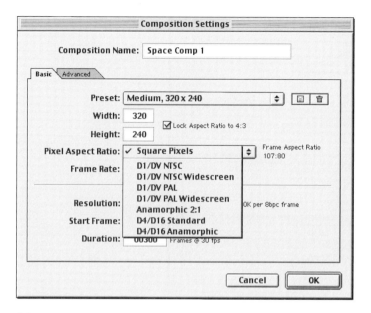

11. Make sure **Pixel Aspect Ratio** is set to **Square Pixels**.

NOTE | Determining Pixel Aspect Ratio

Most display devices in computer graphics use square pixels. This means that the height and width of the pixels are exactly the same. However, many video systems and anamorphic film projects, use display systems that are not square. The height of a non-square display system is not the same as its width, and these pixels are rectangular in shape.

How do you determine when you need to use square pixels or choose another option? The basic rule is this: If you are working on a project that will not be output to video or film, use square pixels.

If you are working on a video project, determine which video format you are using and select it from the menu. In the United States, the most common video format is D1/DV NTSC. In Europe, the most standard video format is D1/DV PAL.

If you are working on a film project, talk to your supervisor before deciding to use square pixels or Anamorphic 2:1. Unless you are a multimillionaire making your own film, you will have a supervisor. If you are a multimillionaire making your own film, hire someone who has a great deal of experience in motion picture visual effects as a consultant before making a determination. Although there are standard operating procedures, many film productions have special ways of doing things. Motion picture production is very expensive, and making assumptions can lead to formidable difficulties.

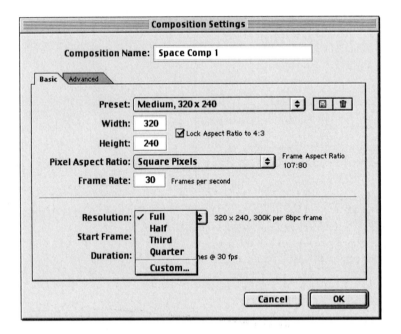

12. Make sure **Resolution** is set to **Full**.

This is a display option. Setting it to Half, Third, Quarter, or Custom would allow you to preview compositions at a lower resolution than the width and height that you set for the composition. Displaying a lower resolution allows After Effects to preview your animation more quickly than it would at higher resolutions. In this chapter we'll start with full resolution for display; throughout this book, however, you'll see the effect of changing to a lower display resolution.

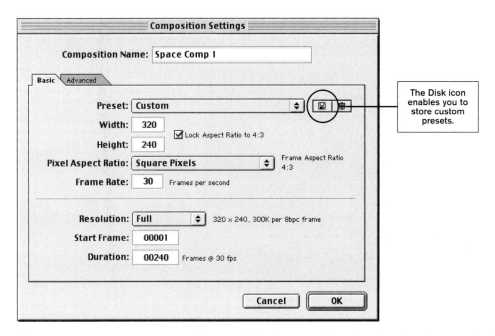

13. From the **Preset** menu, choose **Custom**. With Custom selected, click the **Disk** icon to the right of the Preset menu.

The Disk icon enables you to store custom presets.

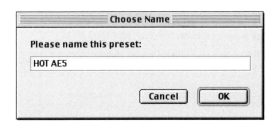

14. Name this preset "**HOT AE5**," and click **OK**.

You now have a preset that will work with all the exercises in this book. If you ever want to delete this preset, simply click the Trashcan icon to the right of the Disk icon while the preset is selected in the menu.

15. In the **Composition Settings** window, click **OK** to accept these option settings.

At this point you're presented with the Composition and Timeline windows. Notice that your composition is listed in the Project window. Whenever you create or open a composition, both the Composition and Timeline windows open also. Likewise, closing either of these windows closes both windows.

---

16. Save your project with **Command+S** (Mac) or **Control+S** (Windows)

---

17. Make sure **Space Comp 1** is highlighted in the **Project** window, and choose **Composition > Composition Settings**, or use **Command+K** (Mac) **Control+K** (Windows).

The Composition Settings window reopens. If you ever need to change your composition settings, you can change them at any time.

---

18. Click **Cancel** to close the Composition Settings window without changing the previous settings. Leave the project open for the next exercise.

Frames, Timecode, or Feet and Frames Settings?

The exercises in this book suggest that you work with frames as the time setting in the Project Settings window (**File > Project Settings...**). That is what you learned to do in the previous exercise. There are times, however, when you will be asked to work with **timecode** or with **feet and frames**.

The Start Frame and Start Timecode settings can be critical when working on a video project. Video editors, for example, use timecode as a system to log all editing decisions. You may be asked to start a title sequence or animation at a certain point in time, based on timecode numbering. Timecode specifies the exact hour, minute, second, and frame within a video piece.

`0:01:48:03`

Here is a starting point displayed as timecode. Notice the colons separating the numbers. The first number is the hour (0) followed by a colon. The second number is the minute (01) followed by a colon. The third number is the seconds (48) followed by a colon. The last number is the frame (03).

To set timecode as the display style, choose **File > Project Settings** and select **Timecode Base**. Set the Start Timecode value in the Composition Settings window based on the needs of the individual shot.

If you are working on a film project, you may need to use **feet and frames** as your display style. Historically, film editors find it convenient to measure time in feet and frames due to the mechanical aspects of film.

In 35mm motion picture film, one foot of film contains 16 frames. Ten feet of film contains 160 frames. One hundred feet of film contains 1,600 frames, and so on.

Today most visual effects facilities use frames as the standard measure of time. If you need to display feet and frames in After Effects, you can do so by choosing **File > Project Settings** and selecting **Feet + Frames**.

TIP | Creating a New Composition

You can create a new composition directly from the Project window in two ways. One way is simply to click on the **New Composition** icon at the bottom of the Project window.

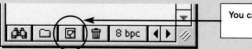

You can click the New Composition icon to create a new composition.

The second method is to drag a footage item to the **New Composition** icon. This method creates a new composition based on the resolution of the source material. If the source material is a QuickTime movie, the frame rate will be set from the QuickTime settings.

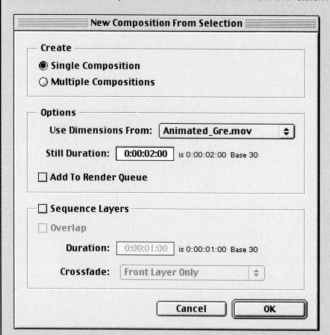

If you drag multiple items at once on to the New Composition button, the New Composition From Selection dialog box will open. The **Options: Use Dimensions From** menu will appear with those files listed. From the menu listing, you can select any of the individual files from which to base the dimensions of the new composition.

2. ——————Getting Footage into the Composition

Now that you've made a composition, you're probably wondering what to do with it. The first step is to bring some footage into it, and the next step is to learn to animate that footage. In this exercise you will learn to bring footage into a composition. In the next chapter, you'll learn how to animate footage in a Composition window. You cannot animate footage without a Timeline, and you cannot gain access to a Timeline without a composition. Understanding the relationship among the project, composition, and Timeline is key to understanding After Effects. This exercise should be a great help in unfolding the mystery of why you need all these things!

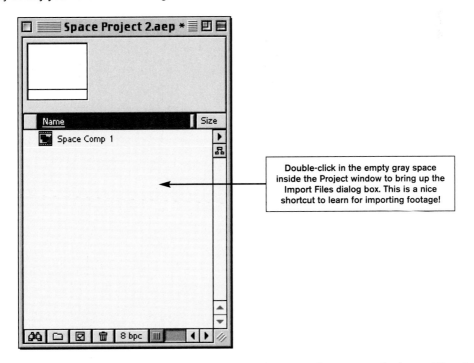

Double-click in the empty gray space inside the Project window to bring up the Import Files dialog box. This is a nice shortcut to learn for importing footage!

1. Double-click inside the blank area in the Project window. This causes the Import Files dialog box to open.

In the last chapter you learned to import footage using the menu item File > Import > File. The way you learned to import footage in this step is a useful alternative.

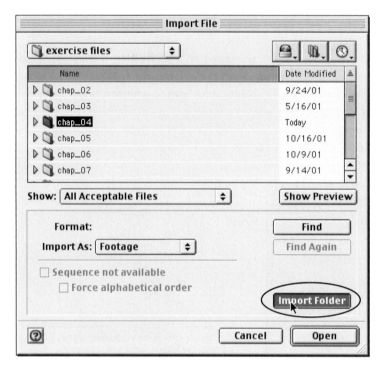

2. When the **Import File** dialog box appears, navigate to the **exercise files** folder. Select **chap_04** and click **Import Folder**. This will import the entire folder of footage in one action.

In the last chapter, you learned how to import Illustrator, Photoshop, and QuickTime documents sepa-rately. There's no need to import them separately, however—you can import an entire folder of footage at once or individual footage items, depending on your needs.

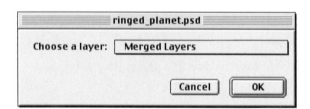

3. You'll be asked to choose a layer for several of the footage items. Click **OK** to each request.

After Effects asks if you want to choose to Merge Layers or select a specific layer. Unless you want to select a specific layer from a Photoshop file, you will always answer OK to this query.

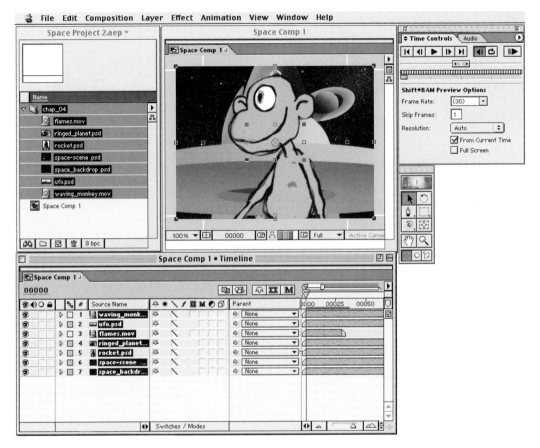

4. Twirl down the **chap_04** twirly to reveal the footage that you just imported. All of the footage should be selected. Drag this footage into the Timeline window; it should all move there at once. Notice that the Composition window now has artwork inside of it. **Note:** You can drag individual footage items into the Timeline window or drag multiple items at once. To deselect items in the Project window, simply click inside the gray area where you don't see any footage or compositions listed.

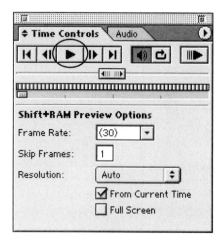

5. Click the **Play** button on the **Time Controls** palette. You'll see the monkey waving his arm in the Composition window. The footage that you're seeing inside the composition is created from all the layers in the Timeline window. You will be learning much, much more about layers and animating footage in future chapters.

6. Click the **close** box of the Timeline window to close both the Composition and Timeline windows. These two windows are tied at the hip! Close one, and the other closes too.

7. Double-click the **Space Comp 1** listing inside the Project window. This reopens the Composition window.

8. Choose **File > Save**. When you save the project, it saves all the footage references and the composition, so there's no need or way to save those things separately. Leave the project open for the next exercise.

3. ——————Importing a Photoshop File as a Composition

So far, you have learned how to create a composition from scratch and how to import footage into a composition. Next, you'll learn a great technique related to Photoshop files. The After Effects Timeline has layers, and Photoshop files have layers. Wouldn't it be cool if you could compose the layers in Photoshop and have them appear as you composed them inside After Effects? Well, you can, and this exercise shows you how.

1. Double-click inside the gray area of the Project window to open the **Import Footage** dialog box.

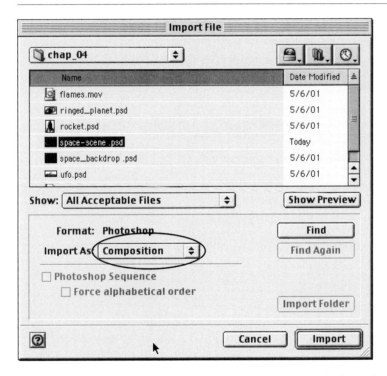

2. Navigate to the **exercise files** folder, then to the **chap_04** folder, and open it to look inside. Select the file called **space-scene.psd**. Choose **Import As: Composition** and click **Import**.

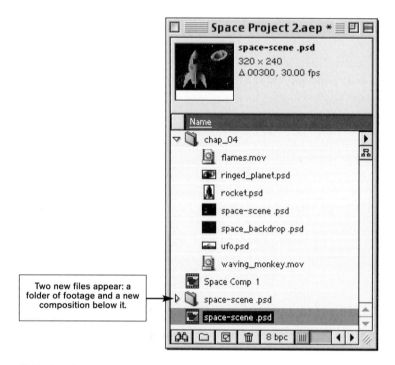

3. Notice that two new files appear inside your Project window—a folder called **space-scene.psd** and a composition named **space-scene.psd**. Double-click on the compositon called **space-scene.psd** to open it. It's OK that your other composition is still open.

Whenever you import a Photoshop document as a composition, After Effects produces two files in the Project window—the footage folder and a composition. Both files take on whatever name the Photoshop document had.

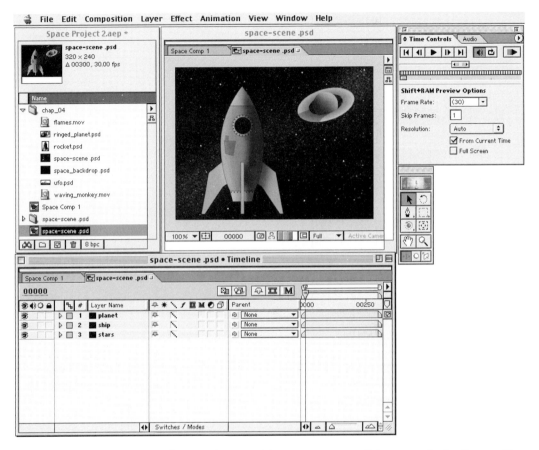

Notice that you can have two (or more!) compositions open at once. Tabs appear in the Composition and Timeline windows with the name of each composition. This illustrates that you can also have multiple compositions inside a project. Often, when you're working on a big project, you might choose to separate elements into individual compositions or keep different versions active within a single project.

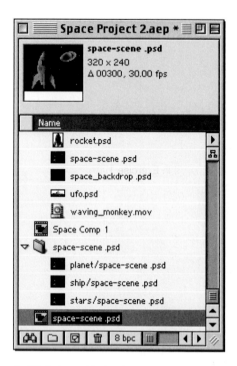

4. Click the twirly for the **space-scene.psd** folder to see its contents. It contains the three layers of the composition as three separate footage items. If you import Photoshop footage as Merged Layers, as you've done in past exercises, you won't be able to access individual layers as you can now.

5. Save and close the project file.

Test Yourself on This Chapter!

Try this short review of this chapter and the previous one, to be sure that you know how to set up a project and a composition without reading our directions. The following suggested steps are intentionally vague to allow you to test your new knowledge. If you need a refresher on how to do any of these tasks, reread the pertinent exercises in this chapter and Chapter 3.

A. Create a new project and save it to the **HOT AE Projects** folder that you created in Chapter 3.

B. Import the artwork from the folder called **chap_04** folder

C. Create a new composition, using the **HOT AE5** preset you created in Exercise 1.

D. Drag the footage that you imported from your project window into the Timeline window.

E. Save and close the project.

That's a wrap for this chapter. You've learned how to make a composition, which might not seem like much but is a very important part of learning After Effects. These steps were necessary skill builders to get you ready to create animation. In the next chapter, you'll be at the point where it all comes together in the form of a moving composition! See you there.

5.

Timeline, Keyframes, and Animation

| What Is a Keyframe? | Setting Keyframes |
| What Is a Property? | Animating Multiple Properties |
| Using Bézier Handles with Motion Paths |
| Mixing Spatial Interpolation Types | Anchor Points |

chap_05

After Effects 5.0/5.5
H•O•T CD-ROM

Because After Effects is a motion graphics tool, creating motion is at the heart of its power. A professional animator and motion graphics artist needs to know how to create movement that is deliberate and complex. Some kinds of motion projects require the use of subtle movement, and others require the use of wild and erratic movement. You can achieve this kind of control over your motion by mastering the use of keyframes.

Keyframe action is set up using the Timeline interface of After Effects. You won't believe how deep the science of keyframes is until you read this chapter and work through its exercises. You'll see that some kinds of keyframes can create movement that speeds up or slows down, other kinds of keyframes can create curved paths, and other kinds can smooth movement or make it jerky. Once you complete this chapter, you will have set a foundation for creating motion that will last your entire professional life.

What Is a Keyframe?

Keyframe is an animation term that's been in existence since animation was first invented. It usually describes a point at which something changes.

The best way to plan and design animation is to determine the start point and end point for the action. These start and end points are keys to your animation. If the action is complex, you might need to indicate other points of change as well.

Animators use the concept of keyframes to describe key points of action. Once keyframes are created, the frames in between the keyframes can be created. For example, in traditional hand-drawn animation, an animator can draw two keyframes and then draw the in-between frames. The keyframes act as a guide for all the frames in between.

In computer graphics, you can define the keyframes and have the computer draw the in-between frames for you. Again, the keyframes act as guides for the in-between frames created by your computer.

Most digital artists love animation once they experience the process of setting keyframes, having the computer create all the in-betweens, and viewing the animation on their monitor. Keyframes are a fundamental part of After Effects and provide the tools to create stunning animation.

 MOVIE | keyframes.mov

We've prepared a short movie that demonstrates the use of keyframes in After Effects. Please watch the movie entitled **keyframes.mov** located in the **movies** folder on the **H•O•T CD-ROM** before proceeding to the next exercise.

I. ——————————**Setting Keyframes**

You've learned to import footage into your project, create a composition, and import artwork from the project to the composition. Now it's finally time to start animating! In this exercise you will learn how to set keyframes. You will learn how to create start and end points as keyframes, and you'll preview the results of your animation.

1. Choose **File > Open Project**. Alternatively, press **Command+O** (Mac) or **Control+O** (Windows).

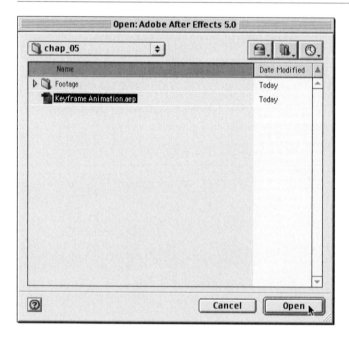

2. Navigate to the **exercise files** folder and open the **chap_05 folder**. Select **Keyframe Animation.aep** and click **Open**.

This is a project file, just like the project files that you learned to make on your own in Chapter 3, "The Project."

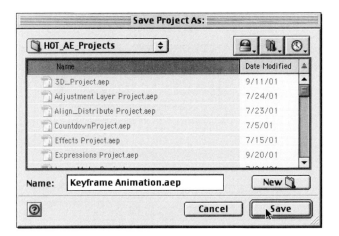

3. Choose **File > Save As**. In the dialog box, navigate to your **HOT_AE_Projects** folder and click **Save**. This saves a copy of the document so you won't alter the original.

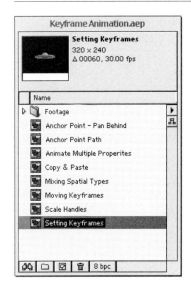
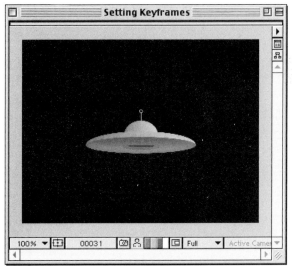

4. In the **Project** window, double-click the **Setting Keyframes** composition to open it.

The Project window contains numerous compositions as well as a Footage *folder. Twirl down the arrow next to the* Footage *folder in the Project window, and notice that it contains a file called ufo.psd. Look at the Timeline window, and notice that it contains a single footage item called ufo.psd, which was imported from the project into the Setting Keyframes composition as a merged Photoshop file. Observe that the UFO image appears in the Composition window.*

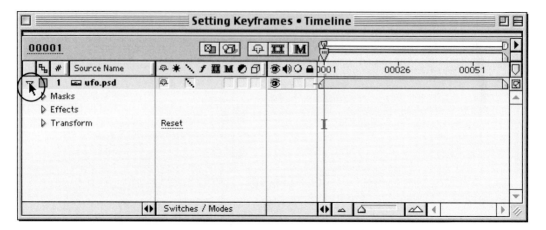

5. In the **Timeline** window, locate the small triangle to the left of the layer named **ufo.psd**. Click on the triangle and notice that it twirls down to display the Masks, Effects, and Transform properties for the layer.

As a nickname, we're going to refer to the triangle used to display properties as the "twirly." Every layer in any Timeline has a twirly, with the exact same properties that you see for this layer. These properties are part of the After Effects interface, and you don't have to do anything special to make them appear.

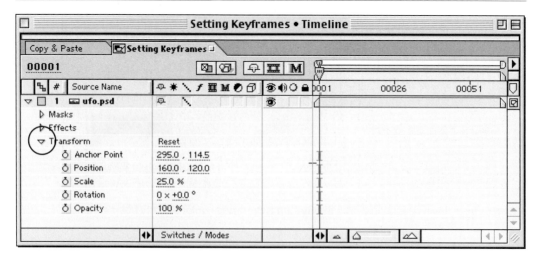

6. Click on the **Transform** twirly to display the Transform properties of the **ufo.psd** layer.

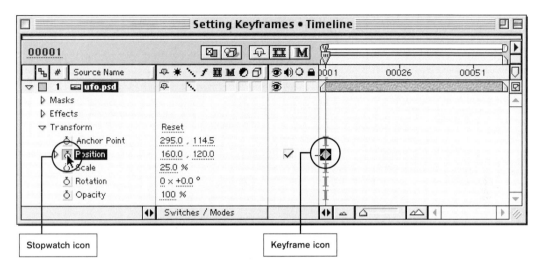

Stopwatch icon

Keyframe icon

7. Locate and click inside the **Stopwatch** icon for the **Position** property. Notice that a Keyframe icon is placed in the Timeline at the current Time Marker position (Frame 1).

Clicking the Stopwatch icon not only inserts a keyframe at the current Time Marker; it also turns on the ability to set keyframes for that property at other locations in the Timeline, as you'll do shortly.

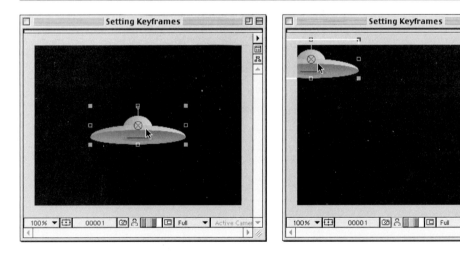

8. In the **Composition** window, click and drag the UFO image to the position shown in the illustration on the right above. This sets the Position property of the image in the first keyframe.

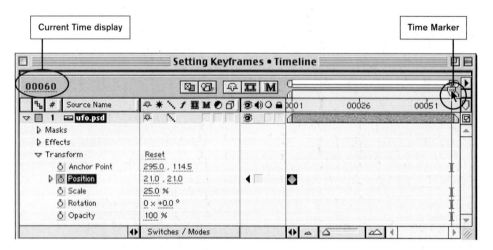

9. In the **Timeline** window, move the **Time Marker** to the last frame (Frame 60). Notice that the **Current Time Display** in the upper-left corner changes based on the current Time Marker position.

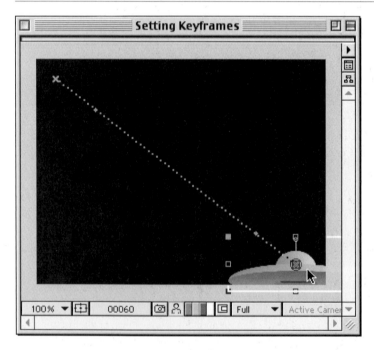

10. In the **Composition** window, drag the UFO image to the position shown above. Notice that a motion path is created between the two keyframe points.

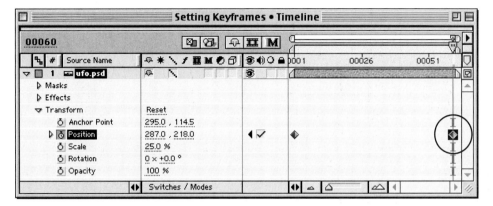

11. In the **Timeline** window, observe that another **Keyframe** icon has been set on Frame 60.

When the Stopwatch is turned on for the Position property, moving the position of artwork in the Composition window will cause a keyframe to be set automatically at the current Time Marker position.

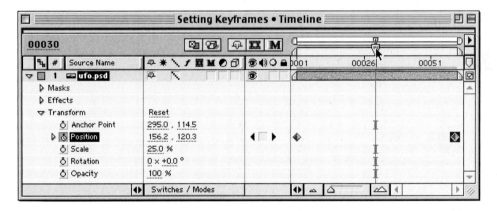

12. Drag the **Time Marker** back and forth to preview your animation.

Dragging the Time Marker back and forth is also called "scrubbing" the Time Marker.

13. Observe your animation in the **Composition** window as you scrub the **Time Marker**.

14. Save your project and leave it open for the next exercise.

What Is a Property?

In the previous exercise, you set keyframes for the Position property. But what exactly is a property?

Every layer in the Timeline has properties. Click the twirly (small triangle) to reveal them.

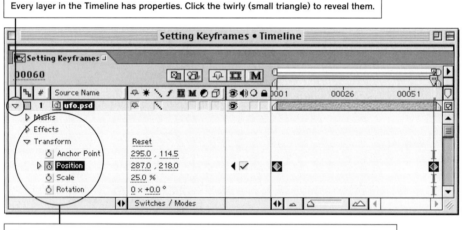

Properties appear below any layer that has its twirly turned down. All layers have properties.

Properties belong to **layers**. Each footage item in the Timeline is referred to as a layer. Think of layers as the individual components that make up your composition.

Each layer has properties that you can access and change on a frame-by-frame basis to animate it. Think of properties as options for a layer. Properties provide the means to change the color, size, position, and many other attributes associated with a layer. The variety of properties in After Effects is impressive, and they are organized into groups to make them easy to find.

There are three primary groups of properties: **Masks**, **Effects**, and **Transform** properties. All property values can be animated by setting keyframes. In this chapter we will be concerned only with setting keyframes for Transform properties. Chapter 10, "*Effects*," provides information specific to the Effects properties. Finally, Chapter 11, "*Masks*," provides additional information on the Mask properties.

2. ————————————Previewing the Motion

A significant part of creating animation is being able to preview the results. In the previous exercise, you watched the motion you created using a technique called scrubbing. In this exercise, you will learn to preview your motion using the Time Controls Play button and RAM Preview button. You'll also learn to rewind your animation, both manually and using the Time Controls Rewind button.

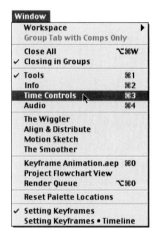

1. If the **Time Controls** palette is not visible, choose **Window > Time Controls** to display it. Alternatively, press **Command+3** (Mac) or **Control+3** (Windows).

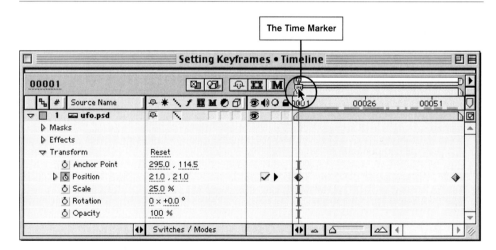

The Time Marker

2. Drag the **Time Marker** to **Frame 1** to manually rewind your animation or press the Home key on your keyboard.

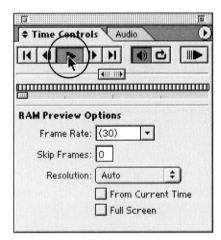

3. In the **Time Controls** palette, click the **Play** button to preview your animation.

4. Click anywhere or press any key to stop playing the looping animation.

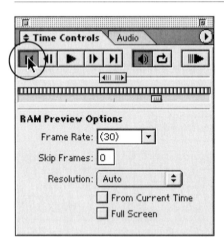

5. In the **Time Controls** palette, click the **First Frame** button to rewind your animation.

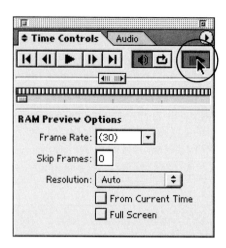

6. Click the **RAM Preview** button to preview your animation. Click anywhere or press any key to stop the preview.

The RAM Preview function causes your computer to store the movie in its memory (RAM) in order to give you a real-time preview. The RAM Preview is much closer to the timing that would occur in video or on film. When you click the Play button without using RAM Preview, After Effects has to render each frame, which can cause the preview to slow down. The RAM Preview is very useful to get a sense of what the final timing of your movie will look like. If RAM preview doesn't work well, it might be because you don't have enough RAM in your computer system. In that case, use the Play button or spacebar to preview your motion.

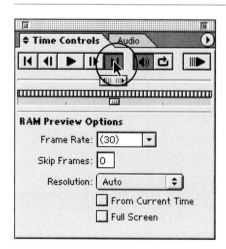

7. Click the **Last Frame** button to stop your animation on the last frame.

3. ——————————Editing the Motion

Remember (if you're old enough) how typewriters didn't have "undo" keys, so if you made a mistake you might have to retype everything? Fortunately, computers are great for editing, and the old days of worrying about changing your mind are gone forever. What good would setting keyframes be if you couldn't make a change? In this exercise you will learn the basics of editing keyframe animation. You'll learn to select individual keyframes and add more keyframes. You'll also learn how to change keyframe values. Nothing is ever cast in stone in After Effects—you can always change your mind (and so can your clients!).

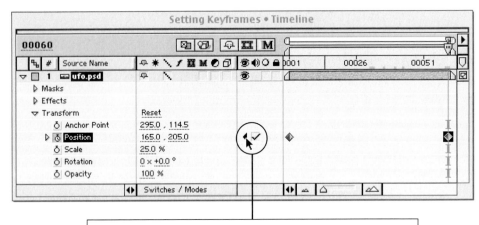

Click the left arrow on the Keyframe Navigator to move the Time Marker to 0.

1. In the **Timeline** window, locate the **Keyframe Navigator**. Click the **left arrow**. Notice that the Time Marker moves to the previous keyframe (Frame 1).

The Keyframe Navigator appears whenever you have keyframes set in the Timeline. Using the right arrow will take you forward to the next keyframe; using the left arrow will take you to the previous keyframe. Note that the right and left Keyframe Navigator arrows will appear only if there are keyframes present to the right or left of the Time Marker's position. Using the Keyframe Navigator arrow is a great way to locate existing keyframes. The only way to change a keyframe is to go to it first, so you'll find the Keyframe Navigator invaluable.

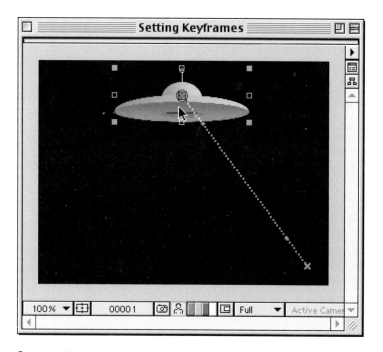

2. In the **Composition** window, click and drag the UFO image to the position shown in the illustration above. Notice that the motion path has changed because you altered the first keyframe. In the **Timeline** window, notice that the Position property values of the **ufo.psd** layer have changed.

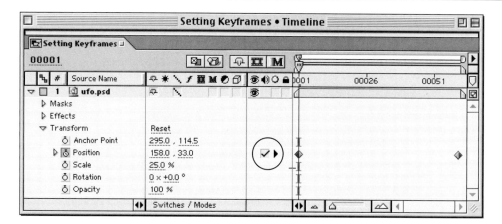

3. Using the **Keyframe Navigator,** click the **right arrow**. Notice that the Time Marker moves to the next keyframe, Frame 60.

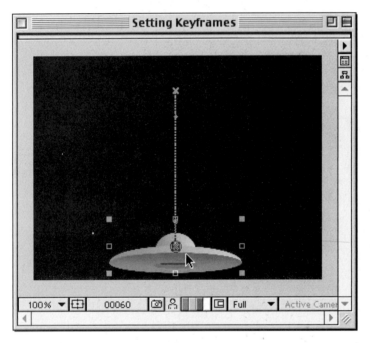

4. In the **Composition** window, drag the UFO image to the position shown above. You've changed the motion path again by editing the keyframe for the end position.

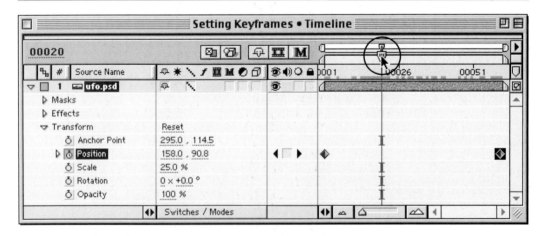

5. Set the **Time Marker** to **Frame 20**. There is no keyframe at Frame 20, but you'll learn how to set one next.

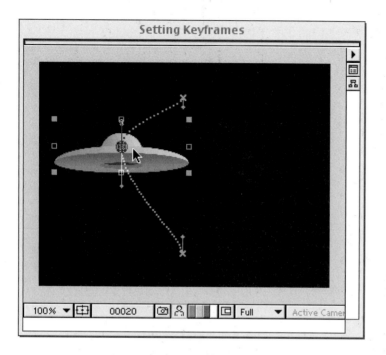

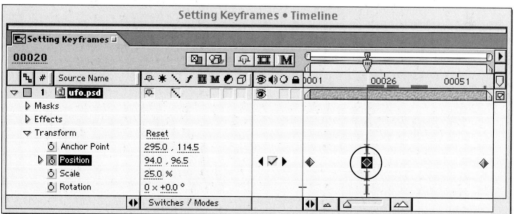

6. Drag the UFO to the left, as shown above. Notice that this adds a new keyframe to your animation at Frame 20.

When you want to create a new keyframe, go to a frame that does not have a keyframe yet and simply move the object, as you did in this step. When you want to edit a keyframe, go to an existing keyframe and move the object.

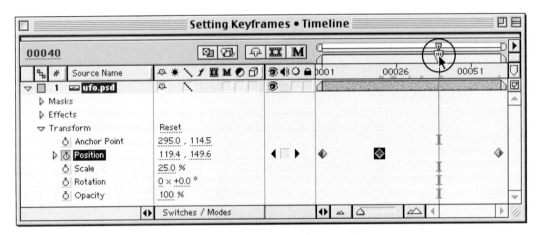

7. Set the **Time Marker** to **Frame 40**. If you notice tiny green marks next to the frame numbers in the Timeline, they represent frames that have been rendered. It's not important to this exercise to understand the green marks yet; they will be explained fully in Chapter 7, "*Previewing Movies.*"

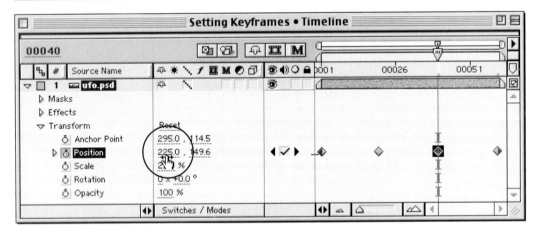

8. Locate the **Position X-axis** value, which represents the horizontal position of the object. Hold your cursor over the X-axis value until the cursor changes into a **hand with a double arrow**. Click and drag to the right to increase the value. Set the value to approximately **225** pixels.

Moving this slider in the Timeline moves the physical object in the Composition window, and is another way to set a keyframe.

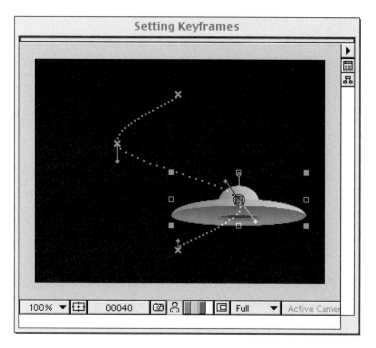

9. Observe the change in the X-axis value in the Composition window.

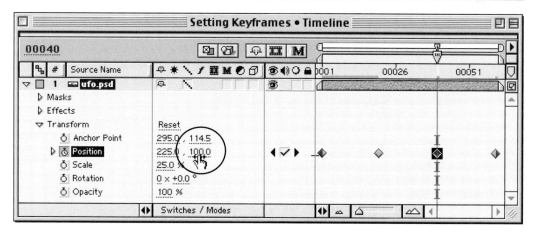

10. Locate the **Position Y-axis** value. Use the **double-arrow cursor** and drag to the left to decrease the Y-axis value. Set the value to approximately **100** pixels.

The Y axis is the vertical dimension.

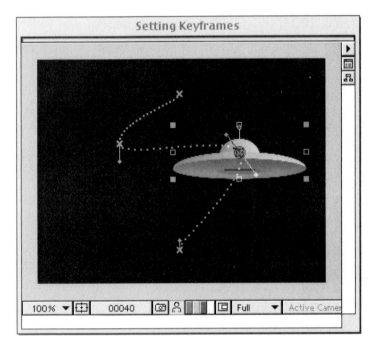

11. Observe the resulting motion path in the Composition window.

---

12. Click the **RAM Preview** icon to view your edited animation.

---

13. Choose **File > Save** to save your **Keyframe Animation.aep** project. Your **Setting Keyframes** composition will be saved automatically along with the project. Choose **File > Close** to close the **Setting Keyframes** composition. Notice that the **Keyframe Animation.aep** project does not close with the composition. Leave this project open for the next exercise.

You may be confused at this point about the relationship between the project and the composition. The composition that you've been working with in this exercise is inside the project file. The composition name is Setting Keyframes, *and the project name is* Keyframe Animation.aep. *The only way to save the composition is to save the project. This is one of the distinctive things about After Effects—the project is what you open and save, not individual compositions. In fact, you cannot open a composition without being in an open project. You'll get used to this, but in the beginning it is confusing to most new users.*

TIP | Typing Property Values

In addition to using the sliders, you can type property values directly into the Timeline. Click the value, and type in the value box that appears. Press **Return** (Mac) or **Enter** (Windows) to enter the value.

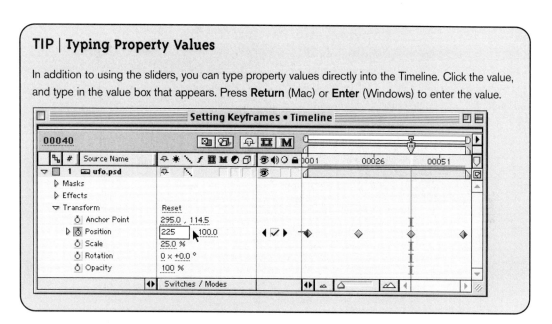

TIP | Double-Clicking a Keyframe Icon to Adjust Values

You can also adjust keyframe values by double-clicking a Keyframe icon.

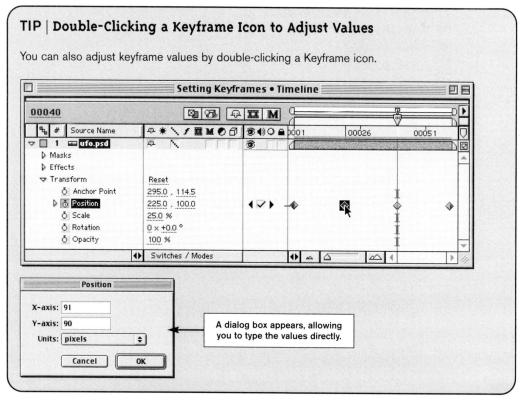

A dialog box appears, allowing you to type the values directly.

4. ——————Copying and Pasting Keyframes

Just as you copy and paste text in a word processor, you can copy and paste keyframes in After Effects. This technique is useful if you've set up a repetitive motion and want to continue with it. In this exercise, you'll use this process to make a light flash on and off.

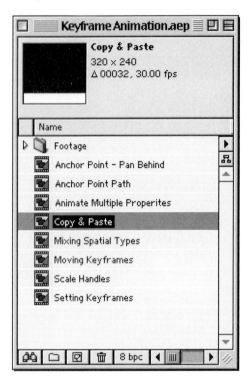

1. In the **Project** window, double-click the **Copy & Paste** composition to open it. This is an empty composition that you will set up yourself.

TIP | Adding a Keyframe via a Check Box

You can add a keyframe by clicking the **Keyframe Navigator** check box. This adds a keyframe wherever the Time Marker is without changing the value of the frame. In effect, it copies the information from the previous keyframe and makes a new keyframe with the same information. This check box can come in handy when you want to hold a value for a specific frame. It's easier to show you how this technique works than it is to tell you, so please watch the following movie!

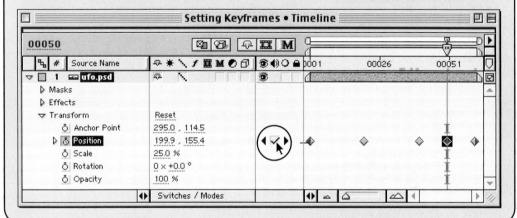

MOVIE | HoldKeyframes.mov

We've prepared a short movie that demonstrates how to set hold keyframes using the Keyframe Navigator in the Timeline. You'll find **HoldKeyframes.mov** in the **movies** folder on the **H•O•T CD-ROM**.

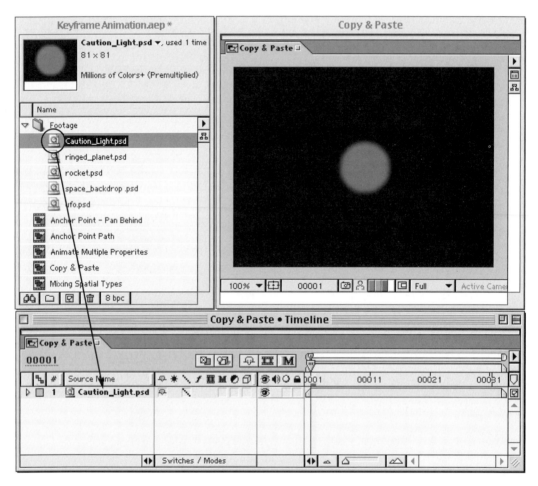

2. In the Project window, click the twirly of the **Footage** folder and locate **Caution_Light.psd**. Drag this file into the **Timeline**. The image of a circle appears in the **Copy & Paste** Composition window.

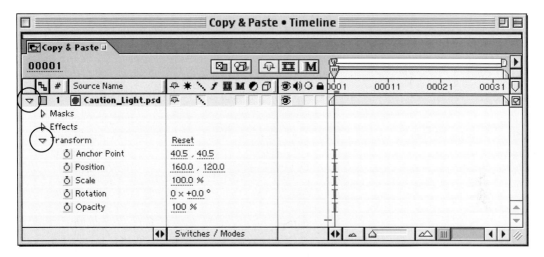

3. In the **Timeline** window, click the twirly next to the layer **Caution_Light.psd**. Click the twirly next to **Transform** to reveal the Transform properties for that layer.

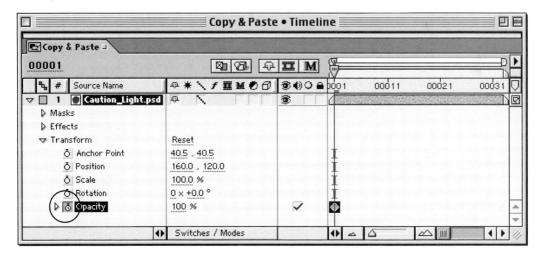

4. Click the **Stopwatch** icon for the **Opacity** property. This sets a keyframe for the opacity of the circle at the current Time Marker, which should be on Frame 1. The circle is currently set to 100% opacity, which makes it fully visible.

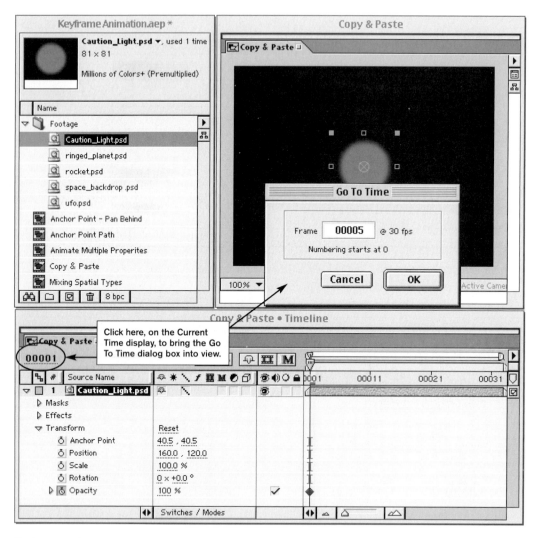

5. Click the **Current Time** display in the Timeline. An alternative way to access this dialog box is Cmd+G (Mac) or Cntrl+G (Windows). This opens the **Go To Time** dialog box. Enter the value **Frame: 00005** and click **OK**. This moves the Time Marker to Frame 5. You can either move the Time Marker to the desired frame in the Timeline window or use this more precise method of specifying the frame in the **Go To Time** dialog box in the future. Either technique achieves the same result.

It's important to move the Time Marker before you make a change to the property. This might take some getting used to, but you will eventually get the hang of it! In the next step, you'll change the property value and a new keyframe will be set.

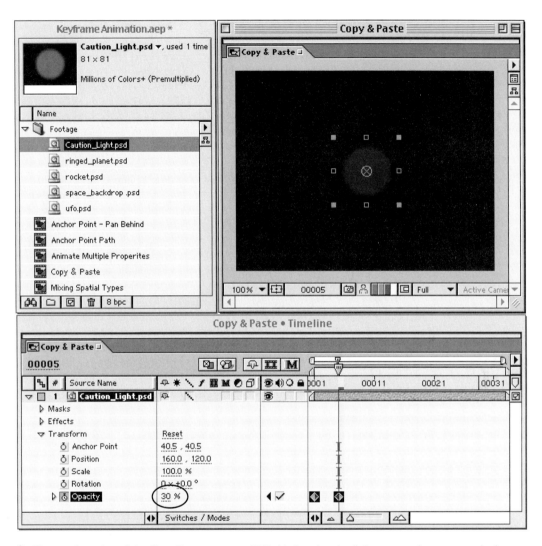

6. Change the value of the **Opacity** property to **30%**. Notice that the light appears less opaque in the Composition window. Also notice that a new keyframe has been set at Frame 5!

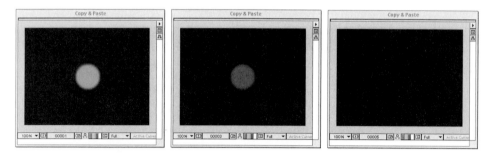

7. Scrub the **Time Marker** over the first few frames and observe the existing keyframe animation. The light fades out quickly. This effect was created by changing the Opacity property from 100% to 30% over two different keyframes.

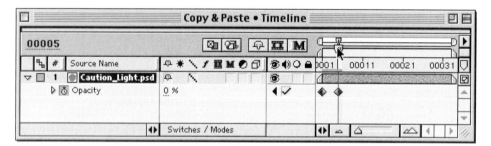

8. In the **Timeline** window, select the **Caution_Light.psd** layer, if it isn't already selected. Press the letter **T** on the keyboard and notice that the Opacity property appears alone, without all the other properties. Observe that the Opacity value is 100% on Keyframe 1 and 30% on Keyframe 5. The shortcut key T allows you to see the one property that you want to change, rather than clicking the twirly and having to navigate through all the different properties before finding Opacity.

9. Hold down the **Shift** key and click the two **Opacity** keyframes to select them both. You will copy these two keyframes so that the fading effect will repeat itself.

10. Choose **Edit > Copy**. Alternatively, press **Command+C** (Mac) or **Control+C** (Windows).

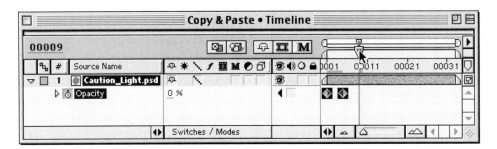

11. Move the **Time Marker** to **Frame 9**. It's important to move the Time Marker before you paste the keyframes into the new location. Keyframes are always pasted wherever the Time Marker resides.

12. Choose **Edit > Paste**. Alternatively, press **Command+V** (Mac) or **Control+V** (Windows). Notice that the keyframes are pasted beginning at the current Time Marker position on Frame 9.

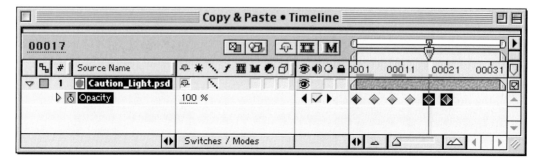

13. Move the **Time Marker** to **Frame 17**. Press **Command+V** (Mac) or **Control+V** (Windows) to paste the keyframes again.

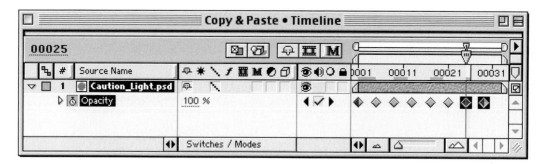

14. Set the **Time Marker** to **Frame 25**. Press **Command+V** (Mac) or **Control+V** (Windows) to paste the keyframes one last time.

15. Click **RAM Preview** in the **Time Controls** palette to see the animation.

16. Save your project and close the **Copy & Paste** composition. Leave the project open for the next exercise.

5. ————————Moving Keyframes

So far, you've set keyframes at the position of the Time Marker. This is the only way to create a keyframe, because the keyframe appears wherever the Time Marker is positioned in the Timeline. Sometimes, after you've created keyframes you might change your mind about where in time you wanted them to occur. The good news is that once you've made a keyframe you can always move it to other frame positions. Moving a keyframe changes the animation relative to the Timeline. In this exercise you'll learn how to move keyframes, and you'll see the effect that has on animation.

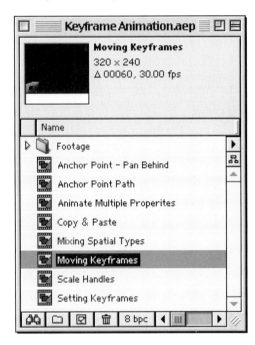

1. In the **Project** window, double-click the **Moving Keyframes** composition. This composition was made ahead of time, and keyframes have been set for both the Position and Scale properties already.

2. Click **RAM Preview** and observe the animation of the rocket moving up through the Composition window and growing smaller.

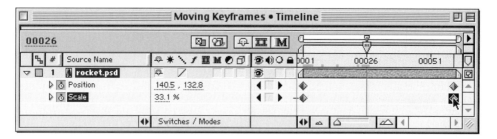

3. Select **rocket.psd** in the **Timeline** window. Press the letter **P**; then hold down the **Shift** key and press the letter **S**. This is a shortcut to reveal the Position and Scale properties without using the twirlies. Click the last **Scale** keyframe (on Frame 60) to select it, and move it to **Frame 26**. Note, the Scale property in After Effects 5.5 shows both X and Y scale percentage values.

4. Click **RAM Preview** and observe the results of moving the Scale keyframe. The rocket now gets smaller more quickly and then continues to traverse the Composition window. You can move the first or last Scale keyframe wherever you want on the Timeline to change the timing of scaling in your composition. The closer together the keyframes are, the faster the scaling; the farther apart they are, the slower the scaling.

5. Save your project and close the **Moving Keyframes** composition. Leave your project open for the next exercise.

***

TIP | Moving Multiple Keyframes

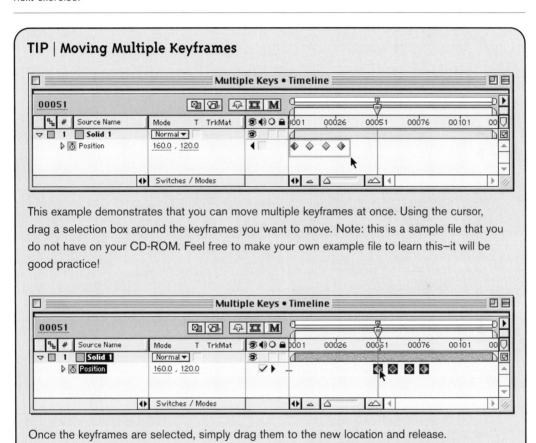

This example demonstrates that you can move multiple keyframes at once. Using the cursor, drag a selection box around the keyframes you want to move. Note: this is a sample file that you do not have on your CD-ROM. Feel free to make your own example file to learn this—it will be good practice!

Once the keyframes are selected, simply drag them to the new location and release.

6. _____Animating Multiple Properties

Most professional animation is more complex than what you've created so far. To achieve more complex motion, you'll want to animate several properties for an individual layer. In this exercise you'll learn to animate the Position, Scale, Rotation, and Opacity properties for a simple title graphic.

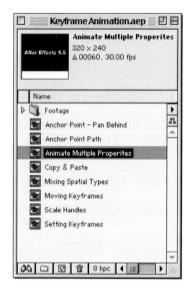 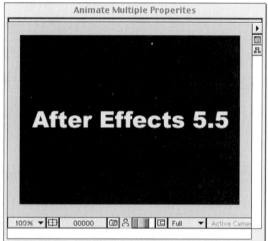

1. Double-click the **Animate Multiple Properties** composition to open it. In the **Composition** window, observe the title graphic.

2. In the **Timeline** window, select the **Title** layer. Press **S** on your keyboard to display the Scale property. Again, you could have clicked the twirly and revealed all the properties, but this shortcut is much faster if all you want to see is the Scale property. Click the **Stopwatch** icon to turn on keyframes.

The Stopwatch must be turned on, or you will not be able to set any keyframes and any change you make will become a global change to the composition. Note, the Scale property in After Effects 5.5 shows both X and Y scale percentage values.

3. Set the **Scale** value to **10%**. In After Effects 5.5, the lock symbol means that if you scale the one X or Y property, the other property will also scale.

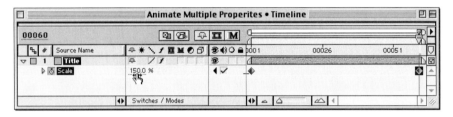

4. Set the **Time Marker** to **Frame 60**. Set the **Scale** value to **150%**.

NOTE | Scale Constrain in 5.5

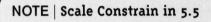

After Effects 5.5 introduces a new icon for the scale property that looks like a lock. This allows you to scale x and y values in equal ratios. With the lock icon turned on (it's a toggle switch), you can increase the scale of x or y and the other property will scale in proportion to those settings.

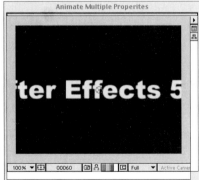

5. Click **RAM Preview** to view the results so far.

6. Move the **Time Marker** to **Frame 1**. Make sure the **Title** layer is still selected, and press **R** on your keyboard to display the **Rotation** property. Notice that the Scale property disappears and is replaced by the Rotation property in the Timeline. Click the **Stopwatch** icon on the **Rotation** property, and then set the **Rotation** value to **−180°**.

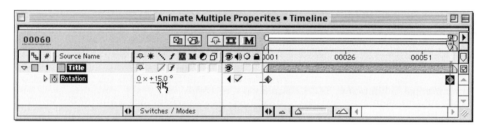

7. Move the **Time Marker** to **Frame 60**. Set the **Rotation** value to **15°**.

8. Click **RAM Preview** to see the results so far.

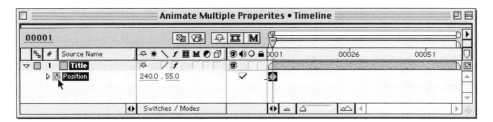

9. Move the **Time Marker** to **Frame 1**. Make sure the **Title** layer is selected, and press **P** on your keyboard to display the **Position** property. Click the **Stopwatch** icon. Set the **X-axis** value to **240** and the **Y-axis** value to **55**.

10. Move the **Time Marker** to **Frame 60**. Set the **X-axis** value to **110** and the **Y-axis** value to **155**.

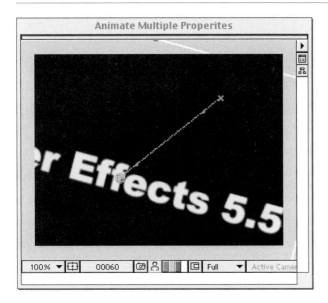

11. Scrub the **Time Marker** to observe the results so far.

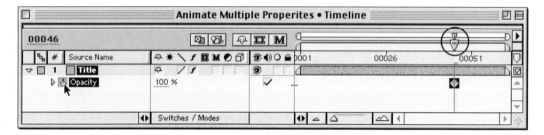

12. Move the **Time Marker** to **Frame 46**. With the **Title** layer selected, press **T** on your keyboard to display the **Opacity** property. Click the **Stopwatch** icon and accept the default value of **100%** for the keyframe.

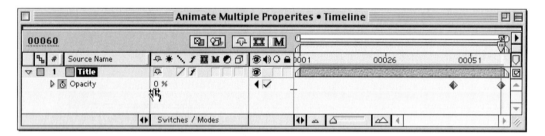

13. Move the **Time Marker** to **Frame 60**. Set the **Opacity** value to **0%**.

14. Click **RAM Preview** to play your animation.

15. Save your project and close the **Animate Multiple Properties** composition. Leave your project open for the next exercise.

Shortcut Keys for Properties

You've seen that you can press keys on the keyboard to display individual layer properties. The following table lists all the shortcut keys for displaying Transform properties. Individual properties are hidden unless you use these shortcut keys, or click the twirly arrow to reveal all the properties at once.

Shortcut Keys to Display Individual Transform Properties	
Shortcut Key	**Property**
A	Anchor Point
P	Position
R	Rotation
S	Scale
T	Opacity

Let's say that you wanted to change the scale and rotation of a layer, and wanted to know the shortcut to show those specific two properties. There's a way to add only the properties you want to see. To display more than one layer property in the Timeline, you must first show a single property. Then, hold down the Shift key and press the shortcut key for the property you want to add to the display. The table below lists all the shortcut keys for adding Transform properties to the Timeline display.

Shortcut Keys to Add Transform Properties	
Shortcut Key	**Action**
Shift+A	Anchor Point
Shifit+P	Position
Shift+R	Rotation
Shift+S	Scale
Shift+T	Opacity

Automatic Keyframe Shortcuts

If you want to set a keyframe automatically while you display a property, press the **Option** (Mac) or **Alt** (Windows) key, along with the shortcut key for the property. This reveals the property you want and sets a keyframe in one shortcut key.

Shortcut Keys for Setting a Keyframe with a Transform Property		
Macintosh	**Windows**	**Property**
Option+A	Alt+A	Anchor Point
Option+P	Alt+P	Position
Option+R	Alt+R	Rotation
Option+S	Alt+S	Scale
Option+T	Alt+T	Opacity

 MOVIE | **Display_Properties.mov**

We've prepared a short movie that demonstrates how to use shortcut keys to display properties in After Effects. It's called **Display_Properties.mov** and is located in the **movies** folder on the **H•O•T CD-ROM**.

What are Bézier Curves and Handles?

The title of this section might sound scarier than it is. **Bézier curves and handles** are something that digital artists love because they give them artistic control. Those of you who are familiar with Illustrator or Freehand will likely be familiar with Bézier curve editing. In After Effects, Bézier curves are used to influence the shape of motion paths. They are also used for other purposes, such as for mask shapes and speed graphs, which you'll learn about in future chapters. If you are not familiar with Bézier curves and points, there's no need to worry—this section will help you out!

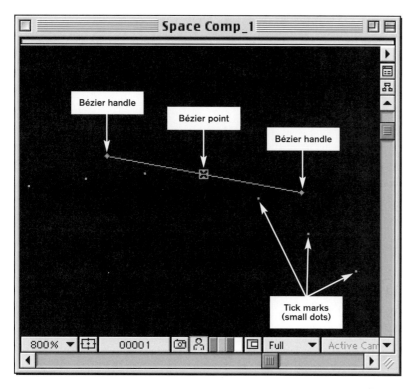

A Bézier curve contains points with control handles. To see the Bézier handles in the Comp window, you must click on a keyframe in the Timeline to select that keyframe. The control handles influence the curves around the Bézier point.

In the image above, the series of tick marks represents the animation path. By dragging the Bézier handles, you affect the Bézier curve and influence the motion path.

Bézier points have two handles: one for the portion of the curve that precedes the Bézier point and another for the portion of the curve that follows the Bézier point.

The scary sounding term **Bézier** comes from the name of a French mathematician, Pierre Bézier. He developed a math formula used to describe curves. After Effects and many other computer graphics programs use this formula. Luckily, you don't have to worry about formulas. All you have to do is click and drag to get the curve you want.

MOVIE | Bézier_Points.mov

We've prepared a short movie that demonstrates the use of Bézier points called **Bézier_Points.mov**, located in the **movies** folder on the **H•O•T CD-ROM.**

7.——————————Using Bézier Handles with Motion Paths

In this exercise you will learn to select Bézier points and adjust Bézier handles to influence the motion path. This gives you added control over the way your objects move and, for that reason, is an invaluable skill.

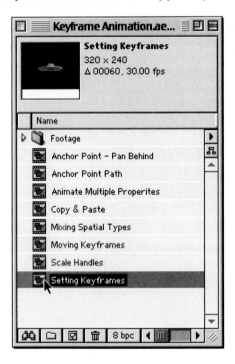

1. In the **Project** window, double-click the **Setting Keyframes** composition to reopen it.

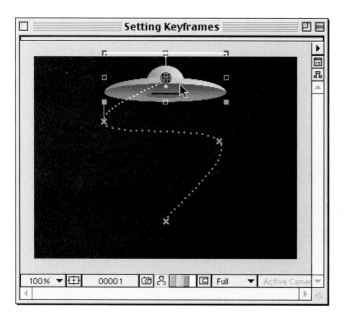

2. In the **Composition** window, click the UFO image to select it. Observe the motion path you created in Exercise 3.

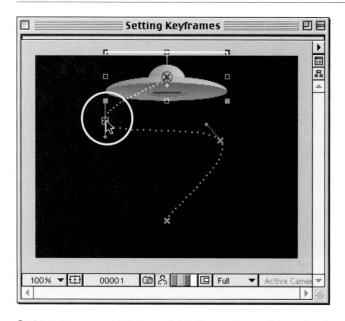

3. Click the second **Bézier point** in the motion path to select it.

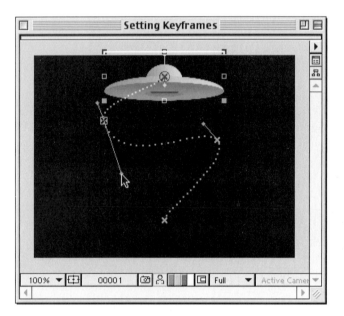

4. Drag the bottom **Bézier handle** down and observe the influence on the motion path. The curve becomes rounder and less angular.

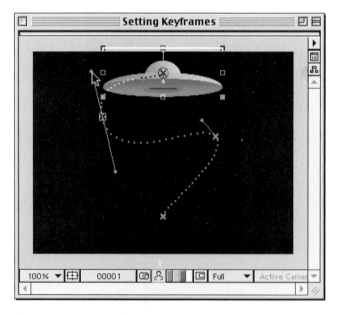

5. Drag the top **Bézier handle** up.

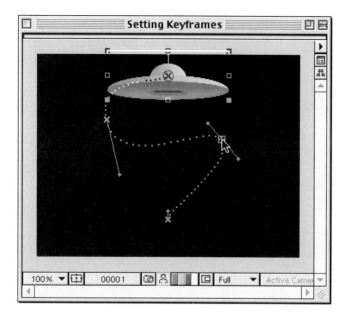

6. Click the third **Bézier point** in the motion path to select it.

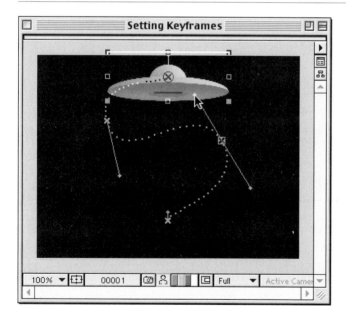

7. Drag both **Bézier handles** out to smooth the curve.

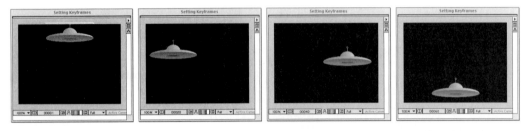

8. Click **RAM Preview** to see the smoothed animation.

9. Save your project, and close the **Setting Keyframes** composition. Leave your project open for the next exercise.

TIP | Auto Orientation

To make the UFO, or any object for that matter, orient to the path as it moves, choose **Layer > Transform > Auto Orient**.

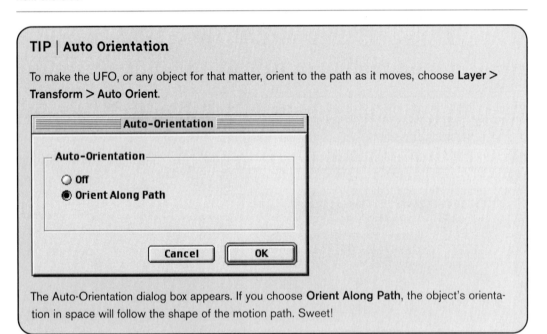

The Auto-Orientation dialog box appears. If you choose **Orient Along Path**, the object's orientation in space will follow the shape of the motion path. Sweet!

Spatial Interpolation Types

The next section will teach you how to control a motion path by learning how to give the path straight lines and curves. This is accomplished with a feature in After Effects called spatial interpolation. Spatial interpolation types are visible in the Composition window because they influence the appearance of the motion path.

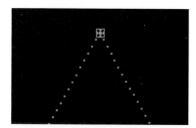

Linear interpolation can be identified by a sharp curve and even distribution of tick marks. There are no handlebar controls in a Linear type. Placing the Pen tool over any keyframe in the Composition window and clicking will toggle the shape between a straight path (like this) and a curved one.

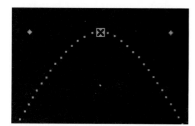

Auto Bézier interpolation can be identified by the smooth curve. There are control handles, but *without* handlebars. (If you attempt to move a control point on an Auto Bézier type, it will be converted to a Continuous Bézier type.) You'll get to try this in the next exercise.

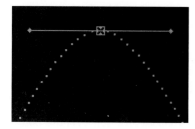

Continuous Bézier interpolation can be identified by the straight handlebars. The handlebars may be of different lengths, but they are always straight.

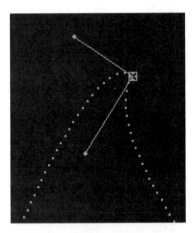

Angled handlebars identify the **Bézier** interpolation type. The angle and length of the handlebars can be adjusted independently. Using the Selection tool, if you hold the Control key (Mac or Windows) on any Bézier handle, you can create this type of path by pulling on the handles in different directions. In order to change a control point from a smooth to a corner point (or vice versa) press Ctrl (Windows) or Control (Mac OS) as you click the point with the selection tool.

Mixing Spatial Interpolation Types

After Effects sometimes uses intimidating terms to explain common tasks. In this exercise, you'll be introduced to a big dose of new, intimidating-sounding terms. We'll explain all of the terms, but we hope they don't get in the way of your understanding. Remember that they are only words. This exercise will teach you something more important than new terms or strange words—it shows you how to make an object move exactly the way you want!

Take the term **spatial interpolation,** for example. The word "spatial" refers to the way an object moves in physical space, such as a Position property. "Interpolation" is what After Effects does to create fluid movement between keyframes. If you set a keyframe to move its position from screen left to screen right, you are affecting its spatial appearance. Interpolation is what makes it move from point A to point B. You may be familiar with the term "tweening" or "in-betweening"; interpolation is the same thing.

The UFO moves from the top of the frame to the bottom using spatial interpolation. The default type of movement is Auto Bézier, which you learned to control manually in the previous exercise. Other types of spatial interpolation methods are possible in addition to Bézier. Often you will need to create straight lines and complex curves within the same motion path. To accomplish this, you must use both linear and Bézier spatial interpolation types on the motion path.

8.——————————**Following a Complex Motion Path**

In this exercise you will create a series of keyframes and make a small object follow the shape of a graphic number 5. When you create a keyframe, the default interpolation type used is Auto Bézier. You will change the interpolation type for each point to make the motion path follow the desired shape.

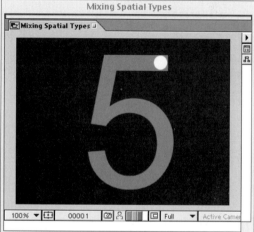

1. In the **Project** window, double-click the **Mixing Spatial Types** composition to open it. Observe the number 5 with a dot in the Composition window.

This composition was created with multiple layers to teach you about spatial interpolation. If you are wondering how you would make your own composition with multiple layers, here are the steps: Import footage into your Project window, create a new composition, and drag the footage items into the composition. Each footage item becomes its own layer. You'll learn more about layers in Chapter 8, "Layers."

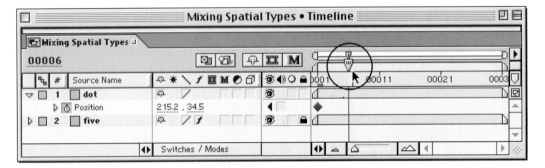

2. In the **Timeline** window, select the **dot** layer and set the **Time Marker** to **Frame 6**. Press the short-cut key **P** to expose the **Position** property. You'll see that one Position keyframe has already been set.

3. Drag the dot to the left, as shown above.

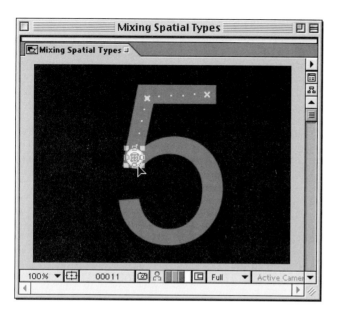

4. Set the **Time Marker** to **Frame 11**. Drag the dot down to the position shown above.

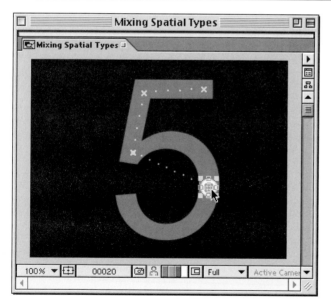

5. Set the **Time Marker** to **Frame 20**. Drag the dot to the position shown above. Notice that the motion path doesn't match the number 5 yet. You'll be going back to fix this shortly.

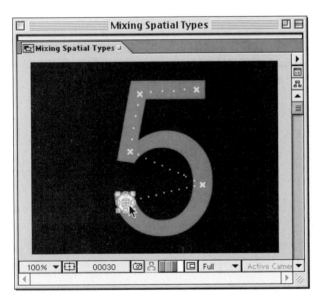

6. Set the **Time Marker** to **Frame 30**. Drag the dot to the end position. The motion path still doesn't match the number 5. You'll fix this in the next step.

7. Select the **Pen** tool from the Toolbox.

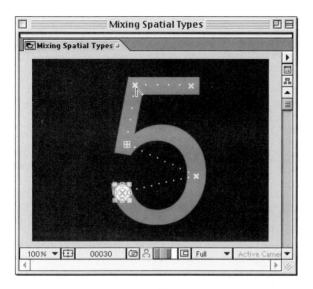

8. Hold the **Pen** tool directly over the second point in the motion path. Ctrl-click (Windows) or Control-click (Mac OS) on the point and notice that the motion path changes to a straight line. That's because clicking on the point converts the spatial interpolation type to **Linear**. If you click a second time, it will toggle between Auto Bézier and Linear. You don't have to remember all the mumbo jumbo terms, spatial and linear, in order to make a straight line. Just remember to use the Pen tool in this manner to make straight lines!

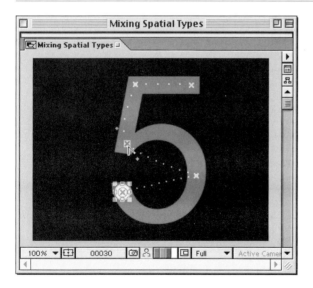

9. With the **Pen** tool, click the third point. Notice that the path changes to have short Bézier handles.

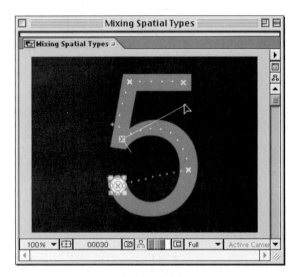

10. Holding the **Option** key (Mac) or the **Alt** key (Windows), move the second handle to the right, as shown in the picture above. Notice that the two handles move independently of one another when using the Bézier interpolation type.

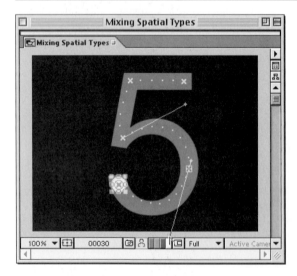

11. Using the **Pen** tool again, click the fourth point in the motion path. This should change it from a straight shape to a curved shape. Move the handles to make the shape round the number 5, as you see above.

 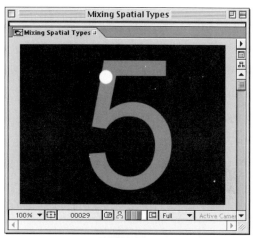

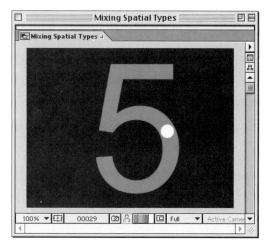 

12. Click **RAM Preview** to view the animation.

13. Save your project and close the **Mixing Spatial Types** composition. Leave your project open for the next exercise.

9. —————————Animating Scale Using Control Handles

You've worked with setting Scale keyframes already, but this exercise will show you a different approach than what you've used so far. Sometimes you may want to change the proportions of an object by making it taller or wider than the original artwork. So far, you've learned to animate scale by setting keyframes and adjusting the Scale values. In this exercise, you'll learn a different method, in which you make the scale changes in the Composition window using the layer control handles.

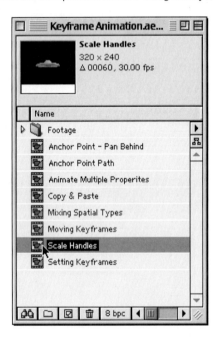

1. Double-click the **Scale Handles** composition to open it.

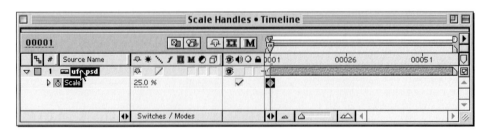

2. Select the **ufo.psd** layer in the **Timeline** window. Press **Option+S** (Mac) or **Alt+S** (Windows) to display the **Scale** property and automatically add a keyframe at the current Time Marker position (Frame 1).

3. Move the **Time Marker** to **Frame 15**.

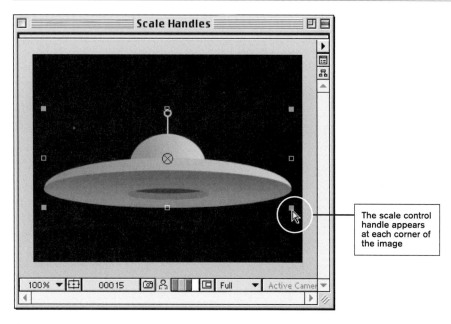

The scale control handle appears at each corner of the image

4. In the **Composition** window, click one of the solid corner **control handles,** hold down the **Shift** key, and drag the UFO until the **Scale** value in the **Timeline** window is approximately **50%**. In 5.5: there is a constrain checkbox for Scale that allows you to constrain proportion while scrubbing x and y values for scale This eliminates the need for holding down the Shift key.

Holding down the Shift key causes both the X axis and the Y axis values to scale proportionally.

WARNING | Constraining Scale Gotcha

In some programs, in order to scale artwork you hold the Shift key down first and then click to select and drag an object. In After Effects, this order is reversed so that you click the object first and then hold the Shift key before you drag.

---

5. Set the **Time Marker** to **Frame 30**.

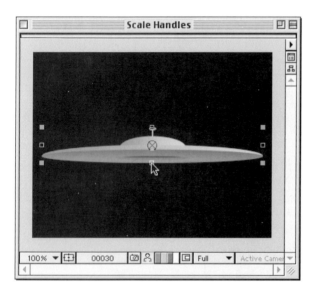

6. Click either the top or bottom center **control handle**, and drag until the **Scale** Y-axis value in the **Timeline** window is approximately **20%**.

7. Move the **Time Marker** to **Frame 45**.

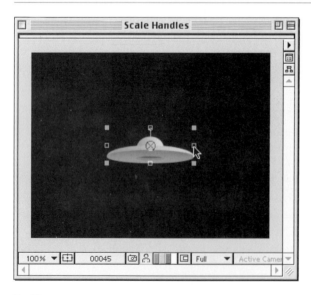

8. Click either the left or right center **control handle**, and drag until the **Scale** X-axis value in the **Timeline** window is approximately **20%**.

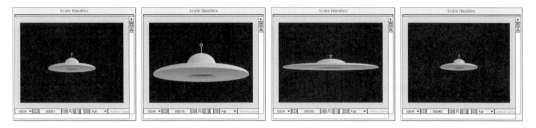

9. Click **RAM Preview** to view the scale animation.

10. Save your project and close the **Scale Handles** composition. Leave your project open for the next exercise.

What Is the Anchor Point?

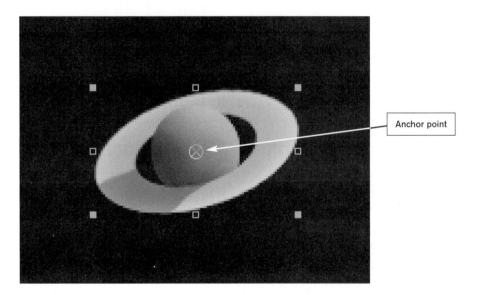

The **anchor point** of an image is a designated point that is used for positioning, scale, and rotation. It is displayed as a circle with an X through it. Each footage item has its own anchor point. By default, After Effects places the anchor point at the center of each footage item. If the object rotates or scales, it will do so around the anchor point.

It is often necessary to move the anchor point to make an object rotate or scale around a point other than the center of the image. Another reason to move the anchor point is to rotate an object around another object. You'll get to move the anchor point in the exercise that follows.

10. ———————————— Animating the Anchor Point Using the Pan Behind Tool

This exercise will give you a real-world example of why you would change the anchor point in an animation. You're going to make the rocket ship rotate around the planet. This sounds like a simple idea, but it will require the use of the anchor point. Why? Because the default rotation axis of the rocket ship is in the middle of the rocket ship. By moving the anchor point, you'll move the axis to the planet, which will cause the rotation to occur around the planet instead of around the rocket itself. If it sounds confusing, trying the exercise will clarify things!

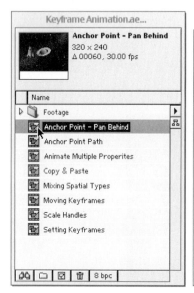
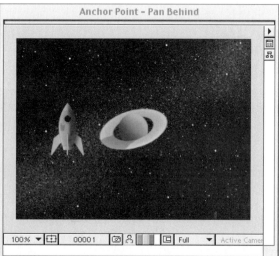

1. Double-click the **Anchor Point – Pan Behind** composition to open it. Notice the rocket and planet images in the Composition window.

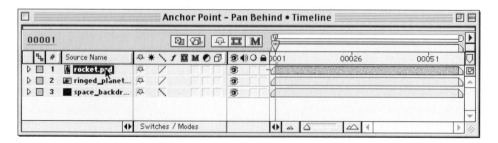

2. Select the **rocket.psd** layer.

3. Select the **Pan Behind** tool from the Toolbox.

4. In the **Composition** window, click the rocket to display its anchor point, and drag the rocket's **anchor point** to the center of the planet. Notice that the cursor changes to a four-pointed arrow shape when you use the Pan Behind tool. **Note:** The Pan Behind tool moves the anchor point of the rocket but doesn't alter the position of the rocket. If you did not use this tool, and simply changed the anchor point position in the Transform properties, the rocket would move along with the anchor point. The Pan Behind tool is very popular for moving the anchor point, because it moves the anchor point without moving the object to which the anchor point is attached.

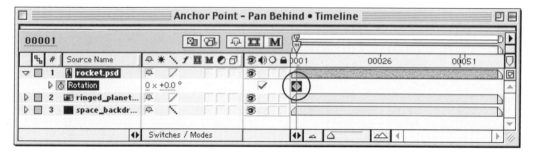

5. Press **Option+R** (Mac) or **Alt+R** (Windows) to display the **Rotation** property and automatically set a keyframe at the current **Time Marker** position (Frame 1).

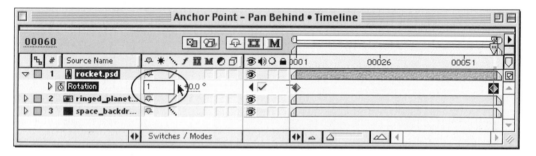

6. Set the **Time Marker** to **Frame 60**, and then set the **Rotation** value to **1**.

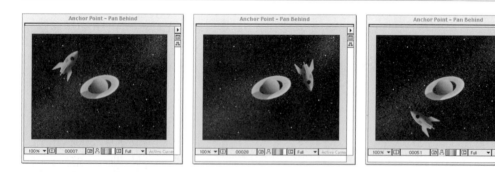

7. Click **RAM Preview** to watch your animation.

8. Save your project and close After Effects.

> **WARNING** | **Pan Behind Alters the Position Motion Path**
>
> If you attempt to use the Pan Behind tool to move the anchor point on a layer with an existing Position motion path, your motion path will be altered. These alterations can be significant. We recommend that while you are learning After Effects, you use the Pan Behind tool to move an anchor point only when the selected layer does not have a Position motion path.

Test Yourself On This Chapter!

This was a critical chapter, in that you've combined the skills you've learned in the past three chapters to create animation—finally! Check your knowledge by trying the following. We're being intentionally vague about how to do these tasks, so you can make sure you have really learned how they are done. If you need to go back to any of the exercises, feel free. This stuff is new, and it really does require practice.

A. Create a new composition, and drag some footage into it.

B. Set two position keyframes to make some artwork move from one part of the Composition window to another.

C. Add two more keyframes to the middle of the animation, so you can move the artwork around on the stage, creating curved and straight paths.

D. Change the opacity and scale of this animation over time.

E. Move the anchor point of one of the objects and create some rotation keyframes so that it spins on an axis other than its own.

Congratulations! You've completed a very important chapter in your work as an After Effects artist. Setting keyframes and anchor points are fundamental skills that you'll use for the rest of your career with After Effects.

6.

Playing with Time

| Spatial Versus Temporal Interpolation |
| Using the Keyframe Assistant |
| Editing the Speed Graph |
| Using the Hold Temporal Interpolation Method |
| Using Roving Keyframes |

chap_06

After Effects 5.0/5.5
H•O•T CD-ROM

This chapter deals specifically with time, or the features that control time in After Effects. As you become more experienced with creating animation, you'll start to recognize the nuances of motion and see how timing plays a critical role. The term "timing" refers to whether objects move quickly, slowly, or change speed in the middle of an animation. An animation that takes 10 seconds has the potential to move at the same speed over the entire 10 seconds, or to start slow, maintain a constant speed, and then go faster at the end, and still only occupy 10 seconds of time. The tools described in this chapter will help you learn how to finesse the timing of your animation. After Effects is one of the most powerful desktop motion graphics tools because of its ability to give you, the animator and motion designer, the utmost control.

Spatial Versus Temporal Interpolation

As you'll soon see, the After Effects interface distinguishes between spatial and temporal keyframes and keyframe interpolation. **Spatial** means space, **temporal** means time, and **keyframe interpolation** describes the types of changes that occur between keyframes. While those terms might sound a little technical or intimidating, their meanings are really that simple.

In After Effects, you can set footage to change in both space and time. Distinct tools are used to adjust the spatial and temporal aspects of your compositions. In the previous chapter you worked primarily with spatial issues in the Composition window. By learning to change the curves of your motion paths, for example, you adjusted the spatial qualities of your animation. In this chapter, you will work with temporal issues in the Timeline window.

The Timeline window is the primary tool for playing with time. Just as you adjust spatial interpolation in the Composition window, you can adjust temporal interpolation in the Timeline window.

All properties have temporal interpolation. In other words, you can adjust the timing of any property. After Effects contains sophisticated tools that allow you to affect time in both subtle and dramatic ways. How you use these tools is up to your imagination and artistic sensibility.

It's been said that timing is everything. Timing is perhaps the most important aspect of animation. Although books can provide information, as an artist you develop a sense of timing through experience. A musician must practice to develop a full sense of rhythm. The same is true for an animator. You develop the subtlety of timing and rhythm through a commitment to the art form.

I. _____Using the Keyframe Assistant

In this exercise you will learn to use the Keyframe Assistant to **ease** the timing of objects. Easing the timing means creating a smooth transition in timing. Rather than having something start moving and continue moving at the same speed, an ease will slowly build acceleration or deceleration. The Keyframe Assistant offers **ease tools** that provide an automated way of easing timing. You'll learn to use the **Easy Ease In** and the **Easy Ease Out** tools to smooth timing changes.

You can see timing changes in the Timeline window by observing the graph associated with time. Through the use of the Keyframe Assistant, you will be introduced to the **Speed graph**, and you will learn to interpret changes in the graph.

1. Open the **Time.aep** project from the **chap_06** folder.

2. Choose **File > Save As**. Navigate to your **HOT_AE_Projects** folder and click **Save**.

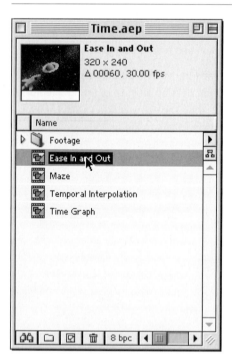

3. In the **Project** window, double-click the **Ease In and Out** composition. This composition was prepared to teach you the principles of this exercise.

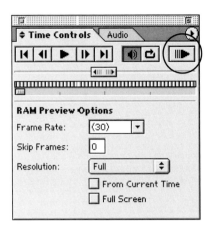

4. Click the **RAM Preview** button on the **Time Controls** palette to view the animation.

Observe that the rocket and the UFO move at a steady, consistent speed. This is called linear timing. There is no acceleration or deceleration in speed with linear timing.

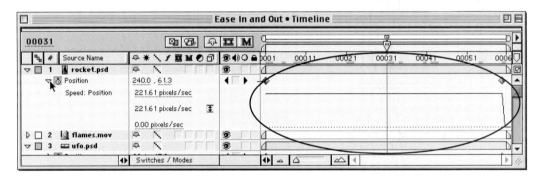

5. In the **Timeline** window, click the **rocket.psd Position** twirly to display the Speed graph for the Position property. Observe the straight line in the graph. This straight line reflects the linear timing of the rocket. This graph is part of the built-in After Effects interface called the Value graph, and it exists on any layer that has keyframed motion in the Position, Rotation, Scale, or Opacity properties.

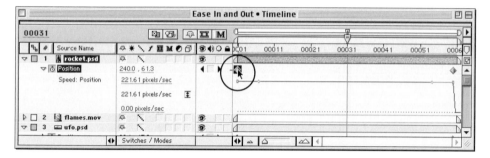

6. Select the keyframe on **Frame 1** of the **rocket.psd** layer.

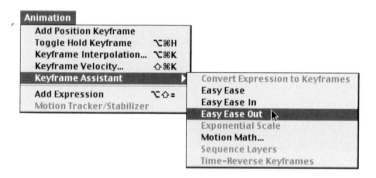

7. Choose **Animation > Keyframe Assistant > Easy Ease Out.**

Notice that the Value graphic has changed, in that it has dipped down at the first keyframe and curved upward at the last keyframe. This indicates that the movement now starts slowly and speeds up.

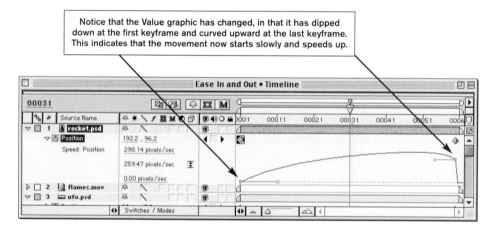

8. Observe that the Speed graph is now curved. This indicates that the movement is no longer linear. At the lower part of the curve, the timing of the object (in this example, the rocket artwork layer) is slowed down. At the higher part of the curve, the timing of the object is faster.

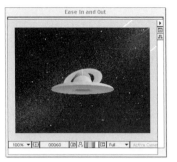

9. Click **RAM Preview** to see the results so far. Notice that the rocket starts slowly and gains speed.

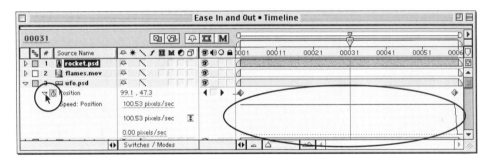

10. In the **Timeline** window, click the **rocket.psd** twirly up to hide that layer's properties. Click the **ufo.psd Position** twirly down to display the Speed graph for that layer. The linear graph reflects the steady, linear timing of the UFO.

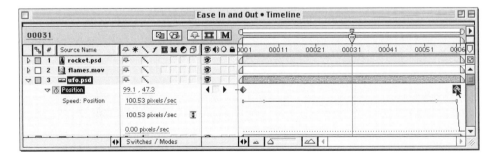

11. Click the last keyframe to select it.

12. Choose **Animation > Keyframe Assistant > Easy Ease In**.

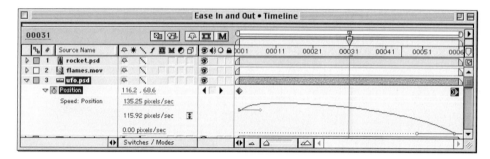

13. Observe that the Speed graph now curves downward. This means that the object starts out moving faster and slows down over time.

14. Click **RAM Preview** to see the animation.

Notice that the UFO slows down at the end of the move. If you can't see the entire animation in RAM Preview, you may not have enough RAM in your computer, or you may need to allocate more RAM to After Effects. You'll find instructions for doing this in the next chapter, "Previewing Movies." Meanwhile, use the spacebar instead to preview everything. Unfortunately, this won't show you a real-time preview, which is what you need in order to judge the timing of your motion.

So, when do you use Ease In and when do you use Ease Out? Use the Ease In function when you want movement to start fast and end slow. Use the Ease Out function when you want movement to start slow and end fast. If you want something other than slow and fast or fast and slow, you'll have to learn how to adjust the timing curves on your own. You'll learn how to do that in the next exercise!

15. Save your project and close the **Ease In and Out** composition. Leave the project open for the next exercise.

NOTE | Speed Dots

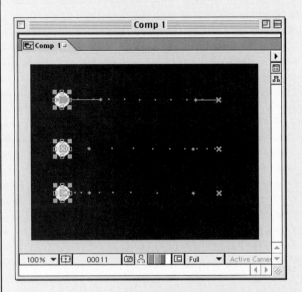

After Effects offers a visual way to see the timing of your animations. When you select an object in the Timeline or Composition window that already has Position keyframe properties set, dots will appear in the Composition window. Each dot indicates a frame in time. The spacing between the dots indicates how fast or slow or evenly paced the keyframed movement is. In the example above, the top circle has evenly spaced dots associated with its motion. This indicates linear movement. The middle circle is using an Ease In, shown by dots that are spaced farther apart at the beginning and closer together at the end. This means that the movement will start out fast and then slow down. The bottom circle is using an Ease Out, and the dots are spaced closer together at the first keyframe and get farther apart at the second. Dots that are closer together mean slower movement, and ones that are farther apart mean faster movement.

The only way to see these dots is to select artwork (that has Position keyframe properties set), either in the Timeline or Composition window. The only way to affect the spacing between the dots is with the Speed graph, which you just learned about!

2. _____Editing the Speed Graph

In this exercise you will learn to work with the Speed graph. You've seen that the Easy Ease In and Easy Ease Out tools will automatically ease timing for you. However, it's often preferable to set the timing exactly as you want it. Here you'll learn to ease animation timing manually.

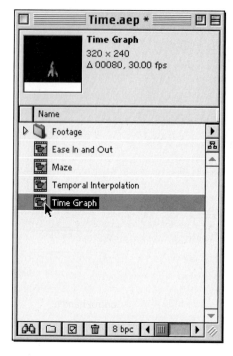

1. Double-click the **Time Graph** composition to open it.

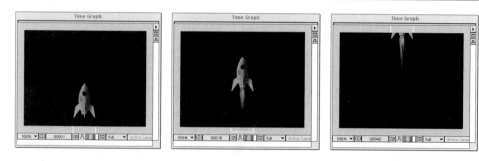

2. Click **RAM Preview** and observe the linear timing of the rocket lifting off.

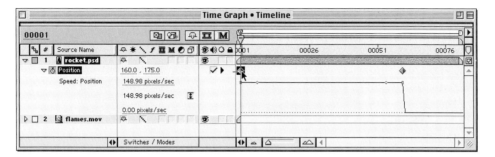

3. In the **Timeline** window, click the first keyframe for the **rocket.psd** layer. Once the keyframe is selected, control handles will appear on the Speed graph.

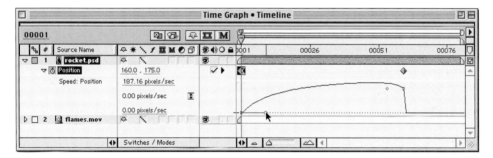

4. Locate the **control handle** for the keyframe on the graph. Drag the handle down to slow the speed of the rocket. Notice that the graph adjusts as you drag and release the control handle.

Dragging the handle down on the graph slows the timing. Dragging the handle up speeds up the timing.

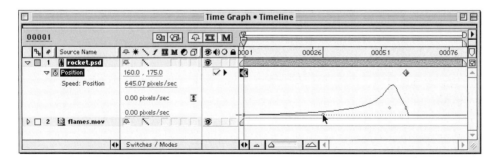

5. Drag the **control handle** to the right to influence more outgoing frames. Notice that the graph adjusts as you drag and release the handle.

Dragging the control handle away from the point influences more frames. Dragging it toward the point influences fewer frames.

6. Click **RAM Preview** and notice that the rocket now lifts off slowly and then speeds up.

7. Save your project, and leave this composition open for the next exercise.

NOTE | Twirlies, Twirlies, and More Twirlies?

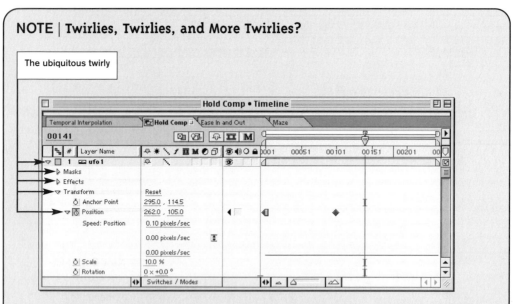

Are you going twirly crazy? What are all those twirlies, and how did they get there, anyway? Every layer in After Effects automatically has properties, and the way to access a property is by using the twirly or a shortcut key. Whenever you drag a footage item on to the Timeline, a twirly automatically appears next to it. All layers, except sound file layers, have the Masks, Effects, and Transform properties. There are twirlies next to each of those properties too! In the Transform property, all the twirlies reveal Value graphs. We've looked at the Speed graph in this chapter. The bottom line is that every layer has a twirly, and if you click it, you might find some hidden treasures or properties to explore. We'll be using twirlies throughout the book, and shortcuts to get to those properties as well.

---

3. ———————Using the Hold Temporal Interpolation Method

In this exercise, you'll learn to use the **Hold interpolation method**. This method is useful when you want movement in an animation to stop and hold. In the process of learning how to use the Hold interpolation method, you'll get more experience building a new composition and setting keyframes.

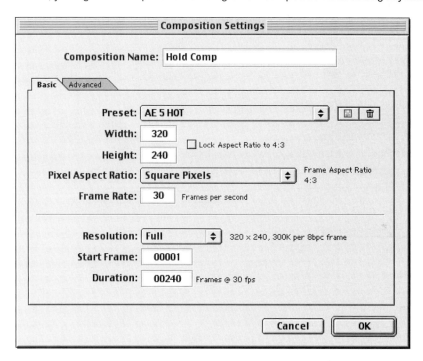

1. Create a new composition. You haven't made a new composition for a few chapters, so let us refresh your memory about how to do it. Choose **Composition > New Composition**. The Composition Settings dialog box opens. Name the composition **Hold Comp**, and select **AE 5 HOT** from the **Preset** menu. If you don't have the preset in your Preset menu, set the Preset menu to Custom, then set the options in the Composition Settings dialog box to match the illustration above. Click the **Disk** icon to the right of the Preset field, and name the preset **AE 5 HOT**. Click **OK**.

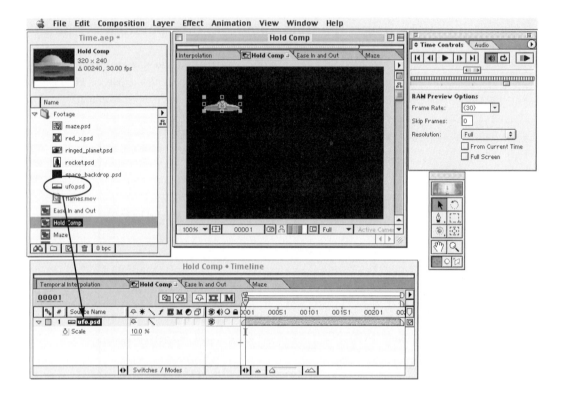

2. Drag **ufo.psd** from the **Footage** folder in the Project window into your Timeline. This artwork is way too big, so set the scale to **10%.** (Hint: The letter S on your keyboard will show you the Scale properties, or you can use the twirly in the Timeline to locate the Transform > Scale properties.) Move the UFO into the position that you see above by dragging it into place in the **Composition** window.

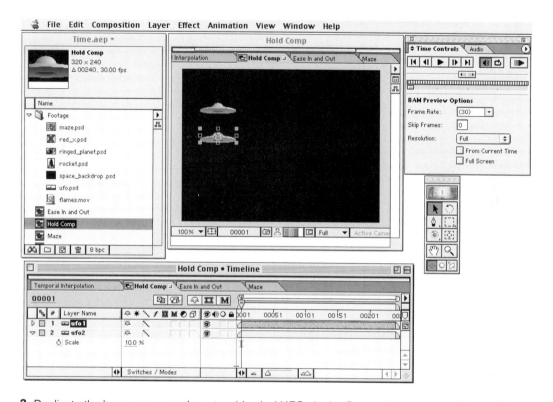

3. Duplicate the layer so you can have two identical UFOs in the Composition window. This is a little easier said than done, so here's how to accomplish it. Select the **ufo.psd** layer in the **Timeline** window, and choose **Command+D** (Mac) or **Control+D** (Windows) to duplicate the layer. A new layer will appear in the Timeline with the same file name. Next, with the copy selected (it appears above the original), use the arrow keys on your keyboard to nudge the copy of the UFO image down in the **Composition** window until it matches what you see in the screen above. Change the file names to **ufo1** and **ufo2** by selecting the layer, using the **Return** key to access the editable name field, and typing new names.

You may not realize what you've just accomplished. By changing the scale in step 2 and not setting a keyframe by not clicking the stopwatch button, you created a global change for the object. This means that it will be 10% scale throughout any animation unless you change your mind, set keyframes, and make changes to the scale between keyframes. By duplicating the object with the global scale change, you now have two identical small UFO images. After Effects professionals often use this duplicate and rename technique to save time.

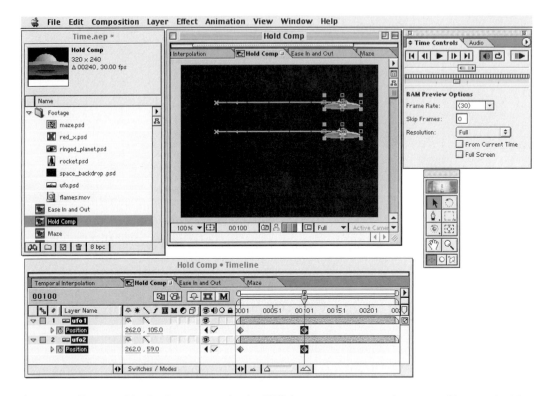

4. Next you'll set position keyframes to make the UFO layers move across the screen. You can do this to both layers at once–joy! Here's how: Select both layers, using your **Shift** key, and press the letter **P** on the keyboard. This causes the Position property to appear on both layers. Alternatively, you could twirl all the twirlies down, but what a hassle! Then click the **Stopwatch** icons for both layers to set start keyframes. Move the **Time Marker** to **Frame 100**. Select both UFO objects in the composition by using your **Shift** key, and move one to the right. They should both move together, and two identical keyframes will be set.

You could have done this keyframe animation to one UFO layer and then duplicated the layer. There are always multiple ways to do things in After Effects. You'll find that sometimes you think through the most efficient workflow and other times you'll change your mind as you're working. After Effects will let you work easily either way.

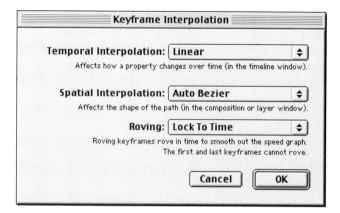

5. Select the keyframe on **Frame 1** in the Timeline for the layer **ufo1**. Choose **Animation > Keyframe Interpolation**. Alternatively, press **Command+Option+K** (Mac) or **Control+Alt+K** (Windows).

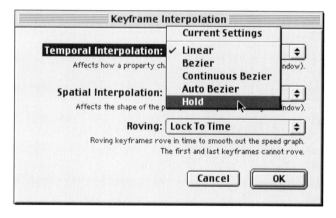

6. In the **Keyframe Interpolation** dialog box, select **Hold** as the **Temporal Interpolation** type. Click **OK**.

This sets the first keyframe as a Hold interpolation keyframe. You'll see the result when you preview the motion in the next step. As you can see, the Keyframe Interpolation dialog box is rather complex. Be sure to read the chart at the end of this chapter to understand its settings.

7. Click **RAM Preview** and observe the change in timing between the two UFOs. In particular, notice that the **ufo1** layer holds in time before appearing at the next keyframe. The Hold interpolation keyframe type is used to make objects stop or jump from frame to frame. If you wanted to make **ufo1** move on the first frame, you could change the keyframe interpolation type back to linear or another type of interpolation. You can also mix and match interpolation types within an animation if you set numerous keyframes.

8. Save your project, and close this composition.

NOTE | Temporal Interpolation Icons

When you change the timing of your animation using the Speed graph, different icons for keyframes show up in the Timeline window. It is not necessary to memorize these icons, but if you are curious about what they mean, read through the following chart.

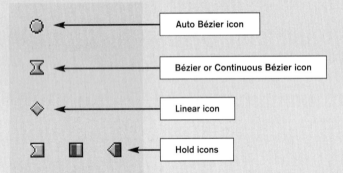

The shape of the Keyframe icon in the Time graph represents the temporal interpolation type. If you ever want to change a temporal keyframe interpolation type, select the keyframe you want to change and choose Animation > Keyframe Interpolation. This will cause a dialog box to appear, in which you can choose another temporal interpolation type.

Interpolation Icons and Functions

Icon	When to Use
Auto Bézier: Round icon.	This type of interpolation maintains a smooth transition between different keyframes. The Speed graph will show handles, and automatic curves will be applied.
Bézier or **Continuous Bézier:** Icon indented on both sides. The Bézier and Continuous Bézier types share the same icon.	Any time you change the curves on the Speed graph, manually or through the Ease In or Ease Out functions, the icon changes to reflect a Bézier or Continuous Bézier interpolation type. The difference between the two (Continuous Bézier and Bézier) is that Continuous Bézier handles adjust both sides of the curve, while Bézier handles adjust each side of the curve separately.
Linear: Diamond icon.	This is the default temporal interpolation type. Use this interpolation method when you don't want the velocity speed of movement to change.
Hold: Icon always flat on the right side. Different situations with nearby keyframe types create different types of hold icons. The indented Hold icon is most often displayed. The square Hold icon is not normally displayed. The half diamond, half square icon is sometimes displayed when the first or last frame of a composition is a Hold interpolation type.	Use the Hold interpolation method when you want movement to stop or pause.

It's not important to memorize what these icons look like. You'll probably be more interested in making your artwork move the way you want it to visually than in worrying about what icon is on your Timeline. Still, you might notice that the icons for keyframes change, and this is a handy chart to refer to if your curiosity gets aroused.

_____**Using Roving Keyframes**

When you set multiple keyframes, it can be hard to get the speed of the movement to be equal and even. This exercise demonstrates this issue. To make the X shape go around the maze in this example, you would have to set numerous keyframes. The trouble is, the physical distance that the X has to travel from keyframe to keyframe varies. Some of the moves are very short, and others are longer. It's hard to know where to set the keyframes on the Timeline, because you aren't going to spend the time to measure the distance, divide it into frames, and figure out where to set your keyframes. Wouldn't it be cool if After Effects provided a way to mathematically figure out even timing for you?

It does, of course! The **roving keyframes** feature addresses this issue. Roving keyframes ensures that the speed from keyframe to keyframe is consistent, even if you didn't set it up that way to begin with. In this exercise you will learn to use roving keyframes by applying the Roving Keyframe command to a prepared composition. If you don't have a good sense of when you'd want to use roving keyframes, this exercise will give you an example.

1. Double-click the **Maze** composition to open it.

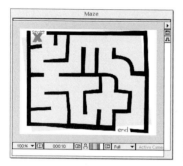 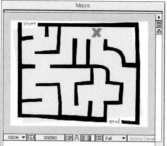 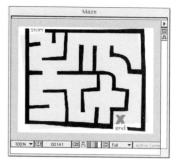

2. Click **RAM Preview** and observe the X moving through the maze. Notice that the timing of the movement is not even. The X speeds up and slows down.

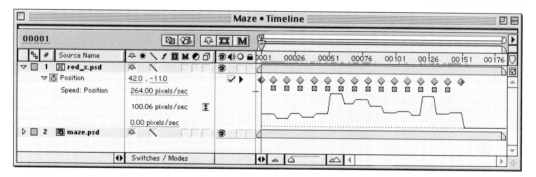

3. In the **Timeline** window, observe the Speed graph. The high portions of the graph are where the **red_x.psd** layer is moving faster. The low portions of the graph are where the **red_x.psd** layer is moving slower. Also observe that all the keyframes except the first and last have little check boxes beneath them. **Note:** You might wonder how the check boxes got here? If you click the twirly for Position to reveal the speed graph, these check boxes are part of the After Effects interface. A check box that is marked indicates that the accompanying keyframe is frozen and cannot move across time. You'll learn what this means in the following steps.

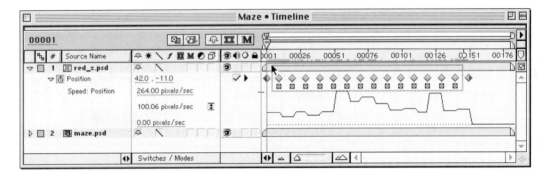

4. With your cursor, drag a selection around all the keyframes that have the little check boxes underneath. This should select all of these keyframes at once. Alternatively, you can hold the **Shift** key down to select each keyframe, but the dragging method is faster.

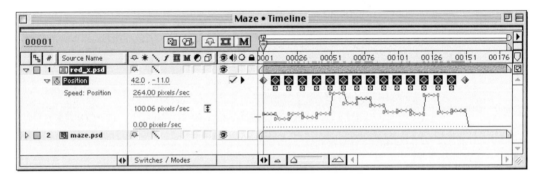

All of the keyframes with check boxes should now be selected.

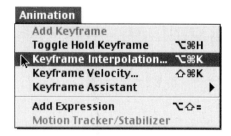

5. Choose **Animation > Keyframe Interpolation**. Alternatively, press **Command+Option+K** (Mac) or **Control+Alt+K** (Windows).

As you can see, the Keyframe Interpolation dialog box is rather complex. Be sure to read the chart at the end of this chapter for an explanation of the various options.

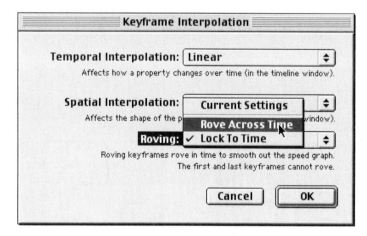

6. In the **Keyframe Interpolation** dialog box, locate the **Roving** option and select **Rove Across Time**. Click **OK**.

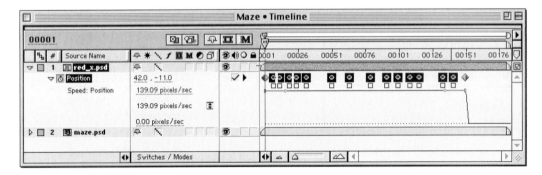

7. In the **Timeline** window, observe that the selected keyframes have been moved and the check boxes are now cleared. Also observe that the Speed graph is flat and even. This kind of timing would have been really difficult to figure out manually!

Clearing the little check box allows a keyframe to "rove across time". This means that After Effects will move the keyframes that you set manually to mathmatically adjust itselve to even increments of time. The position of the keyframes on the Timeline will not look even, but After Effects will even out the timing that it takes to get from each point in the composition. This smooths the timing of movement when the distance of travel between points is varied.

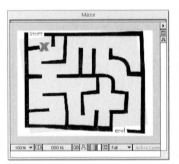
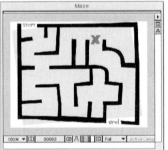
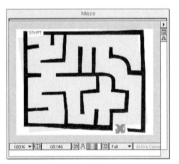

8. Click **RAM Preview** to see the result of the roving keyframes.

9. Save your project, and close After Effects.

What Is Keyframe Interpolation?

The term "interpolation" refers to the process of creating changes between keyframes. It's often referred to as "tweening" in animation terminology.

The Keyframe Interpolation dialog box is where temporal and spatial attributes can be set for keyframes. You can access this dialog box by choosing Animation > Keyframe Interpolation. It is necessary to select single or multiple keyframes before you access this dialog box. Any changes you make in the dialog box will be applied to the selected keyframes. You can mix keyframe interpolation types on different keyframes on a Timeline.

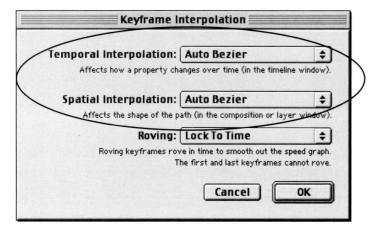

In the Keyframe Interpolation dialog box, you can choose whether you want to use temporal interpolation or spatial interpolation. All properties have temporal interpolation. Of the Transform properties, Opacity is the only one that doesn't have spatial attributes, since its changes are marked by time only, not by space. Here's a chart that explains all the settings in this complex dialog box.

Keyframe Interpolation Dialog Box Settings	
Category	**Option**
Temporal Interpolation: Affects how a property changes over time in the Timeline window.	**Linear:** Creates a uniform rate of change between keyframes. Linear keyframes can be used to form a corner or sharp turn in the graph line. This is useful for giving a mechanical or rhythmic feel to animation timing.
	Bézier: A completely manual type. The two control handles operate independently of one another in both the motion path and Value graph. Use this type when you want manual control of the timing in and out of the keyframe.
	Continuous Bézier: Creates a smooth rate of change through a keyframe, but you set the positions of the control handles manually. Use this type where you want smooth change in time and you need specific control.
	Auto Bézier: Creates a smooth rate of change through a keyframe. You cannot manually adjust the handles of an Auto Bézier point. The handles adjust automatically based on the nearest keyframes, and create smooth transitions through the Auto Bézier point. Use it when you want a smooth change in time and do not need manual control. **Note:** If you do adjust the Auto Bezier handle manually, that action' will convert it to a Continuous Bezier keyframe.
	Hold: Creates an abrupt change. Use it when you want an image to appear or disappear suddenly. It's also useful when you want a strobe effect. It can hold any point in time steady until the next keyframe.
Spatial Interpolation: Affects the shape of the path in the Composition window.	**Linear:** Creates a straight motion path.
	Bézier: Identified by angled handlebars. The handlebars can be adjusted independently in both angle and length.
	Continuous Bézier: Identified by the straight handlebars. The handlebars may be of different length, but they are always straight.
	Auto Bézier: Identified by the smooth curve. There are control handles, but without handlebars. (If you attempt to move a control point on an Auto Bézier type, it will be converted to a Continuous Bézier type.)

Keyframe Interpolation Dialog Box Settings *continued*	
Category	**Option**
Roving: Roving keyframes rove in time to smooth out the Speed graph. The first and last keyframes cannot rove.	**Lock to Time:** The default setting for Roving. This setting allows you to set the keyframe position on the Timeline.
	Rove Across Time: Changes the position of the keyframe on the Timeline to mathematically smooth out the speed of motion. Use this when you want After Effects to create a consistent speed between multiple keyframes

TIP | Cycle Through Temporal Keyframe Types

You don't have to invoke the complicated Keyframe Interpolation dialog box to change the temporal keyframe setting in your Timeline. Simply Command-click (Mac) or Control-click (Windows) on a keyframe, and you'll see the icon change. You can cycle through all the different temporal and spatial keyframe interpolation types this way much more easily than going to a dialog box!

That's it! This chapter is done. Remember that learning the tools of timing is a skill, but the real talent is how you apply your skill to the art of animation. This takes experience, but you now have what it takes to develop your talent.

That's it! This chapter is done. Remember that learning the tools of timing is a skill, but the real talent is how you apply your skill to the art of animation. This takes experience, but you have now taken your first steps towards gaining it!

7.

Previewing Movies

| The Time Controls Palette | Types of Previews | Play Modes |
| Skipping Frames | Lowering Preview Resolution |
| Changing Resolution in the Composition Window |
| Defining a Region of Interest | Setting a Work Area |
| Wireframe Previews |

chap_07

After Effects 5.0 / 5.5
H•O•T CD-ROM

You've already had a little experience previewing your animations using the Play and RAM Preview buttons in the Time Controls palette, as well as learning to scrub the Time Marker in the Timeline window. It's hard to believe that there's much more to previewing than what you've already learned, but surprise—there is! Numerous options for previewing exist that vary depending on whether you want to save time and see a very quick playback or you want to see every detail possible during playback.

Between these two extremes of fast or accurate are mix-and-match settings within the preview features of After Effects that can be tuned to maximize the type of detail you're looking for and minimize the time it takes to see the results. This chapter demonstrates a number of scenarios that will help you understand when and how to use different preview settings.

The Importance of Previewing

To preview animation in the olden days of filmmaking, you had to photograph your hand-drawn cels, send the film from the camera to a lab, and wait until the following day just to see what you were doing! The computer has made life much easier, but there is a science involved with previewing.

When you create animation and keyframe settings in After Effects, the program has to render what each frame should look like. The rendering process can take a long time if you have a lot of layers, effects, or property settings. While this is barely noticeable when you're looking at a single frame, it is possible that After Effects will have trouble keeping up with rendering complicated compositions that contain many frames. For this reason, the speed of your previews can become a problem. This chapter covers a lot of techniques to speed up the preview and rendering process.

The Time Controls Palette

You've already worked with the **Time Controls palette** in previous chapters. Like most things in After Effects, the Time Controls palette is a lot deeper than you might think at first glance. This chapter gives you the opportunity to really learn its features. The following chart describes the various controls on this palette.

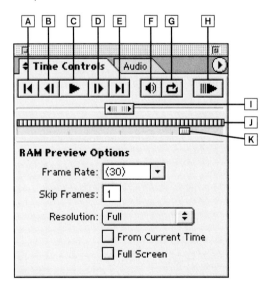

The Time Controls Palette	
Option	**Description**
A. First Frame	Like a rewind button on a VCR, this button will always move the Time Marker to the first frame.
B. Frame Reverse	Allows you to view the composition in single-frame increments in reverse.
C. Play	Plays the composition. It doesn't play in real time, but it plays as fast as it can (which is sometimes slow :)).
D. Frame Advance	Allows you to view the composition in single-frame increments going forward.
E. Last Frame	Moves the Time Marker to the last frame in the composition.
F. Audio	This button needs to be depressed to hear audio. (Audio is audible only using the RAM Preview button, not the Play button.)
G. Loop	Allows you to watch the same composition over and over (and did we say over?). Clicking this button repeatedly accesses the Play Once and Palindrome play modes.
H. RAM Preview	Causes After Effects to do its best job to show you the composition at its true speed. It might take a moment for the program to render the preview, but once it does it will play back faster than using the Play button.
I. Jog control	Move this slider forward or backward to view many frames quickly. It doesn't play smoothly, but gives you a big picture idea of what your composition looks like.
J. Time indicator	A reference bar that equates to the entire length of your composition.
K. Shuttle control	Like the Jog control, this slider lets you view more frames of the composition at once, so you can get a better idea of what is in it. It offers more precise control than the Jog control, however, in that you can move the slider in smaller increments.

The Time Controls palette is the main tool for controlling previews. As you'll see in this chapter, settings in the Composition and Timeline windows also affect the previewing of movies.

NOTE | You Need RAM for RAM Preview

It's very common to have problems with the RAM preview stopping before it has finished displaying your entire composition. This can be due to a few causes. First, you might not have enough RAM in your computer to run the entire composition. You can solve this problem by buying more RAM or by using some of the workarounds you'll learn about in this chapter, such as skipping frames or lowering the preview resolution. Another option is to render a final movie, which you'll learn how to do in Chapter 16, "*Rendering Final Movies.*"

Though not a problem on Windows machines, on Macintosh systems running Mac OS 9 and earlier, you need to allocate RAM to the After Effects program. The minimum RAM allocation is set automatically, but it might not be set high enough to allow satisfying RAM previews.

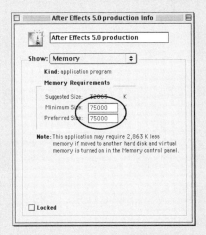

Setting a higher RAM allocation on a Mac is done by selecting the program application icon on your hard drive and choosing File > Get Info > Memory. Change the Minimum Size to be as high as you can set it. You'll need to know how much RAM you have available in order to do this successfully.

You can view how much available memory your Mac has by selecting About This Computer under the Apple menu in the upper left corner of your computer. You must be in the Finder to do this. For more information on checking and allocating RAM, consult the documentation that came with your Macintosh.

Types of Previews

There are four different types of previews: **manual**, **Standard**, **RAM**, and **Wireframe**. The following chart gives an in-depth description of each type and tells how to access these features.

Preview Types and Uses	
Preview Type	**Use**
Manual	Manual preview is used primarily when you want to step through your animation a frame at a time to analyze motion or when you want to set the current time to a specific frame. The Time Marker playhead in the Timeline window, and the Shuttle playhead and the Frame Reverse/Frame Forward buttons in the Time Controls palette are all manual preview types.
Standard	Standard preview is accessed by either clicking the Play button in the Time Controls palette or pressing the spacebar on your keyboard. This mode is useful if you want to see every frame. You can use it to analyze motion at slower than real-time playback. You can also choose to use Standard preview when you are running low on available RAM and you need to see the entire animation play from beginning to end.
RAM preview	RAM preview is most useful when you need to see real-time playback. It is located on the Time Controls palette. You can set up two RAM preview modes and switch between them to optimize your workflow. The best use of the two modes is to set one for high image detail and the other for low image detail. Using higher image detail will cut down on the number of frames that can be played back from RAM. Based on your available system RAM, you may also choose to skip frames to optimize the playback.
Wireframe	Wireframe preview should be used when you need real-time preview and image outlines will provide enough detail to allow for broad compositional choices. Wireframe previews use relatively little RAM and can be valuable when you have numerous frames but very little available RAM. This method can enable you to view a long animation piece in its entirety. You access Wireframe settings on the Composition > Preview menu.

NOTE | Comp or Composition?

Many After Effects professionals use two terms: **comp** and **composition**. They are the same thing—the term "comp" is short for "composition." "Composition" is used in the more formal context, such as when referring to the Composition window. "Comp" is used in the more informal context, such as when you refer to creating a new comp, opening a comp, or closing your comp.

_____Play Modes in the Time Controls Palette

Three **play modes** are available in the Time Controls palette. These three modes determine whether you see your animation preview once, in a continuous loop, or playing forward and backward continuously.

Although you probably won't need to change play modes often, each of the play modes in After Effects is necessary at times. In this exercise you'll see how to access the three play modes, and you'll learn the reasons to use each one.

1. Copy the **chap_07** folder from the **H•O•T CD-ROM** to your hard drive.

2. Open the **Preview.aep** project from the **chap_07** folder.

3. Double-click the **clown.psd** composition in the **Project** window to open it.

This composition was made in advance for you. It is 75 frames long and contains a different layer for each feature of the clown. The layers are animated using Scale, Position, and Rotation properties. It also contains a live-action layer of grass called grass.mov. *This footage was shot in Lynda's front yard with a digital video camera and imported into After Effects. If you want to practice making compositions, feel free to reconstruct this composition at another time, using the contents of the* footage > clown.psd *folder.*

4. In the **Time Controls** palette, click the **Loop** button until it displays the **Loop** icon (shown above). As you click this button, it cycles through different icons. You will learn about them all in the course of this exercise. Make sure you click until you see the icon for the loop feature. Click the **RAM Preview** button to play your animation.

Choosing the Loop icon causes your animation to continue to loop until you click on the screen or press a key on the keyboard. This play mode is generally the most useful for analyzing motion.

5. Click the **Loop** button until it shows the **Play Once** icon (shown above), and click **RAM Preview**.

In Play Once mode your animation plays through once and stops. This mode is good if you are the type who likes to see something once through and quickly get on to making changes. It can also be useful for presenting work to a client for a first impression.

6. Click the **Loop** button again to display the **Palindrome** icon (shown above), and press the **spacebar** on your keyboard. Pressing the spacebar is a shortcut for pressing the Play button to preview an animation.

The Palindrome mode plays forward and backward continuously. This mode can be good for analyzing complex motion. It can sometimes help to see an action in reverse, perhaps running slowly, to understand the subtleties of the motion.

7. When you're finished watching the animation, press any key to stop the preview. Return the icon to the **Loop** mode, which is the default setting for the Time Controls preview.

8. Close the Composition window for the **clown.psd** composition, but leave the **Preview.aep** project open.

2. _____**Skipping Frames for Faster RAM Previews**

You'll sometimes find yourself creating huge, ambitious projects that take a long time to preview. This exercise focuses on a great method for speeding up preview playback –skipping frames.

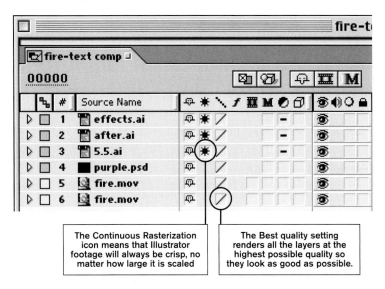

The Continuous Rasterization icon means that Illustrator footage will always be crisp, no matter how large it is scaled

The Best quality setting renders all the layers at the highest possible quality so they look as good as possible.

1. Double-click **fire-text comp** in the **Project** window.

This composition was created in advance for this exercise. It contains Illustrator and QuickTime footage items. All of the footage is set to Best quality, so it looks as good as it possibly can. The Best quality setting is located in the Switches panel and is discussed in Chapter 8, "Layers." Although this setting makes the artwork look great, it makes the composition take longer to render in RAM preview. The Illustrator items are set in the Timeline to Continuous Rasterization, which means that they'll look crisp even if the artwork is scaled large. This also makes the composition difficult to render. This composition was designed to demonstrate what happens when you have artwork that is difficult to preview using RAM Preview.

2. Move the **Time Marker** to any frame in the **Timeline** and notice that the arrow cursor animates with black and white for a moment. This is a visual indicator that After Effects is rendering and cannot show the final frame. Moving the Time Marker to any other point in the Timeline will cause the same result.

3. Move the **Time Marker** to the **first frame** of the composition. Click the **Play** button. You'll see that After Effects struggles to play this animation. This is what happens as you start to work on larger and more complicated compositions, and it is a common issue for every After Effects artist.

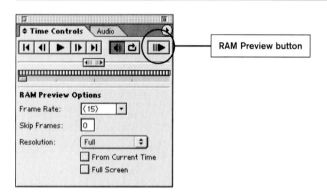

RAM Preview button

4. Click the **RAM Preview** button. It will take After Effects a while to build the preview. Once it is ready to play, it will likely not play all the way through, unless you have a lot of RAM.

See that green line at the top of your Timeline window? That is After Effects' visual display of how many frames it can play in RAM. That green line will appear, disappear and redraw itself every time you preview a change to your Timeline. It indicates that those frames have been rendered.

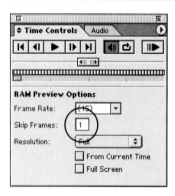

5. Enter a value of **1** into the **Skip Frames** field of the **RAM Preview** options. Click the **RAM Preview** button again. It should take only half as long to prepare this preview. It should also play all the way through now. If it doesn't, enter a value of **2** into the **Skip Frames** field.

The Skip Frames feature is a way to help you see an entire composition, even if you don't have enough RAM to play every frame. This preview technique is useful when you want to see a real-time preview, but you don't care about seeing each individual frame. It gives you an accurate sense of timing but not an accurate sense of appearance.

6. Set the **Skip Frames** option back to **0**. Save your project and leave this composition open for the next exercise.

> ## NOTE | More About the Skip Frames Option
>
> Setting the Skip Frames option to 1 causes the preview to display one frame and then skip one frame. This process continues for the length of the preview.
>
> During RAM preview, the message in the Time Controls palette will say "Playing on 2's." This message means that the frames that aren't skipped are being displayed twice to maintain proper speed for the composition playback.
>
> Skipping frames can help preserve RAM. Every frame skipped preserves memory. However, the more frames you skip, the less smooth the preview. If you need to preserve RAM, it is best to start by skipping one frame and seeing whether this preserves the amount of RAM necessary for your playback.
>
> Another reason you may choose to skip frames is that this option will speed the time it takes to render your preview. Just setting the option to skip one frame will cut the preview rendering time in half.

> ## NOTE | More RAM Questions
>
> You might be curious about other RAM limitations. If RAM is such a big problem, how does it affect your ability to create After Effects projects or the ability for your audience to see your final movies? Let's separate some of these issues to clarify matters.
>
> First of all, insufficient RAM can affect your RAM Preview, but there are several ways around this problem. RAM preview is simply a very handy feature that helps you see your animations quickly as you're working. If you don't have enough RAM in your computer or allocated to your program, however, there are other options. The Play button, the Jog control, and the Shuttle control on the Time Controls palette will all allow you to preview your work; they just won't play as *fast* as the RAM preview will.
>
> The amount of available RAM won't have much of an impact on your ability to create and render After Effects compositions. You can create very complicated movies in After Effects using the minimum RAM requirement of the program. You can also render final movies in After Effects without much RAM. The real issue with RAM is related to using the RAM preview only (and to some of the 3D features that you'll learn about in Chapter 13, "*3D Layers*").

3. _____Lowering Preview Resolution

After Effects treats resolution a little differently than programs that are geared toward outputting files for print. Everything that you bring into After Effects should be prepared at 72 dots per inch (dpi), or it will be converted to that resolution automatically once it is brought into a composition. Instead of dots per inch, After Effects measures resolution in pixels per inch. You set the resolution for a composition in the Compositions Settings dialog box. Whatever resolution is set there is considered to be full resolution by After Effects. In our example for this exercise, the full resolution is 320 x 240 pixels per inch.

In the following steps you will learn about the **RAM Preview Resolution** option. This option allows you to preview your animation at a lower resolution than the full resolution assigned to the composition. It increases playback speed, and so it's another method for speeding things up. You can combine skipped frames with lowered resolution settings, but we're showing you these features one at a time so you'll understand them better.

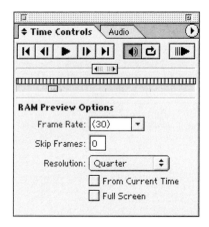

1. Make sure **fire-text comp** is still open. In the **Time Controls** palette, make sure the **Skip Frames** option is set to **0**. Set the **Resolution** to **Quarter**. This takes whatever resolution After Effects is set at (in this case, 320 x 240) and reduces it by 75 percent.

2. Click the **RAM Preview** button.

All frames are rendered at quarter resolution and previewed in real time. This setting is good for previewing all the frames in your composition while preserving RAM. It also speeds up preview rendering time because lower-resolution images are quicker to render. The down side is that the moving footage doesn't look nearly as good at quarter resolution. It does give you a good indication of motion, though it gives a bad indication of appearance.

3. Save the project to your **HOT_AE_Projects** folder, and close this composition.

TIP | Frame Rate Settings Can Speed Rendering Too

Occasionally you will want to preview your movie faster or slower than the composition settings. To do this, use the **Frame Rate** option. This technique can provide another way to analyze motion.

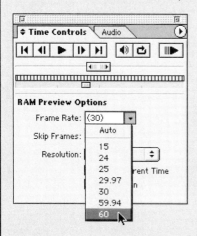

In the Time Controls palette, set the Frame Rate option to 60 frames per second. Click the RAM Preview button. The animation plays back at twice the speed of the composition setting.

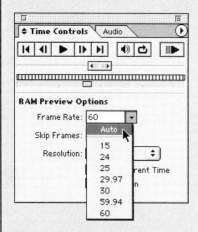

Set the Frame Rate option to Auto. The option displays (15), the composition frame rate setting. The Auto Frame Rate option automatically adjusts the frame rate to match the composition settings.

TIP | Using the Shift+RAM Preview Option

Now that you've learned how to set up the RAM preview with all of its different settings, you might want to take advantage of **Shift+RAM Preview**. This option allows you to work with two different kinds of RAM previews. You can set the first RAM preview to be full resolution, not to skip frames, and to use a high frame rate. Do this by setting the RAM Preview options accordingly.

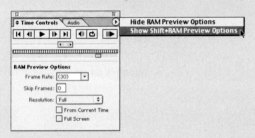

If you want, you can then set up a second type of RAM Preview, called Shift+RAM preview. You access this setting by clicking the arrow at the top right of the Time Controls palette and choosing Show Shift+RAM Preview Options.

Once you've done this, the Time Controls palette will indicate that you are setting the Shift+RAM Preview options. Make your changes to the Frame Rate, Skip Frames, and Resolution options. Once you're finished, click the arrow at the top right of the Time Controls palette again and choose Show RAM Preview Options. Now you'll have two different options set for previewing.

You can access the standard settings simply by clicking the RAM Preview button. If you want to access the Shift+RAM Preview settings, hold down the Shift key and click the same button. Voila—you've got two groups of settings with which to preview. Sweet!

4. ——————————Changing Resolution in the Composition Window

You can change the **Resolution setting** in the Composition window as an alternative to changing the RAM Preview resolution in the Time Controls palette. When you make this change in the Composition window, it affects the way the Composition window appears all the time, until you change it back to full resolution. When you change the setting in the Time Controls palette, the Composition window will look normal, but the RAM Preview will display with the lower resolution. Why change the resolution in the Composition window? If your composition has a lot of render-intensive filter effects, like Blur or Motion Blur, and the Composition window is set to full resolution, After Effects will take a long time to render a still frame. This gets very cumbersome when you're trying to position objects and set keyframes. For this reason, knowing how to use the Composition window's Resolution setting is an important skill.

1. Open **large space comp** from the Project window.

This composition was created at 640 x 480 pixels and is larger than other compositions you have worked with so far in this book. After Effects can create compositions with resolutions as high as 30,000 x 30,000 pixels, which is well beyond anything you would ever need! The 640 x 480 resolution is a common one that is often used for video and CD-ROM development. The trouble is, a 640 x 480 composition is difficult to render at times. This particular composition has some Motion Blur and Best quality settings added to it, which make it challenging to render as well. You will learn about motion blur in Chapter 10, "Effects."

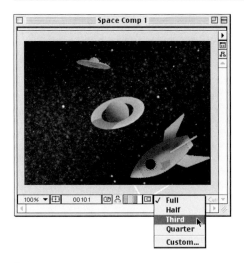

2. Press the **spacebar** to play the composition and notice how slow it is. In the **Composition** window, click the **Resolution** drop-down menu and choose **Third** from the available options. Press the **spacebar** to play the composition. Notice that the image looks noticeably degraded but that the animation plays more quickly.

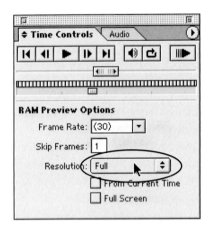

3. In the **Time Controls** palette, set the **Resolution** option to **Full**. Click the **RAM Preview** button.

Your animation plays back at full resolution, even though it is still changed in the Composition window to the Third resolution setting. The RAM Preview Resolution option is independent of the Composition window's Resolution setting. You can make a resolution change in either spot—in the RAM Preview options of the Time Controls palette or the Composition window. That way, when you press the spacebar, the Composition window setting will play (currently set to Third). If you click the RAM Preview button, the composition will play at its current setting, which is Full resolution.

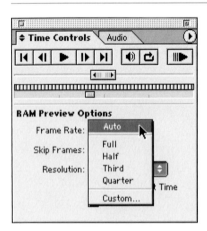

4. In the **Time Controls** palette, choose **Auto** as the **Resolution** setting. Click the **RAM Preview** button.

The animation plays back at Third resolution. The Auto setting allows the RAM Preview to use the same resolution as the current Resolution setting in the Composition window.

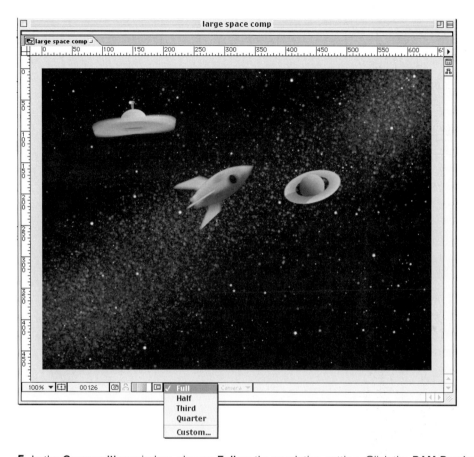

5. In the **Composition** window, choose **Full** as the resolution setting. Click the **RAM Preview** button.

With the RAM Preview resolution set to Auto, the preview adjusts to full resolution. Now the playback will be slower, and it might not be able to play all the frames again.

6. Save your project, and leave this composition open for the next exercise.

MOVIE | resolution.mov

If you still have questions about changing the resolution in the Time Controls palette versus the Composition window, please watch the movie entitled **resolution.mov** located in the **movies** folder on the **H•O•T CD-ROM**.

5. ——————————Previewing a Region of Interest

Defining a **region of interest** allows you to preview a specific area of the image. By specifying a smaller area for preview, you decrease the rendering time and speed up your workflow. This method also allows you to visually concentrate on the details of a limited area.

A region of interest is very easy to use. Once you've set it up, it is always available and can be toggled on or off at the click of a button. In this brief exercise, you'll learn everything about the Region of Interest option.

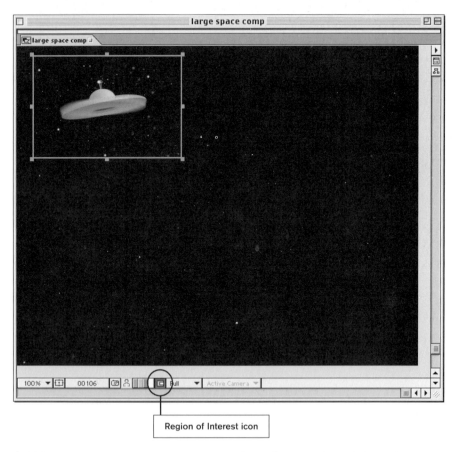

Region of Interest icon

1. Make sure **large space comp** is still open. In the **Composition** window, click the **Region of Interest** icon. The cursor changes to a marquee tool. Drag in the upper left corner to define a region of interest. Use the control handles on the resulting bounding box to adjust the size of the region. Once you complete the shape, everything else will disappear except the area you selected.

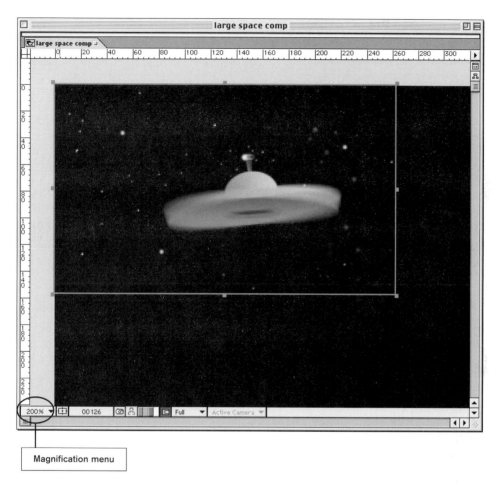

Magnification menu

2. In the **Composition** window, set the **Magnification** to **200%**. Scroll the image to view the region of interest. Press the **spacebar** to view your animation.

3. Set the **Magnification** to **100%**. Click the **Region of Interest** icon to toggle the region of interest off.

4. With the region of interest toggled off, hold down the **Option** key (Mac) or **Alt** key (Windows) and click on the **Region of Interest** icon. This clears the region of interest. The marquee tool appears again so you can draw a new region of interest.

5. Save your project in the **HOT_AE_Projects** folder, and leave this composition open for the next exercise.

NOTE | When Should You Use RAM Preview?

RAM Preview is preferable to using the spacebar or Play button on the Time Controls palette, because it gives you a better sense of how fast your animation plays in real time. You won't always need to know that, however. There are times when you'll just want to check movement, not timing. It's fine to use any preview method you want—RAM Preview simply offers the fastest preview of them all.

Limiting Previews with Work Area Settings

Sometimes, if your animation is long, you might want to preview only a small section that you are in the process of refining. You can do this by using the **work area** settings in the Timeline window. In the following exercise you will learn to use the work area. First you'll learn the keyboard shortcuts, and then you'll learn to set the work area by simply dragging the handles.

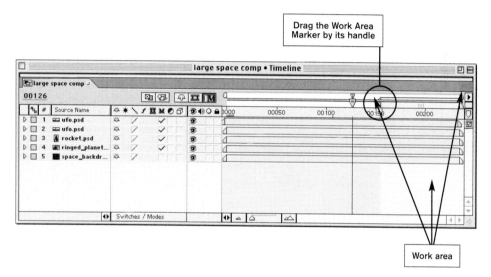

Drag the Work Area Marker by its handle

Work area

1. Make sure **large space comp** is still open. Drag the **Work Area Marker** in the **Timeline** to begin the work area at **Frame 150**.

2. Click the **RAM Preview** button in the **Time Controls** palette. You'll see that the preview includes only the frames within the work area. The animation should start playing on Frame 150, at the beginning of the work area, instead of on Frame 1. This is useful if you want to preview a small section of your Timeline. If the animation won't play in full, try lowering the resolution in the **RAM Preview** options to **Half** or lower.

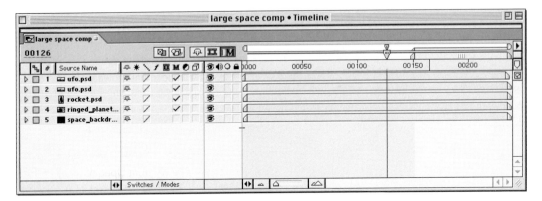

3. Drag the **left** Work Area Marker to **Frame 1** and the **right** Work Area Marker to **Frame 240** so that the work area begins on the first frame and ends on the last frame of the composition.

4. Click **RAM Preview** in the **Time Controls** palette. You'll see a preview of the new work area. If the animation won't play in full, try lowering the resolution in the **RAM Preview** option to **Half** or lower. Sometimes you have to combine techniques. If you make this change, be sure to set it back to **Auto** once you've finished this exercise.

5. Save your project and close the **large space comp** window. You won't need it again in this chapter.

7. Wireframe Previews

Sometimes in a preview, you want to focus on the motion of your objects and not so much on their appearance. In such cases you can use a more-specialized type of preview that allows you to see a **wireframe** of your artwork instead of the full-pixel version. A wireframe outline will typically conform to the shape of the different layers of artwork in your composition. This mode shows a white outline that gives you a quick impression of the shape of your artwork, but without the color, fill, effects, and texture.

Using a wireframe setting is useful for previewing motion quickly, because the computer doesn't have to render as much information as it does in other modes. There are two different types of wireframe previews: basic wireframe and wireframe with motion trails; you'll learn to use both in this exercise.

1. Double-click on the **clown.psd** composition in the **Project** window to open it.

2. Click the **Play** button in the **Time Controls** palette to view the animation.

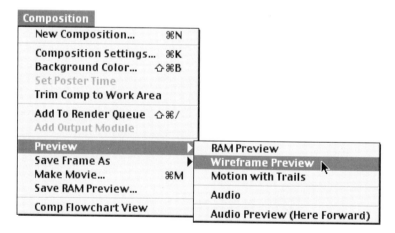

3. Choose **Composition > Preview > Wireframe Preview**.

This setting enables your composition to play in real time because After Effects doesn't have to render much content to the screen. In this preview it's easy to see the compositional relationship between all of the objects while viewing the animation in its entirety. This setting is used when you have a complicated animation and you want to see parts that are hidden by other objects. It's also faster for the computer to generate than full frames, so it's used sometimes as a quick-and-dirty preview method.

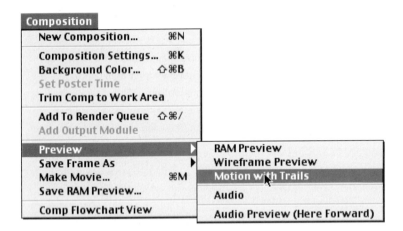

4. Choose **Composition > Preview > Motion with Trails**. This type of preview shows a wireframe view that repeats with every frame, leaving a trace of its motion. It's useful for observing the motion paths of your objects as they are moving.

5. Save your project, and close After Effects.

That's all there is to previewing with wireframes. You won't use this feature all the time; you'll want it only when you have a complicated composition that takes a long time to render. If you want to go back to using the standard previewing options, simply click the Play or RAM Preview button, and the preview will return to normal.

Eeek! Which Setting Should You Use?

At this point, you've been introduced to a lot of different preview settings, and you might be confused as to which setting to use when. It's a good practice to be aware of the following items when previewing animation. You can use this chart as a checklist when setting up a preview. With a little time, this list will become second nature.

Summary of Preview Settings		
Location	**Feature**	**Reason to Use**
Timeline window	Set the *work area* in the Timeline and use RAM Preview in the Time Controls palette.	Useful to reduce the number of frames shown during a preview when you have a long animation that takes too long to render.
Composition window	Select a *Resolution* option—Full, Half, Third, Quarter, or Custom.	Useful when the static preview takes a long time when you are trying to move an object.
Composition window	Set the *region of interest*.	Useful if you want to focus on one small part of your screen only.
Time Controls palette	Select a *play mode*—Play Once, Loop, or Palindrome.	Useful for choosing whether to watch something over and over, forward and backward, or just once.
Time Controls palette	Select *RAM* or *Shift+RAM* preview options	Helpful for previewing in real time. Being able to access a secondary group of settings with the Shift key is useful for easily toggling between an accurate or a fast preview.

Another chapter under your belt! Getting used to previewing movies and using the options takes time and working experience. You won't necessarily need everything you've learned right away, but it will come in handy as you work on larger projects. So give yourself some time to absorb everything here, and feel free to return to this chapter when you want to remember exactly how a preview option functions.

8.

Layers

Layer Basics	Labeling	Switches?	Shy Layers	Solo Button
Quality Switch	Continuous Rasterization	Motion Blur
Moving and Trimming Layers	Trimming Layers	Splitting Layers
Time Stretching and Frame Blending	Time Remapping
Replacing Layers	Sequencing Layers	Solid Layers	Layer Modes

chap_08

After Effects 5.0/5.5
H•O•T CD-ROM

You might be used to the concept of layers from programs like Photoshop and Illustrator. In After Effects, many of the same principles apply, yet its use of layers is much more complicated than in programs that deal only with still images.

Layers reside in the Timeline of After Effects, and they relate not only to what appears visually in your composition, but also to the timing of your graphics and animations. This chapter will expose you to the power that layers hold. Some of the things you'll learn to do here include moving layers, renaming layers, replacing layers, trimming layers, sliding layers, and organizing layers. It's a long chapter but an invaluable part of your After Effects education.

I. _____ Layer Basics

You've used layers throughout the preceding chapters; in the following exercise we'll start with a couple of items that you've seen before, and then we'll quickly move into new territory. You'll learn how to rename a layer and to change the stacking order of layers, using the keyboard to lock and unlock layers. In the process, you'll get practice in making a composition and importing a layered Photoshop file.

1. Choose **File > New > New Project** to create a new project.

2. Choose **File > Save As**. Navigate to your **HOT_AE_Projects** folder, give it the name **Layers.aep**, and click **Save**.

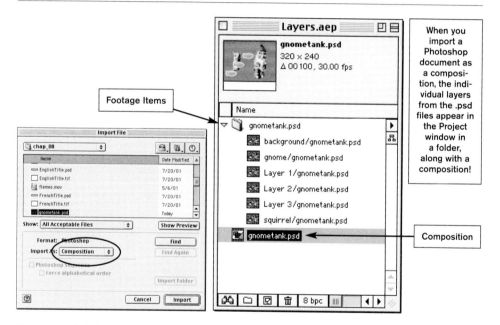

3. Double-click inside the empty **Project** window to bring up the **Import File** dialog box. Navigate to the **chap_08** folder and select the file called **gnometank.psd**. In the **Import As** list, select **Composition**; then click the **Import** button. Both a footage folder and a composition should appear in the Project window, both named **gnometank.psd**. This is a way to bring a layered Photoshop file into After Effects as a composition. Twirl down the **arrow** on the **gnometank.psd** footage folder in the Project window to see that each layer in the Photoshop file has been imported as a separate piece of footage.

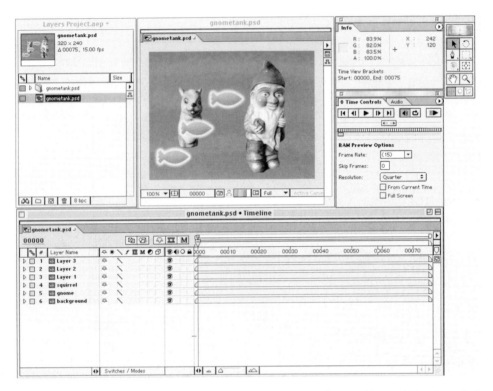

4. Double-click the **gnometank.psd** composition to open the Composition and Timeline windows.

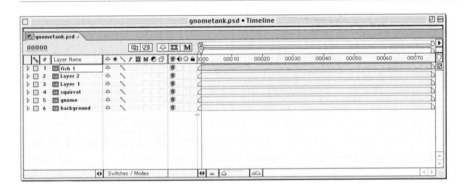

5. In the **Timeline** window, select the top layer, named **Layer 3**, and press **Return**. Rename the layer **fish 1**. Now that you know how to rename layers, change the name of **Layer 2** to **fish 2** and the name of **Layer 1** to **fish 3**.

Sometimes you'll want to rename layers that get imported from Photoshop, or you'll simply change your mind about a layer's name that you brought in from any source. Now you know how to do this.

6. Change the size of the composition preview by choosing **50%** from the pop-up magnification menu, shown circled above. Click and drag each fish so it is in the invisible area of the Composition window. This is how you set artwork to a position that is out of view. The fish will animate into view and exit out of view from left to right. This is the first step in accomplishing such an animation.

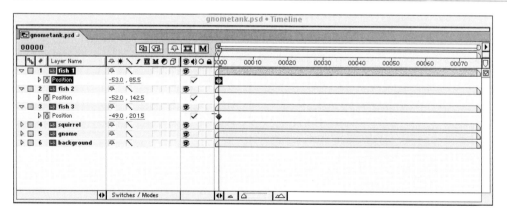

7. Hold down the **Shift** key and select **fish 1**, **fish 2**, and **fish 3** in the **Timeline** window. Press the **P** key to reveal the Position property of each layer. Click the **Stopwatch** icon for each layer.

8. Move the **Time Marker** to the last frame of the Timeline.

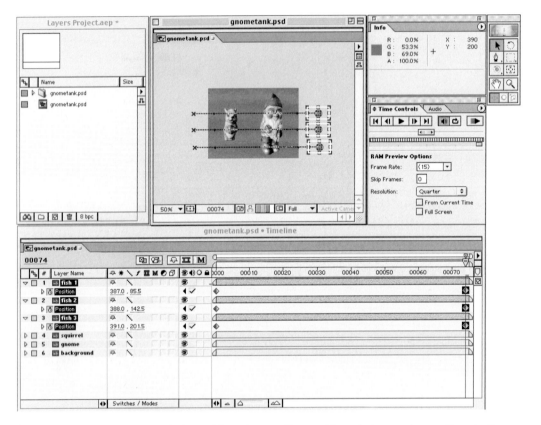

9. Use the **Shift** key to select all three objects in your Composition window, and move them to the other side of the Composition window, as shown here. You can do this by holding down the Shift key and dragging the items or by using the arrow keys. This should set the second keyframe on all three layers.

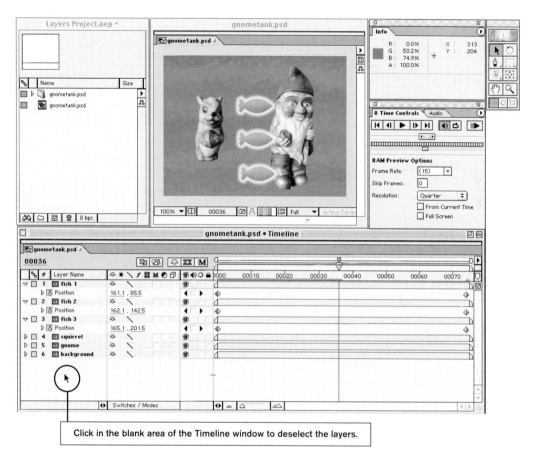

Click in the blank area of the Timeline window to deselect the layers.

10. Change the scale of the Composition window back to **100%**, and watch the animation you just created by pressing the **spacebar**. If you don't want to see the motion paths as you preview the movement, deselect the layers by clicking in an empty area of the Timeline window.

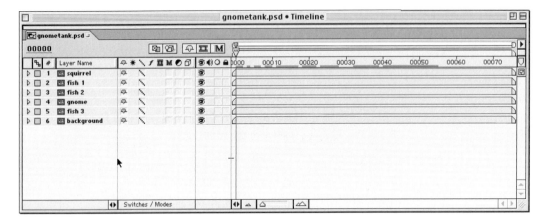

11. Click and drag the **squirrel** layer so that it is at the top of the stack. Move the **gnome** layer so it is above **fish 3**. Watch the animation to see how the stacking order of the layers changes the preview in the Composition window. After Effects stacks its layers from bottom to top, with the topmost layer being in front of all other layers.

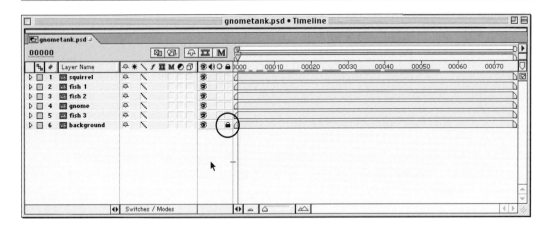

12. Since you wouldn't want the background layer to be animated, click in the **Lock** switch area of the **background** layer, as you see above. This is a great way to ensure that you don't accidentally move or bump a layer that you want to stay still.

13. Save the composition, leaving it open for the next exercise.

TIP | Using the Keyboard to Change the Stacking Order

The following table shows keyboard shortcuts you can use to change the stacking order of the layers in a composition.

Stacking Order Keyboard Commands		
Stacking Change	Mac	Windows
Move down one level	Command+[	Control+[
Move up one level	Command+]	Control+]
Move to bottom of stack	Command+Shift+[	Control+Shift+[
Move to top of stack	Command+Shift+]	Control+Shift+]

2. ————————**Labeling Layers**

All layers have color-coded labels. You probably haven't paid too much attention to these labels; they are displayed in the Timeline window in the second column from the left and are just little squares. You can assign and control the color coding of each layer.

Labels can help you identify layers when you are working with large projects. For example, you could assign one label color to layers that contain type and another to layers that contain photographs. Once layers have color codes, they can be selected using the label color. Label colors can help you keep from losing your mind when you need some method of organizing a lot of content. In this exercise you'll learn how to assign label colors and then select layers based on the label assignment.

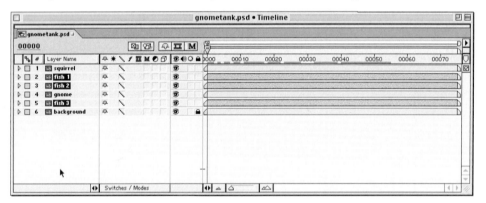

1. With the composition still open from the last exercise, hold down the **Command** key (Mac) or **Control** key (Windows) and click **fish 1**, **fish 2,** and **fish 3**. Clicking while holding down the Command or Control key allows you to select noncontiguous layers.

Observe the column of color squares to the left of the Level # column. At the moment, they are all pink, which is the default color code for layers. You'll learn to change the color of selected layers in the next step.

---

2. Choose **Edit > Label > Red** and notice that the color codes on all the selected fish layers turn red.

---

3. Click the **squirrel** layer to select it. **Choose> Edit > Label > Select Label Group**. Notice that all layers with the same label color are selected in the Timeline window. Also notice that a locked layer is not selected unless you unlock it, which is why the background layer is not selected.

---

4. Save and close the project.

NOTE | Label Preferences

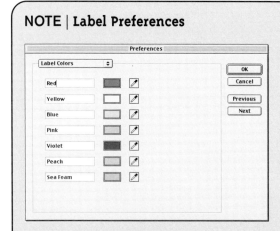

You can change the available label colors and names by choosing **Edit > Preferences > Label Colors**. Label Preferences aren't under the Edit menu in OS X; they're under the After Effects menu. To rename a label, type in a color name. You can also use the eyedropper or click on a color field to access the color picker to change a label color.

What Are Switches?

Switches allow you to display layers in After Effects in different ways. Depending on your work process, you may want to use switches to hide layers from display in the Timeline, turn off the sound from an audio layer, or show only an individual layer in the Composition window. Switches give you options for working with After Effects to make your work process as efficient as possible. They affect the preview and final rendering of your movie.

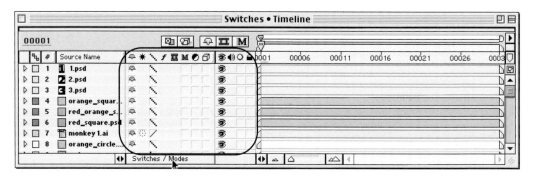

Switches are located in the Timeline window. Each layer has its own set of switches that affect only that layer.

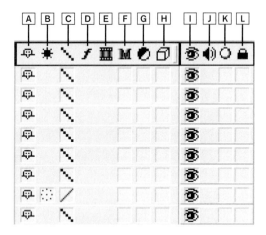

Switches form columns of options for your layers. Pictured above are some of the switch options you might use most often. You've already been introduced to the Lock switch. In the exercises that follow, you'll learn about more switch options, and we'll introduce you to others throughout the rest of this book.

Here's a handy chart that explains the meaning of each switch. The letters correspond to the labels in the illustration above. **Tip:** If you forget what the name of a switch is, you can see its Tool Tip by hovering the pointer over any of the switch icons.

Switch Functions	
Switch Name	**Definition**
A. Shy Layers	Allows you to turn off a layer in the Timeline window, even though it will still be visible in the Composition window. This allows you to limit the number of layers that are visible to make it easier to work with a complicated Timeline. The shy layers can be turned on and off with the click of one button, making it easy to enable and disable them. You'll work with shy layers in the next exercise.
B. Continuous Rasterization	Allows vector artwork to rasterize when different transformations are applied, causing it to have a crisp appearance. You'll get to work with this switch a little later in this chapter.
C. Quality	Toggles to specify either Draft or Best quality. The default is Draft quality. You can click on this switch to see the effect that the two settings produce. The Quality setting is especially noticeable when artwork is transformed using scaling or rotation.
	continues on next page

Switch Functions *continued*	
Switch Name	**Definition**
D. Effects	Allows you to turn effects off temporarily so they don't have to be rendered. You don't lose your effects settings when you turn them off. You'll work with this switch in Chapter 10, "*Effects*."
E. Frame Blending	When you use the time mapping or time stretching features (you'll learn to do so later in this chapter), the result is that After Effects holds frames, which often results in jerky movement. Frame blending smooths out the jerkiness by creating *dissolves* between different frames.
F. Motion Blur	Uses After Effects' built-in motion blur feature, which emulates a motion picture camera that uses a long exposure. You'll learn to use this feature later in this chapter.
G. Adjustment Layers	Allows you to apply effects to more than one layer at a time. You'll learn to work with adjustment layers in Chapter 10, "*Effects*".
H. 3D Layer	A 3D layer can move in three-dimensional space. You'll learn to work with 3D layers in Chapter 13 "*3D Layers.*"
I. Video	Available only if your layer contains movie footage. This switch toggles the video on or off.
J. Audio	Available only if your layer contains audio. This switch toggles the audio on or off.
K. Solo	Allows you to easily isolate one or more layers and turn all the other layers off. It saves you the effort of turning off the layers you don't want to see. This switch turns off the visibility of layers in the Composition window, while the Shy Layers switch turns off the visibility of a layer or layers only in the Timeline window.
L. Lock	Allows you to lock a layer so it cannot be moved or edited. This is useful when you want to ensure that a layer doesn't change.

3. ——————————**Using Shy Layers**

When you have a composition with a lot of layers, it's sometimes helpful to turn off a layer or layers in the Timeline but to leave the artwork itself visible. This eliminates visual clutter in the Timeline when you're trying to focus on setting keyframes. When you mark a layer as shy, it can be hidden from display in the Timeline window until you're ready to display it again.

Shy layers are still active in your composition and display normally in the Composition window. They are just hidden from view in the Timeline window so you can concentrate on the task at hand without scrolling up and down in search of the layers that need attention.

When you have a layer or group of layers that you're happy with and you aren't planning on tweaking them anymore, mark them as shy. You can use this technique as a checklist: to remind yourself which layers still need work. The visible layers are the ones that need attention before you complete your composition.

In this exercise you'll learn to mark shy layers and to hide or display all shy layers using the Enable Shy Layer button.

> **1.** Open the **Switches.aep** project from the **chap_08** folder. Navigate to your **HOT_AE_Projects** folder and click **Save** to create a copy of it there. In the **Project** window, double-click the **switches comp** composition to open it and its associated Timeline.

> **2.** Play the composition to view the animation.

> *Notice that quite a few layers and properties are open in the Timeline. Once your Timeline gets to this level of complexity, it becomes difficult to work with an individual layer.*

Click the Shy Layers icon for each layer except layer 3. Notice that the icon
changes when you click it. This indicates that the layer is set to shy.

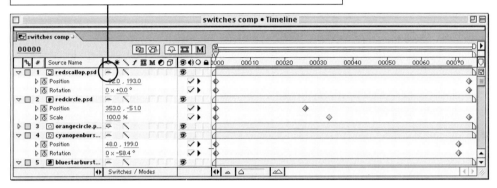

3. Click the **Shy Layers** switch for all of the layers except layer 3, **orangecircle.psd**. Nothing noticeable will happen in the Timeline or composition yet, except that the icons for the Shy Layers switch will
change to identify each of the layers as shy. When a layer is shy, the icon looks flat (as though the guy
is hiding), and when it isn't shy it shows a picture of him with his nose peeking out.

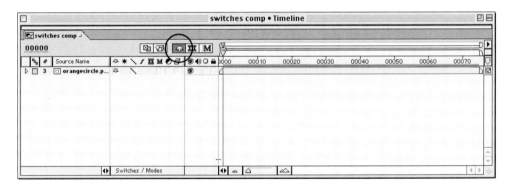

4. Click the **Enable Shy Layer** button at the top of the Timeline window. Observe that the shy layers
you created in Step 3 are now hidden in the Timeline window. Click the **Enable Shy Layer** button
again to toggle it off (so all of your layers are displayed).

Why would you do this? In this example, the orangecircle *layer is the only layer that doesn't animate.*
To add animation keyframes to it, you might want to isolate it so you aren't distracted by all the other
layers in the Timeline window. Once you've worked on it and set keyframes, you'd want to see all the
other layers again, which you could do easily by clicking the Enable Shy Layer button at the top of
the Timeline window. Shy layers offer a way to organize your Timeline when it gets too cluttered with
layers and property settings.

5. Save **switches comp**, leaving it open for the next exercise.

4. _____Using the Solo Switch

The **Solo switch** provides a quick way to hide certain layers temporarily and to leave selected layers turned on. Unlike shy layers, which remain visible in the Composition window when they're turned off in the Timeline, solo layers hide the artwork in the Composition window but leave it visible in the Timeline window.

Sometimes it's useful to see a few layers together. Fortunately, despite its name, soloing is not limited to displaying just one layer at a time. In this exercise you will learn to solo individual and multiple layers. You'll also learn how to stop soloing layers and return to normal display.

1. You should still have the **switches comp** open from the last exercise. Click on the **Timeline** to make it active. Select all the layers by using the shortcut keys: **Command+A** (Mac) or **Control+A** (Windows). Press the letter **P**. All the layer properties should disappear. If you press the letter P twice again, they will appear and disappear.

That was a pretty cool shortcut, but what happened and why did it work? The first time you pressed the letter P, all the layers displayed the Position property. The second time you pressed it, all the properties were hidden. The shortcut to show a layer property functions like a toggle key. It reveals and hides the property. This is a great technique to quickly collapse your Timeline!

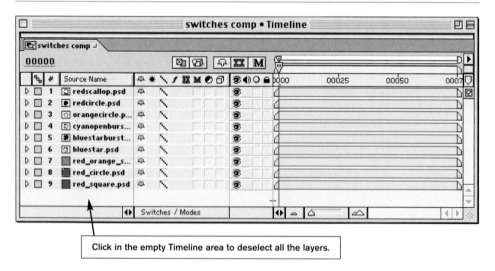

Click in the empty Timeline area to deselect all the layers.

2. Deselect all the layers by clicking in an empty area of the Timeline window.

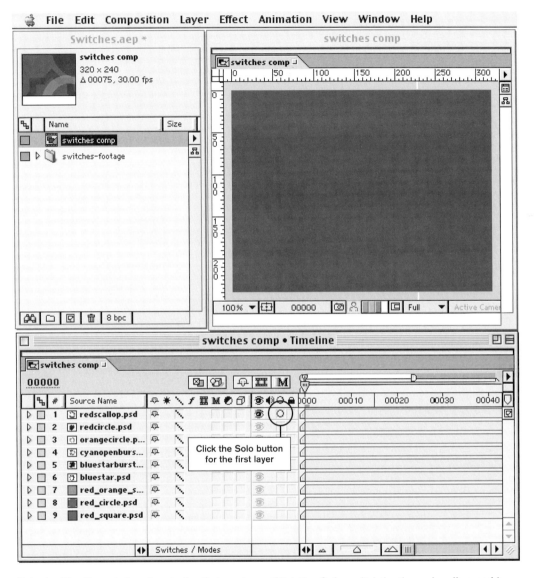

3. In the Timeline window, locate the **Solo** column. Click the **Solo** switch for the **redscallop.psd** layer to solo the layer in the Composition window. Notice that the other layers are no longer displayed!

Why would you want to turn off all the other layers in the Composition window? You may want to work on this individual layer without the distraction of all the other artwork on the screen.

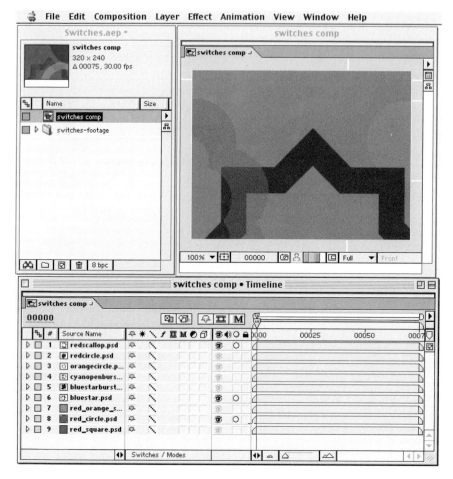

4. Click the **Solo** switch for the **bluestar.psd** and **red_circle.psd** layers. These layers turn on, and the previous solo layer stays on as well.

Note: You can select multiple layers and then click the Solo switch of any of the selected layers to turn on soloing for all selected layers.

---

5. Click the **Solo** switch for the top layer (**redscallop.psd**) and leave your mouse button depressed. With the mouse button down, drag straight down the **Solo** switch column to clear all active Solo switches. Once they are cleared, the artwork for all of the layers will reappear in the Composition window.

The Solo switch is actually a toggle, meaning that you can also click each individual Solo icon to clear soloing for the corresponding layer.

---

6. Save and close the **Switches.aep** project. You won't be needing it again.

---

5. _____Using the Quality Switch

In this exercise you will learn to use the **Quality switch**. This switch toggles the quality for artwork on a layer between the Best and Draft settings. As a rule, Best quality looks better but takes longer to render.

Pixel-based images such as those originating from Photoshop, also known as **raster** images, are affected by the Quality switch setting. If you scale or rotate a pixel image, the Best setting will improve the quality of these types of images. This exercise demonstrates when to use the Best setting and how to do so.

1. Create a new project by choosing **File > New > New Project**. Navigate to your **HOT_AE_Projects** folder, give it the name **Quality.aep**, and click **Save**.

2. Double-click inside the empty **Project** window to launch the **Import File** dialog box. Navigate to the **chap_08** folder and select **small3.psd**. Click the **Import** button and click **OK** to merge layers. The file will appear as footage inside the Project window. This is a Photoshop document, also known as a raster image.

Note that this import method brings in a flattened .psd file, while the method you learned in the Exercise 1 – Layer Basics brought in a Photoshop file as a composition. It's up to you to know the different importing methods and to choose accordingly, depending on whether you want a flattened footage element or layers brought in as separate footage items. In this exercise, we want you to have a single flattened .psd layer.

3. Click the **New Comp** button at the bottom of the Project window. The **Composition Settings** dialog box opens. In the **Composition Name** field, enter the name **raster comp**. The other settings for the composition should be carried over from the last composition you made; they don't need to be changed. Click **OK**. The Timeline and Composition windows open.

4. Click the **Composition** window to make it active. Choose **Composition > Background Color**. Click inside the **color swatch** to change the color from black to blue in any of the color pickers that appear. You can change the background color of any composition at any time. Now you know how!

5. Drag the **small3.psd** artwork into the **Composition** window, and position it so it fills the entire window. You can drag footage into the Composition window or the Timeline window, and it will appear in both windows at once.

When the Quality switch slants to the right, it is set to Best Quality.

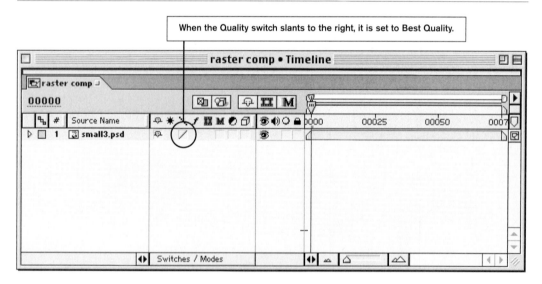

6. Click the **Quality** switch for the **small.psd** layer to change it to Best quality (the line will slant up to the right). Switch it back and forth, and then return it to Draft quality (slanted up to the left). At this point, you shouldn't see a difference in the Quality settings. The next steps will show you when and why you would want to change this switch.

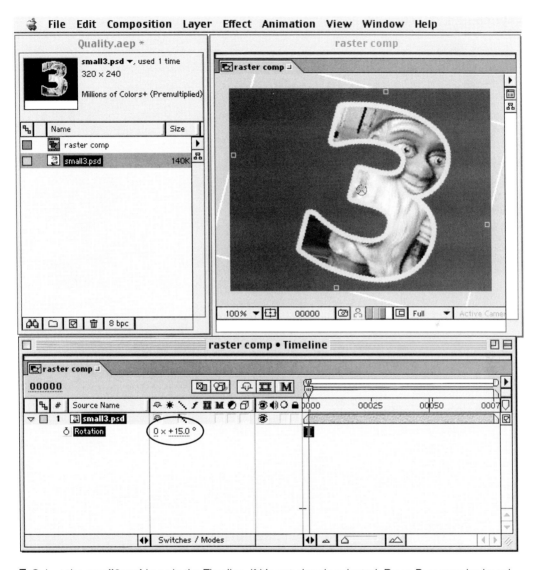

7. Select the **small3.psd** layer in the Timeline, if it's not already selected. Press **R** on your keyboard to display the Rotation property. Set the Rotation value to **15** degrees. Notice that the edges look jagged now.

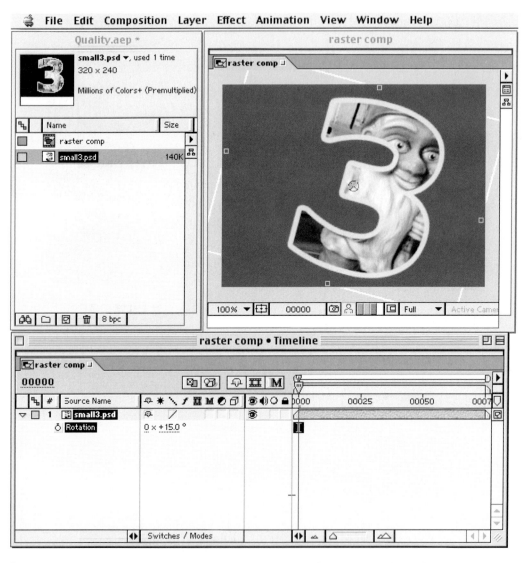

8. Click the **Quality** switch to set the layer to Best quality. Notice that all the jaggedness disappears!

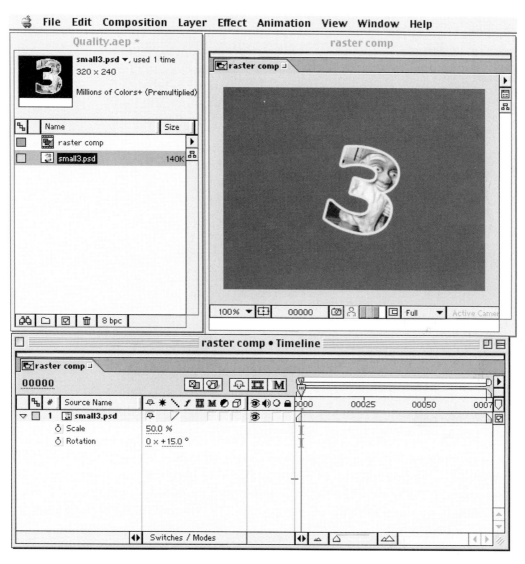

9. Hold the **Shift** key down and press the letter **S**. This should open the Scale property, while leaving the Rotation property visible. Change the **Scale** to **50%** and toggle the **Quality** switch back and forth. You'll see what a big difference Best quality makes when the scale or rotation properties change.

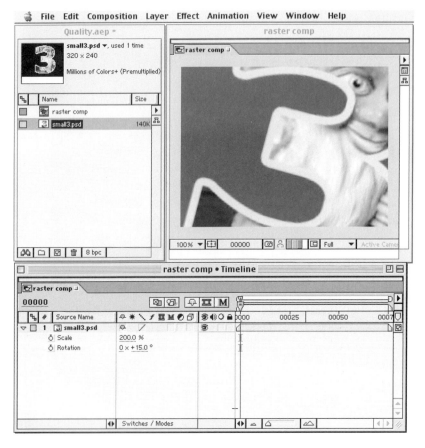

10. Change the **Scale** property to **200%** and toggle the **Quality** switch. You'll see that the Best quality setting helps the image look much better. Note, however, that whenever you scale a raster image larger than its original size, the image will look a little out of focus. It's always best to prepare your Photoshop artwork bigger than what you will need if you plan to animate the Scale property. The Best quality setting helps improve the appearance, but it can't totally compensate for a raster image that is scaled larger than 100%.

In summary, the Quality switch will make a difference to your source footage only if the footage is scaled or rotated. Many After Effects artists leave the Quality switch set to Draft mode to speed up rendering. When you make a final movie (which you'll learn to do in Chapter 16, "Rendering Final Movies"), you can set the overall Quality setting to Best quality and override the switch setting so that your movie will look the best it can. Otherwise, the Quality switch is usually toggled to Best quality occasionally to check the quality, but is left in Draft mode otherwise to allow the work to go faster.

11. Save this project, and leave it open for the next exercise. Close **raster comp**.

6. _____The Quality Switch vs. Continuous Rasterization

Vector images, such as the type created by Adobe Illustrator, do not consist of pixels. When After Effects displays vector images in the Composition window, it converts the vector information to pixels. The Quality switch will determine whether the vector image is displayed in Draft or Best quality. The difference between the two settings is quite noticeable when working with vector images.

As you learned in the previous exercise, if you scale an image larger than 100%, the Best quality setting will improve its appearance, but it will still look out of focus. If you are working with raster images, there is no way around this problem except to remake your artwork larger so you won't have to scale it in After Effects. With vector images, however, there is a solution to this problem, and it's called **continuous rasterization**. The switch that controls this feature is located next to the Quality switch, and it allows vector artwork to scale to any size and always look perfectly crisp. You'll gain working knowledge of this important feature by following this exercise.

1. Import **starmonkey.ai** into your project from the **chap_08** folder. Click **OK** to merge the Illustrator layers as you import the .psd items. You should know how to do this by now; if you don't, please revisit Step 1 of the previous exercise.

---

2. Create a new composition and name it **vector comp**. Bring **starmonkey.ai** into the **vector comp**. You should know how to do this now without a lot of instruction. If you don't, please revisit the previous exercise.

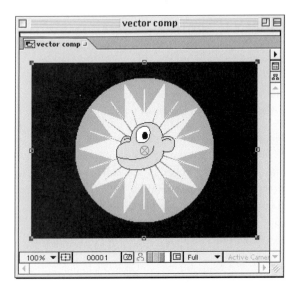

Notice that the monkey looks bad?

3. Click the **Quality** switch in the **Timeline** for the **starmonkey.ai** layer, and the monkey will look crisp.

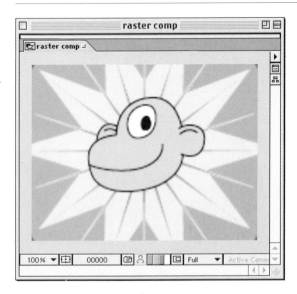

4. Change the scale of the monkey to **200%**. **Hint:** The **S** key on your keyboard will bring forward the Scale property setting.

Observe that the monkey image looks quite blurry at this point.

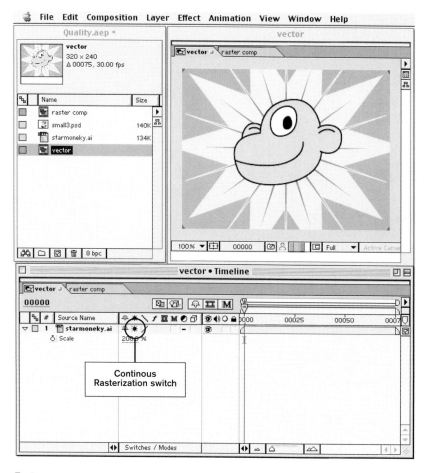

5. Click the **Continuous Rasterization** switch to improve the quality of the vector image. Presto chango; it's beautiful!

The Continuous Rasterization switch is available only for vector-based footage items. If you reopen the raster comp composition you made earlier, you'll see that this switch is missing for raster images. This switch will cause a vector image to look pristine at any scale or rotation setting. It does slow down previews and work, however. You can test this by creating an animation in this composition using different scale settings on different keyframes and activating the Continuous Rasterization switch. If you preview your animation, you'll see that it takes quite a bit longer to render with continuous rasterization in effect. For this reason, most After Effects artists use the Continuous Rasterization switch sparingly until the composition is rendered to a final movie.

6. Save and close this project.

What Is Motion Blur?

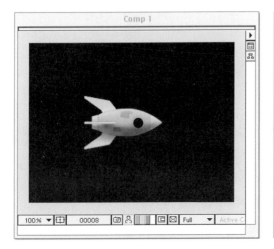 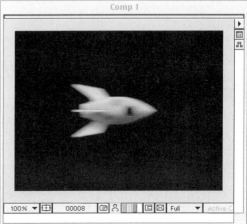

If an object is in motion when it is photographed, any recorded motion will be seen as blur. This is called **motion blur**. For example, if you take a picture of someone on a bicycle speeding past you on the street, the photograph may be blurred if the camera shutter is open long enough to record motion. In the images above, the rocket on the left shows no motion blur and the rocket on right has some blurring.

Cameras have shutters that expose film to light. When the shutter is open, the image is recorded onto film. When you use your snapshot camera, the clicking sound you hear while taking a picture is the sound of the shutter opening and closing. The shorter the time that the shutter is open, the less motion is recorded onto the film image. The longer the shutter is open, the more motion is recorded into the film image.

In motion picture photography, motion blur is useful and usually desirable. In everyday life, we don't see the world as individual snapshots; we see continuous motion. Fast-moving objects are naturally blurred to our eyes. When a series of images is projected in a movie theatre, fast-moving action appears natural to our eyes because motion blur caught by the camera helps to blend images together and produce the perception of smooth action. Introducing motion blur can produce a natural feel to animation created in After Effects.

After Effects offers a very useful tool for smoothing motion by creating motion blur, as you'll see in the next exercise.

7. —————————Applying Motion Blur

The **Motion Blur switch** can be used to make quick movements in your animations look more realistic. After Effects makes it easy to apply motion blur. In this exercise you will learn to use the Motion Blur switch and the Enable Motion Blur button.

1. Choose **File > Open Project**. Alternatively, press **Command+O** (Mac) or **Control+O** (Windows). Select the **Motion Blur.aep** project from the **chap_08** folder and click **Open**.

2. Select **File > Save As**. Navigate to your **HOT_AE_Projects** folder and click **Save**.

3. Double-click on **Space Comp 1** to open it. Press the **spacebar** to play the animation so you can see how it looks before you apply motion blur.

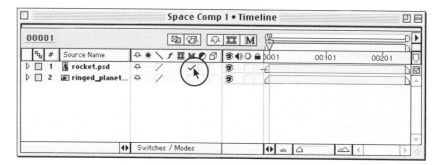

4. In the **Timeline** window, locate the **rocket.psd** layer, and then locate the column for the Motion Blur switch, indicated by a capital M icon. Click the **Motion Blur** check box to turn on motion blur for the **rocket.psd** layer. You won't notice any change in the composition yet.

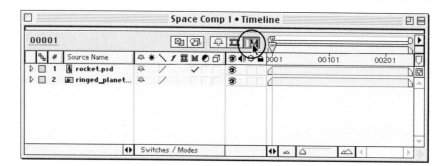

5. At the top of the Timeline window, locate the group of buttons to the left of the Time Marker slider. The button with the capital M is the **Enable Motion Blur** button. Click on this button to enable motion blur. In the Composition window, motion blur is applied to the rocket image.

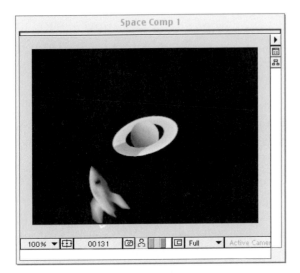

6. Use the Time Marker to move to **Frame 131**. Toggle the **Motion Blur** switch off and on, and notice that this turns motion blur off and on in the Composition window.

In After Effects the Motion Blur switch is very intelligent. It applies more motion blur to the parts of the object that are moving faster. The rocket fin on the left has more motion blur than the fin on the right. This is because the fin on the left has to travel a greater distance to make the sharp turn.

7. With motion blur still on, press the **spacebar** or click **RAM Preview** in the **Time Controls** palette to view your animation.

You'll probably notice that your animation takes longer to render than it did before you added motion blur. Remember to increase your RAM allocation if you can't see the RAM preview, or simply press the spacebar if you don't have enough RAM installed in your computer.

TIP | Motion Blur and Rendering

Motion blur slows down rendering to the screen. When you are designing a composition, it's generally best to enable motion blur only when you want to check the effect it has on the image. The Enable Motion Blur button turns motion blur on or off. The Motion Blur switch selects motion blur for specific layers. To speed your workflow, switch on all the layers that will need motion blur, and then enable or disable motion blur with the Enable Motion Blur button.

---

8. Save and close your project.

Moving and Trimming Time in Layers

You can control two basic items when working with layer time. First, you can define where a layer starts in your composition, and second, you can control how many frames of a layer are actually used.

When you import footage and add it to your composition, by default, the new layer starts on the frame at the current Time Marker position. Of course, you often need to change where the layer starts, which you can accomplish by sliding the layer duration bar to the right or left on the Timeline. This is called **moving** a layer.

The layer added to your composition has a default frame length, as well. Sometimes you need to shorten the length of a layer. This is known as **trimming** a layer.

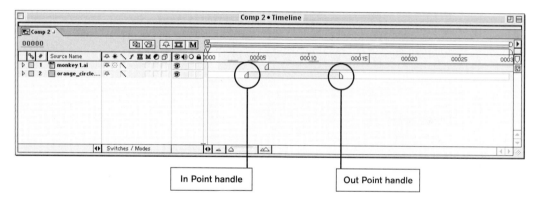

In Point handle

Out Point handle

In this example, the top layer has been moved, and the second layer has been trimmed. Observe that the moved layer (the top one) has an In point handle, but the Out point handle is off the screen in the Timeline window. You can move a layer in time to the right, but not to the left. That's because the In point can never move before the first frame of the composition. Notice that the trimmed layer (the bottom one) has a white bar to its left and right. That is a visual cue that a layer has been trimmed. It indicates that the handles can be pulled back out to their original duration.

After Effects provides several means to accomplish these two essential tasks. You'll learn some new tricks and shortcuts as you work through the next exercises.

8. ————————In and Out Points In Layers

In this exercise you will first learn to move the point at which a layer starts and stops in the Timeline. The starting point is called the **In point** and the stopping point is called the **Out point**. You'll learn to drag a layer in the Timeline to change the In and Out points.

1. Create a new project by choosing **File > New > New Project**. Choose **File > Save As**. Name the project **Sky Project.aep** and navigate to your **HOT_AE_Projects** folder and click **Save**. Import the following footage items from the **chap_08** folder: **sky.mov**, **sky1.psd**, and **sky2.psd**. Click **OK** to merge the Photoshop layers as you import the .psd items.

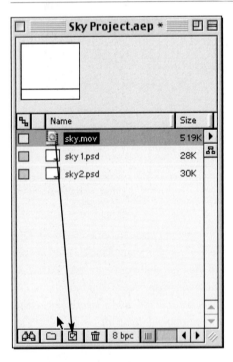

2. Drag **sky.mov** onto the **New Comp** icon. This creates a new composition with the same settings (and name) as the movie. Observe that the Composition and Timeline windows both open in the process and that the layer **sky.mov** already exists in the Timeline.

This is a great technique for making a new composition if you have movie footage and you want the composition to be the same length in both frames and frame rate as the movie file. If you want to check out the composition settings, choose Composition > Composition Settings. You'll see that the settings are different from those of other compositions you've made. The compositions got all these settings automatically from the movie footage.

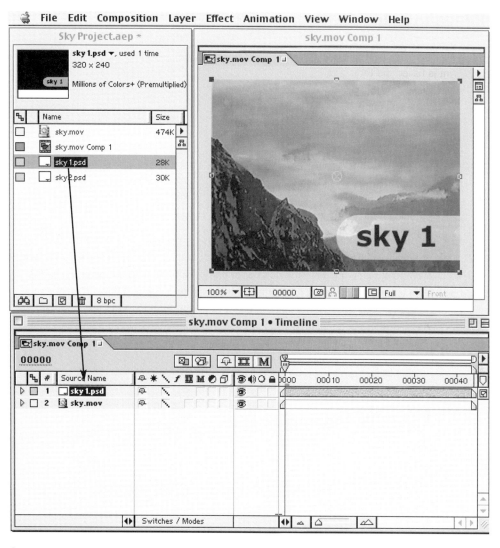

3. Drag **sky1.psd** from the **Project** window to the **Timeline** window. Make sure to place it above the **sky.mov** layer. Press the **spacebar** to watch the composition. Notice that the **sky1.psd** artwork is visible over the movie footage in the Composition window. This artwork was created in Photoshop and was saved on a transparent layer. The areas that were transparent in Photoshop are also transparent in After Effects. Also notice that there is an abrupt cut in the movie footage midway through and that a different moving cloud image appears. This abrupt change is built into the movie footage, and you'll add a different title to begin when this new footage appears in the steps that follow.

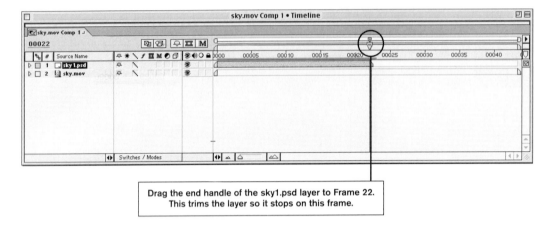

Drag the end handle of the sky1.psd layer to Frame 22.
This trims the layer so it stops on this frame.

4. Scrub the **Time Marker** to the point in time where the abrupt sky change occurs in the movie (**Frame 22**). Pull the right handle of the **sky1.psd** layer to the left to match the Time Marker. You have just adjusted this layer's Out point, trimming the number of frames of footage in this layer. Press the **spacebar** to watch the composition so far. Notice that the lettering turns off at the same point as the abrupt change in the movie footage. Observe that there is a white bar to the right of the Out point. This means that you could drag the handle back to the right, and the footage would reappear all the way to the end of that bar.

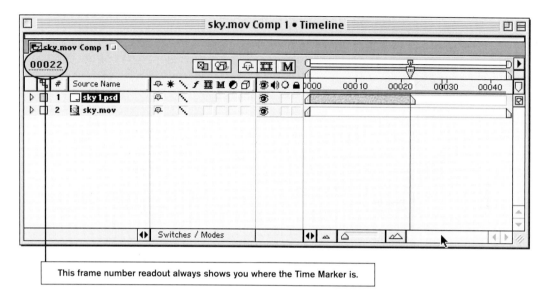

This frame number readout always shows you where the Time Marker is.

5. Make sure the **Time Marker** is still at **Frame 22. Hint:** You can easily see what frame the Time Marker is on by looking at the readout in the upper left corner of the Timeline window. An alternative to moving the Time Marker to a specific frame is to press **Command+G** (Mac) or **Control+G** (Windows) to see the **Go To Time** dialog box and type in a number.

---

6. Drag **sky2.psd** into the **Timeline** and make sure it is the top layer. Notice that it appears in the Timeline window at exactly the same position as the Time Marker.

After Effects always sets the In point of any footage item in the Timeline to the same position as the Time Marker when you bring the footage from the Project window. If you ever accidentally bring footage in at the wrong In point, you can always slide the layer's duration bar to the right or left to make a change.

---

7. Save and close this project.

---

9. _____Keyboard Methods for Trimming Layers

Trimming is a method that is useful when you want to shorten a layer within the composition. You can trim an Out point or an In point in After Effects. The neat thing about trimming is that you can always change your mind.

The difference between moving and trimming footage is that when you move footage, you don't change its physical length in the Timeline; you just move it. With trimming, you can shave off time from the beginning or end of a layer. You trimmed footage in the previous exercise using the layer handles. In this exercise, you'll learn to trim footage using the Time Marker and bracket keys.

1. Open the **trimming.aep project** from the **chap_08** folder, and double-click the **Trimming** composition to open it.

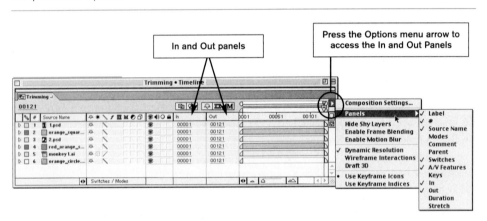

2. Click the **Options** menu arrow at the upper right corner of the Timeline window and select **Panels > In**. Repeat this process and select **Panels > Out**. This will cause the In and Out panels to appear in your Timeline window. These panels are not necessary for performing trimming functions, but they give you numeric feedback about where your footage starts and ends. To make these panels go away, repeat the same process, and they will toggle off. Leave them on for now.

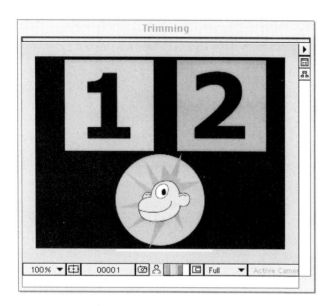

In the Composition window, notice the images. They don't move at all, even though they are on the Timeline for 121 frames! You're going to make the numbers and the monkey turn off and back on over time by using trimming methods.

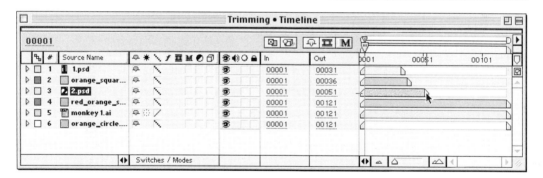

3. Drag the right layer handle for the **1.psd** layer and set the Out point to **Frame 31**. Use the Out panel as a frame reference.

Drag the right layer handle for the **orange_square.psd** layer and set the Out point to **Frame 36**.

Drag the right layer handle for the **2.psd** layer and set the Out point to **Frame 51**.

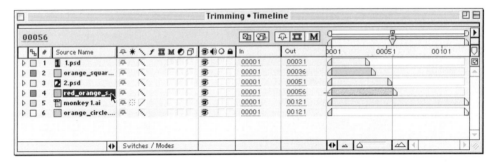

4. Select the **red_orange_square.psd** layer. Set the **Time Marker** to **Frame 56**. Press **Option+]** (Mac) or **Alt+]** (Windows). Notice that the Out point is trimmed to the current Time Marker position. This is a shortcut key to trim the Out point of any layer, based on the location of the Time Marker.

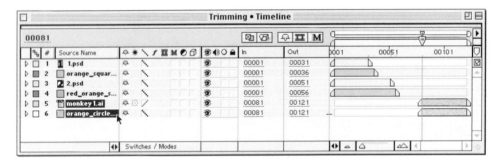

5. Shift+click to select the **monkey1.ai** and **orange_circle.psd** layers. Set the **Time Marker** to **Frame 81**. Press **Option+[** (Mac) or **Alt+[** (Windows). This keyboard shortcut will trim the In point of any layer, based on the location of the Time Marker.

The In points of both selected layers are trimmed to the current Time Marker position. This is the quickest way to trim multiple layers to the same In or Out point.

6. Press the **spacebar** to see your animation.

7. Save and close your project.

TIP | Using the Bracket Keys

The left and right bracket keys are important in After Effects. You can use them to move layers, change the stacking order, and trim layers. Here is a chart that summarizes the different types of bracket key commands.

Bracket Key Commands			
Command Type	**Command**	**Mac**	**Windows**
Move	Move In point to Time Marker	[	[
Move	Move Out point to Time Marker	]	]
Stacking order	Bring Forward	Command+]	Control+]
Stacking order	Send Backward	Command+[	Control+[
Stacking order	Bring to Front	Command+Shift+]	Control+Shift+]
Stacking order	Send to Back	Command+Shift+[	Control+Shift+[
Trim	Trim In point to Time Marker	Option+[	Alt+[
Trim	Trim Out point to Time Marker	Option+]	Alt+]

NOTE | Using In and Out Panels

You can enter values into the In and Out panels, and your footage will move to the frame position you enter. The In or Out panels in the Timeline window cannot be used to trim footage. Although they will display the current trimmed points, the In and Out panels are useful only for *moving* layers or to display the numeric In and Out point frame values of footage.

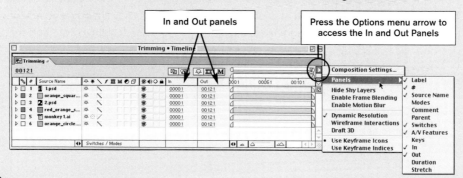

In and Out panels

Press the Options menu arrow to access the In and Out Panels

IO. _____Splitting Layers

Most of the time, when you drag a footage item into your composition, you want that footage to be used as a single layer in your composition. There are times, however, when that isn't the case. For example, let's say that you want an item to travel in front of a layer and then behind the same layer. You might, for instance, want a spaceship to go in front of a planet in one part of your animation and then behind the planet in another. The long way to do this would be to duplicate the spaceship layer, put it above and below the planet layer, and trim its In and Out points correctly.

After Effects offers a much simpler way of dealing with such a situation by **splitting** a layer. When you split a layer, the layer is split into two pieces. The two pieces contain all the properties that were origi- nally on the single layer. Each piece is actually a whole layer that is placed in your Timeline window and trimmed automatically according to the Time Marker position. This is a real timesaver. In the following exercise, you'll learn how to split a layer and when you'll need to split a layer.

1. Choose **File > Open Project**, navigate to **Split Layer Project.aep** in the **chap_08** folder, and click **Open**.

2. Choose **File > Save As**. Navigate to your **HOT_AE_Projects** folder and click **Save**.

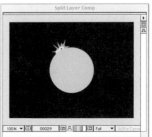
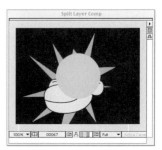

3. If the Composition window is not open, double-click **Split Layer Comp** in the **Project** win- dow. Scrub the Time Marker and notice that the monkey goes behind the orange circle twice. This is appropriate for the first half of the movie. However, the monkey should go in front of the orange circle during the second half of the movie. You're going to learn how to split the layer to achieve this effect.

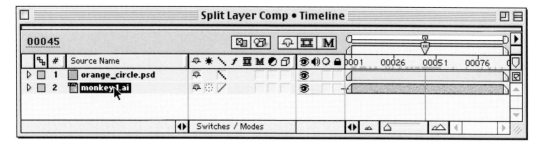

4. Set the **Time Marker** in the Timeline to **Frame 45**, and select the **monkey1.ai** layer. We chose frame 45 because that is the first frame where we want the monkey to appear in front of the circle, instead of behind the circle.

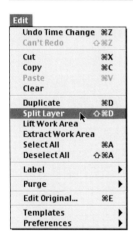

5. Choose **Edit > Split Layer**.

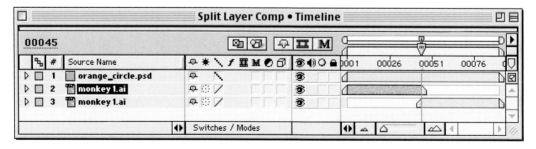

After the split, your Timeline window will look like this. Notice that the layer automatically duplicated itself and set In and Out points to line up exactly on the frame at which you specified that the layer be split.

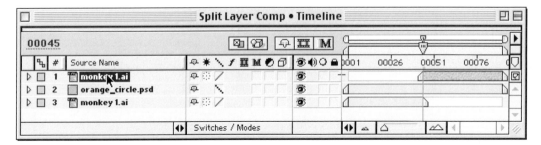

6. Drag the second half of the split **monkey1.ai** layer above the **orange_circle** layer.

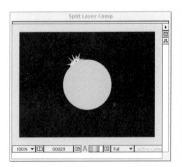 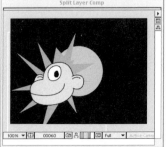 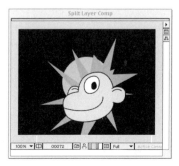

7. Click **RAM Preview** in the **Time Controls** palette and check out the split layer action. Sweet! That was so much more painless than duplicating and trimming, don't you agree?

8. Save your project and close it.

II. ————————Time Stretching and Frame Blending

You've learned how to trim (shorten) layers, but what about stretching layers? There's hardly anything that After Effects can't do, so this is possible, of course! This exercise will show you how to define, set, and adjust the duration of layers.

1. Open **Time Stretch Project.aep** from the **chap_08** folder. It contains two footage items, a QuickTime movie and a Photoshop document.

2. Create a new composition that is 30 frames long, and name it **short comp**. You should know how to do this now without our instruction.

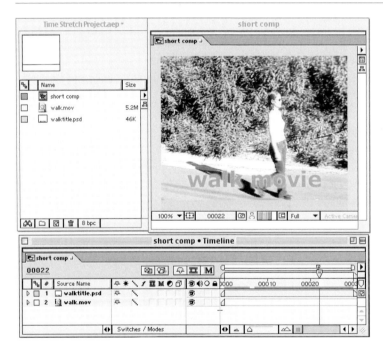

3. Drag the two footage items into this composition. Make sure that **walktitle.psd** is above **walk.mov** in the **Timeline** window. Play the composition by pressing the **spacebar**.

Notice that the Photoshop layer stops at Frame 30 and that the movie footage item extends longer and seems to get cut off by the short length of the composition. That's because a still footage item, such as a Photoshop or Illustrator document, is automatically set to the duration of whatever composition it is inserted into. The movie footage has a fixed time associated with it. You can change the length of the composition to fit the movie, or you can resize the movie to fit the length of the composition. You'll learn to do both in this exercise.

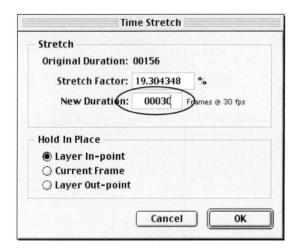

4. To change the length of the movie, select the layer **walk.mov**. Choose **Layer > Time Stretch**. This will open the **Time Stretch** dialog box. Enter a **New Duration** of **00030** frames and click **OK**. You will see that the **walk.mov** footage is now only 30 frames long in the Timeline. If you play the composition by pressing your **spacebar** key, you'll see the woman walking quite a bit faster than before. That's because the footage of her walking has been compressed to 30 frames from 156 frames. How did After Effects do it? By dividing 156 by 30 and discarding the frames that weren't needed. In this case, you've used Time Stretch to shorten duration of the layer. It might not seem like the term "stretch" in "Time Stretch" should be appropriate, however, Time Stretch can be used to shrink as well as stretch. You'll get to do both operations over the next few exercises.

You can stretch or shrink the duration of footage based on entering frame values or percentage values. Hold in Place means that After Effects will stretch or shrink the duration of the footage to make sure the In point is preserved, the Out point is preserved, or the current Time Marker position (Current Frame) is preserved, depending on the option you choose.

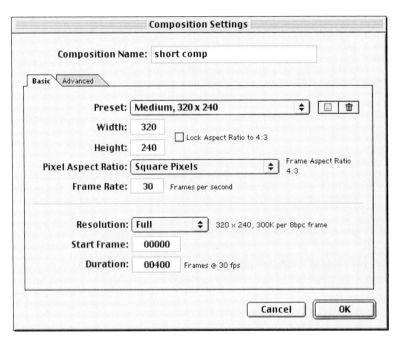

5. Change the length of the composition by choosing **Composition > Composition Settings**. Enter **00400** frames for the **Duration** setting. This will lengthen the composition to 400 frames. Click **OK**.

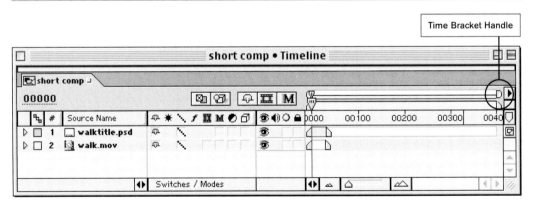

6. Move the Time bracket handle to the right to reveal all 400 frames in the Timeline. You can always zoom in and out on your Timeline by using this handle. Try stretching it back and forth to see what we mean. Move it back to the end of the composition when you are finished. Notice that the two layers are much shorter than the length of the Timeline. That's because the layers were automatically set to the original duration of the composition. Now that you've changed the composition's duration, the layers no longer fit to size.

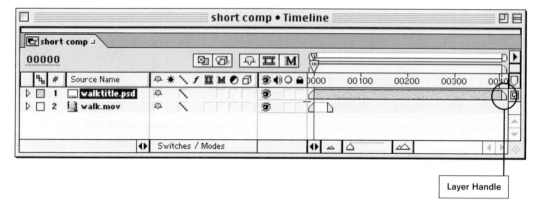

Layer Handle

7. Move the layer handle for **walktitle.psd** to the end of the length of the composition. If you press the **spacebar**, you'll see that the title now extends much longer than the walk movie. While the .psd layer has a movable handle, **walk.mov** does not. That's because movie footage has to be time-stretched to change its duration. Still footage is always a lot more flexible than movie footage.

8. Select the **walk.mov** layer and choose **Layer > Time Stretch**. Enter a **Duration** value of **00400** frames and click **OK**. Watch the composition by pressing the **spacebar**.

Now the walk is very, very slow. You would walk slow too if you'd been time-stretched! How is After Effects achieving this? It's repeating frames by dividing 126 (the original length of the movie) by 400. Most of the frames are being repeated two to four times. A good way to see this is to step through the composition by clicking the Next Frame button on the Time Controls palette, as you'll do in the next step.

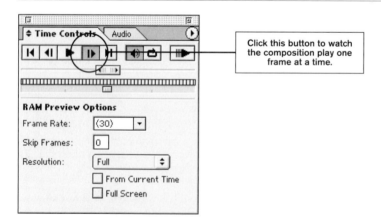

Click this button to watch the composition play one frame at a time.

9. Click the **Next Frame** button on the **Time Controls** palette to step through the frames. Notice that many poses of the walk are held for more than one frame. After Effects has a solution for this, believe it or not. It's called **frame blending**, and you'll get to try it in the next step.

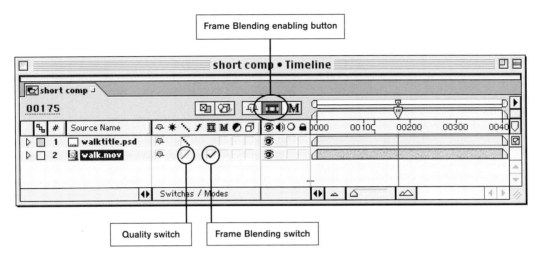

Frame Blending enabling button

Quality switch

Frame Blending switch

10. Click the **Quality** switch and the **Frame Blending** switch for the **walk.mov** layer, and then click the **Enable Frame Blending** button. Step through the animation again, using the **Next Frame** button on the **Time Controls** palette. You'll see that After Effects has created soft opacity transitions between the held frames.

11. Click the **Ram Preview** button on the Time Controls palette and watch the final results. Turn off the **Frame Blending** switch and the **Enable Frame Blending** button and watch again. The frame blending feature makes time-stretched footage look significantly better!

*You can set up frame blending with the switch but turn off the Enable Frame Blending button to speed up rendering while you're working on your project. **Note:** Frame blending works only on moving footage—it has no effect on still frames.*

12. Save and close this project.

I2. —————————Time Remapping

Time remapping is a feature in After Effects that lets you change the way time is interpreted for a live action clip. Using the same walk footage that you worked with in the previous exercise, you'll see how time remapping lets you speed up and reverse the footage layer over time. This effect isn't used that often, but when you need something like this, there is no better tool to do the job!

1. Open the project **timeremapping.aep**. It's an empty project because you're going to import the footage and create the composition. Save this project in your **HOT_AE_Projects** folder so you don't overwrite the original.

2. Import **walk.mov** from the **chap_08** folder.

3. Drag this footage onto the **New Comp** icon. This creates a composition that's exactly the right length and frame rate. The composition is automatically named **walk.mov Comp 1**, and the Timeline and Composition windows open automatically. Whenever we work with live action in a project, we usually like to create the composition using this technique because of all the behind-the-scenes work that After Effects does for you.

4. Select the **walk.mov** layer in the **Timeline** window and choose **Layer > Enable Time Remapping**. Nothing happens—or so you think. You won't see the effect of this feature until you twirl down some twirlies. Wheeeee!

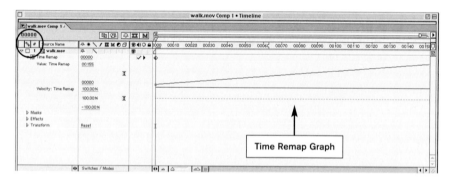

Time Remap Graph

5. Click the twirly for the **walk.mov** layer. You'll see a **Time Remap** property. Click the twirly for that too, and your screen should look like the one above.

Notice that an initial keyframe has been set and that the Stopwatch icon is active. This happens automatically when you enable this feature. The Time Remap property shows a graph, called the Time Map graph, that represents the length of the layer. The graph shows a gradual incline, which means that the movie footage plays at the expected speed. You are going to add keyframes to this graph to change all that.

Keyframe checkbox

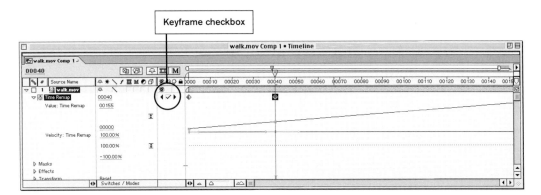

6. Move the **Time Marker** to **Frame 40** and click the **Keyframe Navigator** check box. This inserts a keyframe at Frame 40. Nothing else happens (yet).

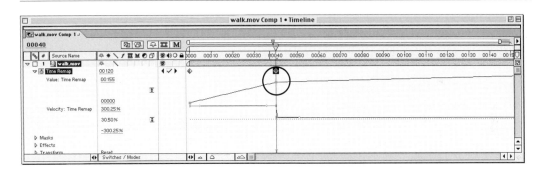

7. Now that you've placed a keyframe on Frame 40, you'll see a handle appear on the graph at that frame. Move the handle up to approximately to the point you see above.

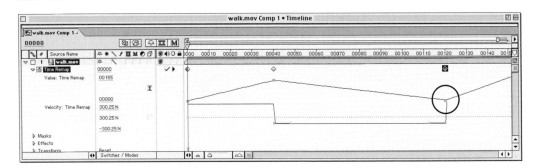

8. Add another keyframe by moving the **Time Marker** to **Frame 120** and clicking the **Keyframe Navigator** check box. On this new keyframe, move the graph down to approximately to the point you see above.

9. Play the animation, and you'll see that the time of this movie speeds up, slows down, and reverses. That's what time mapping does, folks! Feel free to add more keyframes and move the graph to new places. Time will just get more and more distorted!

NOTE | More About the Time Map Graph

You might be wondering what kinds of results you can get by making changes to the Time Map graph. Here are some visual examples that might help you out.

This Time Map graph will play at a constant speed.

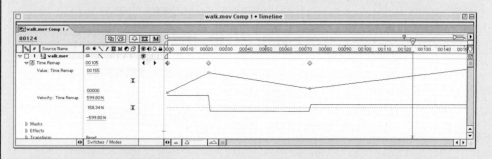

The steep incline at the beginning of this graph will speed the footage up. The decline in the graph will cause the footage to play in reverse. The gradual incline at the end will cause it to play at a constant speed.

---

10. Save and close this project.

I3. ——————————Replacing Layers

After Effects allows you to set up a layer in the Timeline, set keyframes and change properties, and then swap out different footage for the layer. This new footage will retain all the animation and property settings of the old footage. Why would you need to do something like this? Imagine that you are working for a motion graphics design company. Your job might be to design an English and a French version of a main title sequence.

Replacing titles could get rather complicated if you had to start from scratch and replace each English title with a French title. You would have to rework the position keyframes for each title, add mask properties, add effects properties, add the layer options, etc.

Luckily, After Effects makes replacing a layer very easy. All of the properties and options of the original layer are automatically applied to the new layer. In this exercise you will see how easy it is to replace a layer.

1. Choose **File > Open Project**, navigate to **Replace Layer.aep** in the **chap_08** folder, and click **Open**. **Title Comp** will open automatically.

2. Choose **File > Save As**. Navigate to your **HOT_AE_Projects** folder and click **Save**.

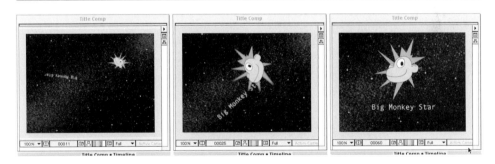

3. Press the **spacebar** to preview the animation.

In the next steps you will learn to use the Replace Layer command. When a layer is replaced, all of the animation and keyframes applied to the original layer continue to work with the new layer.

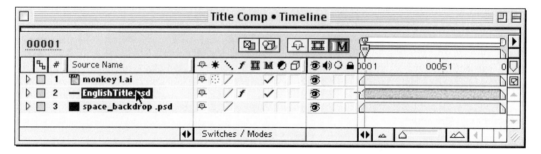

4. In the **Timeline** window, select the **EnglishTitle.psd** layer.

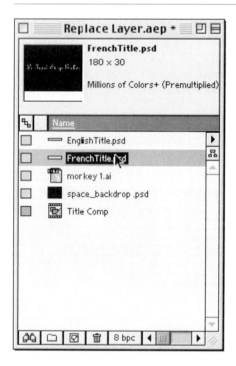

5. In the **Project** window, select the **FrenchTitle.psd** footage. Press **Option** (Mac) or **Alt** (Windows) and drag the French title footage from the **Project** window to the **Timeline** window. Release the footage in the Timeline.

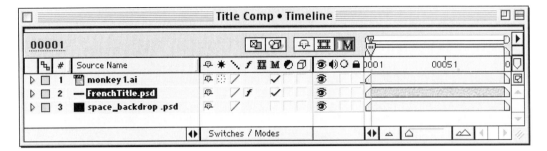

Notice that the **EnglishTitle** layer is replaced by the **FrenchTitle** layer in the Timeline window.

It doesn't matter where you drop the FrenchTitle.psd *footage in the Timeline, because After Effects knows that it should replace the* EnglishTitle.psd *layer. Why? Because you selected that layer before you dragged the replacement layer into the Timeline.*

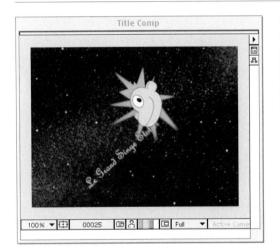

6. Press the **spacebar** to preview your work, and notice that the French title uses the original animation This technique is used for a lot of purposes besides language translations. You might design a template for a title sequence and just swap out the appropriate titles. If you have a commercial, you might make the same animation for different products and just swap them out. To review, here are the steps needed to replace footage: Select the layer you wish to replace in the Timeline, and **Option-drag** (Mac) or **Alt-drag** (Windows) the replacement footage from the Project window into the Timeline. Practice this on your own so you really understand how it works. You'll use this timesaving technique often in your real work.

7. Save your project and close it.

14. _____Sequencing Layers

Quite often in motion graphics, you want to create a sequence of frames, in which the first piece of art-work shows on screen, followed by each successive piece of artwork playing in order. When you learned how to move and trim layers, you saw that you can accomplish something like this by having layers start and end on different frames. The manual method of sequencing layers would be to move each layer in the Timeline to sequentially follow another. However, After Effects provides a way to select layers and sequence them automatically in the Timeline.

After Effects also provides options to overlap the layers rather than simply have one end and the next begin. When you overlap layers, a certain number of frames can be transitioned with crossfades. This is a lovely transitional device that filmmakers use all the time. In the following exercise, you'll learn to sequence layers, overlap them, and crossfade the overlapping layers.

1. Create a new composition by choosing **File > New > New Project**.

2. Choose **File > Save As**. Name the file **Sequence.aep**. Navigate to your **HOT_AE_Projects** folder and click **Save**.

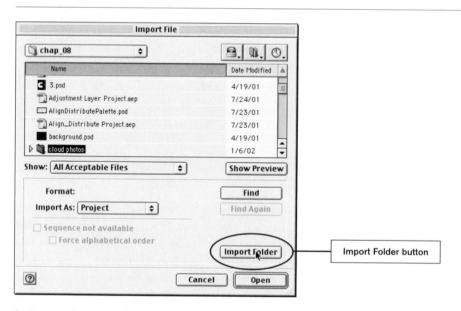

3. Double-click inside the empty **Project** window to launch the **Import File** dialog box. Select the folder called **cloud photos** from the **chap_08** folder. Click the **Import Folder** button. This brings an entire folder of images into your project.

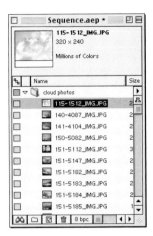

4. Deselect the folder by clicking away from it in the **Project** window. Click the twirly arrow to see the list of images that are inside the folder. If you click on an image, you will see a thumbnail appear at the top of the Project window with some information about the document.

This folder contains 18 different cloud photos that were imported into Photoshop from a digital still camera. They were all sized identically in order to work well in a 320 x 240 After Effects composition, and you will soon learn how to create a slideshow from these still images using the sequence layers feature. Because there are 18 images and we'd like each image to be on the screen for 15 frames, we can figure out the composition length by multiplying 18 (images) x 15 (frames duration) = 270 (frames of composition). In the next step, based on this information, you will create a new composition that is 320 x 240 and 270 frames long.

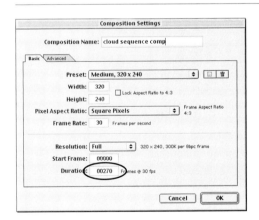

5. Click the **New Comp** button in the Project window to create a new composition. Name it **cloud sequence comp**, and set the rest of the settings to match the screen above. Click **OK**. An empty Timeline and Composition window will open.

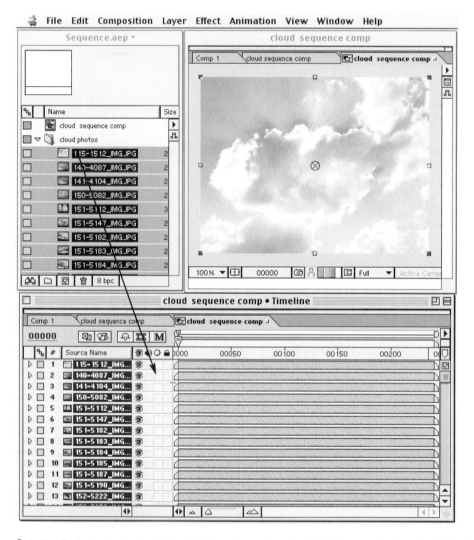

6. In the Project window, hold the **Shift** key down to select all 18 images in the **cloud photos** folder. Drag them all together into the Timeline. Warning: Make sure you don't select the cloud sequence comp you just made when you select these images. If you do, the images will not be able to be dragged into the composition.

Notice that all 18 layers are 270 frames long. After Effects automatically creates a duration for still footage that is the length of the composition. As you have already learned, you can trim this footage to be a different length, and you can also stretch footage to be longer than a composition. For the purpose of this exercise, we want each layer to be 15 frames long so that we can create a slide show. You'll do this next.

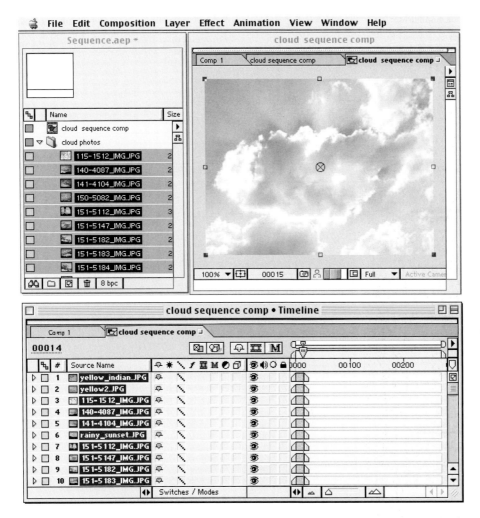

7. Position the **Time Marker** at **Frame 14**. If all the layers are not still selected, choose **Command-A** (Mac) or **Control-A** (Windows) to select them. Press the keyboard shortcut **Option-]** (Mac) or **Alt-]** (Windows). This trims each layer to be 15 frames long because the composition started at frame 0 and you trimmed the footage at frame 14.

You can see why keyboard shortcuts for trimming are useful. Sure, you could have dragged 18 handles to Frame 14, but why do that when you can automate the whole process? Now that the layers are trimmed, you'll learn to automatically position each layer in a sequence on the Timeline.

8. With all the layers still selected, choose **Animation > Keyframe Assistant > Sequence Layers**. The **Sequence Layers** dialog box appears; click **OK**. The settings in this dialog box will be explained shortly.

Notice that the layers are now perfectly positioned on the Timeline to create a 15-frame sequence 18 times. Press the spacebar to preview the animation. It might be cooler if there were little cross-fades between each pair of layers, don't you think? You've learned how to set Opacity property keyframes—can you imagine the labor involved in manually setting keyframes for this kind of animation on 18 frames? Of course, there's a better solution, which you'll learn next.

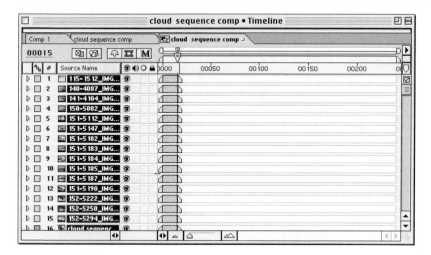

9. Press **Command-Z** (Mac) or **Control-Z** (Windows) twice to return the layers to their trimmed state before they were sequenced. You screen should look like the one above. It's important that all 18 layers are selected, as shown.

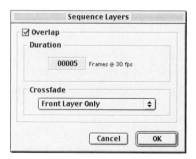

10. Choose **Animation > Keyframe Assistant > Sequence Layers**. This time, don't click OK when the Sequence Layers dialog box opens until you select the **Overlap** check box. Set the **Duration** to 00005 frames and the **Crossfade** to **Front Layer Only**. Check out the chart at the end of this exercise to understand all the possible settings in the Sequence Layers dialog box. Click **OK**.

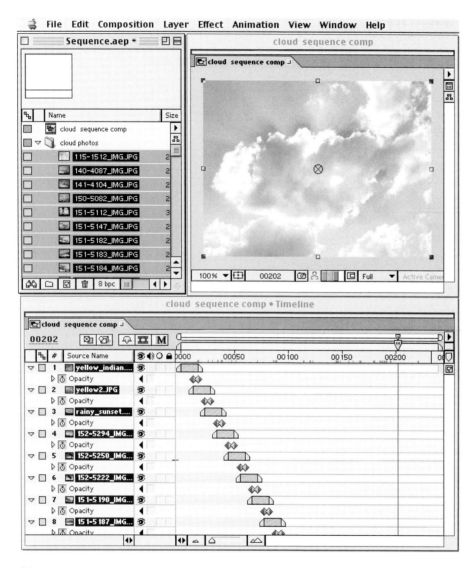

11. Press the **spacebar** to play the composition, and notice the crossfades between the layers. Press the **T** key (to reveal the Opacity settings) and notice that each layer has keyframes automatically set for opacity changes. Wow! After Effects has just saved you a lot of work, eh?

Notice that the composition is now too long for the animation. That's because, with the overlapping of each layer by 5 frames, the footage no longer takes up the entire 270 frames. The last frame containing an image is Frame 202. Fortunately, you can also trim a composition! The next step will show you how.

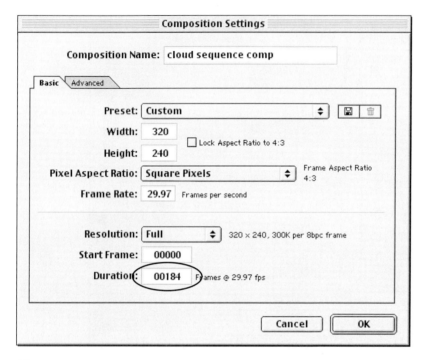

12. Choose **Composition > Composition Settings** and change the **Duration** to 0202 frames. Click **OK**. When you do, you'll see that your composition has been shortened. Now when you play the slide show, the composition will end at the same time that the images do.

13. Save and close your project.

NOTE | The Sequence Layers Dialog Box

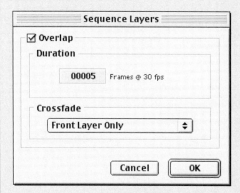

In this last exercise, you worked with the sequence layers feature of After Effects. The Sequence Layers dialog box has many options. Here's a handy chart that outlines what they are.

Sequence Layers Dialog Box

Option	Description
Overlap	Allows you to overlap two adjacent layers with a crossfade. This causes each layer to look as though it is fading in or out or both in and out. The crossfade is controlled by the Crossfade setting.
Duration	Indicates the number of frames over which the overlap of layers occurs. You can enter any value into this field that does not exceed the duration of the layer.
Crossfade: Front Layer Only	Fades out at the end of the layer's duration. Opacity keyframes are automatically set that last for the duration of the overlap. For a layer that is 15 frames long with a 5-frame overlap, the fade-out will occur from frames 10 to 15.
Crossfade: Front and Back Layers	Fades the layer in at the beginning and out at the end of the layer's duration. Opacity keyframes are automatically set that last for the duration of the overlap. For a layer that is 15 frames long with a 5-frame overlap, the fade-in will occur from frames 1 to 5 and the fade-out will occur from frames 10 to 15.

What Is a Solid Layer?

As you have probably figured out by now, After Effects doesn't have paint tools like Photoshop. The standard workflow is to create assets outside of After Effects and import this footage into the Project window. There's one exception to the lack of artwork creation tools in After Effects, and that is when you want to create a solid layer.

A **solid layer** is exactly what it sounds like—a layer that contains a solid-colored shape. You can make a solid layer of any size, from 1 x 1 pixel up to 32,000 x 32,000 pixels. The color can be any color of your choosing. Why would you want a solid layer? They are useful when you want a quick graphic in the shape of a rectangle. Later in the book, you'll also see that solid layers can be masked to create shapes other than rectangles.

At first it would seem that having a layer of a solid color would be of minimal use—say, only for a background color. However, because solid layers have all of the properties of a normal layer, you'll find yourself using them all the time. You can add effects, masks, and transformations to solid layers and make them useful in many ways.

In the following exercise, you'll learn how to create solid layers and change their color, dimensions, and settings. You can make solid layers smaller than the shape of your composition so they don't cover up other layers of artwork, or you can make them partially transparent so you can see through them. All of the properties of a solid layer can be animated as well.

I5. ————————Creating Solid Layers

In this exercise you will create a solid layer, change the settings, and animate the properties.

1. Choose **File > New > New Project**. Alternatively, press **Command+Option+N** (Mac) or **Control+Alt+N** (Windows) to create a new project.

2. Choose **File > Save As** and save your new project into the **HOT_AE_Projects** folder as **Solid Layers Project.aep**.

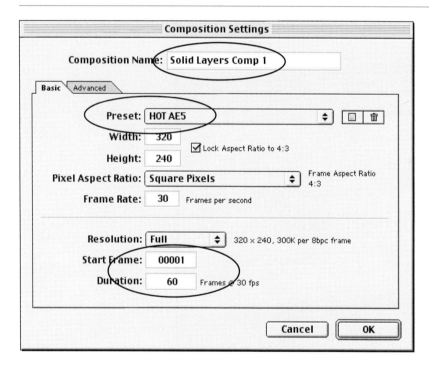

3. Choose **Composition > New Composition**. You can also press **Command+N** (Mac) or **Control+N** (Windows) or click the **New Comp** button at the bottom of your Project window. There are three ways to create a new composition—take your pick!

Name the composition **Solid Layers Comp 1**. Select the **HOT AE5** preset from the drop-down menu in the **Preset** field. Set the **Duration** to **60** frames. Click **OK**.

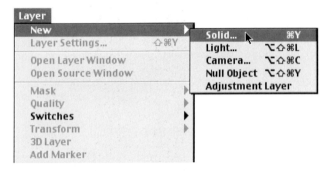

4. Choose **Layer > New > Solid**. As an alternative method, press **Command+Y** (Mac) or **Control+Y** (Windows).

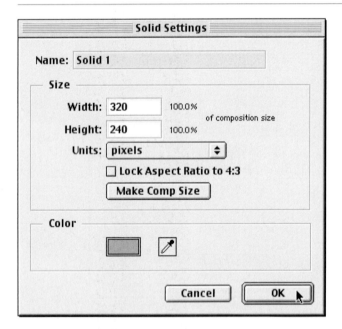

5. In the **Solid Settings** dialog box, accept **Solid 1** as the name for the solid layer. Make sure the **Width** is **320** and the **Height** is **240**. Notice the color in the **Color** block. This will be the color of your solid layer. Click **OK**.

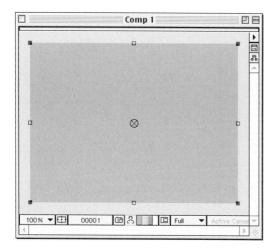

Your Composition window should look like this. If it does not, it is probably because a lighter or darker color was left as the default color in the Solid Settings dialog box. In the following steps, you will learn to change the color and other settings of a solid layer.

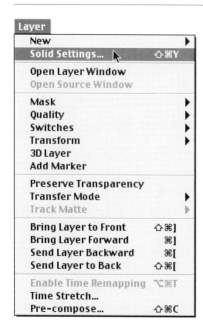

6. Choose **Layer > Solid Settings**. As a keyboard shortcut, you can use **Command+Shift+Y** (Mac) or **Control+Shift+Y** (Windows). This reopens the Solid Settings dialog box that will enable you to make a color change.

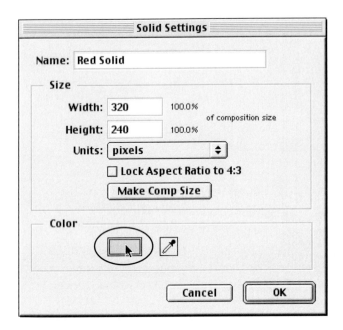

7. Rename the solid layer **Red Solid**. Click the color well to access the color picker.

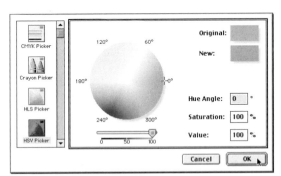
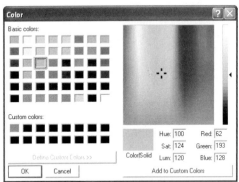

8. On the **Macintosh**, the **HSV Picker** will appear. Click and drag in the color circle to select a **red** color. Drag the **Value** control slider to **100%**. Make sure the saturation is set to **100%**. Click **OK**, and then click **OK** again to close the **Solid Settings** dialog box. In **Windows**, the **Basics** color chart will appear. Click on the **red** rectangle or choose a color of red from the spectrum and click **OK**. Click **OK** again in the **Solid Settings** dialog box.

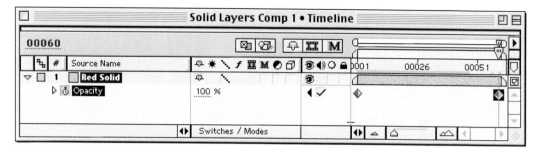

9. In the **Timeline** window, select the **Red Solid** layer and press **T** on your keyboard as a shortcut method to display the **Opacity** property. Click the **Stopwatch** icon. Make sure the **Time Marker** is on **Frame 1**, and set the **Opacity** to **0%**. Press **K** to move the **Time Marker** to the last frame of the composition. Set the **Opacity** to **100%**.

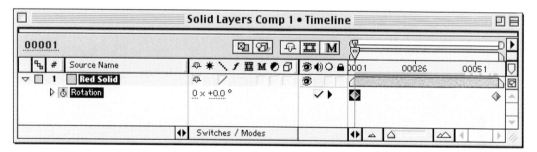

10. With the **Red Solid** layer selected, press **R** to display the **Rotation** property. Press **J** to move the **Time Marker** to the first frame. Click the **Stopwatch** icon. Press **K** to move the **Time Marker** to the last frame. Set the **Rotation** to **90** degrees.

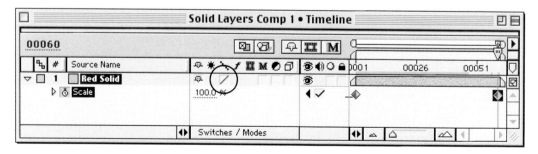

11. Press **S** to display the **Scale** property. Press **J** to move the **Time Marker** to the first frame. Click the **Stopwatch** icon and set the **Scale** to **1%**. Press **K** to move to the last frame. Set the **Scale** to **100%**. Click the **Quality** switch to set it to Best quality. Solid layers preview much better at Best quality.

 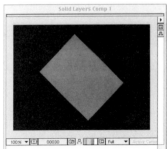 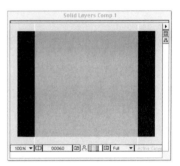

12. Click **RAM Preview**. Notice that the solid layer responds to all property settings just as imported footage does.

In the following step you will learn to change the dimensions of a solid layer.

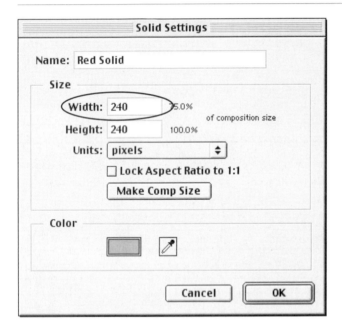

13. Choose **Layer > Solid Settings**. As a keyboard shortcut, you can use **Command+Shift+Y** (Mac) or **Control+Shift+Y** (Windows). In the **Solid Settings** dialog box, set the **Width** to **240**. Click **OK**.

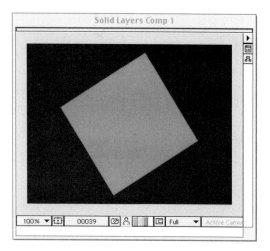

14. Press the **spacebar** to watch the animation, and observe the square dimensions of the solid layer.

15. Choose **Layer > New > Solid**. As an alternative method, press **Command+Y** (Mac) or **Control+Y** (Windows).

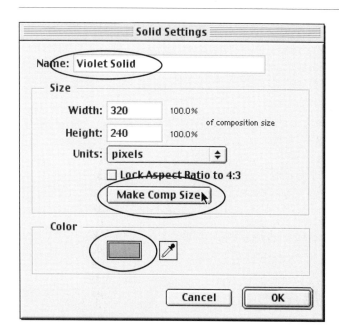

16. Change the name to **Violet Solid**. Click the **Make Comp Size** button, and observe that the Width and Height settings change to match the composition size. Click the color block.

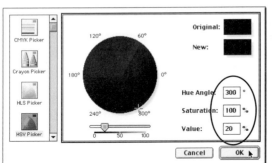 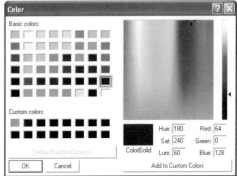

17. On the **Macintosh**, set the **Hue Angle** to **300** degrees, the **Saturation** to **100%**, and the **Value** to **20%**. In **Windows**, select the violet rectangle from the **Basics** color chart. Click **OK**, and then click **OK** again in the **Solid Settings** dialog box.

18. In the **Timeline** window, drag the **Violet Solid** layer under the **Red Solid** layer. In the **Composition** window, notice that the new solid layer displays at the composition dimensions.

Our hope is that this exercise has given you some idea of the capabilities of a solid layer. You'll work with these layers in other chapters as well, to get other ideas that demonstrate their usefulness. For now, you could make an abstract moving composition with lots of animating rectangles set to different scales, opacities, and rotations. In future chapters, you'll learn to combine solid layers with other footage, text, and effect elements.

19. Save and close this project.

Aligning and Distributing Layers

There will be times when you have multiple layers that need to be aligned mathematically. You could use a ruler and sit and calculate what constitutes perfect distribution and alignment, but it's much easier to let the computer do these sorts of tasks for you!

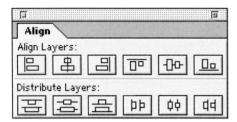

In After Effects, layers can be moved using the Align palette. You access this palette by choosing **Window > Align and Distribute**.

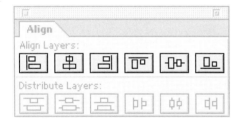

The top row contains the alignment buttons. Alignment indicates that artwork on layers is lined up. The icons in this row represent left, vertical center, right, top, horizontal center, and bottom alignment.

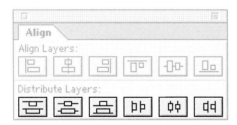

The bottom row contains the distribution buttons. To distribute something means to space it evenly. You can space multiple pieces of artwork by using the icons in this row, choosing from vertical top, vertical center, vertical bottom, horizontal left, horizontal center, or horizontal right distribution.

16. ——————**Using the Align Palette**

In this exercise you will get to use the alignment and distribution tools for the first time. This example, of a menu system, would be useful if you were doing a design for a DVD interface or for a title sequence. It is just one of numerous examples in which the align and distribute features of After Effects are useful.

1. Open the **Align_Distribute Project.aep** file from the **chap_08** folder.

2. Choose **File > Save As**. Navigate to your **HOT_AE_Projects** folder and click **Save**.

3. In the **Project** window, double-click on **menu comp**, if it isn't already open.

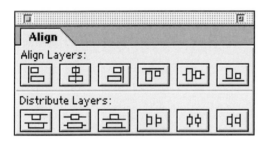

4. Choose **Window > Align & Distribute**. This opens the **Align** palette. Warning: Your Align_Distribute Project listing also appears under the Window menu. Be sure to click Align & Distribute, not the project name!

Study the Align palette. The top row contains the alignment icons. The bottom row contains the distribution icons.

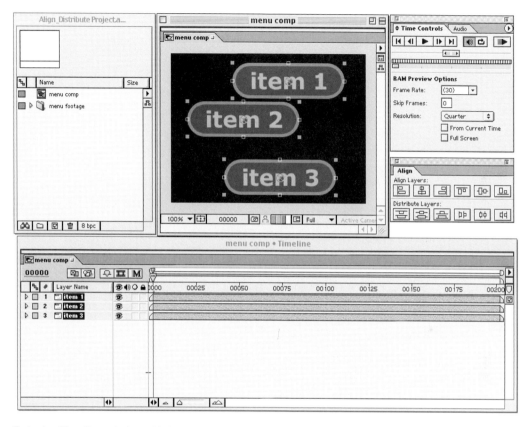

5. In the **Timeline** window, **Shift+click** to select all the layers. Notice that they also become selected in the Composition window. **Tip:** Alternatively, you could **Shift+click** on the images in the **Composition** window. This would also select them in both places.

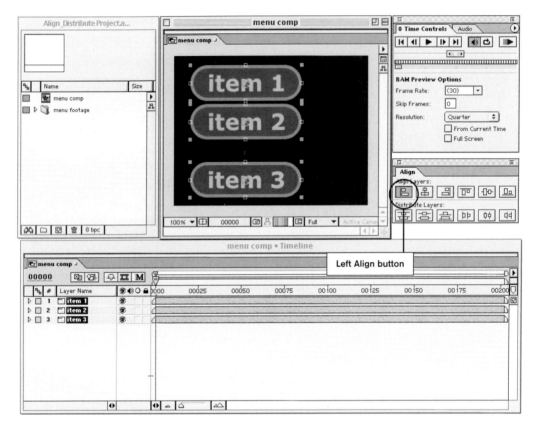

6. Click the **Left Align** button, and notice that the menu items move to align with the left edge of the button shape.

Notice that when you specify left alignment, the selected layers align with the selected object that is farthest to the left. The far left edge does not move—it is used to identify the alignment edge.

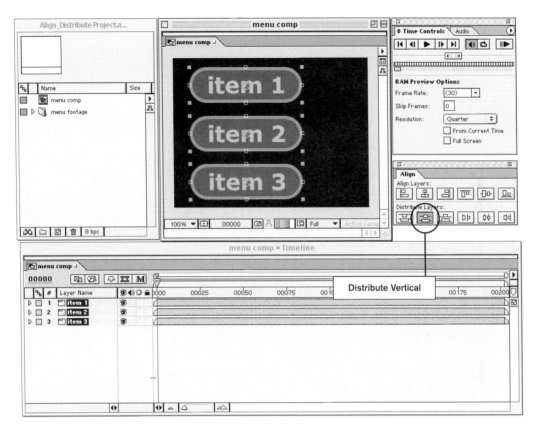

7. Click the **Distribute Vertical Center** button, and notice that the menu items are distributed evenly from top to bottom. This button spaces the centers of the items evenly, starting from the most extreme vertical positions.

This sure beats aligning the objects by hand! This technique is useful for static or animated graphics. In the next few steps, you'll see how you can incorporate this alignment technique to create an animation of the menu items flying in the screen.

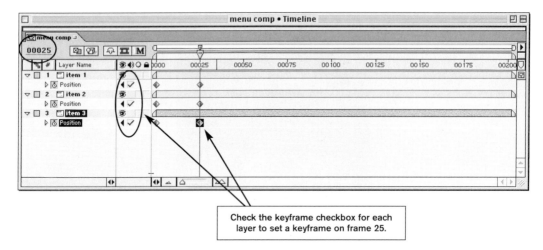

Check the keyframe checkbox for each
layer to set a keyframe on frame 25.

8. With all three layers still selected, press **Option+P** (Mac) or **Alt+P** (Windows) to reveal the Position properties. Notice that the Stopwatch is active and that a check mark already appears in the Keyframe Navigator check box. This happens automatically when you use the Option/Alt shortcut keys. Move the **Time Marker** to **Frame 25**, and select the **Keyframe Navigator** check boxes for each layer. This inserts a keyframe of the current position for each layer at Frame 25.

9. Move the **Time Marker** back to the first frame (press the letter **J** to accomplish this).

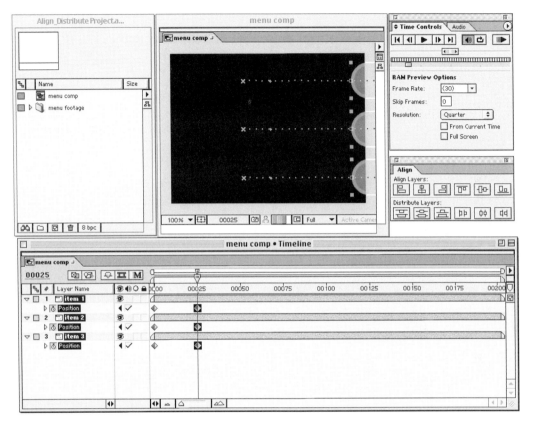

10. Reselect all three objects, using the **Shift+click** method. Hold the **Shift** key down and use your **right arrow** key to move the artwork to the right. Repeat this process until the artwork is moved off the screen. Since two keyframes have been set and the layers are selected, you should see the motion path of the animation you just created.

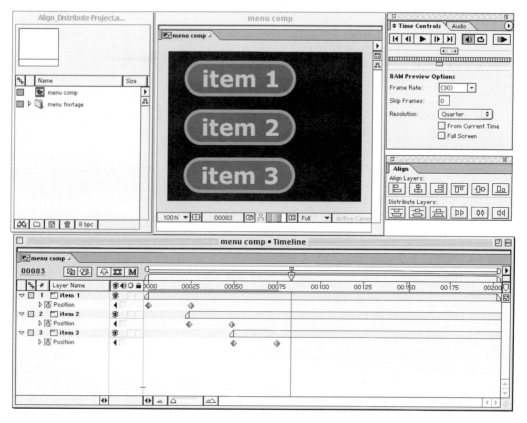

11. Deselect all the layers by clicking away from them in the Timeline. This will deactivate the motion path preview. Press the **spacebar** to view what you've done so far. Try moving the layers as you see here by dragging them, and watch the animation again. This staggers the timing of each layer.

NOTE | Reversing Keyframes!

Let's say you wanted to reverse the direction of the position keyframes. Can you do it? Of course, this is After Effects! Simply select the keyframes you want to reverse by holding down the shift key. Choose Animation > Keyframe Assistant > Time Reverse Keyframes.

---

12. Once you've seen the results of your efforts, save and close this project.

TIP | Using the Keyboard to Move a Layer

You can move a layer by selecting it in the Timeline window and using the keyboard arrow keys. Pressing an arrow key moves the selected layer or layers 1 pixel in the direction of the arrow. Holding the Shift key down while pressing an arrow key moves the selected layers 10 pixels.

NOTE | Distributing Layers of Different Sizes

The Vertical Top, Vertical Bottom, Horizontal Left, and Horizontal Right distribution buttons become important when one of your objects is of a different size than the rest.

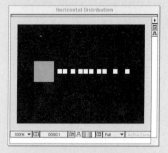

The example above shows a horizontal group of squares before distribution. The large square on the left will create different results when selected with the smaller squares for distribution.

 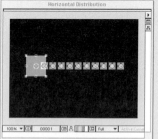 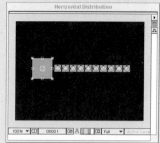

Shown above are the results of Horizontal Left, Center, and Right distribution. The Left option arranges the objects so that their left edges are an equal distance apart, causing the small squares to overlap the large square. The Center option distributes the centers of all the squares evenly, without regard to the edges. The Right option creates the same size gap between all of the squares.

continues on next page

NOTE | Distributing Layers of Different Sizes *continued*

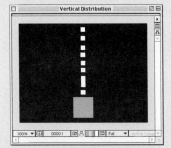

Above is an example of squares arranged vertically before distribution.

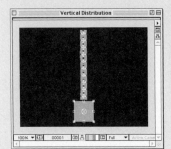  

The three examples above show the results of applying a Vertical Top, Center, and Bottom distribution to the group of squares. Each option spaces the edges and centers of the small squares differently relative to the big square.

When distributing objects of different sizes, try each distribution option to decide which relationship suits the visual needs of your composition.

What Are Layer Modes?

You may have worked with **layer modes** in Photoshop before, and if you have, you'll find that they are quite similar in After Effects. Layer modes affect the way that multiple layers in the Timeline appear when composited (or combined) in the Composition window. A normal layer, if put on top of another normal layer in the Timeline, will cover the lower layer completely. If set to a layer mode, however, the top layer will interact with the layer beneath it to change its appearance.

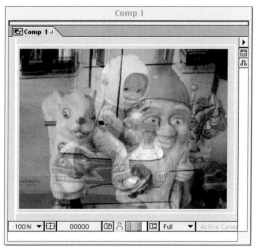

If the top layer is set to Normal mode, it obscures the layer(s) beneath it. If the top layer is set to Multiply mode, the layer beneath it shows through. Layer modes offer alternative compositing effects in multilayered After Effects documents.

Layer modes are created by mathematical formulas that add, subtract, multiply, and divide pixels. Depending on the formula used, a different result occurs. Most After Effects artists use layer modes in an experimental way. It's hard to remember what each layer mode does, and it's much easier to try different ones to search for a desired effect.

Here's a handy chart that explains what the different layer modes do.

Layer Modes		
Visual	**Mode**	**Description**
	Normal	Covers the layer(s) beneath it.
	Dissolve	In order for Dissolve to work, the layer to which it is applied must contain transparent pixels. This can be achieved with a mask or an alpha or by lowering the opacity. The result is that random pixels of the layer(s) beneath this layer will appear. If you set keyframes with different values for the Opacity property for the top layer, this layer mode will animate in After Effects. It is actually the Opacity property that is animating, however, as you cannot set keyframes for layer modes.
	Dancing Dissolve	Looks identical to Dissolve, except that the random pixels will change over time. This creates an animated flicker effect. As with the Dissolve layer mode, the top image must have transparent pixels.
	Add	Combines the colors of the top and underlying layers, resulting in a lighter color than the original.

continues on next page

Layer Modes *continued*		
Visual	**Mode**	**Description**
	Multiply	Multiplies and divides the color value from the layer beneath, resulting in a darker image than the original.
	Screen	Multiplies the inverse brightness of the colors for the top and underlying layers. The result is never darker than original.
	Overlay	Preserves the lights and dark areas of the layer colors while mixing colors between layers.
	Soft Light	Darkens or lightens colors, depending on the original layer color. Changes depending on whether the underlying color is lighter or darker than 50 percent gray.
	Hard Light	Produces different results depending on the lightness or darkness of the pixel values.

continues on next page

	Layer Modes *continued*	
Visual	**Mode**	**Description**
	Color Dodge	Results in a lot of pure whites and blacks and creates a brighter result than the original layer.
	Color Burn	Creates a darker result than the original layer; pure white does not change the underlying color, while pure black is preserved.
	Darken	Gives preference to the darker of the two images. Will cause color shifts.
	Difference	Subtracts the values of the top layer's underlying color.
	Exclusion	Similar to the Difference filter but with lower contrast.

continues on next page

Layer Modes *continued*		
Visual	**Mode**	**Description**
	Hue	Combines the luminance and saturation of the underlying colors with the hue of the layer colors.
	Saturation	Combines the luminance and hue of the underlying colors with the saturation of the layer colors. Has no affect on grayscale images.
	Color	Combines the luminance of the underlying colors with the hue and saturation of the layer colors. Grays are preserved.
	Luminosity	Combines the hue and saturation of the underlying colors of one layer with the luminancy of the layer colors. The effect is the opposite of what the Color mode achieves.

17. ——————————Layer Modes

Layer modes add, subtract, divide and multiply pixel values of different layers together. Because After Effects is programmed to do this in many different ways, you have a wide variety of blending modes to choose from. These modes are used to create special effects in the way images look when they are composited together. There really isn't a practical use for them; it is more of a visual effect that you might choose to use when you want your movie footage to look different from normal. This exercise will let you experiment with layer modes.

1. Open **layermodes.aep** from the **chap_08** folder.

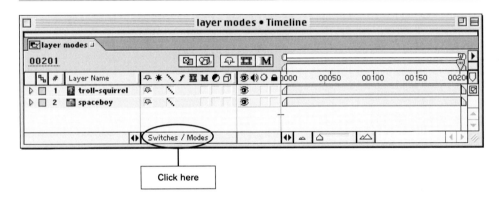

Click here

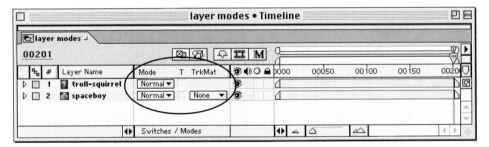

2. Click the words **Switches/Modes** to toggle to the Modes panel. This is a somewhat hidden button in After Effects (aren't ya glad ya got this book?). Try clicking it a bunch of times—you'll see that it toggles on and off. Make sure you leave it set to the Modes panel when you're finished clicking.

3. Change the **troll-squirrel** layer from Normal to the Multiply mode by displaying the Mode menu on the top layer. You always apply the layer mode to the layer above the one you want to affect.

Tip: As an alternative method, select the layer and then choose Layer > Transfer Mode > Multiply. This Transfer Mode menu contains the same list found in the Mode pop-up menu. Layer modes are also known as transfer modes.

4. Experiment with other modes, and see what they do. There is no better way to learn which ones you like than to experiment. You might also try lowering the opacity on the **troll-squirrel** layer, which will have varying effects with different layer modes. When you are finished, save and close this project.

Note: Some of the layer modes were omitted from the Layer Modes chart, as they relate more to the chapter on masking. Those left out include Stencil Alpha, Stencil Luma, Silhouette Alpha, and Silhouette Luma, as well as Alpha Add and Luminescent Premul.

TIP | Changing Layer Modes

Unlike layer properties, layer modes cannot be animated over time using keyframes. If you wish to use another layer mode on the same layer at any point in a Timeline, split the layer and apply a new layer mode. You learned how to split a layer earlier in this chapter.

This chapter was a biggie! As we said, layers are quite a bit more complex in After Effects than in other programs. I guess you believe us now! Have yourself a nice break before moving forward to the next chapter.

9.
Parenting

| Parenting Layers | Attaching Children to a Parent |
| Animating Children and Parents | Animating Null Objects |

chap_09

After Effects 5.0/5.5
H•O•T CD-ROM

In programs such as Photoshop or Illustrator, you might be familiar with "grouping," "linking," or "nesting" objects. These features allow you to address multiple objects as a single object in order to edit, move, or organize them. After Effects doesn't use these same terms, but it does offer some of these same functions in its parenting features.

Parenting allows one layer to inherit the Transform properties of another. This means you can animate the anchor point or the Position, Scale, or Rotation properties of one parent object, and the attached child object's properties will be animated in the same way. The only Transform property that does not work with parenting is Opacity.

This chapter covers how to use the After Effects parenting features and gives some examples that show why you would want to use them. Parenting is one of the new features of the After Effects 5.0/5.5 release that has caused legions of users to upgrade. It's no wonder, since the tasks you'll learn to do easily with parenting used to take much longer and were much harder to perform.

Parenting Layers

In parenting, one layer is assigned as a **parent**, and another layer or multiple layers are assigned to be the **child** or **children**. The Transform properties of the parent layer are inherited by any layer that you assign as a child. This might mean, for example, that if a parent layer had a Rotation property set to 30 degrees, the child layer would also rotate 30 degrees, even though you hadn't set the child's Transform properties to do so. A child layer can have only one parent, but a parent layer can have any number of child layers within the same composition.

In this section you will learn how to assign parenting to a layer. You'll also learn how to adjust the child layer to work appropriately with the parent. (This is beginning to sound like a psychology book! However, it's much easier than psychology.)

I. _____Attaching Children to a Parent

Assigning a parent layer to a child layer is very easy in After Effects. However, once you've attached a child layer to a parent, you may need to make adjustments to the child layer's anchor point to position the child properly with respect to the parent. For example, if you wanted an arm [child] to attach to a body [parent], you'd need to set the anchor point of the arm at the shoulder point. Often when you attach a layer to another as a child, its default anchor point (the center of the object) is not where you really want it to be.

In this exercise, you will assign the rocket layer as the parent and the flame footage as the child. Setting the rocket layer as the parent will allow the flames to animate with the rocket. As you'll see, the Position, Scale, and Rotation properties of the flame layer will all be affected by the rocket layer's Transform properties.

The flame footage is a QuickTime movie that is 30 frames long. It is too short to play for the entire duration of the composition. However, the flames were designed to play as a continuous loop, and After Effects provides a way to loop movies.

Before assigning the parenting, you will first learn how to use the **Interpret Footage** dialog box to loop the flame movie. This dialog box provides options for each footage item in the Project window.

1. Choose **File > Open Project** and navigate to the **chap_09** folder. Choose **Space Project.aep** and click **Open**. Double-click **Space Comp 1**, if it is not already open This will open the Timeline and Composition windows.

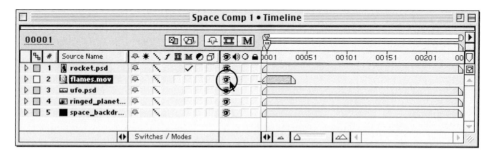

2. In the **Timeline**, click the **Video** switch for **flames.mov** to display the flame footage. Scrub the **Time Marker** and notice that the flame footage is shorter than the rocket footage.

In the next steps you'll learn how to loop the flames for the duration of the shot, using the Interpret Footage dialog box.

3. In the **Project** window, select the **flames.mov** footage from the **Movies** folder inside the **chap_9** folder. In the following steps, you'll learn how to make this footage loop to last longer. This process has to start in the Project window, where you select the footage you want to loop.

4. Choose **File > Interpret Footage > Main**. As an alternative method, press **Command+F** (Mac) or **Control+F** (Windows).

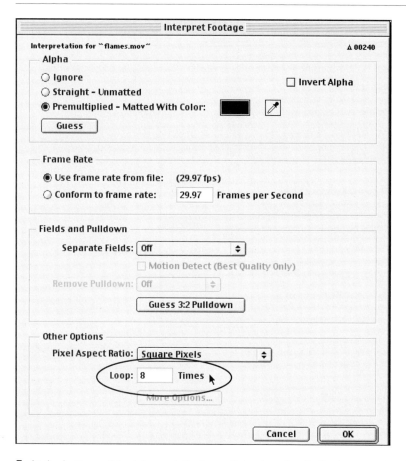

5. At the bottom of the **Interpret Footage** dialog box, locate the **Loop** option. Enter **8** as the number of times to loop, and click **OK**. **Note:** The value 8 was chosen to make the 30-frame movie last 240 frames. The Interpret Footage dialog box is explained in a chart starting on page 271. See the note regarding the Interpret Footage dialog box at the end of this exercise.

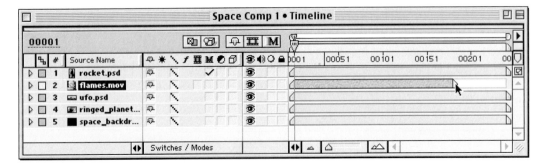

6. Scrub the **Time Marker** and notice that the footage now stretches for the duration of the shot. It does this by looping (repeating) itself.

In the next steps you'll assign the rocket.psd *layer as the parent of the* flames.mov *layer.*

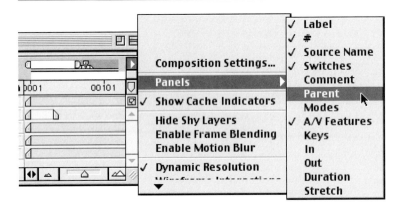

7. Open the Timeline window menu by clicking the **arrow** at the top right of the **Timeline**, and choose **Panels > Parent** to display the Parent panel in the Timeline.

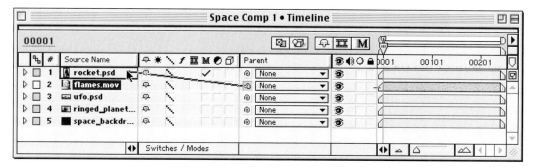

8. Locate the **Pick Whip** icons in the **Parent** panel. *(The Pick Whip is the spiral icon)* Click the Pick Whip icon and drag the resulting line from the **flames.mov** layer to the **rocket.psd** layer. This method of dragging the Pick Whip from one layer to another is how you create a parent-child relationship. Everything in the child layer (**flames.mov**) takes on the Transform properties of the parent layer (**rocket.psd**). You establish which layer is the parent and which is the child through this tool. You always drag the child to the parent to establish this relationship.

Notice that the Parent panel pop-up menu now lists the 1.rocket.psd *layer as the parent for the* flames.mov *layer.* **Note:** *The* 1. *in* 1.rocket.psd *indicates the layer's stacking order in the Timeline.*

NOTE | Pick Whip? What?

You might wonder what the heck a Pick Whip is and why Adobe chose to use this funny term. The "pick" in Pick Whip stands for picking a relationship between layers. The "whip" part of the term was chosen because of how the line behaves between the layers if you change your mind and don't select anything. It animates, kind of like a whip at a rodeo. Hey, engineers have senses of humor too!

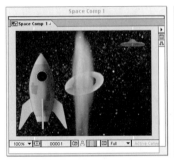  

9. Scrub the **Time Marker** and observe that the flame movie now follows along next to the rocket ship animation. The Position, Scale, and Rotation properties of the rocket's layer are now applied to the flame's layer properties! That's what happens when you parent something—the Transform properties (except Opacity, sadly) are applied to the child layer. The fact that the flame and rocket are not positioned properly yet will be addressed in the following steps.

Move the anchor point to the top of the flame artwork

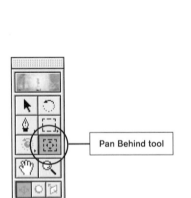

Pan Behind tool

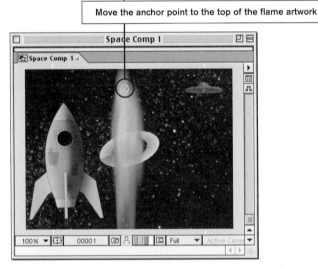

10. Select the **flames.mov** layer in the **Composition** or **Timeline** window to see its anchor point (the target in the middle of the artwork). You'll need to move this point so the position of the flame and the rocket line up. Select the **Pan Behind** tool, and click and drag the anchor point to the top of the flame artwork, as you see above.

11. Switch back to the **arrow** cursor in the **Toolbox**, and move the flames below the rocket in the **Composition** window, as you see above.

---

12. Press the **spacebar** to play your animation. The flame should now track the rocket ship perfectly! By parenting the **flames.mov** layer to the **rocket.psd** layer, you avoided having to animate the flames to make them match the motion of the rocket. This is a new feature in After Effects that is considered a key reason to upgrade to the 5.0 or 5.5 version.

---

13. Save your project in the **HOT_AE_Projects** folder and close it.

NOTE | The Interpret Footage Dialog Box

In the last exercise, you learned to loop the flames.mov footage to make it last longer. This was done through the Interpret Footage dialog box. This dialog box is used when you want to change footage from the way it was originally imported. You can use it to change the number of times footage repeats, or loops; the frame rate; or the way After Effects honors the alpha channel. You don't need to use this dialog box all the time — only when you want to change your footage in some way. Often you'll use it to make a change while you're in the middle of a project, as we did in the previous exercise when we realized that the footage wasn't long enough to last the duration of the composition.

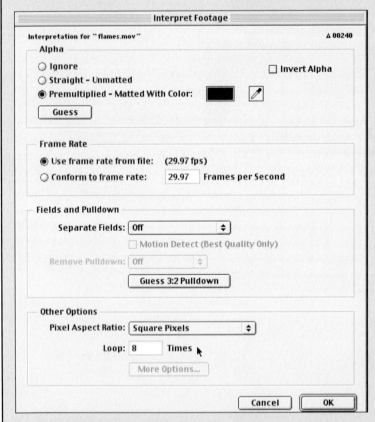

You can access the Interpret Footage dialog box by selecting any footage item in the Project window and choosing **Command+F** (Mac) or **Control+F** (Windows). The following chart describes the options in this dialog box.

The Interpret Footage Dialog Box

Category	Option	Description
Alpha	Ignore	When you import an image or movie that is partially transparent, that transparency information is stored in the footage's alpha channel. If Ignore is checked, After Effects will ignore the transparent parts of the image or movie, and they will appear as a solid color.
	Straight–Unmatted	After Effects treats footage files that contain alpha channels in one of two ways: straight or premultiplied. When you import footage, After Effects makes a guess, and it almost always guesses right. The only time you need to use this option is when you want to alter the way After Effects has treated your alpha channel—for example, if you don't like the way your footage looks once it's in a composition and you want to make a change.
		For footage with a straight alpha channel, the program you used to generate the footage must have built a straight alpha. Few programs use this kind of alpha channel. Many 3D programs generate straight alpha channels because these kinds of alphas can be placed over any background color without predisposition.
	Premultiplied– Matted with Color	Most alpha channels created in common graphics applications like Photoshop and Illustrator are premultiplied. With a premultiplied alpha channel, a footage item keeps the transparency information in the alpha channel. A premultiplied alpha channel is also known as matted alpha with a background color. The colors of semitransparent areas, such as feathered edges, are shifted toward the background color in proportion to their degree of transparency. The background color, in this instance, is defined in the authoring program, such as Illustrator or Photoshop.

continues on next page

	The Interpret Footage Dialog Box *continued*	
Category	**Option**	**Description**
Alpha *(continued)*	Invert Alpha	This option will invert the alpha channel mask, so every thing that was originally masked will be reversed, and will show, while everything that wasn't masked will be.
Frame Rate	Use frame rate from file	This setting applies only to movie footage. It uses the original frame rate of the footage.
	Assume this frame rate	This setting applies only to movie footage. It changes the original frame rate of the movie to any new frame rate that you enter.
Fields and Pulldown	Separate Fields: Off	When footage is transferred to video or originates from video, it contains two fields for every frame: an upper field and a lower field, to be exact. So for every frame of video, there are two fields. These two fields are "interlaced," meaning that they are blended and combined into a single frame during the video recording process. There are times when you want to separate one interlaced frame of video into two separate fields. The Separate Fields: Off setting does not separate the fields; it leaves them untouched.
	Separate Fields: Lower Fields First	When importing video footage, After Effects tries to guess which of the fields came first in the interlacing process. If the footage looks funny, use this option to reverse the "field order" (lower first or upper first) of the interlacing process. This problem is most often obvious when motion in video does not appear smooth.
	Separate Fields: Upper Fields First	Same as the Lower Fields first setting, except that this places the upper field first.
	Motion Detect (Best Quality Only)	Increases the quality of rendered footage that has its fields separated.
		continues on next page

	The Interpret Footage Dialog Box *continued*	
Category	**Option**	**Description**
Fields and Pulldown *(continued)*	Remove Pulldown: Off	Pulldown becomes an issue with footage that originated as film (35mm, 16mm, or 8mm that was shot at 24 frames per second) and was transferred to video using a Telecine process at 29.97 frames per second. If you choose to remove pulldown, After Effects will convert the video footage into 60 separate frames per second (each frame representing one video field). This setting is useful for rotoscoping live action (drawing on top of or tracing video footage).
	Guess 3:2 Pulldown	This option is important when your footage originated on film and was transferred to video using a Telecine process. After Effects' Guess 3:2 Pulldown process will convert every 4 film frames into 10 video fields, making the math for the transition from film to video work.
Other Options	Pixel Aspect Ratio: D1/DV NTSC (0.9) D1/DV NTSC (0.9) D1/DV PAL (1.07) D1/DV PAL (1.07) Anamorphic 2:1 (2) D4/D16 Standard (0.95) D4/D16 Anamorphic (1.9)	Your computer graphics files produce images composed of square pixels, but many video formats use nonsquare pixels. There may be times when you incorporate live action into your After Effects project that was originally produced with a nonsquare format. That's okay—After Effects can mix square and nonsquare pixels, but you have to tell it what footage is not square during the import process. You do that with this option. By importing the footage with the proper setting (you must know how the footage was originally shot), you allow After Effects to preserve its pixel aspect ratio. When you output to a final movie, you can also choose whether to output square or nonsquare pixels, depending on the setting you use in the Time Sampling area of the Render Settings dialog box, accessed from the Render Queue. You'll learn about the Render settings in Chapter 16, "Rendering Final Movies."
	Loop	You can set the number of times footage will repeat. The footage will become longer in the Timeline as a result.

TIP | Changing or Removing a Parent

To specify a different layer as a child's parent, use the Parent panel pop-up menu to select another layer.

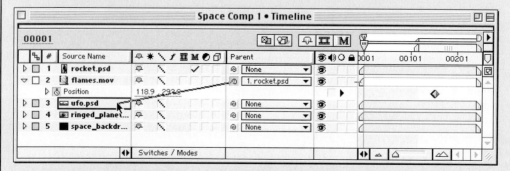

As an alternate method, drag the Pick Whip icon for the child layer to another layer. The new layer will be selected as the parent.

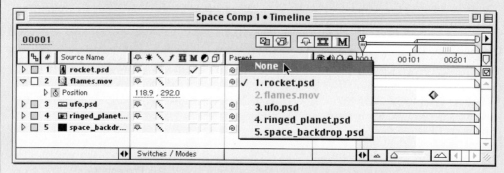

To remove a child's parent, choose None from the Parent panel pop-up menu.

2. _____Preparing for Parenting

In the last exercise, you practiced how to connect a child (**flames.mov**) to a parent (**rocket.psd**) layer. The child took on all the Transform properties that had been specified for the parent. It's also possible to animate children independently from their parents. You will learn how to do that in the following exercises. First, however, some preparation work has to go into this process. When planning this type of animation, you have to give thought to how pieces of artwork fit and move together. This often involves changing the anchor point of some of the pieces so that they rotate, scale, or move in the correct manner. In this exercise, you'll learn how to import a layered Illustrator file, and you will practice changing anchor points and parenting. Once the document is prepared properly, you'll learn to animate the parent and children independently in a subsequent exercise.

1. Create a new project and double-click inside the empty **Project** window to bring forth the **Import Footage** dialog box. Navigate to the **chap_09** folder and choose **wavingmonkey.ai**. For the **Import As** option, choose **Composition**. The **wavingmonkey.ai** document is a layered Illustrator file. You can bring layered Illustrator files in as compositions in exactly the same way that you bring in layered Photoshop files.

2. Save the project file as **wavingmonkey.aep** to the **HOT_AE_Projects** folder.

3. Double-click the **wavingmonkey.ai** composition inside the **Project** window to open it. This will open the Timeline and Composition windows.

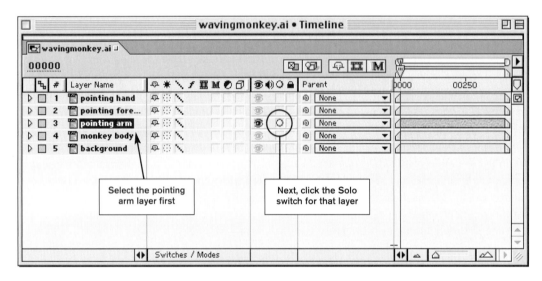

4. Select the **pointing arm** layer, and click the **Solo** switch. This will cause all the other layers to turn off so you can see the arm layer all by itself. The anchor point needs to be moved to line up with the shoulder of the monkey. You'll do this next.

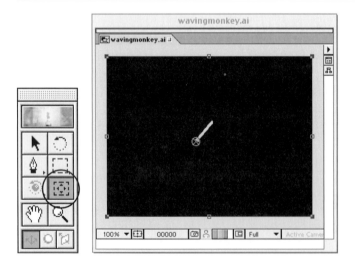

5. Using the **Pan Behind** tool, click and drag the **anchor point** inside the **Composition** window to match what you see here. **Note:** The layer must be selected for the anchor point to be visible in the Composition window. Moving the anchor point will affect future animations, as the Transform properties Rotate, Scale, and Position all use the anchor point position as a reference point.

6. Click the **Solo** switch for the **pointing arm** layer to turn it off. The Solo switch made it easier to isolate this layer in order to see and move its anchor point.

7. Select the **pointing forearm** layer, click its **Solo** switch, and move its anchor point, using the **Move Behind** tool, to the position you see here. Click the **Solo** switch again to toggle it off once you complete this task.

8. Select the **pointing hand** layer, click its **Solo** switch, and move its anchor point, using the **Move Behind** tool, to the position you see here. Click the **Solo** switch again to toggle it off once you complete this task.

You've finished changing the anchor points on the objects. If you think about your own shoulder, arm, forearm, and hand, and where those joints pivot, you'll see that you've just created the anchor points to mimic human (and monkey!) anatomy. Soon you'll animate the hand of the monkey, and you'll see how the anchor point adjustments play an important role in the success of your movie.

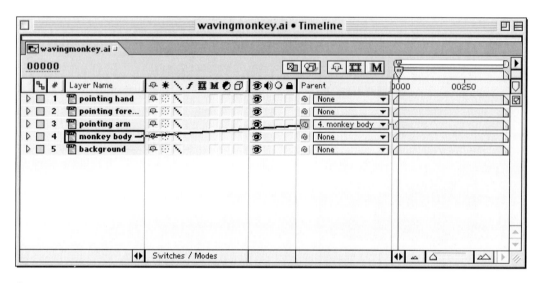

9. In the **Timeline**, using the **Pick Whip**, attach the **pointing arm** layer to the **monkey body** layer.

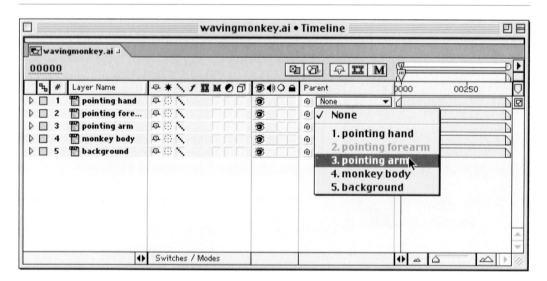

10. Next, you'll attach the **pointing forearm** layer to the **pointing arm** layer. As an alternative, you can use the Parent panel pop-up menu instead of the Pick Whip to achieve this. Click on the **Parent panel** menu for the **pointing forearm** layer, and select **3. pointing arm** from the list. The **3.** indicates that this is the third layer in the stack. This tells the **pointing arm** layer to be the parent for the **pointing forearm** layer.

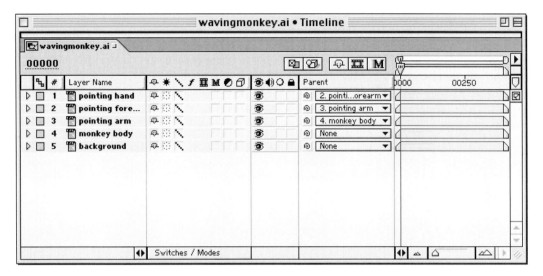

11. Next attach the **pointing hand** to the **pointing forearm** layer. Do this using the Pick Whip or the Parent panel menu item method—either way achieves the same result!

12. Save the project and leave it open for the next exercise.

In the first exercise, there was only one parent (the rocket) and one child (the flames). Here you can see that a layer can be the child to one layer and the parent of another! You'll see this come together in the next exercise.

3. —————————**Animating Children and Parents**

In the first exercise, you saw how the animation of a parent affected the child. This exercise sets up a more complicated set of relationships. You've done the hard part of setting the anchor points and parenting. Now enjoy the fun of making it all move!

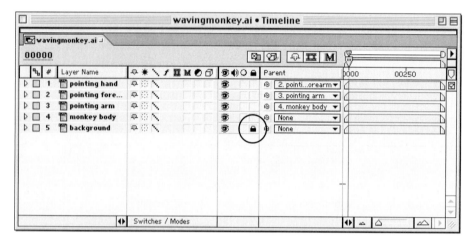

1. Lock the **background** layer by clicking the **Lock** switch. This prevents the background layer from being moved accidentally during the animation you are about to program.

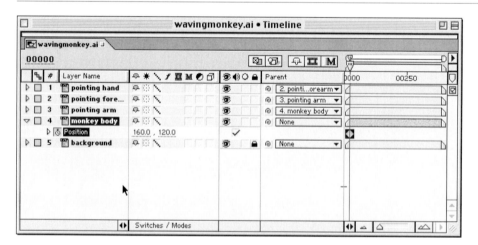

2. In the **Timeline**, select the **monkey body** layer and set a position keyframe. There are many ways to do this—you could either twirl all the twirlies down and click the **Stopwatch** icon or press **Option+P** (Mac) or **Alt-P** (Windows). The Option or Alt keystroke shortcut sets the stopwatch for you!

3. Select the **arrow** cursor from the **Toolbox** (it is stuck on the Pan Behind tool from the last exercise), and move the monkey to the left side of the branch, as you see here. This sets the start position for the monkey in a different place than before.

Notice that the monkey and all the child layers moved at the same time. Even though you set only the monkey body layer as the parent for the pointing arm layer, the pointing forearm and pointing hand layers moved as well. That's because they're all indirectly linked to the monkey body through the hierarchy of parenting. The pointing arm layer is the child of the monkey body layer. The pointing forearm layer is the child of the pointing arm layer, which is the child of the monkey body layer. The pointing hand layer is the child of the pointing forearm layer, which is the child of the pointing arm layer, which is the child of the monkey body layer. All the layers are ultimately related to monkey body as the master parent.

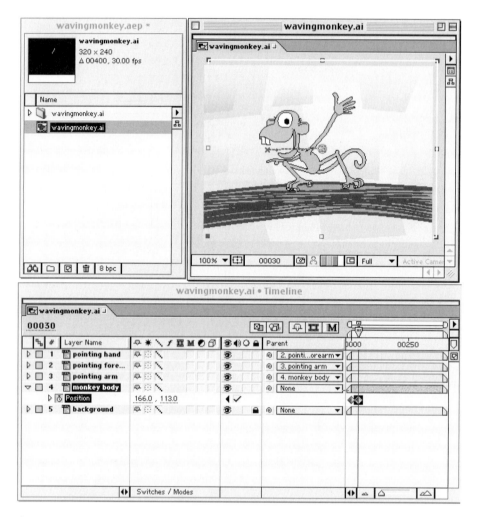

4. In the **Timeline**, move the **Time Marker** to **Frame 30**. Move the monkey to the middle of the branch, as you see here. You should now see two keyframes set in your Timeline.

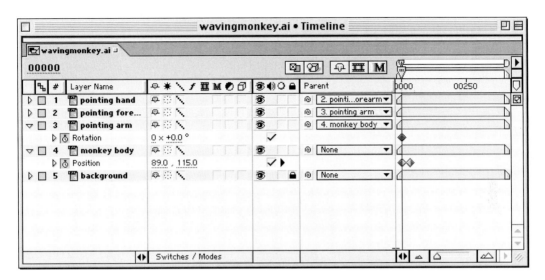

5. Move the **Time Marker** back to **Frame 0**. Select the **pointing arm** layer and set a **Rotation** keyframe. You really should know how to do this now on your own! Notice that this Rotation keyframe is on Frame 0 as well. A keyframe is always set on whatever frame the Time Marker was on when you set it.

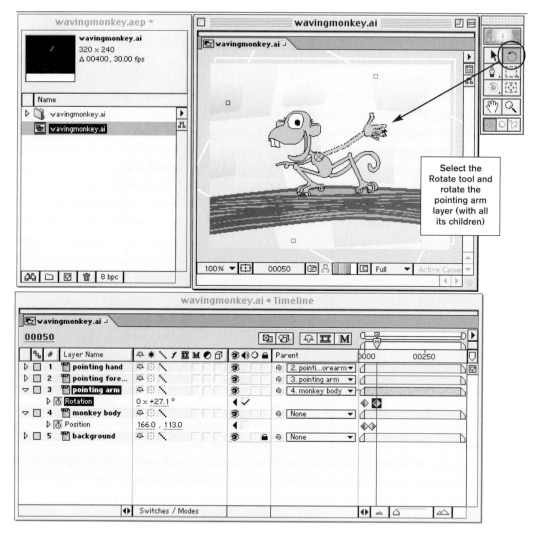

6. Move the **Time Marker** to **Frame 50**. Select the **Rotation** tool from the **Toolbox**. Click and drag the arm on your screen so that it looks like ours above. The pointing arm child will now animate independently from its parent, taking all its children with it.

As you rotate the pointing arm, notice that it rotates all the other children that are attached to it. The parent doesn't move because you haven't told it to. Children can be animated separately from their parents, but if the parent moves, so do the kids!

7. Move the **Time Marker** to **Frame 0** and set a **Rotation** keyframe for the **pointing forearm** layer. This sets a start keyframe at Frame 0.

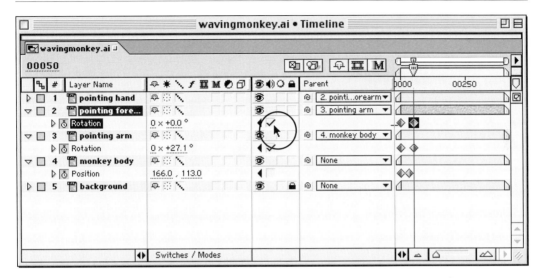

8. Move the **Time Marker** to **Frame 50** and click to put a check in the **Keyframe** check box. This holds the start position for the **pointing forearm** layer so that it stays still from Frame 0 until Frame 50.

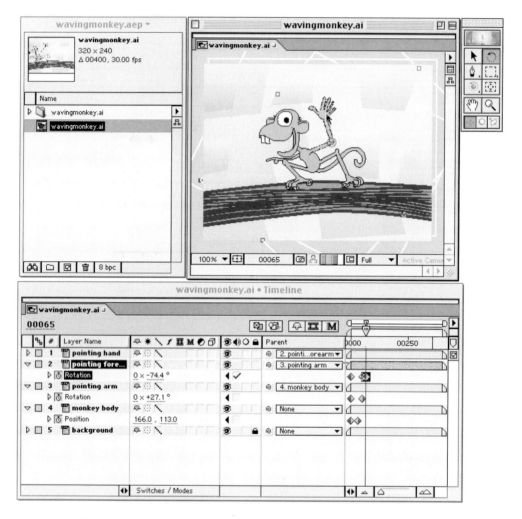

9. Move the **Time Marker** to **Frame 65** and, with the **pointing forearm** layer selected, use the **Rotation** tool to move it into the position you see above.

As you rotate the pointing forearm, notice that it rotates all the other children that are attached to it. The other parents don't move because you haven't told them to.

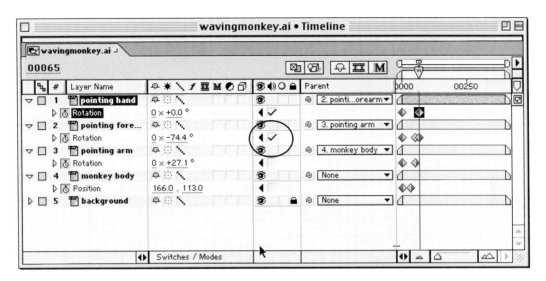

10. Move the **Time Marker** to **Frame 0** and select the **pointing hand** layer. Set a **Rotation** keyframe. Move the **Time Marker** to **Frame 65** and click to put a check in the **Keyframe** check box. This sets the rotation so that it will not move at all from Frame 0 to Frame 65.

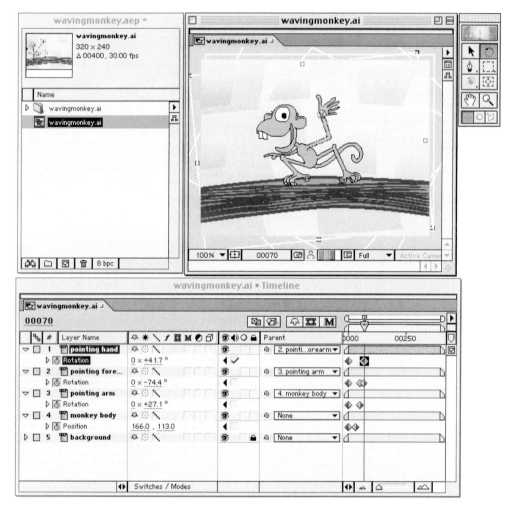

11. Move the **Time Marker** to **Frame 70**, and move the **pointing hand** layer with the **Rotation** tool as shown above.

This is the last child in the hierarchy. It can move all by itself without moving the other parents.

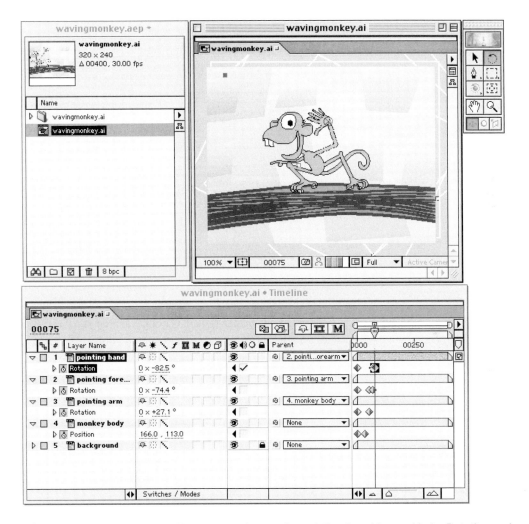

12. Move the **Time Marker** to **Frame 75** and move the **pointing hand** layer with the **Rotation** tool as shown above.

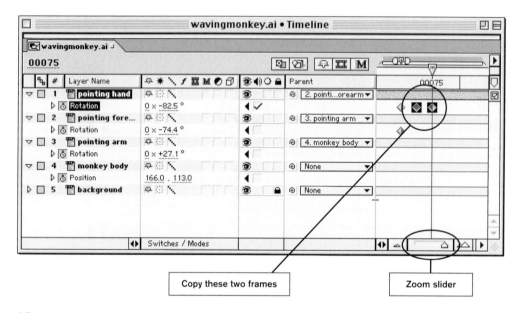

Copy these two frames   Zoom slider

13. Using the **Zoom** slider, zoom into the **Timeline** so you can get a closer look at Frames 70 and 75. Hold the **Shift** key and select the keyframes on **Frames 70 and 75** for the **pointing hand** layer. Copy them by pressing **Command+C** (Mac) or **Control+C** (Windows).

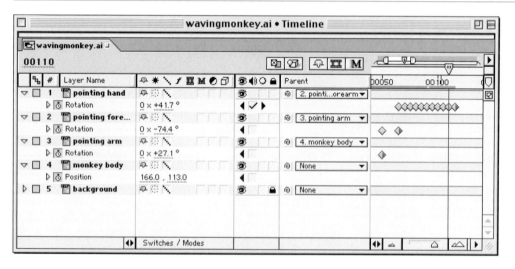

14. Move the **Time Marker** to **Frame 80**, and **paste** the copied keyframes. Move the **Time Marker** to **Frame 90** and **paste** again. Keep advancing the Time Marker by 10 frames and pasting until you've pasted a few more times.

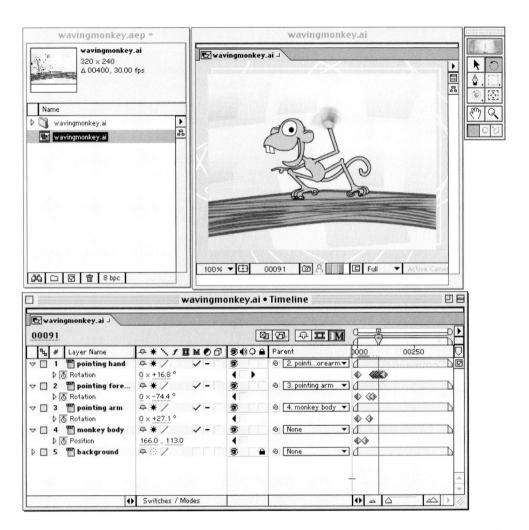

15. Rewind and use **Ram preview** to test your work. Try using the **Continuous Rasterization**, **Best Quality**, and **Motion Blur** switches and you'll see a big improvement in appearance. Don't remember how to do those things? Check the last chapter.

When you use Ram preview to test again, you'll see that it takes much longer to render but looks much better. Save this project and close it when you're finished looking at your handiwork. We've included a finished version of this project, if you want to look at it, called finished-wavingmonkey.ai.

4. _____Using a Null Object as a Parent

Null object is an intimidating term for an invisible object. Even the concept of an invisible object is a bit hard on the brain—why would anyone need or want something that wasn't visible? Our hope is that this exercise will provide a concrete example of when you might want to use a null object. In this example, you will create a null layer—in other words, a layer with an invisible object inside of it. The objects that are visible will be attached to the null layer, making them the children and the null layer the parent. The parent will be told to move and the children will follow. The reason, in this example, to use the invisible object to control the movement of the visible objects is that they already move using Position keyframes. Adding the null object's movement to the already moving children achieves a compound movement that is otherwise impossible. You'll see what we mean as you work through this puzzle.

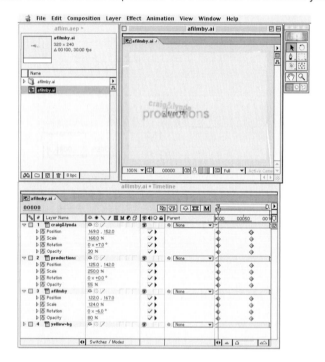

1. Open the **afilmby.aep** project from the **chap_09** folder. Double-click the **afilmby** composition to open the Composition and Timeline windows. Select all the layers and press the **U** key. This is the keyboard shortcut that shows all the properties that have been animated in the composition. You will see that Position, Scale, Rotation, and Opacity properties have been applied. Deselect the layers so you don't see the motion paths. Play the composition to see what it looks like, and then click the **Rewind** button on the **Time Control** panel to return to **Frame 0**. Select all the layers again and press **U**. This will collapse all the properties so your layers take up less space.

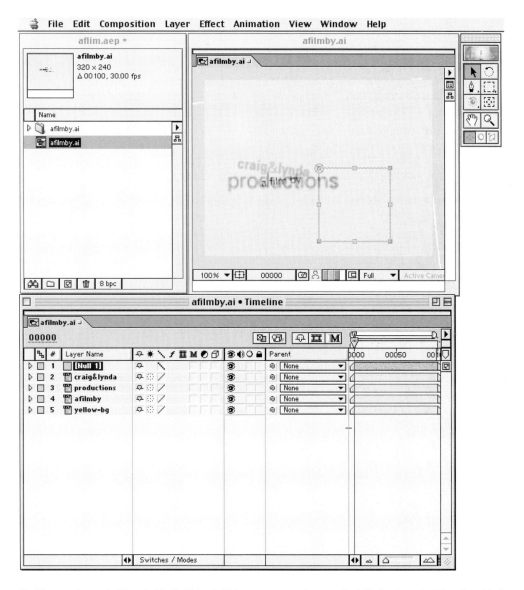

2. Choose **Layer > New > Null Object**. This puts a new layer called Null 1 into the Timeline. Notice that an outlined box appears inside the Composition window. This box appears only in the Composition window. If you use the RAM preview feature or make a movie (which you'll learn to do in Chapter 14, "*Rendering Final Movies*"), this outlined box will disappear. Meanwhile, however, the outlined box is important because you need to see the null object even though you don't want anyone else to see it.

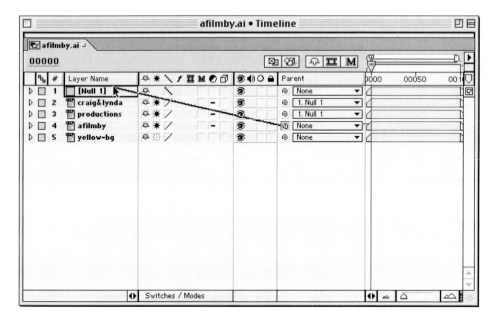

3. Attach the layers **craig&lynda**, **productions**, and **afilmby** to the **Null 1** layer.

4. Lock the **yellow-bg** layer so you don't accidentally move it. Select **Null 1** in the **Timeline**, and move it upward in the **Composition** window, as you see here. Because other layers are assigned to be children of the Null 1 layer, they will move too!

5. Set a **Position** keyframe for **Null 1** at **Frame 0**.

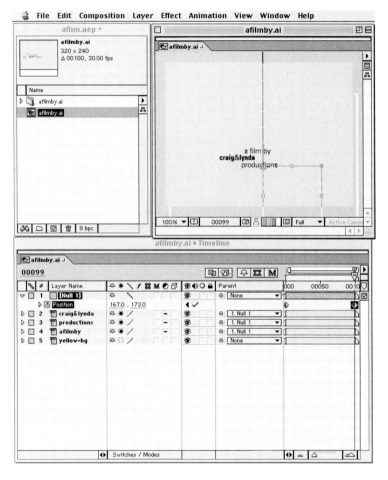

6. Move the **Time Marker** to the **last frame**. Move the **Null 1** layer to the bottom of the screen, as you see in the Composition window above.

7. Use **Ram preview** to see the motion. The null object has allowed you to create compound motion—the type has its own motion, and the null object offers the opportunity to add another motion path to the animation. This would be very hard to do any other way. You can probably imagine how useful this would be for title sequences, type treatments, and other kinds of artwork.

8. Save and close the project; you're done!

That's a wrap for this chapter, folks! We hope you see the tremendous possibilities that parenting features offer, from both a practical and an aesthetic perspective. Now onward to the next chapter, where you'll learn about adding another powerful feature—effects.

10.

Effects

Applying Effects	Multiple Effects
Text Effects	Drop Shadow Effect
Adjustment Layers	Pre-compose	Effects Palette

chap_10

After Effects 5.0 / 5.5
H•O•T CD-ROM

You might be familiar with the terms "filters" and "layer effects" in Photoshop. These are mini-applications, called plug-ins, that you can use to change the appearance of artwork, such as brightness, contrast, color, blur, etc. After Effects contains plug-in filters, just as Photoshop does, only they're much better! Why? Because you can animate them over time, and they have many keyframable settings that can add endless variations of visual alterations to your animations.

In this chapter, you'll learn to apply effects and control their settings. You'll see the interaction among multiple effects, and you will learn how to control this interaction. Warning: This chapter is really fun :).

On the other hand, there is no physical way we could take you through all of After Effects' effects and settings. The book would be much fatter than the one you're holding, because the variations are practically endless. It's our hope that this chapter will open your eyes to the power of effects so that you become inspired to try them all on your own. It might take a lifetime, but hey, you'll enjoy yourself, so who cares?

What Are Plug-ins?

You can think of **plug-ins** as little programs that work within After Effects. After Effects is written to allow these special external programs to plug into After Effects and work their magic.

All "effects" are actually plug-ins. They reside in a special folder within the After Effects folder on your hard disk.

Adobe supplies a great number of effects that ship with After Effects. Other companies also create plug-in effects that can be used in After Effects. You can add any number of effects to your plug-in folder.

Many Photoshop plug-ins also work with After Effects. If you are interested in learning more about plug-ins, consult the User Guide that came with your program, or choose **Help > Contents and Index**.

I. ————————**Applying Effects with Animation over Time**

During this exercise, you will create a new project and apply four effects: **Blur**, **Brightness & Contrast**, **Color Emboss**, and **Lens Flare**. You will learn how to animate and control each effect with its unique options.

As you work through this exercise, notice how the effects are organized for easy identification. After Effects groups the various types of effects together to speed selection.

1. Choose **File > New > New Project** to create a new project.

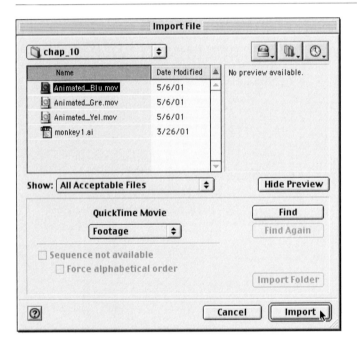

2. Choose **File > Import > File**. As an alternate method, press **Command+I** (Mac) or **Control+I** (Windows).

Open the **exercise_files** folder and then open the **chap_10** folder. Select **Animated_Blu.mov** from the file list. Click **Import**.

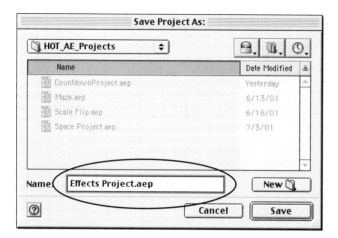

3. Press **Command+S** (Mac) or **Control+S** (Windows) to save your new project. Navigate to the **HOT_AE_Projects** folder. Type **Effects Project.aep** as the name and click **Save**. **Tip:** You can name a project file in uppercase or lowercase, with spaces or without. Project file names are free of the restrictions that apply to files that will be published to the Web.

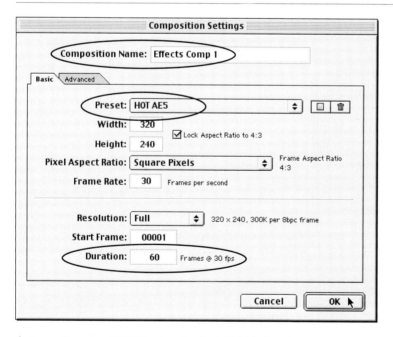

4. Press **Command+N** (Mac) or **Control+N** (Windows) to create a new composition. Type **Effects Comp 1** as the composition name. Set the **Preset** to **HOT AE5**. Set the **Duration** to **60** frames. Click **OK**.

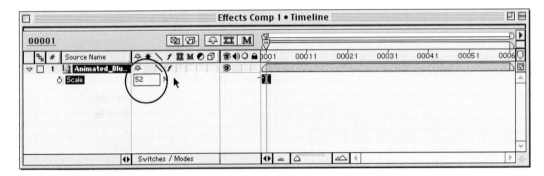

5. Drag the **Animated_Blu.mov** footage from the **Project** window to the **Timeline** window. This movie was made in After Effects and was saved as a QuickTime movie. You'll learn how to do this in Chapter 16, "*Rendering Final Movies*." Press **S** to display the **Scale** property. Set the scale to **52%**. Press **S** again to hide the Scale property.

Note: Since there is no plan to animate the Scale property in this movie, you don't need to set the Stopwatch. You set keyframes only when you know that you will use different settings over the duration of a composition. If you change the scale without setting the Stopwatch and initiating keyframes, as you did here, it simply means that the footage will hold this new setting throughout the entire Timeline.

6. Choose **Effect > Blur & Sharpen > Gaussian Blur**.

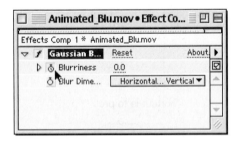

7. When the **Effect Controls** palette opens, click on the **Blurriness Stopwatch** icon to turn on keyframes, and set a keyframe on **Frame 0**. Set the **Time Marker** to **Frame 60**, and set the **Blurriness** to **20**.

NOTE | Where Are the Effects Keyframes?

You've probably gotten used to setting keyframes in the Timeline. However, you can also set keyframes for effects in the Effect Controls palette. In fact, we prefer to use the Effect Controls palette to set keyframes, because it offers a more robust feature set than the Timeline—for example, you can turn individual effects off and on, and you can reorder them. You'll learn to do this in the following exercises.

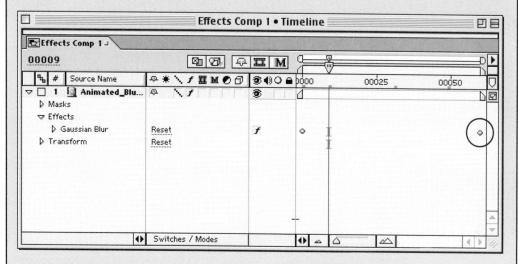

Twirl down the Effects twirlies to see the keyframes in the Timeline.

The keyframes are visible in the Timeline; you just need to twirl down the twirlies to see them under the Effects properties. To do this, click the twirly once to hide the Scale properties, and then click it again to see the properties for Effects. Click the Transform twirly to hide the Transform properties, and click the Effects twirly to reveal these properties. A shortcut is to press the letter **E** for Effects. This would show only the Effects settings and would hide the others.

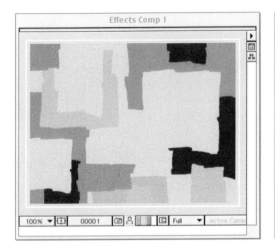
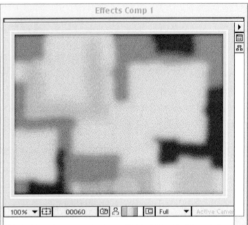

8. Press the **spacebar** to preview the blur effect animation. The blue background movie animates from 0 blur to a blur that is 20 pixels horizontal and vertical.

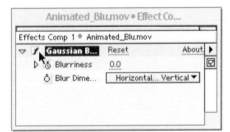
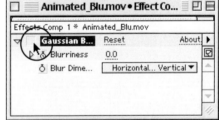

9. Locate the **Effects** switch in the **Effect Controls** palette. Click it to turn off the Gaussian Blur effect. Scrub the **Time Marker** to verify that the effect is off. Set the **Time Marker** to Frame 1.

The Effects switch is useful because it allows you to set an effect and then turn it on and off. Since certain effects take a long time to render, this can save time while you're editing the animation.

10. Choose **Effect > Adjust > Brightness & Contrast**.

11. Click the **Brightness Stopwatch** and **Contrast Stopwatch** icons to set a keyframe on **Frame 1**.

12. Set the **Time Marker** to **Frame 60**. Set the **Brightness** to **−40** and the **Contrast** to **45**.

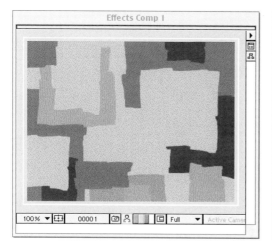 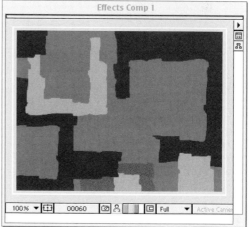

13. Press the **spacebar** to preview how the brightness and contrast animate over time.

14. Click the **Brightness & Contrast Effect** switch to turn off the effect. Set the **Time Marker** to **Frame 1**.

In the Effect Controls palette, you can turn both the Gaussian Blur effect and the Brightness & Contrast effect on and off. This lets you look at each effect independently and also lets you see how the effects look when combined together.

15. Choose **Effect > Stylize > Color Emboss**.

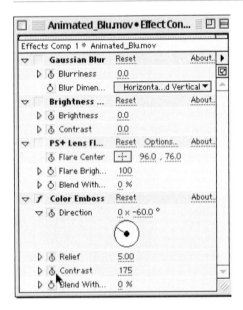

16. Click the **Stopwatch** icons for **Direction**, **Relief**, and **Contrast**. Set the **Direction** to **−60** degrees, the **Relief** to **5**, and the **Contrast** to **175**.

17. Move the **Time Marker** to **Frame 60**. Set the **Color Emboss Direction** to **−135**.

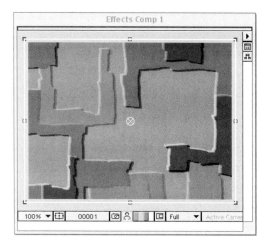 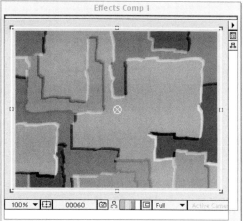

18. Click **RAM Preview** and observe the Color Emboss effect.

19. Click the **Color Emboss Effect** switch to turn the effect off. Set the **Time Marker** to **Frame 1.**

Finally, you will apply the Lens Flare effect.

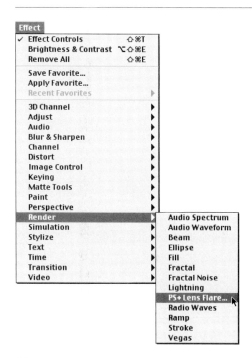

20. Choose **Effect > Render > PS+ Lens Flare** (Lens Flare in After Effects 5.5).

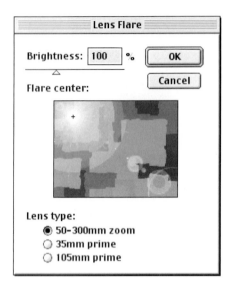

21. In the **Lens Flare** dialog box, drag the **Flare Center** to the upper left corner of the image. Click **OK**. **Note:** this dialog box does not exist in After Effects 5.5. You can adjust the flare center inside the Composition window.

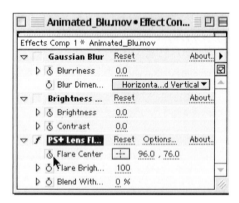

22. In the **Effect Controls** palette, click the **Flare Center Stopwatch** to set a keyframe.

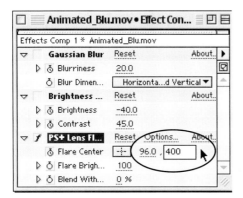

23. Move the **Time Marker** to **Frame 60**. Set the **Flare Center's Y-axis** value to **400**.

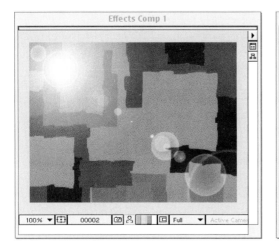
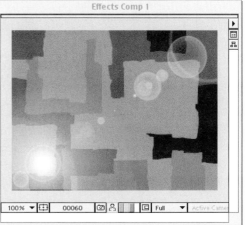

24. Click **RAM Preview** and observe the Lens Flare effect.

25. Click the **PS+ Lens Flare Effect** switch to turn the effect off.

All of the effects should be switched off at this point. This exercise exposed you to only four effects out of hundreds available for After Effects. You can explore other effects after you've finished this chapter. It's amazing how many different "looks" you can achieve using effects. They are a huge tool in your After Effects visual creation palette.

26. Save your project and leave it open for the next exercise.

2. _____Multiple Effects: Rearranging the Order

You've probably used filters in Photoshop before, so it might surprise you to learn that the effects in After Effects are more flexible. That's because you can rearrange the order of multiple effects after you've applied them, changing the appearance of the effects. This ability offers unprecedented flexibility.

To change the relationship between effects, you simply change the order of the list. In this exercise you will learn to control multiple effect interaction by rearranging the **rendering order** in the Effect Controls palette.

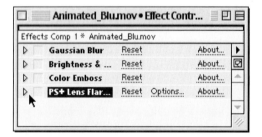

1. Click the **twirly** for each effect to hide the controls. This will make it easy to select each effect and reorder the list.

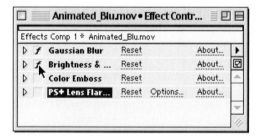

2. Click the **Effect** switch to display the **Gaussian Blur** and **Brightness & Contrast** effects.

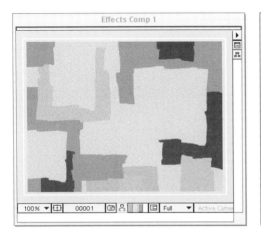 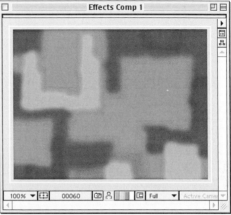

3. Click **RAM Preview** and observe the result of animating multiple effects.

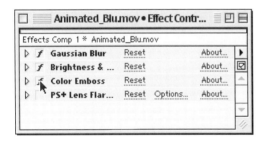

4. Click the **Color Emboss Effect** switch to turn it on.

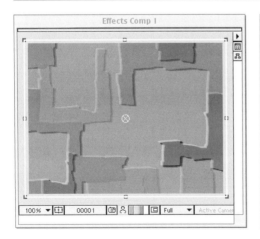 

5. Click **RAM Preview** and observe the additional effect in action.

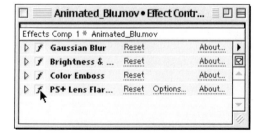

6. Click on the **PS+ Lens Flare Effect** switch to turn it on.

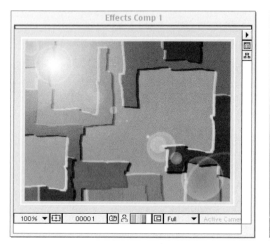
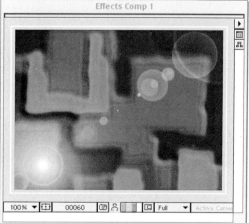

7. Click **RAM Preview** and observe the results.

In the following steps, you will rearrange the rendering order of these effects.

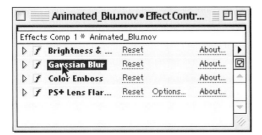

8. Move the **Time Marker** to **Frame 60**. Drag the **Gaussian Blur** effect to the second position in the render order list. Note that the stacking order of effects is different from the stacking order of layers. Whatever effect is on the bottom of the stack is applied last.

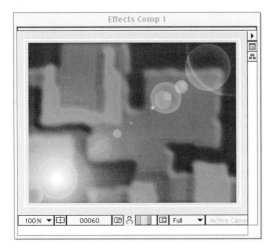

9. Observe the change in the image. This order reduces edge artifacts and creates a more pleasing image. Click **RAM Preview** or press the **spacebar** to preview the movement.

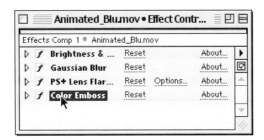

10. Drag the **Color Emboss** effect to the fourth position in the render order list.

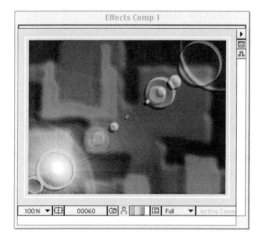

11. Click **RAM Preview**. You'll see that the Color Emboss effect is now applied to the Lens Flare effect as well. At this point, the interaction and control you have by using the rendering order will probably begin to make perfect sense.

In the following steps, you'll add another effect and rearrange the rendering order. This effect is available only in the production bundle, so if you don't see it listed in your menu, skip to step 19.

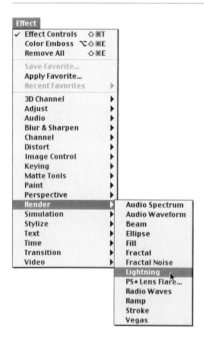

12. Choose **Effect > Render > Lightning**.

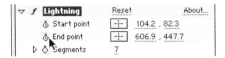

13. Move the **Time Marker** to **Frame 1**. In the **Effect Controls** palette, click the **Stopwatch** icons for the **Lightning start point** and **end point** to set the first keyframe at the default values.

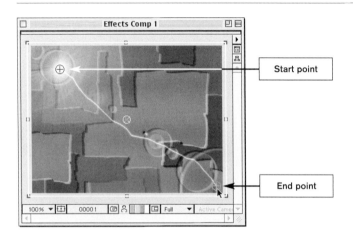

14. In the **Composition** window, drag the **start point** and **end point** to match the diagonal position of the Lens Flare effect.

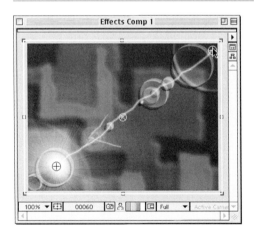

15. Move the **Time Marker** to **Frame 60**. In the **Composition** window, again drag the **start point** and **end point** to match the diagonal position of the Lens Flare effect. Click **RAM Preview** to view the animation.

Now you will continue to rearrange the effects rendering order.

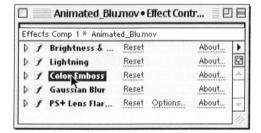

16. In the **Effect Controls** palette, click the **twirly** for the **Lightning** effect to hide the controls. Drag the **Lightning** effect to the second position, and drag the **Color Emboss** effect to the third position in the render order list.

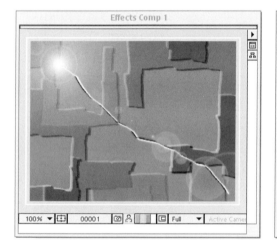
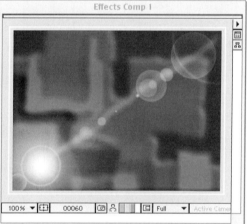

17. Click **RAM Preview** and observe the results of the render order. The Lightning effect is now embossed and blurred, while the Lens Flare, being rendered last, is unaffected.

To complete your composition, you'll reorder the Lightning effect to be rendered last.

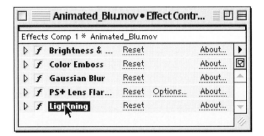

18. Drag the **Lightning** effect to the last position in the render order list. Click **RAM Preview** and observe the final results.

The interaction between all of the effects based on the rendering order is probably quite clear now. However, if you need additional time to let the concept sink in, feel free to try different rendering orders with these effects. As you start to gain more experience with After Effects, you will see that you can change your mind at any time without damaging anything that you've already set up. It's a great freedom! When finished, return to the rendering order shown in step 18 above.

19. Close the composition, but leave the project open for the next exercise.

NOTE | Resetting and Deleting an Effect

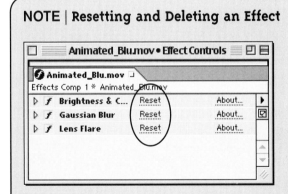

If you are ever unhappy with settings that you've created, you can reset the effect to clear all your settings. To the right of every effect in the Effects Control palette is a Reset switch. Click this switch and voila—your settings will disappear. If you ever want to delete an effect, simply select it in the Effects Control palette and press your Delete key.

NOTE | Turning Off Effects

You can turn off effects in two places—the Effect Controls palette and the Timeline. It doesn't matter where you do it or whether you do it; this feature exists for your convenience only. You've seen how to turn effects off in the Time Controls palette. In order to turn them off in the Timeline, you must make the Effects properties visible. The quickest way to do this is to select the layer that contains the effects and press the letter **E**.

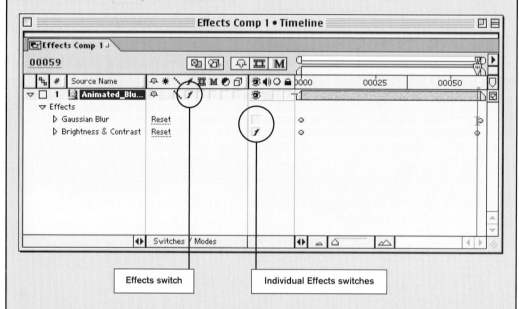

Effects switch   Individual Effects switches

The Timeline has two different areas to turn effects on and off. The Effects switch in the Switches panel will turn all effects off. The individual switches for each effect are beneath the video switch and can be turned on and off for each effect used in a layer.

3. ⎯⎯⎯⎯⎯⎯**The Basic Text Effect**

Basic Text is one of the most useful and commonly used effects that After Effects offers. That's because you can set type using this filter, eliminating the need to use an outside program, such as Illustrator or Photoshop, for creating text. It's better than using Photoshop or Illustrator because the text stays dynamic (meaning that you can change it at any time, even after you've set keyframe-based animations with it!), and it scales dynamically, meaning that you don't have to worry about setting the type too big or too small in an outside program. The text you specify in this filter will be placed on a straight line, and you can animate the Position, Fill & Stroke, Size, Tracking, and Line Spacing controls. Follow along to learn how.

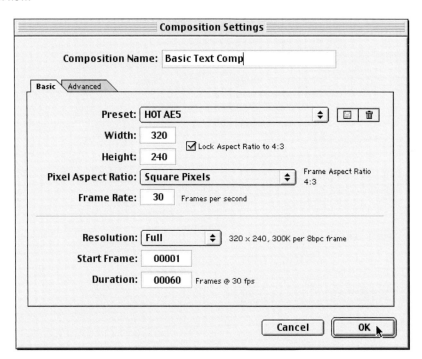

1. Create a new composition by clicking the **New Comp** icon at the bottom of the **Project** window.

In the **Composition Settings** dialog box, type **Basic Text Comp** as the composition name, use the **HOT AE5** preset, and set the **Duration** to **60** frames. Click **OK**.

2. Choose **Composition > Background Color** to change the background color of the composition from black to a **light yellow**.

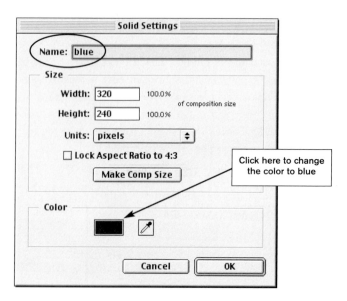

3. Choose **Layer > New > Solid** to create a new solid layer. Name the layer **blue**, and match your set-tings to what you see here. Click the **color well** to change the color to **dark blue**.

4. With the **blue** solid layer selected, choose **Effect > Text > Basic Text**. **Note:** In order to apply the Basic Text effect (or any effect for that matter), you must first select a layer.

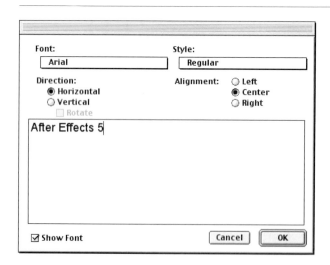

5. In the **Basic Text Options** dialog box, type **After Effects 5** as the text to display. Set the font to **Arial**, the style to **Regular**, the direction to **Horizontal**, and the alignment to **Center**. Click **OK**.

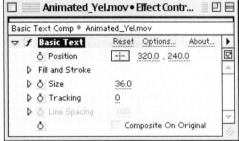

Your Composition window displays the text, and the Effect Controls palette opens. Notice that the After Effects 5 *text color is red and that the* blue *solid layer appears to be gone. The default behavior of the Basic Text effect is to cause whatever layer it is on to disappear and to be set to a red color. You'll learn to change this shortly!*

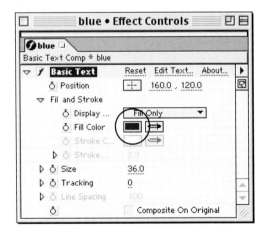

6. In the Effect Controls palette, make sure that the **twirly** for **Fill and Stroke** is turned down to reveal those settings. Click inside the **color swatch** to access your color picker, and choose a **dark green**. Click **OK**. Notice that the text is now green. **Note:** You can change this color at any time! Leave it green for the exercise, but it's important to recognize that this is part of the power of using Basic Text instead of text from Illustrator or Photoshop.

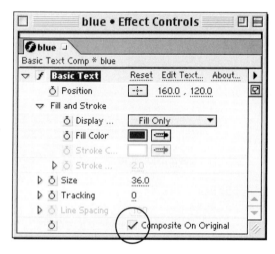

7. Click the check box for **Composite On Original**. Now you should see the blue solid layer again! Sometimes you'll want to use the background color of the solid layer, and sometimes you won't. You can apply the Basic Text effect to *any* layer, even a movie. Knowing that this feature exists is the important part; whether you choose to use it or not is your creative choice!

8. In the **Timeline** window, click the **Quality** switch to select **Best** quality; this will make your text anti-aliased.

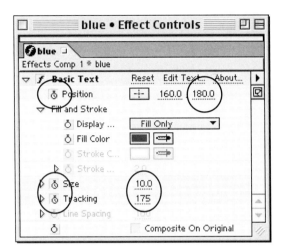

9. With the **Time Marker** set to **Frame 1** in the Timeline, click the **Position, Size,** and **Tracking Stopwatch** icons to turn on keyframes in the Effect Controls palette.

Set the **Position Y-axis** to **180**, the **Size** to **10**, and the **Tracking** to **175**. Observe that the text in the Composition window changes to reflect these settings. **Tip:** To see the keyframes that you just set in your Timeline, press **E** (for Effects) and click the **Text Effect** twirly.

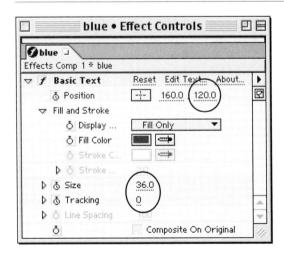

10. Set the **Time Marker** to **Frame 60.** Set the **Position Y-axis** to **120**, the **Size** to **36**, and the **Tracking** to **0**.

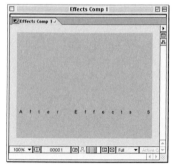

11. Click **RAM Preview** or press the **spacebar** to play your animation. The settings you chose caused the type to animate in scale, position, and tracking (the spacing between letters). This sure beats setting keyframes for each letter, eh?

12. Save your project. Close the **Basic Text** composition, and leave After Effects open for the next exercise.

NOTE | Can You Animate Color?

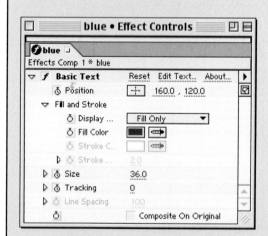

Using the Basic Text filter, can you animate color? You betcha! You can animate *any* property setting in the filter that has a Stopwatch icon. Simply set the keyframes (come on, you know how!). For your information, these are the properties that can be animated using the Basic Text effect: Position (X and Y), Fill and Stroke (fill color, stroke color, stroke width, and the display of the Fill and Stroke properties), Size, Tracking, Line Spacing (the distance between multiple lines of type, otherwise known as leading), and Composite On Original.

4. ————————The Numbers Effect

There are special provisions in After Effects to display numbers.. This effect can be used, for example, when you wish to display a frame number or timecode value within the composition.

The **Numbers** effect can also be used in many other ways as well. It can display the date, the time, or the number of seconds in your composition. Or it can flash random numbers across the screen in a project involving, say, a commercial for a financial institution. You may not use the Numbers effect often, but when you need it, it can be a lifesaver.

In this simple exercise you will create a new composition and apply the Numbers effect. The techniques you'll learn apply to any number format.

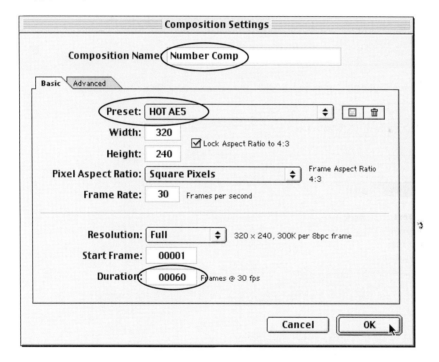

1. Create a new composition. You should know how by now!

In the **Composition Settings** dialog box, type **Numbers Comp** as the composition name, use the **HOT AE5** preset, and set the **Duration** to **60** frames. You don't have to type in the zeros before 60, but you can if you want to! Click **OK**.

2. In your **Project** window, import **Animated_Gre.mov** from the **chap_10** folder, and click **Import**. This is a QuickTime movie that was created for this exercise.

3. Drag the **Animated_Gre.mov** footage onto the **Timeline** window.

4. With **Animated_Gre.mov** selected, choose **Effect > Text > Numbers**.

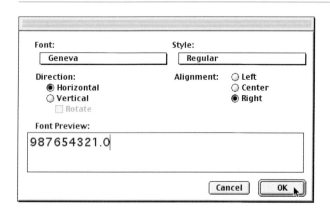

5. In the **Numbers Options** dialog box, accept the defaults and click **OK**.

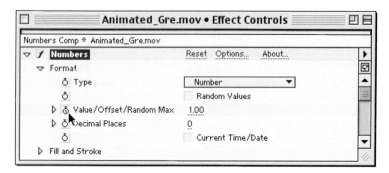

6. In the **Timeline**, set the **Time Marker** to **Frame 1**. Adjust the **Effect Controls** palette to make it wider for easy visibility.

Click the **Format** twirly to display the Format options.

Click the **Value/Offset/Random Max Stopwatch** icon to turn on keyframes. Set the value to **1**.

Set the **Decimal Places** value to **0**.

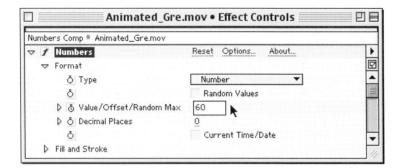

7. Set the **Time Marker** to **Frame 60**. Set **Value/Offset/Random Max** to **60**.

8. Scrub the **Time Marker** and observe that the numbers change synchronously with each frame number. Notice that the numbers jerk around. If you uncheck **Proportional Spacing** in the **Effect Controls** palette, they will not jump any more.

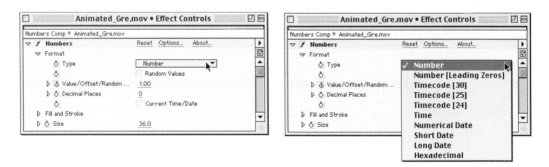

9. Click the **Type** option pop-up menu. Observe the number types available.

This is where you would select a different number type if, for example, you wanted to display the date, time, etc.

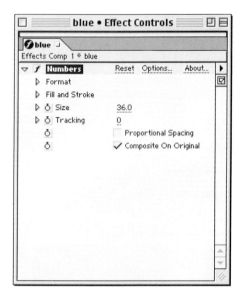

10. Click the **Format** twirly to hide the Format options. Click the check box next to **Composite On Original**. This causes the background of the **Animated_Gre.mov** layer to reappear.

The Options, Fill and Stroke, and Composite On Original tools that you learned in the Basic Text exercise all work the same way with the Numbers effect. In other words, anything that has a Stopwatch icon can be animated!

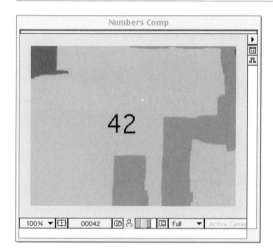

11. Click **RAM Preview** to watch the numbers animate over the background layer, instead of on top of the solid layer.

---

12. Save your project. Close the **Numbers Comp** composition, and leave After Effects open for the next exercise.

TIP | Random Values

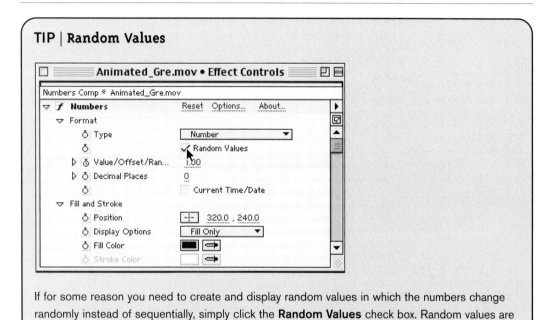

If for some reason you need to create and display random values in which the numbers change randomly instead of sequentially, simply click the **Random Values** check box. Random values are used a lot in mock computer readout animations.

5. ———————The Path Text Effect

The **Path Text** effect offers an easy way to animate text along a path. A path can be defined as a straight line, a Bézier curve, a circle of any diameter, or even a mask, which you will learn how to make in Chapter 11, "*Masks*."

The Path Text controls provide a variety of animation possibilities. In this exercise, you'll learn to move text along a path by creating keyframes for the left or right margin controls. You'll also get to set keyframes for the curved path, to make the text look as though it's waving. The possibilities that this (and other filters) offer are endless—this is just a starting point from which you can explore many other animation options.

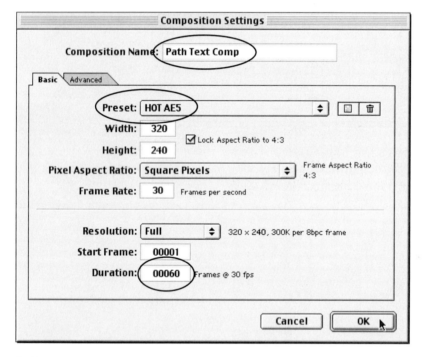

1. Create a new composition. In the **Composition Settings** dialog box, type **Path Text Comp** as the composition name, use the **HOT AE5** preset, and set the **Duration** to 60 frames. Click **OK**.

2. Drag the **Animated_Gre.mov** footage from the **Project** window onto the **Timeline** window. We'd like you to realize, however, that you could use any still or movie footage.

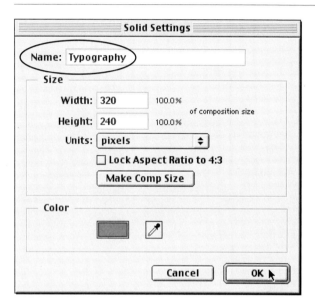

3. Choose **Layer > New > Solid**. Leave the settings at their defaults, change the name to **Typography**, and click **OK**. You'll be applying the Path Text effect to this solid layer. Solid layers are often used for text and number effects. Since you have to apply an effect to a layer, solid layers are perfect for the job if you don't want to use other footage items.

4. Choose **Effect > Text > Path Text**.

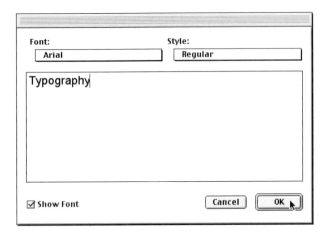

5. In the **Options** dialog box, type **Typography** and click **OK**.

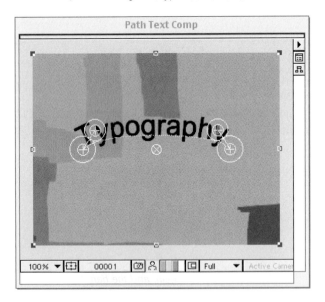

Your type appears in red letters on a curved path with control points. The curved path and red color are the default settings of this effect; they are applied when you don't change any of the settings. The solid layer is now transparent and the background layer is visible. These are also default settings—the solid layer will disappear unless you select Composite On Original. Don't select it, though; seeing through to the layer beneath is the effect we're going for in this exercise. As we've said before, this is a creative decision that you can make on your own when you're designing your own project.

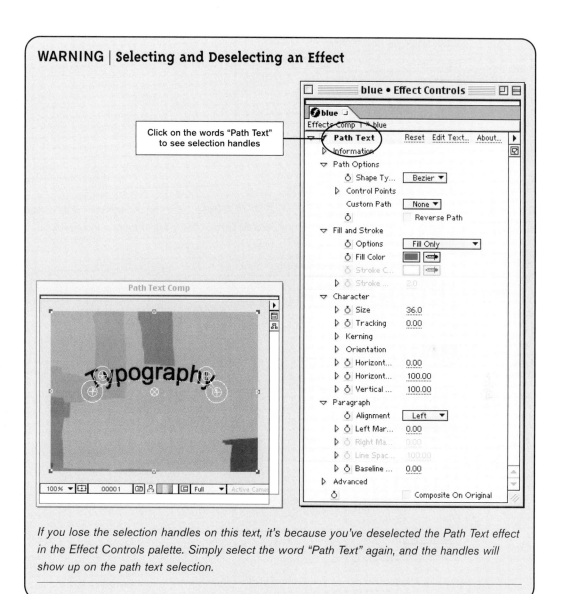

WARNING | Selecting and Deselecting an Effect

Click on the words "Path Text" to see selection handles

If you lose the selection handles on this text, it's because you've deselected the Path Text effect in the Effect Controls palette. Simply select the word "Path Text" again, and the handles will show up on the path text selection.

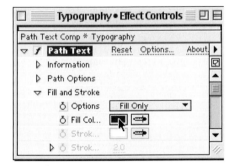

6. Click the **Fill and Stroke** twirly to display the controls. Select any fill color you like by clicking the **color selector** or **color dropper**. When finished, click the **Fill and Stroke** twirly again to hide the controls.

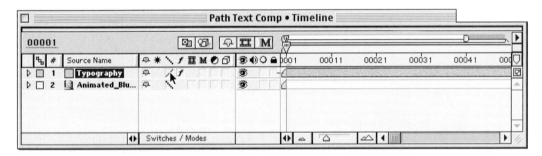

7. In the **Timeline** window, click the **Quality** switch for the **Typography** layer to select Best quality.

In the following steps you will learn to animate text along a curved Bézier path.

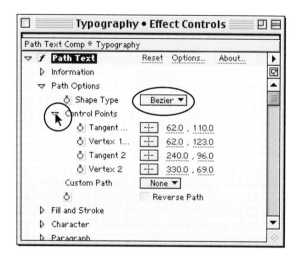

8. Click the **Control Points** twirly to display the controls. You're not going to set any keyframes just yet, so don't click any Stopwatch icons. Remember, when you change a setting without clicking the Stopwatch icon, it simply changes the setting for the entire length of the composition.

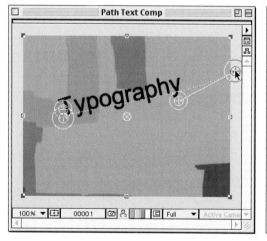 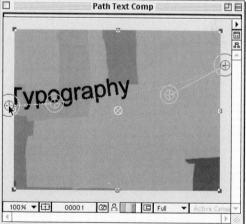

9. Drag the **right Vertex** (large control point) to the upper right. Drag the **left Vertex** to the middle left.

You'll see that the Vertex values change in the Effect Controls palette as you drag the points.

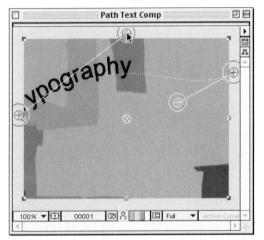
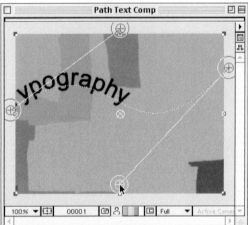

10. Drag the **left Tangent** (small control point) to the top center. Drag the **right Tangent** to the bottom center. Again, you'll see the Tangent values change in the Effect Controls palette as you drag. When you're finished setting the path, hide the **Path Options** by clicking the **twirly**.

You can also set Vertex and Tangent values numerically in the Effect Controls palette, but dragging the handles is much more intuitive!

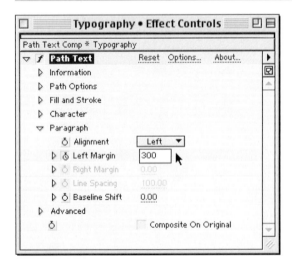

11. Click the **Paragraph** twirly to display the controls. With the **Time Marker** set to **Frame 1**, click the **Left Margin Stopwatch**. Set the **Left Margin** to **300**.

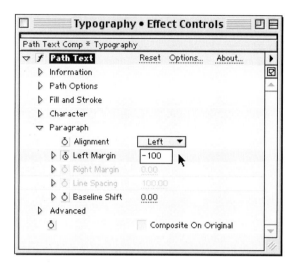

12. Set the **Time Marker** to **Frame 60**. Set the **Left Margin** to **–100**.

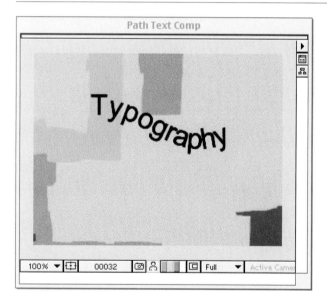

13. Click **RAM Preview**. Your text animates smoothly along the curved path.

14. Leave this project open for the next exercise.

6. _____The Drop Shadow Effect

The **Drop Shadow** effect is one of the most commonly used effects in many graphics programs. In this exercise, you will create a new composition, import a footage item, and apply the Drop Shadow effect to one layer.

1. Create a New Composition. Type **Drop Shadow Comp 1** as the name. Select the **HOT AE5** preset and set the **Duration** to **60** frames.

2. Import **monkey1.ai** from the **chap_10** folder. Click **Import**. In the dialog box that follows, click **OK** to accept importing Merged Layers.

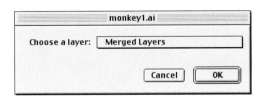

You have just imported an Illustrator document. The choice of Merged Layers means that you are bringing in a flattened Illustrator file instead of separate layers (if there are layers). Choose Merged Layers when you don't want separate layers to import.

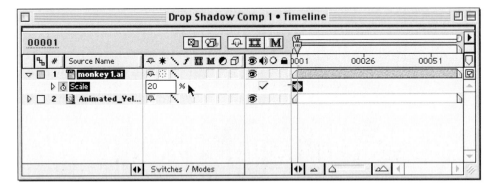

3. Drag the **monkey1.ai** footage and the **Animated_Gre.mov** footage from the **Project** window to the **Timeline** window. Select the **monkey1.ai layer** and press **S** to display the **Scale** property. Click on the **Stopwatch** icon and set the **Scale** value to **20%**.

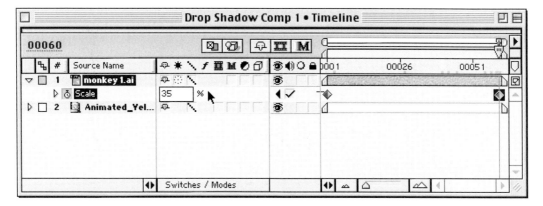

4. Press **K** on your keyboard. This is a shortcut method to move the Time Marker to the last frame in a composition. Set the **Scale** value to **35%**. Press **S** again to hide the Scale property.

5. Choose **Effect > Perspective > Drop Shadow**.

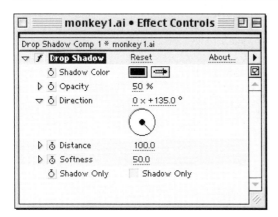

6. In the **Effect Controls** palette, click the **Distance** and **Softness Stopwatch** icons to turn on keyframes. Set the **Distance** to **100** and the **Softness** to **50**.

Note that you are setting the last frame of the animation before you set the first frame. Many After Effects artists work backward this way, for convenience. There is no wrong or right here; just understand that you can approach setting keyframes in different ways.

7. Press **J** on your keyboard. This is a shortcut method to move the Time Marker to the first frame in a composition. Set the **Distance** value to **20** and the **Softness** value to **2**.

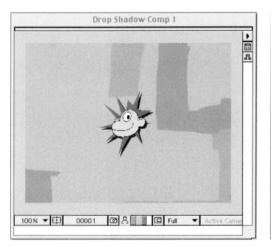
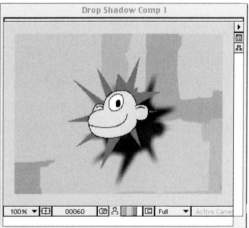

8. Click **RAM Preview** and observe how the Drop Shadow effect animates in distance from the monkey and the edges become softer as it moves forward.

TIP | Use Best Quality for Illustrator Files

When using Illustrator files or other types of vector graphics in your compositions, set the Quality switch to Best to ensure that the preview image is as detailed as possible. If you want to speed up rendering of previews, return to the Draft setting. **Warning:** The Continuous Rasterization switch cannot be used on vector files that have effects applied. The reason? It's a limitation of After Effects–sorry!

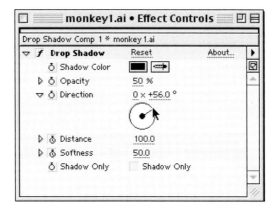

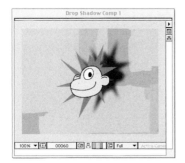

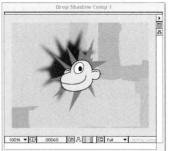

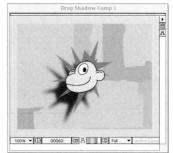

9. Press **K** to move to the **last frame** of the composition. In the Effect Controls palette, drag the **Direction** control around the circle and watch the shadow direction change in response. Set the **Direction** value back to the default **135** degrees.

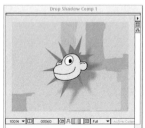
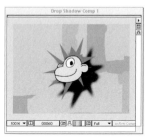

10. Drag left and right over the **Opacity** value and watch the shadow opacity change in the **Composition** window. Set the **Opacity** value back to the default **50%**.

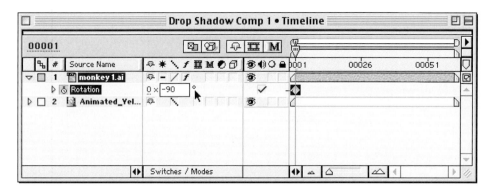

11. Press **J** to move to the **first frame**. In the **Timeline** window, select the **monkey1.ai** layer and press **R** to display the **Rotation** property. Click the **Stopwatch** and set **Rotation** to **−90** degrees.

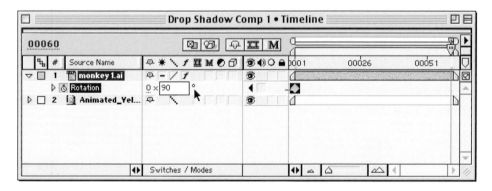

12. Press **K** to move to the **last frame**. Set **Rotation** to **90** degrees.

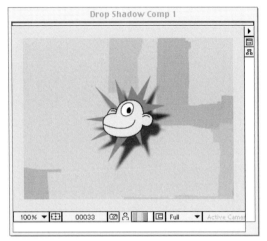
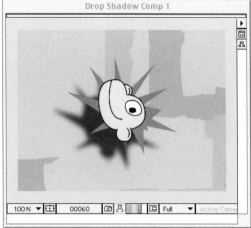

13. Click **RAM Preview**. Observe that the shadow rotates with the monkey.

The default behavior of the Drop Shadow effect causes the angle of the shadow to rotate with the artwork, which is not how a shadow from a light source would really behave. This is a byproduct of the way After Effects renders effects. It is rendering the Drop Shadow first and then the rotation, so that the two are tied. To ensure that the shadow does not rotate with the artwork, you must follow these steps.

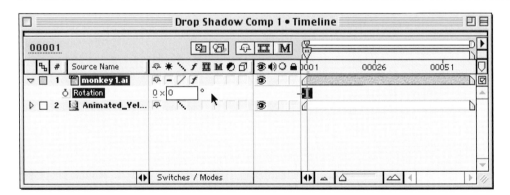

14. In the **Timeline** window, click the **Rotation Stopwatch** to turn off keyframes. Set the **Rotation** value to **0** degrees. Press **R** to hide the Rotation property.

15. Choose **Effect > Distort > Transform**.

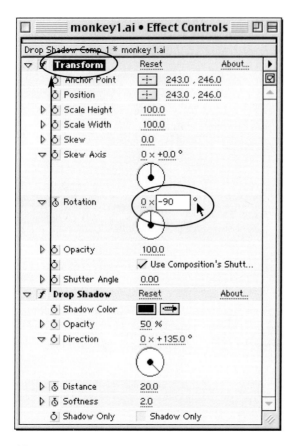

16. In the **Effect Controls** palette, drag the **Transform** effect to the top of the list so that it renders before the Drop Shadow effect.

Press **J** to move to the **first frame**. Set the **Transform** effect **Rotation** value to **−90** degrees. Click the Stopwatch to set a keyframe.

Press **K** to move to the **last frame**. Set the **Transform** effect **Rotation** value to **90** degrees. If you set the Rotation property to animate as an effect, instead of as a transformation, and you put this effect at the top of the stack, you've tricked After Effects into rendering the rotation first and then applying the drop shadow. This is an essential trick to know in order to produce realistic-looking drop shadows!

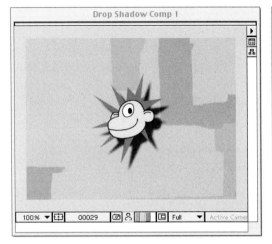
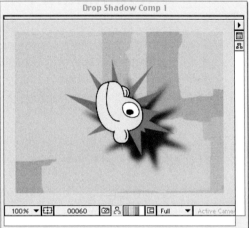

17. Click **RAM Preview** and observe that the direction of the shadow stays at a constant 135 degrees, as desired.

18. Save and close this project. You won't be needing it again.

7.——————————————Adjustment Layers with Effects

In Chapter 8, "*Layers*," we promised we'd get to the subject of **adjustment layers** in the "*Effects*" chapter. We waited because adjustment layers are hard to show without using effects, since they work especially well together. You're probably wondering what the heck adjustment layers are, anyway. They are special layers that affect other layers. If you apply an effect to an adjustment layer, the effect will apply to any and all layers below it. It's best to show you what we mean, so dig in and learn!

1. Open **animals.aep** from the **chap_10** folder. Double-click **animal comp** to open its Composition and Timeline windows. This composition has four layers.

2. Choose **Layer > New > Adjustment Layer**.

A layer called Adjustment Layer *appears at the top of your Timeline window. This layer has no visual effect on the composition—it's as though nothing has happened. You're about to change that!*

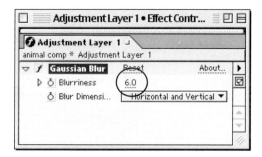

3. With the **Adjustment Layer** selected, choose **Effect > Blur & Sharpen > Gaussian Blur**. Change the **Blurriness** setting to **6.0**.

Notice that all the layers in the composition became blurry. That's the power of an adjustment layer. Any layer below the adjustment layer that contains an effect is affected by the effect. Although we're showing this with the Gaussian Blur effect, it works with any effect!

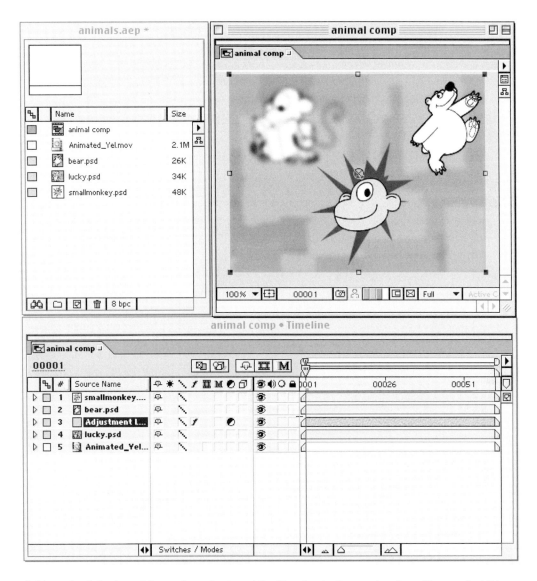

4. Move the **Adjustment Layer** from the top of the Timeline to the number **3** position, so that it is above the **lucky.psd** layer.

Notice that the layers above the Adjustment Layer are unaffected, and the layers below it are still affected. That's how an adjustment layer works. Basically, any time you want to apply the same effect to multiple layers, use an adjustment layer.

5. Save the project to your **HOT_AE_Projects** folder and leave it open for the next exercise.

8. ——————Using Pre-compose with Effects

In the last exercise, you learned how to use an adjustment layer with an effect. In this exercise, you'll see how to combine this with another technique called **precomposing**. You probably didn't know that you can put compositions inside compositions. That's right—a composition can be used as a footage item inside of another composition. Why would you ever want to do such a thing? This exercise will give you a good example.

1. Move the **Adjustment Layer** back to the top position in the **Timeline** of **animal comp**. This will blur all of the layers below it.

Let's say that you wanted to blur the animals in this composition but not the background movie. How would you accomplish this? By putting the animal images and Adjustment Layer *in their own composition and then placing that composition inside this composition, that's how. You'll learn to do this next.*

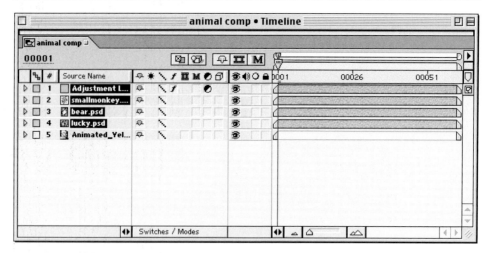

2. Holding down the **Shift** key, click to select the top four layers.

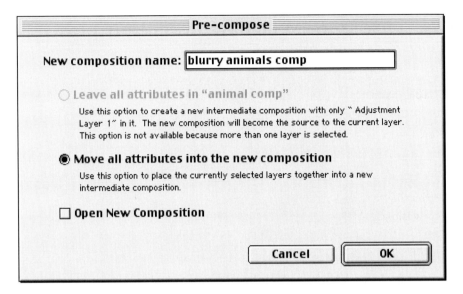

3. Choose **Layer > Pre-compose**. The **Pre-compose** dialog box appears, with **Move all attributes into the new composition** selected. The chart at the end of this exercise explains all of the settings in this dialog box. For now, click **OK** and watch what happens.

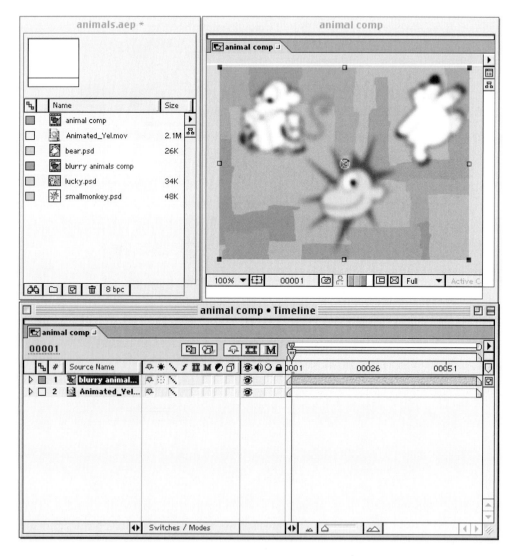

The four layers you selected in the previous step disappeared and were replaced by a composition layer called blurry animal comp. You are probably scratching your head, as this is a difficult concept to comprehend at first glance.

When you choose Pre-compose, After Effects takes those layers, places them in their own composition, and places this new composition inside the original. The result is that the adjustment layer that affected all the layers now affects only the layers in blurry animal comp. The Animated_Yellow.mov layer is unaffected by the Adjustment Layer, because it is in its own composition.

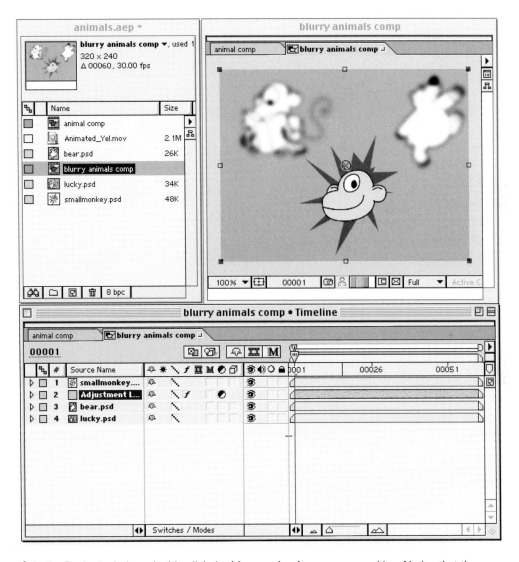

4. In the **Project** window, double-click the **blurry animal comp** composition. Notice that the Adjustment Layer is affecting all the layers below it. Move the **Adjustment Layer** below the **small-monkey.psd** layer. Notice that the **smallmonkey.psd** layer is now unaffected by the Adjustment Layer.

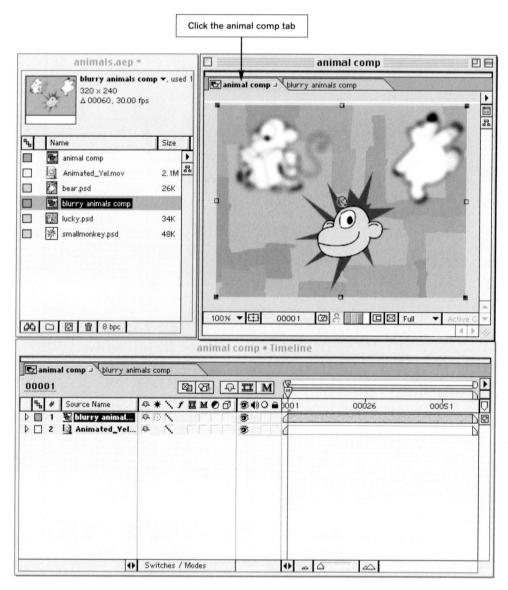

Click the animal comp tab

5. Click the **animals comp** tab in the **Composition** window. Notice that the change you made inside **blurry animals comp** is reflected in **animals comp**. This is the nature of a nested composition, which is what the Pre-compose feature allows you to do.

6. Save and close this project.

The Pre-compose Dialog Box

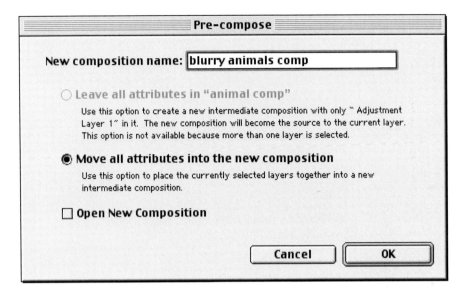

Since this dialog box is new to you, here's a handy description of its features:

Leave all attributes: This option works only with a single layer. Since you had selected multiple layers before choosing Pre-compose, this option was grayed out. It places the single layer into its own composition and places that new composition into the original composition.

Move all attributes into the new composition: This feature is chosen most often. It moves layers, effects, masks, and keyframes into the new composition and places it into the existing composition.

Open New Composition: This setting can be used with either of the other choices. It simply means that the new composition will open. If you don't check this option, you stay in the existing composition and the new composition is nested in the original composition.

NOTE | Parenting Versus Precomposing

You've already learned about parenting, and now you've learned about precomposing. You might wonder when to use which technique. This comparison chart should help.

Parenting Versus Precomposing

Parenting	Precomposing
Parenting can affect all Transform properties except Opacity.	All Transform properties can be precomposed. However, parenting may prove more effective than precomposing much of the time.
Parenting is not useful for effects or mask properties.	Effects and mask properties can be precomposed for all selected layers.
Parenting is useful for creating complex, *dependent* animation such as the orbits of planets in a solar system or the linking of marionette parts for movement.	Precomposing is not always useful for anchor point–based animation. For example, linking the parts of a marionette would not be an effective use of precomposing.
Parenting does not affect the rendering order.	Precomposing can be used to change the rendering order. You learned about the rendering order in the exercise involving the drop shadow rotation. In that exercise, you used the Transform effect to render the rotation before the drop shadow. You could also have also used precomposing to create a composition that rotated the monkey, and then nested that composition inside the composition with the Drop Shadow effect. This is an important use of precomposing.
Parenting does not affect adjustment layers.	Precomposing can control the effect of adjustment layers.
N/A	Precomposed items can be reused inside other compositions.
N/A	Precomposed animations can be updated in one step by editing the original composition.

The chart above can help you identify where you might use parenting rather than precomposing. Parenting affects only the Transform properties (except Opacity). For this reason, parenting is used for animating the motion of objects. As its major strength, parenting provides a very effective way to create animation that is dependent on the motion of other objects within a composition.

Precomposing, on the other hand, provides the most effective means of applying complex changes to a multitude of properties and layers. Effects, masks, adjustment layers, and prerendering are all excellent reasons to use precomposing on a group of layers.

The Effects Palette

New to After Effects 5.5 is the **Effects palette** (not to be confused with the Effect Controls palette you used earlier). There are many effects, and it can be difficult to remember where an effect is located in the menu, or even to remember the exact name of an effect. The Effects palette offers another way to search for and select any effect you want.

To display the Effects palette, choose **Window > Effects**.

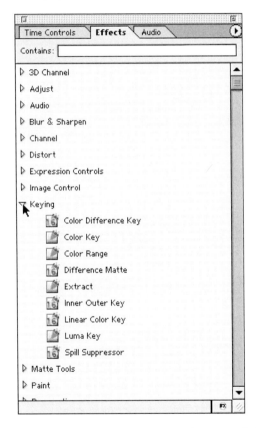

The Effects palette contains all of the types of effects. Click the twirly to display the individual effects available under each type.

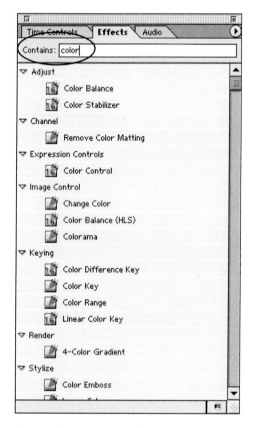

Best of all, you can type in the entry field and the palette will display the name of any effect that has matching letters.

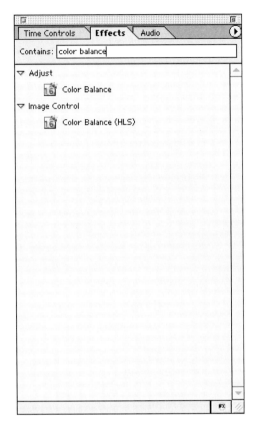

As you continue typing, the window will continue to display the items that match, making it easy to find exactly what you are looking for.

That's another chapter wrap. Be sure to experiment with effects on your own, as we have barely scratched the surface. A great way to learn about effects is to visit discussion boards and learn from other After Effects users. The combinations of effects are literally endless, so don't stop with this chapter!

11.

Masks

Simple Masks	Drawing Masks with the Pen Tool
Locking Masks	Applying Effects	Feathered Masks
Mask Modes	Animating Mask Shapes

chap_11

After Effects 5.0 / 5.5
H•O•T CD-ROM

Masks allow you to define transparent areas for footage items, and they play an important role in motion graphics design. You have imported Photoshop and Illustrator images with transparent masked regions into After Effects. This chapter will show you how to produce these masks in After Effects. Masks are useful for all kind of visual effects and are used often by professional animators.

You'll learn several useful and practical methods for creating, editing, and animating masks. You'll find that you use these masking skills often in your work as an After Effects animator.

I. _____Creating Simple Masks

A **mask** defines the boundary between transparent and opaque areas of a composition. When you draw a mask in After Effects, the area inside the boundary is completely visible, and the area outside the mask boundary is completely transparent. In addition to setting masked regions, After Effects allows you to set masked areas to have different levels of opacity. Masks can be used on still or movie footage.

After Effects allows you to create simple masks with a rectangle or oval masking tool or complex masks using a pen tool similar to the one in Illustrator and Photoshop. This first exercise will focus on making simple masks.

In the following exercise, you will learn to draw a simple mask and adjust its size. You will also learn to invert a mask. Inverting a mask reverses (or inverts) the transparent and opaque areas defined by the mask boundary.

> **1.** Open **Mask Project.aep** in the **chap_11** folder.
>
> *Warning: If you get an error message saying that you don't have the font Verdana, don't worry. This project will still work properly; After Effects will simply substitute a font that you do have.*

> **2.** Choose **File > Save As**. Navigate to your **HOT_AE_Projects** folder and click **Save**.

> **3.** In the **Project** window, double-click on the **Simple Masks** composition to open it.

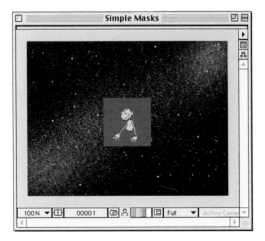

> **4.** In the **Composition** window, press the **spacebar** to preview the monkey animation.
>
> *You're going to place the monkey footage inside the rocket image, which is currently turned off in the Timeline window. In the following steps you will turn the rocket layer on and draw a circular mask that will be used to make the port window transparent.*

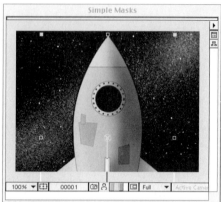

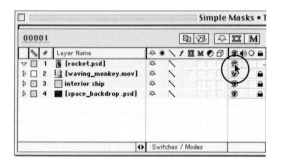

5. Click the **Video** switch to display the **rocket.psd** layer in the Composition window. Observe the solid port window, which is where you will draw the mask to reveal the monkey animation.

This animation was set up for the purposes of this masking exercise. It was created in After Effects (remember the monkey animation from Chapter 9, "Parenting"?), saved as a QuickTime movie (which you'll learn to do in Chapter 16, "Rendering Final Movies"), and imported into this composition. We could have had you create all this yourself, but then it would have been another 30 pages before we could teach you about masking!

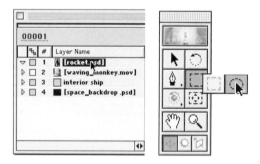

6. Make sure that your **Time Marker** is on **Frame 1**, and that the **rocket.psd** layer is selected. If the **Toolbox** is not visible, press **Command+1** (Mac) or **Control+1** (Windows) to display it. As an alternative, you can choose **Window > Tools**.

Click and hold on the **Mask** tool in the Toolbox to display the Rectangle and Oval Mask tools. Select the **Oval Mask** tool.

In the following steps you will draw the mask in the Composition window and adjust the size of the mask. Go slowly with each step. If you want to undo something, use the Undo command by choosing Edit > Undo. Alternatively, press Command+Z (Mac) or Control+Z (Windows). After Effects' default preference settings will allow you 20 undos, which should be sufficient for any exercise in this book.

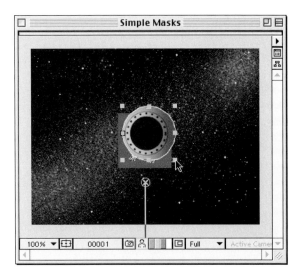

7. Hold down the **Shift** key and, in the **Composition** window, click just above and to the left of the port window of the rocket and drag to create a circular matte around the port window of the rocket. It will look as though the rocket has just disappeared, but don't worry! The mask immediately makes everything outside the mask path completely transparent. You'll fix this in the next step. Don't worry if your circle isn't perfectly matched to the shape of the port shape either. You'll fix this soon as well!

TIP | Using the Shift Key with Rectangle and Oval Masks

Holding down the Shift key creates a perfect circle when you draw with the Oval Mask tool. Likewise, when using the Rectangle Mask tool, hold down the Shift key to create a perfect square.

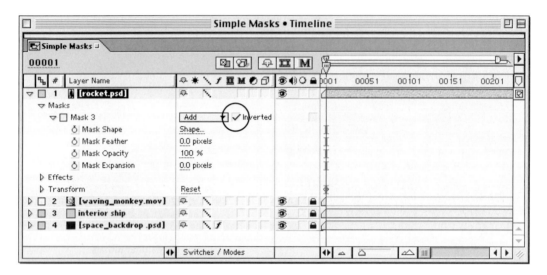

8. Click the **twirly** to the left of **rocket.psd** to display the **Mask** properties. In the **Timeline** window, observe that a mask has been added to the rocket layer.

In the **Switches** panel, locate the **Inverted** switch and click the **check box** to invert the mask. Observe that the mask has been inverted so that it is now completely transparent inside the mask boundary and completely opaque outside the boundary. If the mask you drew doesn't fit properly, don't worry. You'll learn how to adjust its size and position next.

9. In the **Toolbox**, select the **Selection** tool.

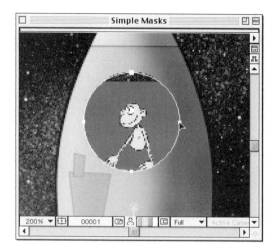 

10. In the **Composition** window, set the **magnification** to **200%**. Double-click any **mask handle** to display the mask bounding box.

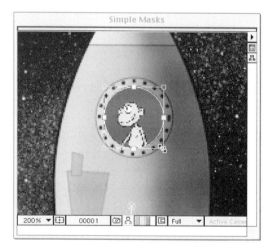

11. Hold down the **Shift** key and drag a **corner scale handle** to adjust the size of the circle mask to fit the port window. When done, click in an empty part of the Timeline window to hide the bounding box.

If you need to reposition the mask, use the Selection tool. If you want to readjust the size of the mask, double-click on any mask handle to display the bounding box and repeat the scale adjustment process.

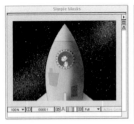  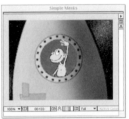 

12. Set the **magnification** back to **100%**. Click **RAM Preview** or press the **spacebar** to view the properly masked animation. Notice that the monkey and rocket move together. They were animated to do this for you, using parenting!

13. Save your project. Close the **Simple Masks** composition and leave your project open for the next exercise.

Drawing Masks with the Pen Tool

In the previous exercise, you learned to create an oval mask using the Oval Mask tool. You can also draw custom masks using the Pen tool, which uses Bézier points to define a mask path. Masks drawn with the Pen tool can be either **closed** or **open** paths.

In a closed path, there is no definite beginning or end. A closed path is continuous; for example, a circle is a closed path.

An open path has different beginning and end points. A straight line is an example of an open path. You'll get to create an open path in the next exercise.

In the next exercise, you will learn to use the Pen tool to draw a free-form Bézier mask. The mask you create will have an open path.

Working with the Selection Tool

The Selection tool has a great deal of functionality when used with paths. One of the tricks to working effectively with After Effects is to understand how the Selection tool works.

What might not be obvious when working with the Selection tool is the fact that it does different things depending on what is currently selected. For example, if the entire mask is selected, the Selection tool will move the mask in the Composition window. However, if a single point or a group of points is selected, the Selection tool will change the shape of the mask. This can be a bit frustrating when you're adjusting a path.

Here's another example: The entire mask is selected and you click on a point to select it individually, but After Effects won't let you select it. This behavior also causes a bit of frustration. You can develop a system, however, that will make these frustrations go away.

The first thing to do is to identify whether the entire mask just individual points are selected or before you attempt to drag a mask path. In a certain respect, this is the hardest part. Once you've trained yourself to become aware of the selection "state," the rest is easy.

The answer to the Selection tool dilemma lies in using keyboard commands that modify Selection tool functionality. There are three keys that will help you when using the Selection tool, and luckily they're easy to remember because you use them all the time:

> Mac keys: **Command**, **Option**, and **Shift**
> Windows keys: **Control**, **Alt**, and **Shift**

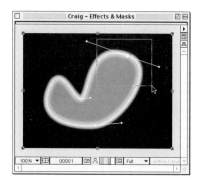

The first trick to learn is what to do if your entire mask is already selected and you want to change the "state" of the mask so you can select single points.

Hold down the **Shift** key and, with the **Selection** tool, draw a **marquee** around any point(s) you want to select. After that, the mask will be in the "individual point" selection state. You can just click on any point within the marquee that you want to select directly. Holding down the **Shift** key allows you to click unselected points and add them to your selected group.

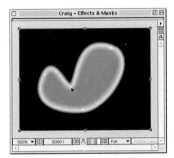

The second trick involves what to do if individual points are selected and you want to select the entire mask.

Press **Option** (Mac) or **Alt** (Windows) and click on the mask. After that, the entire mask will be selected and you can reposition it anywhere you want in the Composition window.

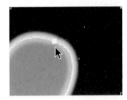 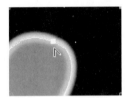

The third trick is to hold down the **Command** (Mac) or **Control** (Windows) key to toggle between the **Selection** tool and the current **Pen** tool. For example, if the Convert Control Point tool is visible in the Toolbox, it will become active if you hold down the **Command** (Mac) or **Control** (Windows) modifier key while using the Selection tool. This can be handy when you are adjusting Bézier points and you want to convert their type from a straight point to a curved one or vice versa.

Finally, remember to **double-click** to display or hide the mask bounding box.

Knowing these tricks will make working with masks much less frustrating. You'll get some hands-on practice in the following exercises, and feel free to revisit this section as you gain more experience with masking in After Effects.

2. ——————————Drawing Bézier Masks Using the Pen Tool

In Chapter 5, "*Timeline, Keyframes, and Animation*," you learned to use the Pen tool to adjust spatial keyframes in motion paths. The Pen tool can also be used to draw Bézier mask paths directly in the Composition window. In this exercise you will open the **Effects Mask** composition, select the Pen tool, and draw a Bézier mask. After drawing the mask path, you will adjust the points to smooth the path.

1. In the **Project** window, double-click on the **Effects Mask** composition to open it.

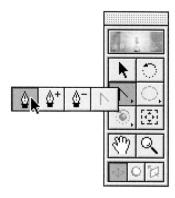

2. In the **Toolbox**, select the **Pen** tool.

In the following steps you will draw the mask path and save it for later. In the next exercise, you will combine that mask path with the text effect.

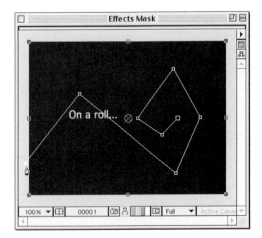

3. In the **Timeline** window, select the **Text Effect** layer. This is a solid layer that has the Text effect applied to it. In the **Composition** window, using the **Pen** tool, start on the right side and click from point to point to draw the mask path that you see above, ending the path on the left side. When you click from point to point, you create a straight path.

You don't have to follow exactly what you see above; just do something that basically resembles this path and it'll be fine.

In the following steps, you will smooth the mask path by converting each point from a straight path to a curved path.

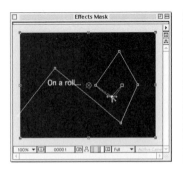 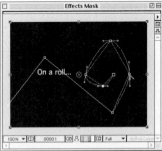 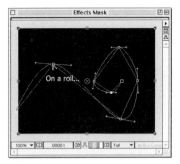

4. With the **Pen** tool still selected, hold the cursor over the **second point** from the right, and observe that the cursor changes to a ^ shape. This is the Convert Control Point tool.

Click on this same point again and observe that the point changes to a curved path.

Using this method, click **each point** and convert it to a curved path point, except the first and the last points in the path.

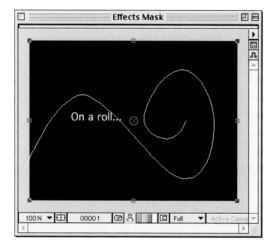

5. Select the **Selection tool** from the **Toolbox** and adjust any points you like. Your finished mask path should be fairly smooth, so the text will flow nicely along the path when you animate it.

6. Save your project and leave it open for the next exercise. So far, you've learned how to create straight and curved paths. Upcoming exercises will build on these skills.

NOTE | Open Mask Paths

Open mask paths, like the one you just drew, are used only with effects. They act as a boundary for an effect, or they can define a path for an effect.

NOTE | Locking Masks

Knowing how to lock and unlock a mask is a nice skill to have, so you don't accidentally edit a mask after going to the trouble of creating it. To display the Lock switch for a mask, you must first display the mask properties.

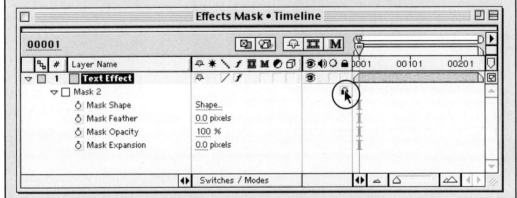

Tip: You can display the Mask Shape property by pressing **M** (once) on your keyboard. This will also display the Lock switch for the mask.

The Lock column and the Lock switch for the mask are located in the Switches panel. Click the **Lock-box** icon to lock the mask. The icon changes to a lock to indicate that the mask is now locked.

3. —————————Using Masks with Text Effects

In the following exercise, you'll apply a Path Text effect to the mask path you created in the last exercise. Once you apply the mask, you'll animate the text along the mask path. This combines techniques you learned from the last chapter with some that you learned in this one. It's all starting to come together!

1. The **Effects Mask** composition should still be open from the last exercise.

2. In the **Timeline** window, select the **Text Effect** layer.

To make this exercise more efficient, we've already applied the text effect to this solid layer.
Tip: *You can add a text effect to any kind of layer—a solid layer, still footage, or a movie. See Chapter 10, "Effects," if you need more info on text effects.*

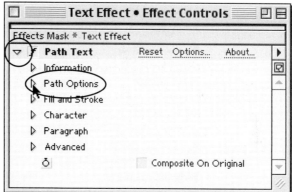

3. Choose **Effect > Effect Controls** to display the **Effect Controls** palette. As an alternate method, press **Command+Shift+T** (Mac) or **Control+Shift+T** (Windows).

In the **Effect Controls** palette, click the **Path Text** twirly, and then click the **Path Options** twirly.

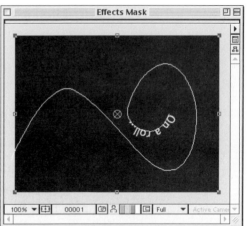

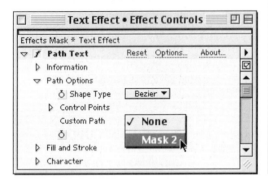

4. Locate the **Custom Path** option and click the pop-up menu to select **Mask 2**. Notice that the text conforms to the path. After Effects automatically names the mask you made in the last exercise Mask 2. You can change the mask's name to anything you want by selecting **Mask 2** in the **Timeline** window, pressing the **Return** key, and renaming it. For this exercise, you can leave it named Mask 2.

This text is oriented upside down. In the following step you'll see how to reverse the orientation of the text by reversing the path.

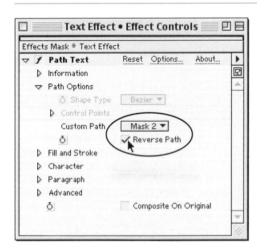

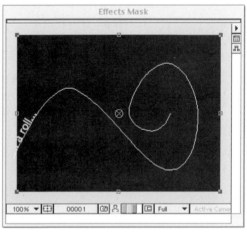

5. Click the **Reverse Path** check box. Notice that the text is now oriented right side up, just as it should be.

Reversing the path affects the text in two ways. One, it reverses the up/down orientation of the text. Two, it reverses the first/last point origin of the text. In the following steps, you'll learn to animate the text along the custom path, using the Left Margin option.

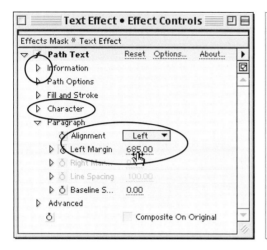
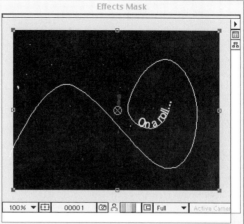

6. In the **Timeline** window, make sure the **Time Marker** is set to **Frame 1**.

In the **Effects Control** palette, click the **Path Options** twirly to hide those properties. Click the **Paragraph** twirly to display the Paragraph properties.

Click the **Left Margin** stopwatch to turn on keyframes. Position your mouse over the **Left Margin** value so that you see the arrows. Clicking inside the value field and dragging to the right will increase the numbers. Do this until the text starts on the right, as in the image above. The value (in this case 685) relates to the relative position of the artwork, so it will be different for every path.

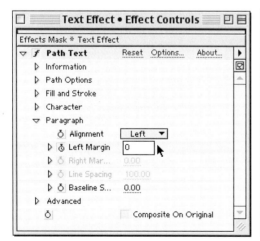
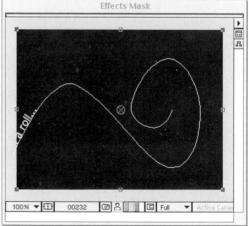

7. In the **Timeline** window, move the **Time Marker** to the **last frame**. In the **Effect Controls** palette, set the **Left Margin** to **0**.

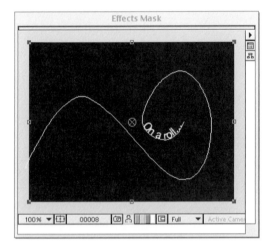

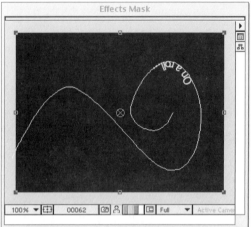

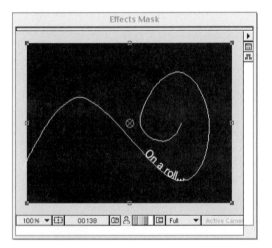

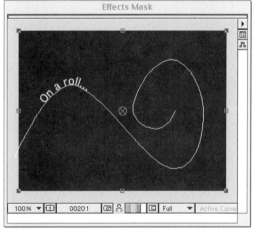

8. Scrub the **Time Marker** or click **RAM Preview** in the **Time Controls** palette to see the results of the animation.

9. Do not close this project; you will need it for the next exercise.

 MOVIE | **effect-path.mov**

To see a movie that demonstrates this exercise, open **effect-path.mov** from the **Movies** folder on the **H•O•T CD-ROM**.

Creating Feathered Masks

So far, you've created a closed path (using the Oval Mask tool in Exercise 1) and an open path (using the Pen tool in Exercise 2). You can create closed paths using the Oval Mask tool, Rectangle Mask tool, or Pen tool. One of the benefits of creating a closed path is that it can be feathered, creating a soft-edged mask, which is what you'll get to try out next.

1. In the **Project** window, double-click on the **Feathered Masks** composition to open it.

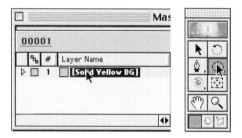

2. In the **Timeline** window, select the **Solid Yellow BG** layer. In the **Toolbox**, select the **Oval Mask** tool. **Note:** You must always select the layer on which you want the mask applied before you create a mask. In fact, the mask tools in the Toolbar are grayed out unless a layer in the Timeline is selected first!

Tip: Press Q on your keyboard to toggle between the Oval and Rectangle Mask tools.

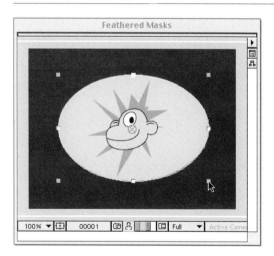

3. Draw an oval mask similar to the one above.

If you want to adjust the position of the mask, drag it with the Selection tool.

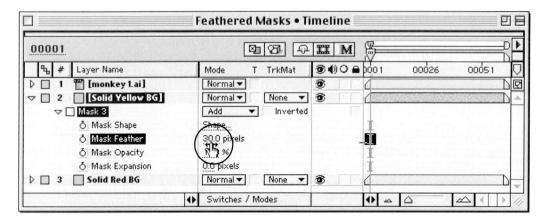

4. Press **MM** on your keyboard as a shortcut to display all of the Mask properties. Set the **Mask Feather** property to **30** pixels. Since you haven't set the Stopwatch icon, this change will last for the duration of the composition. The only reason to set the Stopwatch icon is if you want a property to animate over time.

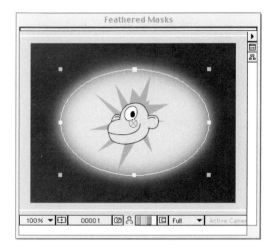

5. In the **Composition** window, notice that the mask path is in the center of the feathered transition.

You can control the feathering along the mask path by using the Mask Expansion property. In the following steps you will reduce the mask expansion. This will move the area from which the feathering originates.

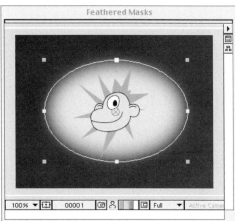

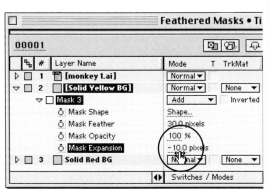

6. Set the **Mask Expansion** property to **−10** pixels.

Positive numbers increase the mask expansion while negative numbers decrease it.

This is the end of the exercise. If you want to experiment more, you could try setting keyframes for the Mask Feather or Mask Expansion properties and changing the values over different keyframes. You can animate any of the Mask properties by clicking the Stopwatch icon, just as you can with any other After Effects property!

---

7. Save your project, and close the **Feathered Masks** composition. Leave your project open for the next exercise.

NOTE | Change to Mask Feather Property in After Effects 5.5

In the release of After Effects 5.5, a small yet nice change was made to the Mask Feather property.

A Lock icon has been added that makes it easy to change the mask feathering uniformly along the X and Y axes, or you can control the two axes separately by clicking the Lock icon to unlock the axes.

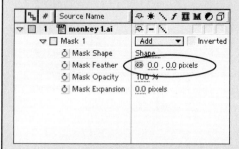

This is useful for making asymmetrical feathered effects.

TIP | Deleting a Mask

How do you delete a mask? It's fairly simple. Hey, everything is simple in life if you know how to do it!

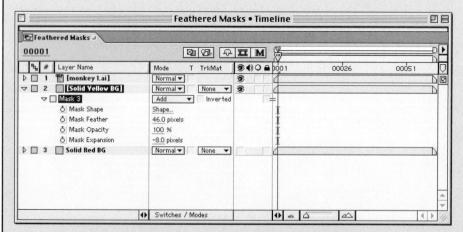

Select the mask by clicking its name in the Timeline. Press the Delete key. This will delete only the mask, not the layer itself!

5. —————Using Mask Modes

More than one mask can be applied to a single layer. In fact, you can apply up to 127 masks to a single layer. While there aren't many instances in which you'd use 127 masks on a layer, there are some interesting effects that can be derived from using multiple masks. When you use multiple masks on a single layer, you can work with **mask modes**. These modes change the appearance of the different mask shapes and can create effects that are quite beautiful and useful. In this exercise you will learn to apply multiple masks and to use mask modes. You'll also learn to use mask opacity with mask modes.

This exercise works with a solid layer. It's amazing how many different "looks" you can get from a solid layer, especially when you're working with masking, feathering, and opacity. You will find that you might use Photoshop and Illustrator less, once you see the power of combining solid layers and masks.

> **1.** In the **Project** window, double-click the **Mask Modes** composition to open it. This is an empty composition. Not for long, though, because you are going to add content to it.

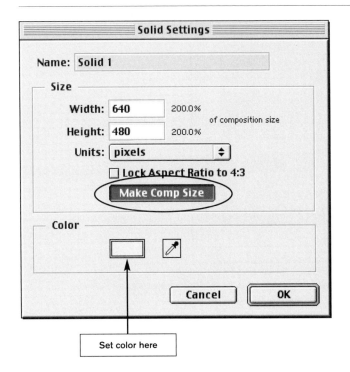

2. Create a new solid layer by choosing **Layer > New > Solid**. This opens the **Solid Settings** dialog box. Pick a **yellow** color and click **Make Comp Size**. Then click **OK**. You should see a solid yellow layer that fits perfectly inside the Composition window.

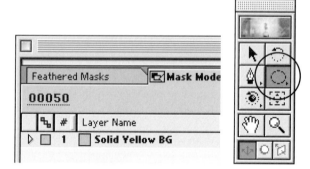

3. With the **solid** layer selected, press the **Return** key so you can rename it **Solid Yellow BG**. In the **Toolbox**, select the **Oval Mask** tool.

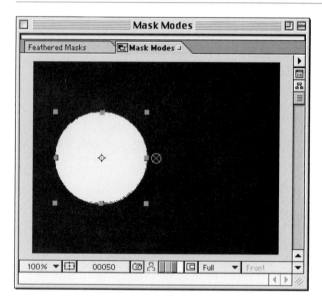

4. With the **Oval Mask** tool, draw a circle on the screen like the one you see above.

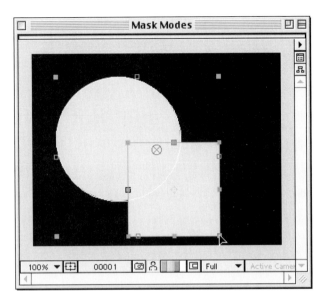

5. Select the **Rectangle Mask** tool. Hold down the **Shift** key and draw a square mask that overlaps the circle. **Note:** The Shift key constrains the rectangle mask to a perfect square. Don't worry too much about getting the positions to match exactly—the idea is to create two masks like the ones you see here.

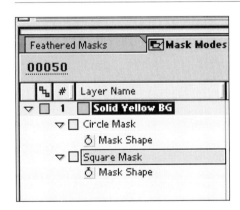

6. Press **M** on your keyboard to display the **Mask Shape** property. Highlight each mask, and then press **Return** (Mac) or **Enter** (Windows). Type **Circle Mask** and **Square Mask** as the new names. Press **Return** (Mac) or **Enter** (Windows) again to complete the renaming process.

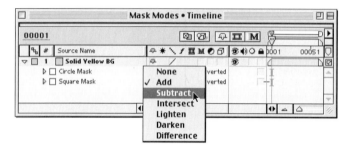 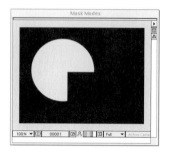

7. In the **Switches/Modes** panel, locate the **Mask Mode** pop-up menu for the **Square Mask**, which is set to **Add** by default. Choose the **Subtract** mode. Notice that the square mask is subtracted from the circle where they overlap.

This pop-up menu is automatically available in the Timeline as soon as you create a mask. Like many things in the Timeline, the Mask Mode menu in After Effects is context sensitive. Add a mask, and the menu appears.

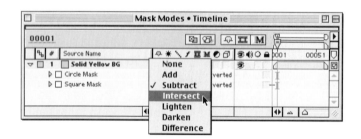 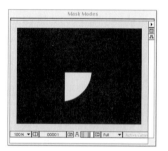

8. Choose the **Intersect** mode for the **Square Mask**. Notice that only the intersecting area of the masks is displayed.

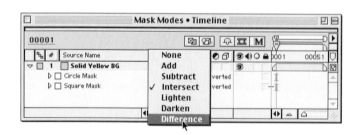 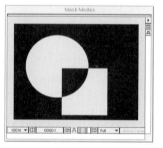

9. Choose the **Difference** mode for the **Square Mask**. Notice that only the areas of the masks that do not overlap are displayed.

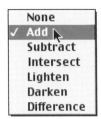 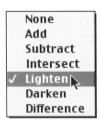 

10. Compare the **Add** and **Lighten** modes for the **Square Mask**. The results appear the same. Some modes work identically on the same artwork. Even though you used a solid layer for this exercise, you could have used a photograph or a movie as your source layer for the mask. If, instead of these solid shapes, you had photographic content that wasn't at full opacity, you would see a different effect if you selected Lighten.

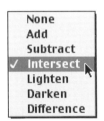 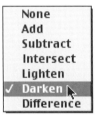 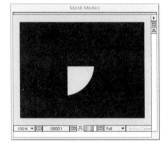

11. Now compare the **Intersect** and **Darken** modes for the **Square Mask**. The results of these modes also appear the same.

The Lighten and Darken modes take on greater significance when acting on masks that have opacities of less than 100%. In the following steps you will draw a triangular Bézier mask and then adjust the opacity of all three masks. After that, you will reapply the Lighten and Darken modes and observe the new results.

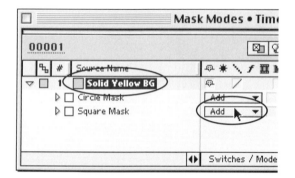

12. Set the **Square Mask** mode to **Add**. Make sure the **Solid Yellow BG** layer is selected, and then, in the **Toolbox**, click on the **Pen** tool.

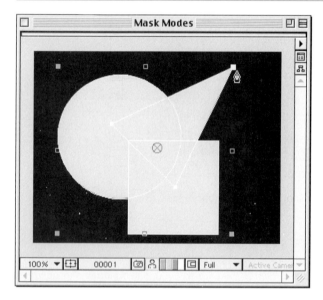

13. Draw a triangle that overlaps the circle and the square. Create this shape by clicking the three points to form the triangle.

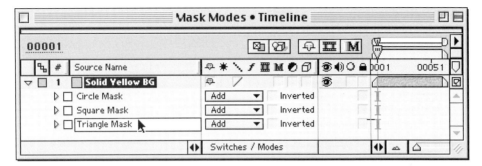

14. Select the new mask, and then press **Return** (Mac) or **Enter** (Windows). Type **Triangle Mask** as the new name. Press **Return** (Mac) or **Enter** (Windows) again to complete the renaming process.

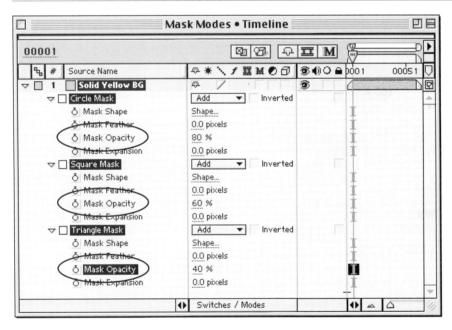

15. Press **MM** on your keyboard to display the **Mask** properties for all the masks. Feel free to adjust the size of your **Timeline** window if you like.

Set the **Circle Mask** opacity to **80%**. Set the **Square Mask** opacity to **60%**. Set the **Triangle Mask** opacity to **40%**.

After setting the opacity values, click the **twirly** next to each of the masks to hide the properties but still display the mask names. Readjust the height of your **Timeline** window if you like.

16. Choose **Edit > Deselect All** to deselect everything. Alternatively, you can press **Command+ Shift+A** (Mac) or **Control+Shift+A** (Windows).

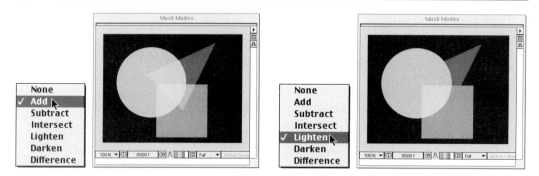

17. Change the **Triangle Mask** mode from its default (Add) to **Lighten**. Compare the results.

The Add and Lighten modes display opacity values differently. In the Add mode, where multiple masks intersect, the opacity values of all intersecting masks are added together. In the Lighten mode, where multiple masks intersect, the highest opacity value is used.

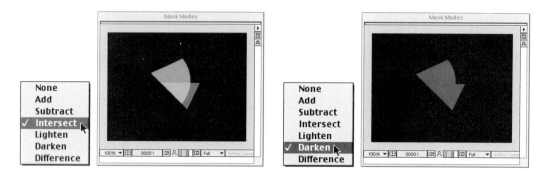

18. Set the **Triangle Mask** mode to **Intersect**, and then set it to **Darken**. Compare the results.

Here again, the opacity values are processed and displayed differently. In the Intersect mode, the opacity of all intersecting masks is added together. In the Darken mode, opacity values are not added together—instead, a single opacity value is used for intersecting multiple masks.

19. Save your project, and then close the **Mask Modes** composition. Leave your project open for the next exercise.

You don't need to worry about memorizing how each of these modes work. With experience you will intuitively understand the results you get from each mode.

Right now, it's primarily important to see what the Add, Subtract, Intersect, and Difference modes do. Of secondary importance is to see that the Lighten and Darken modes won't do anything for you unless you are using masks with opacity values of less than 100%.

Now that you've seen the modes and you have some first-hand experience, you'll be able to incorporate mask modes into your work.

TIP | Changing the Color of a Mask Outline

When working with multiple masks, it can be a good idea to change the color of mask outlines so you can easily identify each one in the Composition window.

 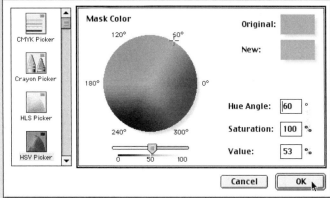

*To change the color, locate the mask in the Timeline window and click on the **color swatch** to the left of the mask name. Pick a new color and click **OK**.*

---

6. _____Animating and Changing Mask Shapes

Mask shapes can be animated. The result creates the impression of one shape morphing into another. In this exercise you'll learn to animate mask shapes and to change mask types.

1. In the **Project** window, double-click on the **Animate Mask Shape** composition to open it.

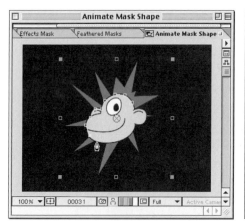 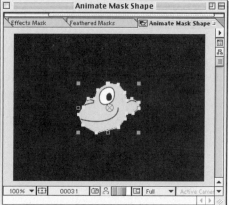

2. With **monkey1.ai** selected in the **Timeline**, select the **Pen** tool from the **Toolbox**. Click around the monkey's head to create a mask that shows his head without the starburst, as you see above.

Note: Click in an empty part of the Timeline to get rid of the mask selection so you can see whether you're happy with the mask. If not, using the Selection tool, double-click on the monkey in the Composition window to see the mask handles. Using the Pen tool, you can modify the points from straight lines to curves or, using the Selection tool, you can move the mask. Keep up this process of clicking in an empty part of the Timeline to see it and fixing it until you're happy with the shape it's taken. This often takes some massaging—few people get it right without a little extra effort.

3. Press **M** to reveal the Mask Shape property. Click the **Stopwatch** icon for the **Mask Shape** property. This will set a keyframe on the first frame.

The shortcut M reveals only the property that has been set (Mask Shape), while the shortcut MM reveals all the different Mask properties. Since we are animating only the Mask Shape property, the shortcut key M is sufficient to show us what we need to see.

4. Move the **Time Marker** to the end of the **Timeline**. Double-click on the **monkey** artwork inside the **Composition** window to open the **Layer In** window (see the tip on the next page). Use the **Selection** tool to move the points of the mask outward, revealing the entire starburst shape. Close the **Layer In** window when you're finished.

If you look in the Timeline, you'll see that this change has set another keyframe. That's because the Stopwatch icon was on! Any change that you make to the mask will create a keyframe as long as you move the Time Marker to a new location. If you think about it, this is how all keyframes are created in After Effects. Set the stopwatch, move the Time Marker, make a change, and you have a new keyframe!

5. The effect that you just created will be more impressive if you change the background color from black to something else. Choose **Composition > Background Color**, and pick a bright orange.

6. Click in an empty part of the **Timeline** to deselect the **monkey1.ai** layer. This will turn off the mask shape. Scrub the **Time Marker** or press the **spacebar** to view the mask shape animation.

7. Save and close this project. You're finished trying out the mask exercises!

TIP | Use the Layer In Window for Better Control

Sometimes, for really tight masking jobs, it's easier to view the mask in the Layer In window. You access this window by double-clicking on artwork in the Composition window.

This launches the Layer In window. It is more intuitive to move anchor points in this view, but you must close the view to see the results of your work, so it's a little inconvenient.

TIP | Toolbox Keyboard Commands

Drawing and adjusting masks often requires many trips to the Toolbox. You can streamline your work process by using keyboard commands to access every tool in the Toolbox.

Toolbox Shortcut Keys	
Key	**Tool**
V	Selection tool
W	Rotation tool
G	Pen tool
Q	Oval / Rectangle Mask tool
C	Camera tools
Y	Pan Behind tool
H	Hand tool
Z	Zoom tool

Use these shortcut keys and you'll find that you spend less time clicking on the Toolbox and more time making creative choices.

That's a wrap on another chapter! Masks are great tools for creating transitions, and you've certainly got the experience now to create a vast array of masks for your projects. Practice on some footage of your own—don't stop with the examples in this chapter. Try masking all kinds of footage, and you'll be amazed by the different kinds of effects you can achieve.

12.

Track Mattes

| How do Alpha Channels Relate to Track Mattes? |
| Creating a Track Matte | Luminance-Based Track Mattes |
| Soft-Edged Track Matte with a Masked Solid Layer |
| Other Masking Modes |

chap_12

After Effects 5.0 / 5.5
H•O•T CD-ROM

The term **track matte** is new to any of you who've never used After Effects before. Actually, many experienced After Effects users do not use track mattes or know what they do. That's because the concept is slightly abstract—better explained with exercises than words!

Imagine that you had a movie that you wanted to appear within some text. This kind of effect would be perfect for a track matte. You would separate the text and movie onto two layers and use a track matte to tell After Effects to use the shape (or alpha channel) of the text as a mask for the movie. The cool thing about a track matte is that you can still animate the associated layers independently. This means that you could have a movie that scaled to different sizes, which also appeared inside text letters, and which shifted its position within those letters. It gets very exciting, and without further abstract description, let's get right to the heart of track mattes to try them out!

What Is an Alpha Channel?

Alpha channels are critical to working with track mattes. Why? Because a track matte has to use the alpha channel of footage in the Timeline in order to work.

The term "alpha channel" sounds a lot more intimidating than it is. The simple explanation is that an alpha channel works invisibly to mask areas of a digital image from Photoshop, Illustrator, and other programs that support this feature. If you work with Photoshop, we're sure you've created documents with alpha channels, even if you weren't aware that you were doing so. Any Photoshop or Illustrator layer containing artwork that employs transparent pixels uses an invisible alpha channel.

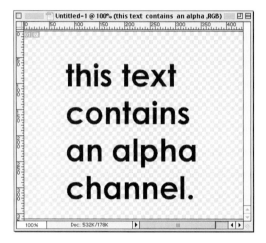

Whenever you create a layer in Photoshop that has shapes and transparent pixels, such as text, for example, the program generates an invisible mask called an alpha or transparency channel. The checkerboard background in Photoshop indicates this type of transparency.

If you could see the alpha channel, it would look like this. It works much as a film negative does: If you shine light through it, the white areas expose the content, while the black areas mask it.

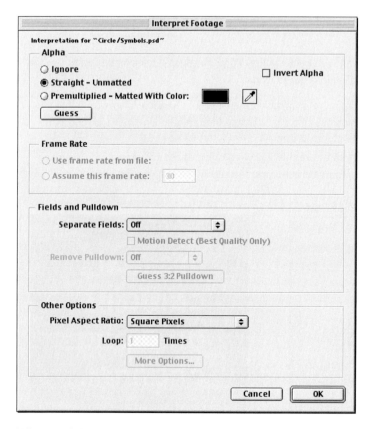

When you bring a file into After Effects, you can choose to merge layers, import a single layer, or import a Photoshop document as a composition. All of these methods preserve the alpha channel. In fact, if you don't want the alpha channel to be honored, you have to go through a little bit of effort. If you ever want to turn off an image's alpha channel, select the image in the Project window, choose **File > Interpret Footage > Main**, and select Ignore.

Masks and mattes in After Effects work in conjunction with alpha channels. The track matte feature in After Effects uses the alpha channel in artwork created in Photoshop, Illustrator, or other software that support this feature.

Importing Alpha Channels from Photoshop Documents

Now that you know that alpha channels are essential to your track matte workflow, you might wonder how to prepare Photoshop artwork and import alpha channels properly. Since this is an After Effects book and not a Photoshop or Illustrator book, we've created the artwork for you to use in the exercises that follow. When you work on your own, however, you will be importing artwork that you've created in other programs. Photoshop and Illustrator files can be imported using a number of options.

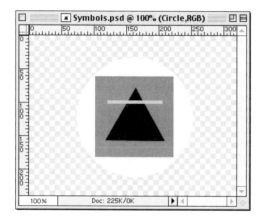 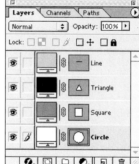

Adobe Photoshop and Illustrator files can contain layers that make up a complete image. The picture above is an image in Photoshop consisting of four individual layers. The Photoshop Layers palette lists each layer from top to bottom: Line, Triangle, Square, Circle.

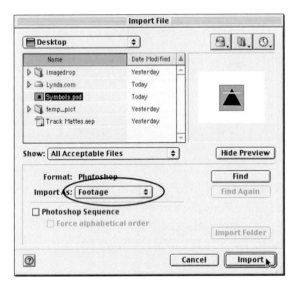

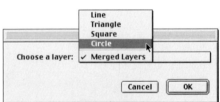

When you import the Photoshop file as footage, you can choose to merge the layers or import each one individually. Choosing the Merged Layers option will combine all of the Photoshop layers into a single footage item. Choosing an individual layer will import only that layer as a footage item.

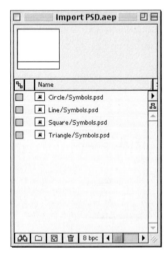

Individually imported Photoshop layers show up in the Project window with their original layer names followed by the name of the Photoshop file.

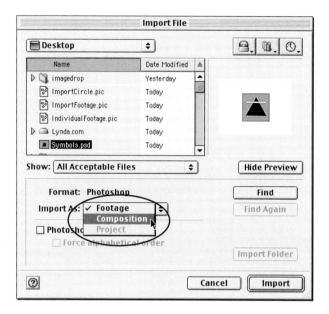

You can also choose to import a Photoshop or Illustrator file as a composition.

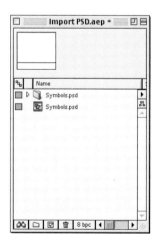

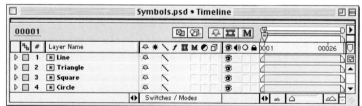

When you import a file as a composition, a new composition is automatically created in the Project window, and the layers are placed in the original stacking order. It's a real timesaver.

In all cases, alpha channel transparency from Photoshop and Illustrator files is imported appropriately into After Effects.

I. ————————Creating a Track Matte

In the following exercise, you will learn to create a simple track matte that places a photograph inside some type.

1. Create a new project and name it **Track Mattes.aep**. Save it in your **HOT_AE_Projects** folder on your hard drive.

2. Double-click inside the empty **Project** window to bring up the **Import File** dialog box. Navigate to the **chap_12** folder. Use your **Control** or **Command** key to select the multiple file names: **largeclouds.psd**, **sky.jpg**, and **sky.psd**. Click **Import**, and then click **OK** to merge layers when prompted.

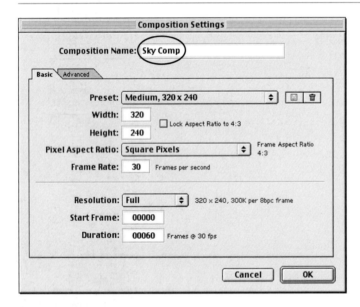

3. In the **Project** window, click the **New Comp** button, which will display the **Composition Settings** dialog box. Name the new composition **Sky Comp**, and enter the settings you see above. Click **OK**.

4. Drag the footage **sky.psd** and **sky.jpg** into the **Timeline** window. Make sure that the type layer, called **sky.psd**, is on top.

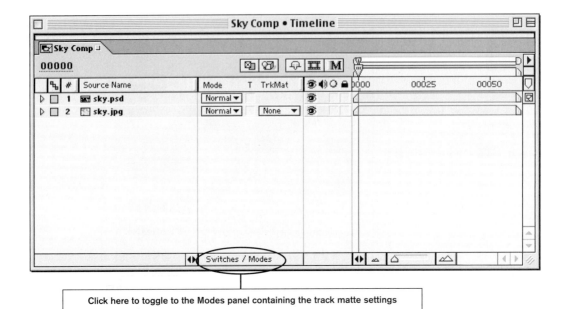

Click here to toggle to the Modes panel containing the track matte settings

5. Click **Switches/Modes** to toggle to the **Modes** panel, where you'll see track matte information. Notice that the switches disappear and that the column headings Mode, T, and TrkMat appear.

As you may recall, you learned what modes do in Chapter 8, "Layers." You'll work with the TrkMat and T settings shortly, and their meanings will be revealed. At the end of this chapter you'll also learn about stencil modes, which you did not learn about in Chapter 8 because they work only with artwork that contains alpha channels.

Note: *The Switches/Modes toggle is part of every Timeline. All you have to do is click that area of your screen and you can toggle between these two groups of settings at any time.*

6. On the **sky.jpg** layer, change the **TrkMat** menu from **None** to **Alpha Matte "sky.psd"**. Notice that the photograph now appears inside the type. The track matte layer is using the alpha channel from the layer directly above it. This is how track mattes work—you put the layer from which you want to pull the matte above the layer that you want affected.

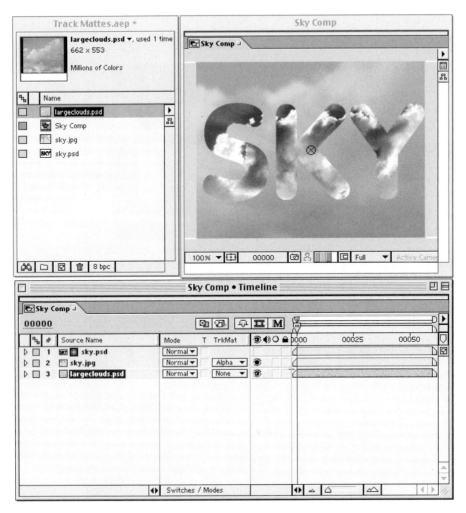

7. Drag **largeclouds.psd** from the **Project** window into the **Timeline** below **sky.jpg**. This layer's TrkMat option is automatically set to None, which means it is unaffected by the type.

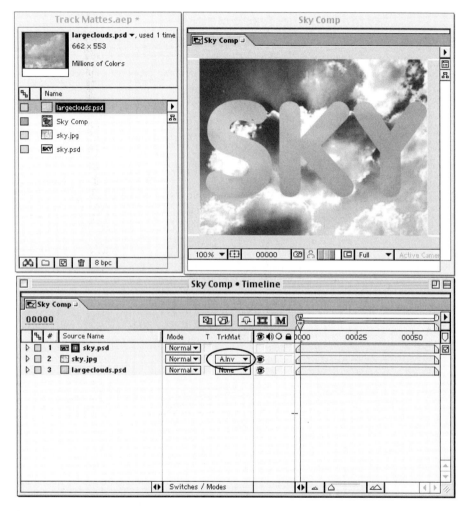

8. Change the **TrkMat** option for **sky.jpg** from **Alpha** to **Alpha Inverted "sky.psd" Matte**. Notice that the type mask is now inverted. Be sure to change it back to **Alpha** when you're finished seeing the change.

Whether you select Alpha or Alpha Inverted as your TrkMat option is a creative decision that depends on the kind of look you're after. The nice thing about this feature is that it's so flexible. There's no harm in trying either setting. You'll learn about the luminance TrkMat settings in a later exercise. The artwork we've used in this exercise (the type) has a great alpha channel, so it's best to work with that kind of track matte here.

9. Save this file and leave it open for the next exercise.

2. ——————————Animating the Track Matte

Since anything and everything can be animated in After Effects, you haven't really touched the power of track mattes until you combine them with some keyframes and set some properties in motion. You'll see in this exercise that you can animate the matte, animate the contents of the matte, or do both!

1. With **sky.psd** selected, reveal the **Position** and **Scale** properties (hint: remember **P** and **Shift+S**?), and change those settings to what you see here. Click the **Stopwatch** icon for both properties—you're going to be setting some keyframes! Change the **Scale** to **38%**, and move the artwork to the position you see above. You can click on the word **SKY** and just move it right in the Composition window. This is the easiest way to set a position without thinking in numbers :).

2. Move the **Time Marker** to the **end** of the **Timeline** (a great shortcut is to press the letter **K**). Change the **Scale** to **100.0%** and the **Position** to **156.0, 165.0**, as you see here. Two keyframes should now be set. Press the **spacebar** to see the effect of moving and scaling the type over time.

It's neat to see the type move through the cloud image of the track matte. Next you'll animate some of the photos for an even neater effect.

3. Move the **Time Marker** back to the **beginning** of the **Timeline** (a great shortcut is to press the letter **J**). Select **sky.jpg** and press **P** for **Position**. Click the **Stopwatch** icon to set a keyframe. Change the **Y** position to **–45**. This moves the image inside the type up on the screen.

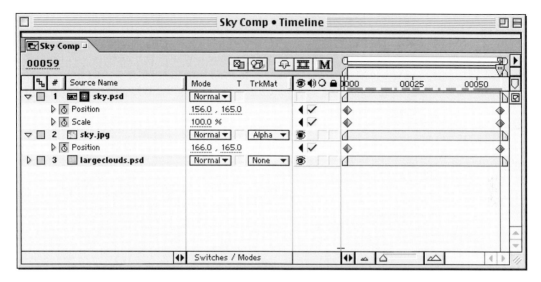

4. Move the **Time Marker** to the **end** of the **Timeline**. Change the **Position** property to **166.0, 165.0**. Press the **spacebar** again to watch your work. Now not only is the type moving but the clouds are moving inside the type.

---

5. Move your **Time Marker** to the **end** of the **Timeline** again. Select **largeclouds.psd** in the **Timeline**. Press **S** to reveal the **Scale** property, and click the **Stopwatch**. That will set a keyframe at the last frame of the Timeline. Move the **Time Marker** to the **beginning** of the **Timeline** and change the **Scale** to **49%**. Make sure you have two keyframes set before you play the animation.

---

6. Press the **spacebar** or click the **Play** button or **RAM Preview** to see your handiwork. You could also put movie footage inside the type, if you used a QuickTime movie instead of a still photo. The variations are endless!

---

7. Close this composition and save the project.

---

3. ————————————**Luminance-Based Track Mattes**

So far, you've had a chance to work with alpha channels and track mattes. This exercise will demonstrate when and why to use a luminance-based track matte. The term **luminance** in After Effects refers to footage that is in **grayscale**. Grayscale source footage can originate from Photoshop, Illustrator, or a QuickTime source. Basically, After Effects treats the grayscale value as it would an alpha channel—black in the grayscale image represents full opacity, while white represents full transparency, and the gray shades in between take on varying degrees of transparency. Why would you use a luminance track matte? They are generally used when you want to make a mask from artwork that doesn't have an alpha channel. It's a convenience to be able to choose from source artwork that contains either grayscale information or an alpha channel. The After Effects program is all about lots of choices to fit any creative needs that might arise!

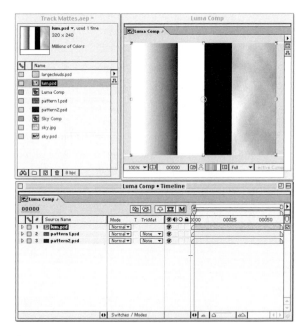

1. Create a new composition, using the same settings as the last exercise (After Effects is "sticky," meaning that all the setting from the last time you created a new composition are still set), and name it **Luma Comp**. Import the artwork **lum.psd**, **pattern1.psd**, and **pattern2.psd**. Click **OK** to merge layers. Drag **lum.psd**, **pattern1.psd**, and **pattern2.psd** from the **Project** window to the **Timeline**. Put the layers in the order you see above.

Observe the lum.psd artwork and notice that it has some areas of pure black, some of pure white, and some mixed grays. This artwork is ideal for understanding how the luminance track matte works against different shades of gray.

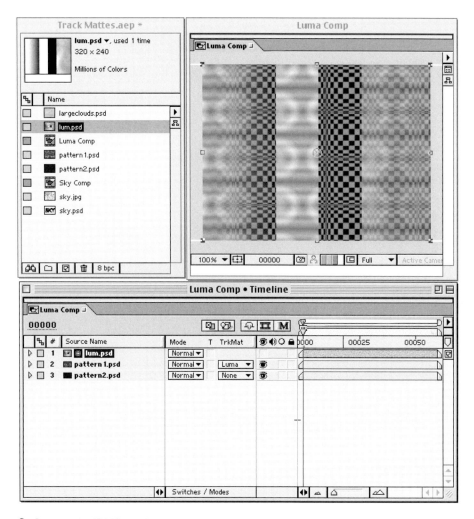

2. Change the **TrkMt** setting of **pattern1.psd** from **None** to **Luma Matte "lum.psd."** Observe that the areas that were pure black knock out **pattern1.psd** completely to reveal **pattern2.psd**. The areas that were pure white fully reveal **pattern1.psd** and hide **pattern2.psd**. The gradient gradually causes one pattern to reveal the other, and the mottled areas of gray show both patterns. The luminance mask is doing its handiwork!

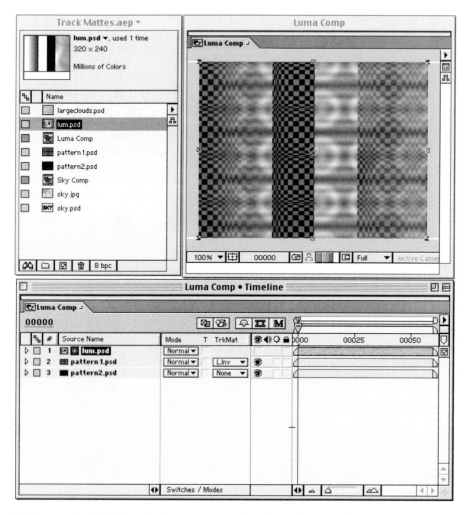

3. Change the **TrkMat** setting for **pattern1.psd** to **Luma Inverted Matte "lum.psd."** Watch the mask change to the opposite of what it was before.

To summarize, luminance mattes are based on grayscale values. Use them when you have source artwork that contains grayscales, and you want to use that artwork as a mask. Remember that you can use movie footage as well as still footage as your mask source. The effects you can achieve with this technique are endless!

4. Close the **Luma Comp** and save this project. You'll make another new composition for the upcoming exercise.

4. ————————**Soft-Edged Track Matte with a Masked Solid Layer**

This track matte stuff gets even better. You can combine the masking skills you learned in Chapter 11, "*Masks*," with what you've learned in this chapter. You'll create a soft-edged matte from a solid layer and feather its edges. Then you'll use that layer to mask another layer. It's easier than it sounds; just try it!

1. Create a new composition and name it **Soft Comp**. Drag **sky.jpg** from the **Project** window into the **Timeline**.

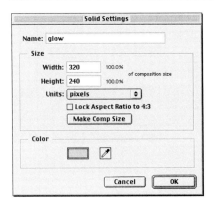

2. Create a new solid layer by choosing **File > New > Solid**. In the **Solid Settings** dialog box, name the solid layer **glow**. The color doesn't really matter, because ultimately the solid layer won't be visible. Pick a bright orange for the heck of it, to make sure you remember how to set the color of a solid layer.

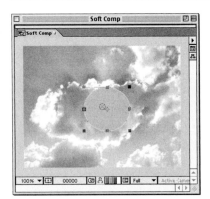

3. Using the **Oval Mask** tool, draw a circle on the solid layer. It will become masked in the shape of a circle, as you see here.

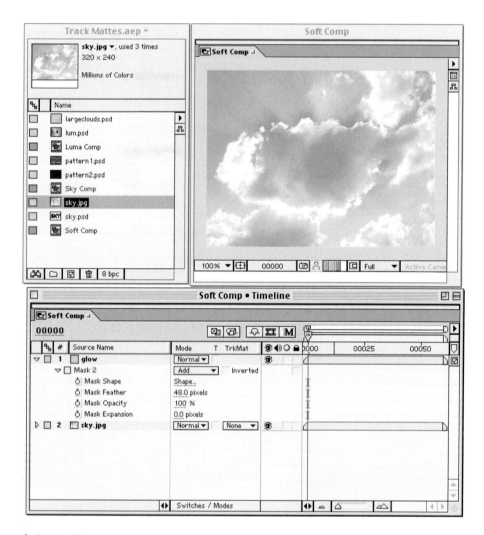

4. Press **MM** to reveal all of the Mask properties. Change the **Mask Feather** to **48** pixels, and click in an empty area of the **Timeline** to turn off the bounding box around the circle.

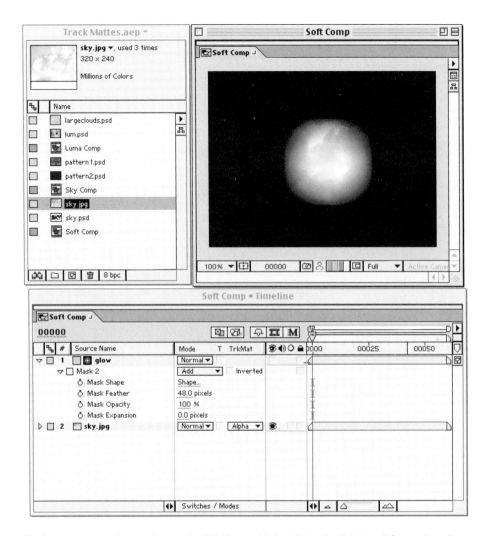

5. On the **sky.jpg** layer, change the **TrkMat** to **Alpha Matte "solid glow"** (even though you named the Solid layer "glow," After Effects remembers that its origins were as a solid layer). The **sky.jpg** layer will appear inside the glow.

When you create a mask on a solid layer, you also create an alpha channel without realizing it. In this instance, the track matte is using the alpha channel from the masked solid layer. This is a very useful technique, because it's so convenient to make masks from solid layers. You don't have to leave After Effects and go to Photoshop to make the glow artwork this way. Time to animate!

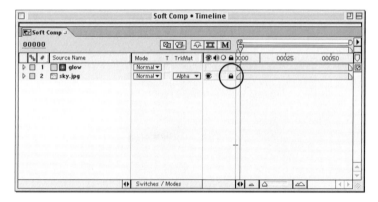

6. With **glow** selected, press **M** to hide the Mask properties. Click the **Lock** switch for **sky.jpg** so you don't accidentally move it.

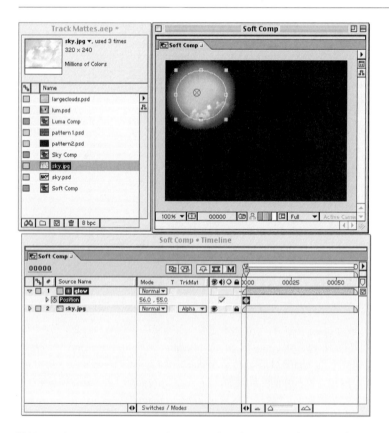

7. With **glow** selected, press **Option+P** (Mac) or **Alt+P** (Windows) to set a keyframe for the **Position** property. Drag the artwork in the **Composition** window as you see above.

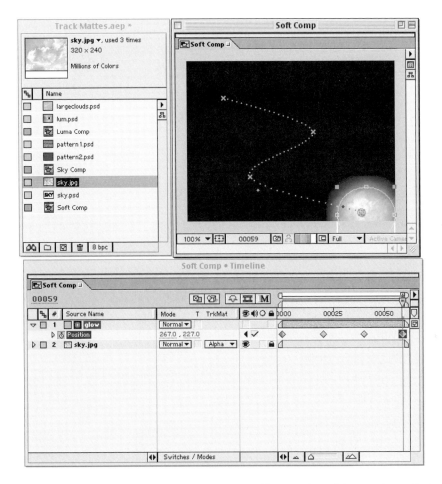

8. Move the **Time Marker** to **Frame 20**, then to **Frame 40**, and then to the **end** of your Timeline, and move your artwork accordingly to create a motion path like the one you see above. This is a good refresher for you to remember how to set multiple keyframes.

---

9. Play the animation and notice that the glow passes over the static cloud image, panning the image as it moves. Sometimes this is what you want, but sometimes you want the artwork to stay fixed inside the glow. You can do that too—we'll show you how next.

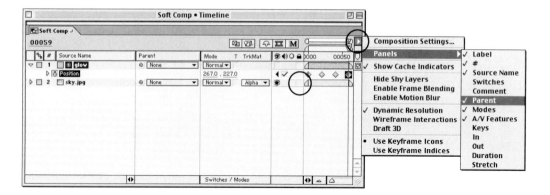

10. Unlock the **sky.jpg** layer in the **Timeline**. In the Timeline's **Options** menu, choose **Panels > Parent** to show the Parent panel.

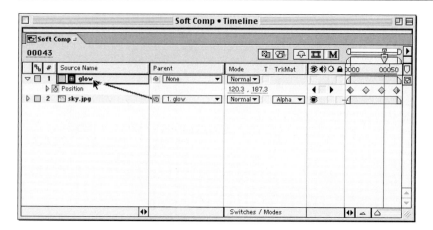

11. Move the **Time Marker** back to **Frame 1**. Point the **Parent** pick whip of the **sky.jpg** layer to the **glow** layer. Now play the animation. It's not as interesting as the previous one, but who knows? You might want to do this in an animation you'll make in the future.

12. Close this composition and save the project.

Other Masking Modes

You learned about modes in Chapter 8, "*Layers*." Modes are used to composite two or more images together to create interesting artistic effects. We've reserved the discussion of a few modes for this chapter because they deal specifically with masking. We find we use masking modes less often than track mattes, but there are times when they are useful. Although the following examples are not hands-on exercises, you have all the artwork shown here in the project you created in this chapter, and you could try them if you want to. Examples and definitions follow in this section.

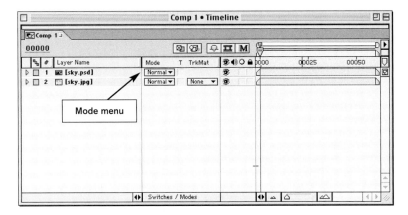

Modes are located next to the T and TrkMat columns of the Modes panel. A Mode menu appears for each layer in the Timeline, and its default is set to Normal. For the most part, modes have nothing to do with masks or alpha channels. A few modes do, however, and they are located toward the bottom of the Mode menu.

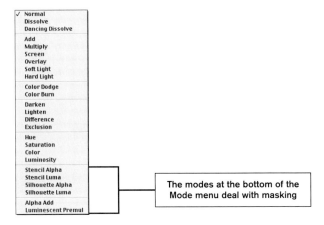

The stencil modes, in general, cut through multiple layers so that you can see all the layers beneath the layer containing the stencil. The source artwork sits on top in the stacking order of layers in the Timeline, and the mode is applied to this source.

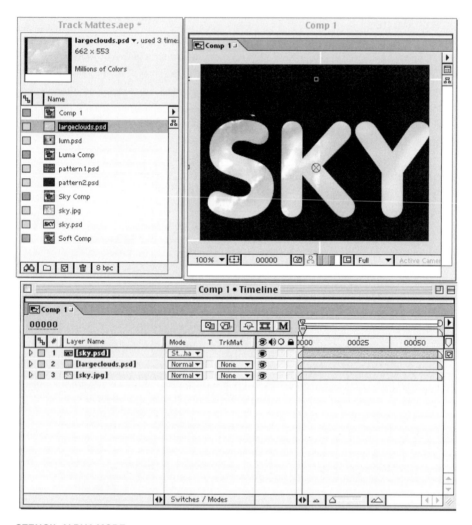

STENCIL ALPHA MODE

Stencil Alpha mode: Cuts through all the layers beneath it (the source footage must contain an alpha channel). In this case, the top layer is set to Stencil Alpha, and the bottom two layers show through.

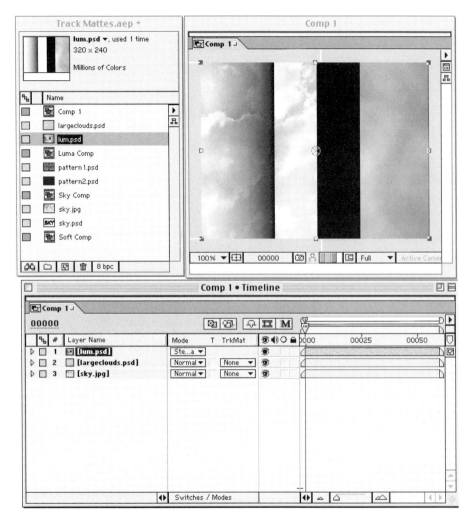

STENCIL LUMA MODE

Stencil Luma mode: Cuts through all the layers beneath it (the source footage will be treated as grayscale; if it's in color, it will be converted). In this case, the top layer is set to Stencil Luma, and the bottom two layers show through.

Silhouette mode: In general, blocks out all layers beneath it, allowing you to cut a hole through several layers at once. The source artwork sits on top in the stacking order of layers in the Timeline, and the mode is applied to this source.

SILHOUETTE ALPHA MODE

Silhouette Alpha mode: The artwork with an alpha channel punches a hole all the way through to the background color of the composition. It cuts through every layer in the composition.

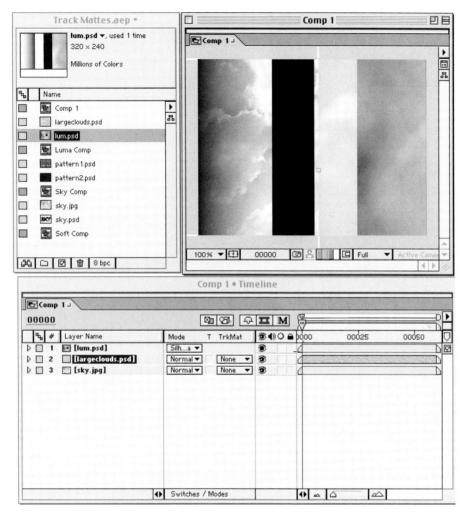

SILHOUETTE LUMA MODE

Silhouette Luma mode: The grayscale artwork (source artwork in color will be converted to grayscale) punches a hole all the way through to the background color of the composition. It cuts through every layer in the composition.

The modes **Alpha Add** and **Luminescence Premul** are described in your user manual. These modes require complicated compositions that are too detailed to stage in the context of this book. We find that only advanced users ever require these features, and they are rarely used even by them!

NOTE | The Preserve Underlying Transparency Option

There is another option in the Modes panel. The *Preserve Underlying Transparency* option is a single check box. Locate the option by finding the letter **T** at the top of the column. (Think "T" for transparency in this case).

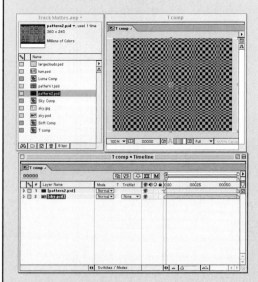 

With this check box turned on for the top layer, the alpha channel from the layer beneath is used to mask the artwork. The Preserve Underlying Transparency option works only if the artwork below the layer with the T option checked contains an alpha channel.

continues on next page

NOTE | The Preserve Underlying Transparency Option *continued*

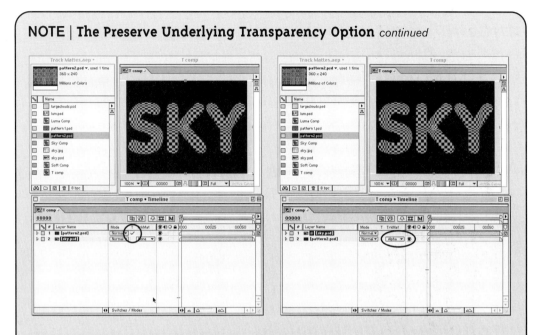

Here's a side-by-side comparison with the same artwork using two different techniques. The example on the left uses Preserve Underlying Transparency, and the example on the right uses a track matte. The results are identical, but the layer order in the Timeline is different.

To use the Preserve Underlying Transparency option, just click the check box. This option has an identical function to alpha channel–based track mattes; it just accomplishes that function differently.

We hope you enjoyed the techniques that you learned in this chapter. Feel free to experiment and try other combinations of artwork for your track mattes. We suggest that you use track mattes with QuickTime movies as source footage, or that you practice working with masked solid layers as your source for track mattes. Honestly, the possibilities are infinite. A little imagination is all you need to combine with the skills you've just learned.

See you at the next chapter, "3D Layers." Rest up, because it's a huge new area for you to learn that will open even more doors for artistic expression.

13.

3D Layers

Making 3D Layers	3D Views	Custom Camera Views
Lighting	Material Options	Adding and Animating Cameras
Animating the Point of Interest	Camera Options and Settings
Previewing 3D

chap_13

After Effects 5.0 / 5.5
H•O•T CD-ROM

3D layers are a new feature in After Effects 5.0/5.5. They are a welcome addition because they bring new levels of design capability to After Effects artists. With this capability, you can create images in After Effects that would have been impossible before.

It's safe to say that working with 3D layers will probably inspire you creatively. Seeing your images move in three-dimensional space, complete with gorgeous lighting, shadows, and camera work, is exciting for anyone working with After Effects. However, there is a lot of new territory to cover for those of you who have never worked in a 3D environment before. Getting to know your way around different views and looking at artwork from the top, left, right, bottom, and front is uncomfortable at first, because it isn't familiar. Likewise, moving artwork along a new axis and dealing with cameras and lights isn't intuitive either. Thankfully, you'll get to try everything firsthand in this chapter, which should demystify these new areas of the program.

3D in After Effects

At heart, After Effects is a program designed to combine two-dimensional images. As you've seen, you can import a variety of digital image files into After Effects. All of these image files have an **X axis** (providing the ability to move from side to side) and a **Y axis** (for the ability to move up and down). These two axes are the two dimensions of digital images.

Other programs that are entirely 3D in nature have the capability to build, animate, and render three-dimensional models. These specialized programs have a different purpose. They are designed to create three-dimensional *objects* that reside in a three-dimensional "world" inside a computer.

After Effects should not be confused with these 3D programs. Artwork in After Effects is two-dimensional and has no depth. By activating a **3D layer** in After Effects, you allow your 2D objects to reside and move in After Effects' 3D world. Basically, After Effects offers a 3D viewing and lighting environment, just like any 3D program would, in which you can move 2D objects. The real difference between After Effects and true 3D programs is the lack of a modeling application. This simply means that you can't create true 3D objects that have thickness and depth; you can create only 2D artwork and move it in a 3D space.

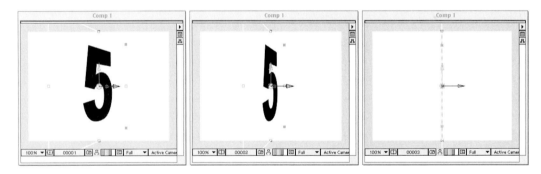

When a 2D object is turned with its side toward the viewer, it disappears completely. That's because 2D objects have no depth. The effect of moving 2D artwork in 3D space is very similar to what you could achieve with a skew tool in a 2D drawing program. The difference is that when you see the artwork in motion, the movement looks as though it is occurring in 3D space. This believable 3D motion is very hard to simulate with a simple skew tool.

What does all this mean? It means that as you design your 3D work in After Effects, you have to keep in mind that you are working with 2D objects. There's no additional thickness in a 2D object when it is displayed in perspective. However, the realistic perspective results that occur inside After Effects' 3D environment are quite astounding. As well, the three-dimensional lighting and shadows provide benefits that can be fully appreciated only when seen in action.

You can do amazing work in After Effects. By understanding the way its 3D layers work, you can create images of striking believability, imaginative stylization, and stunning beauty.

Overview of Making 3D Layers in the Timeline

Basically, all you have to do to turn a regular layer into a 3D layer is click a switch in the Timeline.

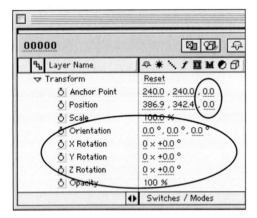

Once you've converted a layer to a 3D layer, additional Transform properties and options are shown in the Timeline:

- The Anchor Point and Position properties display a **Z-axis** option.

- The Orientation property is added.

- Rotation values are separated into X-, Y-, and Z-axis properties.

What is the **Z axis**? Just as the X axis (side to side) and Y axis (up and down) define two-dimensional space, three-dimensional space includes a Z axis. The X axis is the horizontal dimension, the Y axis is the vertical dimension, and the Z axis is the distance, or depth, dimension. With this coordinate system, you can place objects in After Effects' 3D world and use the axis values to define their exact position.

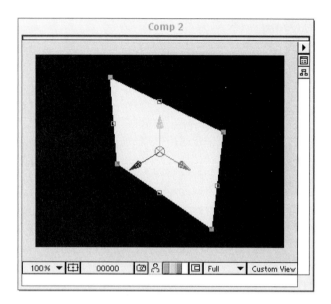

When you select a 3D layer, you'll see three arrows extending from the anchor point. Each arrow is color-coded. The **red** arrow is the **X axis**, the **green** arrow is the **Y axis**, and the **blue** arrow is the **Z axis**.

You can move an object by holding the Selection or Rotation tool over any handle. The letter X, Y, or Z will appear next to the pointer, identifying the axis and allowing you to drag the object.

In the following exercise you'll learn to turn a layer into a 3D layer. You'll also learn to use 3D Transform options.

I. ——————Making 3D Layers

In this exercise, you'll work with a prepared composition that contains two layers, converting them to 3D layers. You'll also use the Position and Rotate properties for each layer. Feel free to take your time and become comfortable with each step.

1. Copy the **chap_13** folder from the **H•O•T CD-ROM** to your hard drive.

2. Open **3D_Project.aep** from the **chap_13** folder.

3. Choose **File > Save As**, navigate to your **HOT_AE_Projects** folder, and click **Save**.

4. Double-click the **Making 3D Layers** composition to open it. This composition has two simple layers: an Illustrator file called **monkey1.ai** and a solid layer named **Gray Solid**.

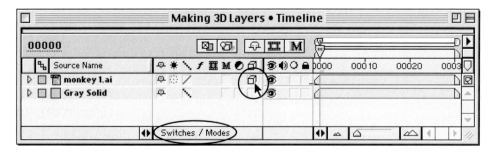

5. In the **Timeline** window, locate the **3D cube** icon in the Switches panel. This is the **3D Layers** switch. Click this switch for the **monkey1.ai** layer. **Note:** If this panel is still showing Track Matte information, it is still set to the Modes panel from the last chapter. Click Switches/Modes to toggle it back to the Switches panel.

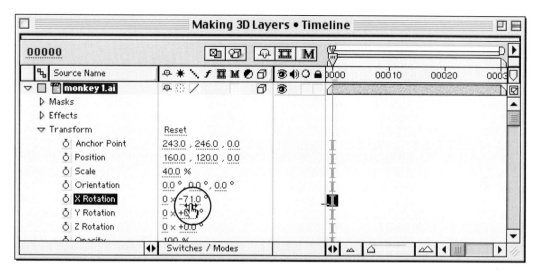

6. Click the **twirly** for the **monkey1.ai** layer to display the properties. Display the **Transform** properties, if they aren't already showing. Place your cursor over the **X Rotation** degrees value, and drag back and forth to see the effect.

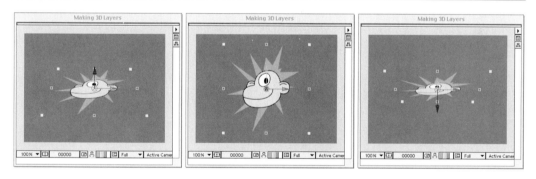

7. Notice that the layer rotates around the X axis. When you are done, return the **X Rotation** value to **0** degrees.

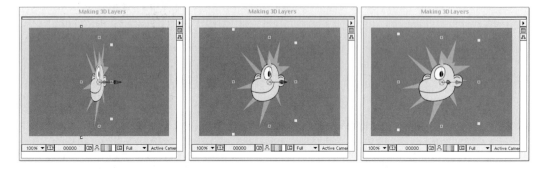

8. Place your cursor over the **Y Rotation** degrees value, and drag back and forth to see the 3D rotation around the Y axis. Return the **Y Rotation** value back to **0** degrees when you are done.

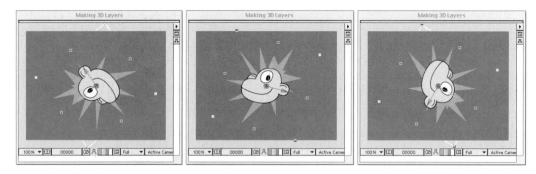

9. Now drag the **Z Rotation** degrees value and observe the image rotate around the Z axis. When you are done, return the **Z Rotation** value to **0** degrees.

Next you'll set keyframes to animate the 3D layer.

NOTE | The Orientation Property

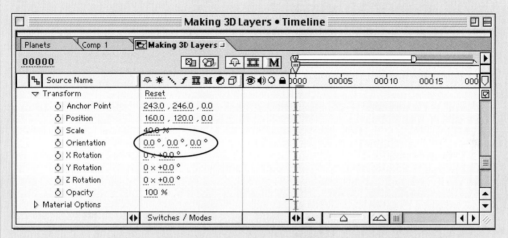

There is another property in the Transform group called **Orientation** that works to rotate a 3D layer. However, it can get confusing if you start using the Orientation property in conjunction with the X Rotation, Y Rotation, and Z Rotation properties to rotate layers.

For this reason, we recommend using the X Rotation, Y Rotation, and Z Rotation properties for animating 3D rotation while learning After Effects. That way, you'll develop a consistent approach to working in 3D.

Later, after you've had a fair amount of experience with 3D, use the Orientation property when you need to set an object in 3D space but do not need to use keyframe animation. The Orientation property moves your object along the shortest rotational path in 3D space. For this reason, Orientation is best used to set a position and leave it, rather than for keyframe animation. If you attempt to use keyframe animation with Orientation, the layer may move in ways you do not intend.

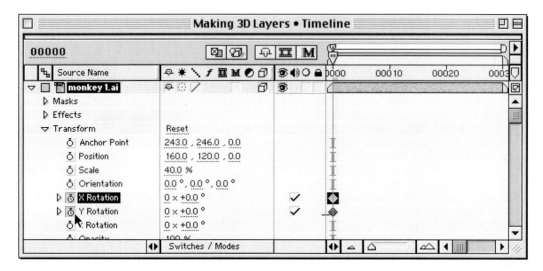

10. Click the **Stopwatch** for the **X Rotation** and **Y Rotation** properties to set keyframes on **Frame 0**. Accept the default value of **0** for both properties.

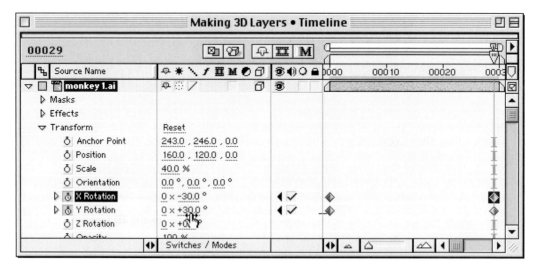

11. Move the **Time Marker** to **Frame 29**. Set the **X Rotation** value to **−30** degrees, and set the **Y Rotation** value to **30** degrees.

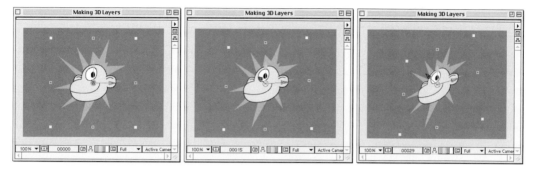

12. Scrub the **Time Marker** or click **RAM Preview** to view your 3D layer in action.

In the following steps, you'll turn the Gray Solid layer into a 3D layer and set property options for it.

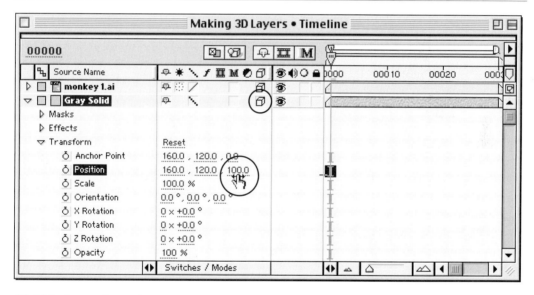

13. Hide the **monkey1.ai** properties by clicking the **monkey1.ai** twirly. Click the **3D Layers** switch for the **Gray Solid** layer.

Display the properties for the **Gray Solid** layer and then display its **Transform** properties by clicking those twirlies. Set the **Position Z-axis** value to **100**. **Note:** 2D layers do not have a Z-axis Position property. This extra field appears only when you set the 3D Layers switch for a layer.

In the Composition window, the Gray Solid layer will get smaller because it is moving away from the current 3D view. In After Effects you view 3D layers from several angles. In the following steps you'll switch the 3D view to see your layers from another viewpoint.

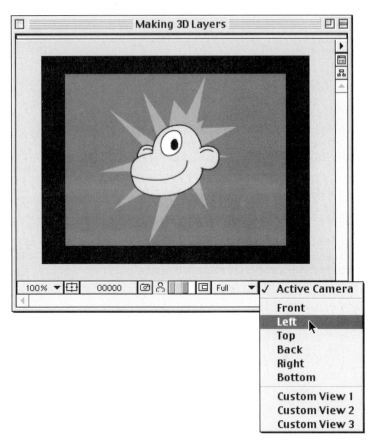

14. Make sure the **Time Marker** is set to **Frame 0**. In the **Composition** window, click on the **3D View** pop-up menu and select the **Left** view.

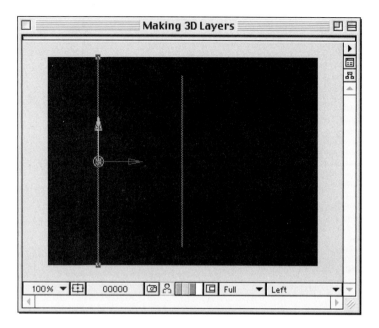

15. Observe the **Left** view. The **Gray Solid** layer is selected and is positioned 100 pixels along the **Z** axis behind the **monkey.ai** layer. Since the monkey.ai and Gray Solid layers are 2D objects without depth, you can see only a line representing each object's position. It may help you to click on each of the two lines to look at the 3D layer handles. The red X-axis handle is pointing directly toward you, the green Y-axis is pointing straight up, and the blue Z-axis is pointing to the right, toward the normal view (the Active Camera).

You will learn all about 3D views in the next section. Here we wanted to give you a preview of seeing your 3D layers from the left side to help you visualize the layers in depth during this exercise.

16. Select the **Active Camera** view from the **3D View** pop-up menu in the **Composition** window to return to the default view. This is the most important view because it is what After Effects will render if you preview or make a movie.

In a future exercise, you'll learn that you can have more than one camera! To begin, however, it's important to understand the principle of an invisible camera through which you are viewing your scene.

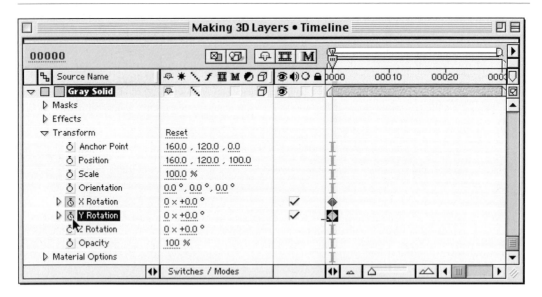

17. In the **Timeline** window, click the **Stopwatch** for the **X Rotation** and **Y Rotation** properties to set keyframes for **Frame 0** of the **Gray Solid** layer. Accept the default value of **0** for both properties.

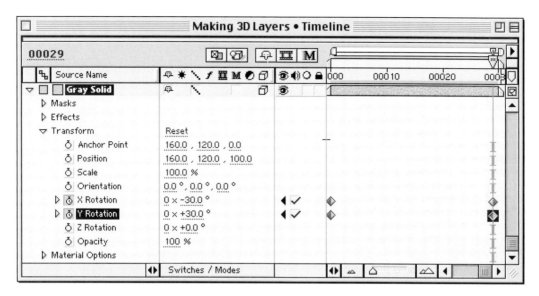

18. Move the **Time Marker** to **Frame 29**. Set the **X Rotation** value to **−30** degrees, and set the **Y Rotation** value to **30** degrees.

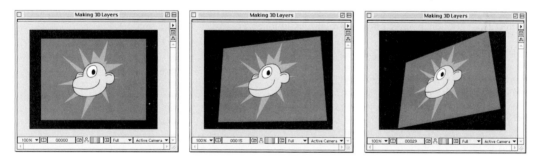

19. Click **RAM Preview** in the **Time Controls** palette to view your 3D animation. Although this result may look just like a simple skew effect to you, After Effects is moving this flat artwork in true 3D space. More-realistic 3D results come later in this chapter, when you learn to animate the lighting and camera.

20. Save your project and leave it open for the next exercise.

Overview of 3D Views

The previous exercise gave you a brief introduction to **3D views**. These views allow you to see 3D layers from different angles in your Composition window. When you first start working with 3D layers, it can be a little disorienting to see any 3D view other than the default view, which is called Active Camera view. With a little experience, though, you'll quickly get comfortable with using different 3D views.

Active Camera is the view that will be rendered when you preview or create a final movie; this is the view that you should use to evaluate your work. The other 3D views are available to aid you in positioning your layers accurately in 3D space.

The Front, Left, Top, Back, Right, and Bottom views are **orthogonal views**. An orthogonal view shows the position of your layers but does not show perspective. This can take some getting used to. Again, with a little experience you'll feel comfortable with these views.

There are three custom views that show your layers in perspective. These views look more natural because they use perspective. They are also quite useful because you can adjust each view position to your liking.

You'll find yourself using all the views, however, because working in 3D space requires that you view objects from many positions while creating your design. You'll also see that orthogonal views, without perspective, are useful because they give you a good idea of object relationships, proportions, and positions. Perspective changes the size of objects, which can be a hindrance at times. For these reasons, the orthogonal views are valuable.

In the following exercise you'll learn to use each view and to move layers in space using the various 3D views. As you'll soon see, using 3D views is the best way to position objects accurately in your 3D world.

2. _____Using 3D Views

In this exercise you'll check out all of the 3D views. The purpose of doing so is to become familiar with each view and how it shows object relationships in the Composition window. By the end of this exercise, you'll be able to relate your objects' positions to each view and understand the view options.

The three custom views can be positioned anywhere you like. You'll learn to create your own custom views at the end of the exercise.

You'll also learn to move and position layers in space using 3D views. This is one of the main tasks when working in 3D. For most people who are new to 3D, positioning objects in 3D space is one of the hardest concepts to get comfortable with.

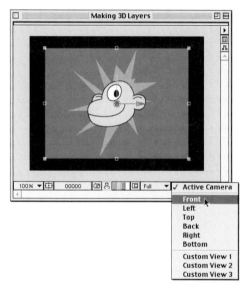
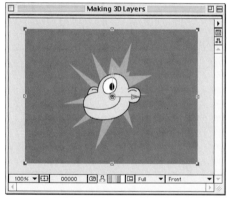

Active Camera view   *Front view*

1. The **Making 3D Layers** composition should still be open. If not, open that file now. Make sure the **Time Marker** is set to **Frame 0** and the **Gray Solid** layer is selected. Select the **Front** view from the **3D View** pop-up menu in the **Composition** window. Compare this view to the Active Camera view.

In Active Camera view, the Gray Solid layer looks smaller than it does in the Front view. That's because there is no perspective in the Front view. When the perspective is taken away, the width (the X axis) and height (the Y axis) are displayed at their full values.

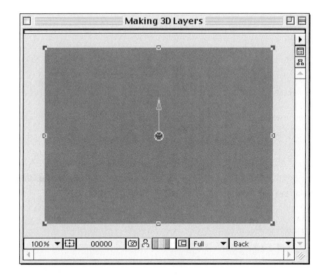

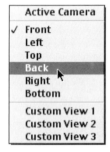

2. Now select the **Back** view from the **3D View** menu. You are looking at the back of the Gray Solid layer, so you can't see the monkey.ai layer. Again, the width and the height of the Gray Solid layer are displayed without perspective.

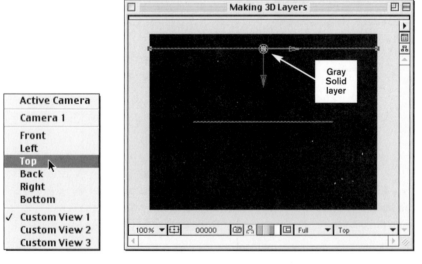

3. Select the **Top** view. You are looking down on the monkey.ai and Gray Solid layer. Note that the Gray Solid layer is selected, so its axis handles are visible. Those handles appear only on layers that are selected.

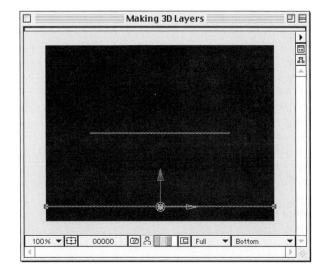

4. Select the **Bottom** view. Now you are looking up at the two layers. The Gray Solid layer is still selected, so its axis handles are visible.

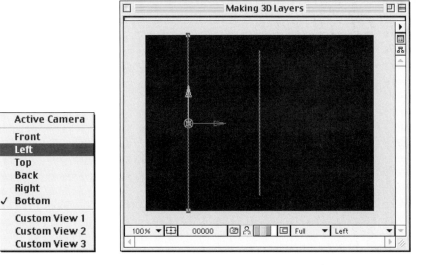

5. Select the **Left** view. You will see the side of the graphics again. The Gray Solid layer is still selected, so its axis handles are visible.

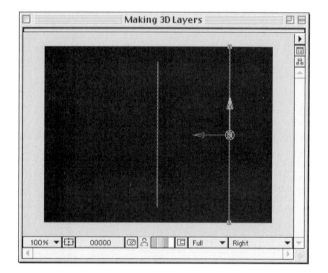

6. Select the **Right** view. This is another side view, from the right side. The Gray Solid layer is still selected, so its axis handles are visible.

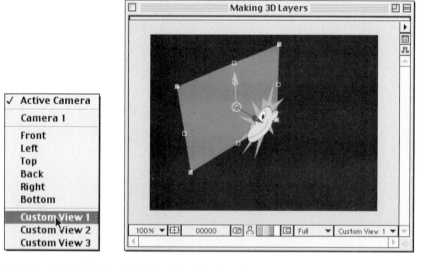

7. Select **Custom View 1**. Notice that this view has perspective. This is After Effects' default Custom View 1. You will learn to create your own custom views soon.

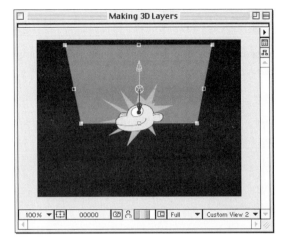

8. Select **Custom View 2**. The default view looks down from the center of the 3D world.

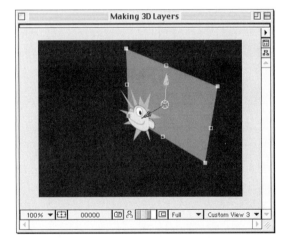

9. Select **Custom View 3**. The default viewpoint is located above and to the right of center.

You've looked through all the possible views for this composition now. These views are available to compositions that contain 3D objects. They make sense to use only when viewing 3D layers, as they are very helpful when you're positioning your objects in 3D space.

10. Save your project. Leave the **Making 3D Layers** composition open for the next exercise.

At this point you should be able to make some sense out of each view. If you are having trouble with this, it's okay. Understanding the 3D views is the hardest part of learning 3D in After Effects. With repetition you'll be able to understand where you are in the 3D world using each view.

3. _____Changing Custom Camera Views

In the previous exercise, you became familiar with views and learned how they can help you see the 3D environment. You can easily change any of the custom camera views while you are working. This exercise will show you how.

1. Select **Custom View 1** from the **3D Views** menu.

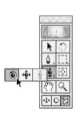  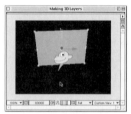 

2. In the **Toolbox**, select the **Camera Orbit** tool. In the **Composition** window, drag the cursor across the window to orbit your view, as you see above. **Note:** This tool is simply changing the view, not moving the artwork!

3. Select the **Track XY Camera** tool to change your view in the X axis or the Y axis. As before, this tool is simply changing the view. The artwork remains in the same position.

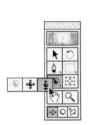

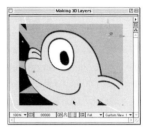

4. Select the **Track Z Camera** tool from the Toolbox and experiment with changing your view in the Z axis, as you see above. The Z axis controls how close or far the camera view is from your artwork. Once again, note that this tool changes only the view of the artwork, not its position.

That's all there is to it. If you toggle between Custom View 2 and Custom View 1, you'll see that Custom View 1 is just where you left it. It will be set to the last view you created until you change it again.

5. To reset the view to the default, choose **View > Reset 3D View**. **Note:** Any change you make to a custom view is permanent until you change it again. Resetting the view will set it back to the default, unless you change it again.

6. Save the project and close this composition. You won't be using it again in this chapter.

Multiple Views in After Effects 5.5

New to After Effects 5.5 is the ability to have multiple views. This feature allows you to have more than one Composition window open, and each window can have its own view settings.

To add a new view, choose View > New View. Alternatively, press Option+Shift+N (Mac) or Alt+Shift+N (Windows).

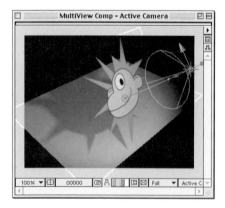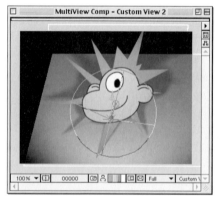

Once you create another view, you can set the 3D view and the magnification of the new window. Shown above are Active Camera and Custom View 2. This Composition already has a light applied to it. Doesn't it look cool? You'll learn to do this very soon!

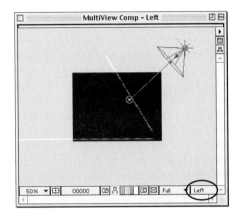

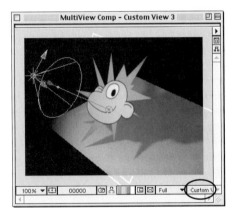

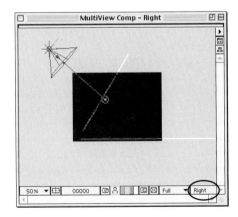

Using this technique in After Effects 5.5, you can add as many different views as you wish. In After Effects 5.0, you have only Custom View 1, 2, and 3.

4.————————Lighting in 3D

So far, everything you've looked at has been very flat. You might still be wondering why 3D is such an exciting feature, if you can achieve a lot of the same effects more easily using a simple skew tool in an illustration program. Adding lights is when working in 3D starts to get magical.

In After Effects, a light is a special type of layer. When you add a light, it shows up in the Timeline window, just as any other layer does. However, lights have their own set of properties, all of which can be keyframed for animation, of course!

After Effects offers several types of lights, but in general you'll probably use the Spot type most often. It provides many options and the greatest range of control. In the following exercise you'll learn how to add lights, adjust the options, and position lights within your compositions.

This is probably one of the most fun exercises in the book. Lighting is a powerful tool that enables you to immediately see dramatic results. It's truly cool!

> **1.** In the **Project** window, double-click on the **3D Lighting** composition to open it. You'll see that it already contains three layers, two of which have 3D layers turned on. If you press the **spacebar** or click the **Ram Preview** button in the **Time Controls** palette, you'll see that the layer **5** has already been animated in 3D. Press the **U** shortcut key to see which properties have been animated for this layer. You'll see that keyframes have been set for the Y rotation.
>
> *You should know how to do this kind of animation based on the first exercise of the book. If you want to practice, turn the 3D Layers switch off in the Timeline, then turn it back on to reprogram this animation on your own! Since this exercise is focused on lighting, we've chosen to do the animation work for you, but don't let that stop you from gaining more practice!*
>
> **2.** Choose **Layer > New > Light**.

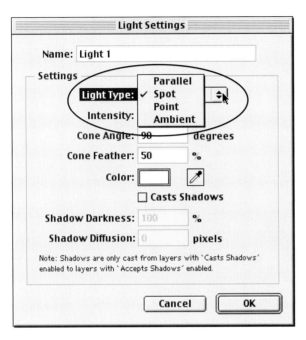

3. In the **Light Settings** dialog box, click the double arrow next to **Light Type** to see the pop-up menu. Notice that there are four types of lights.

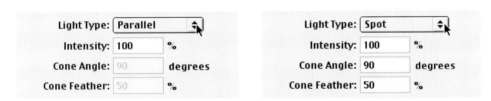

4. Select each type from the menu and observe that only the Spot type offers the Cone Angle and Cone Feather options.

Parallel light is directional, unconstrained light from an infinitely distant source. This type is best used when you want light to fall evenly on all objects and you want the light to come from a specific direction.

Spot light is constrained by a cone. The Spot type is the most useful because you can control all aspects of the light.

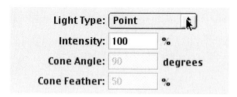 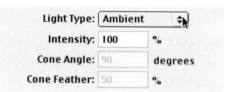

Point light is unconstrained, omnidirectional light. This type is best when you need something like a bare light bulb that lights up whatever is nearby.

Ambient light has no source and casts no shadows. It contributes to the overall brightness of your composition. It is best used as a secondary light to bring up the general lighting level for all objects. Use it sparingly, if at all.

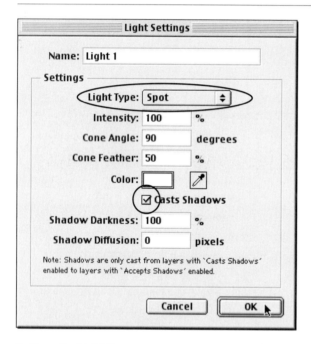

5. From the **Light Type** pop-up menu, select the **Spot** light option. Make sure the **Casts Shadows** option is checked. Click **OK**.

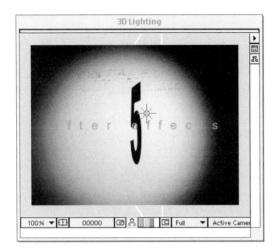

Notice that the light has taken effect but that no shadow is cast on the background. You'll fix this next.

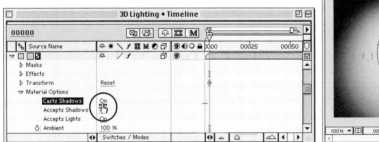

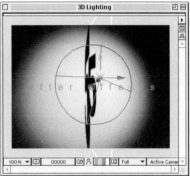

6. In the **Timeline** window, click the twirly to display the properties for the **5** layer, and then click the twirly to display the **Material Options** properties. Click the **Casts Shadows** property to select the **On** value. In the **Composition** window, notice that the 5 layer now casts a shadow. The shadow is quite hard-edged and not very attractive yet. You'll fix this soon.

Note: The layer named after effects *hasn't been turned into a 3D layer, so it does not cast any shadows. Only 3D layers cast shadows in After Effects. You can control whether some layers are 3D and some are not by clicking the 3D Layers switch for each layer, as you did in Exercise 1. For this exercise, leave the* after effects *layer alone and do not convert it to 3D.*

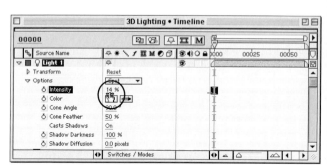

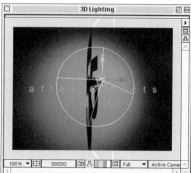

7. In the Timeline window, click the twirly to display the **Light 1** layer properties, and then click the twirly to display the **Options** properties. Drag across the **Intensity** value to see the effect of changing the intensity. Intensity is how bright you want the light to be. When you're done, set the **Intensity** value back to **100%**.

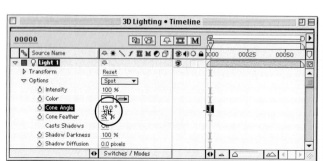

8. Drag across the **Cone Angle** value to see the effect of changing it. Observe that the cone angle constrains the light in degrees. When you're done, return the **Cone Angle** value to **90%**.

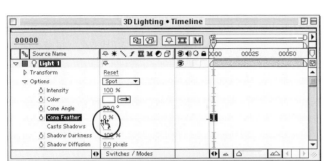

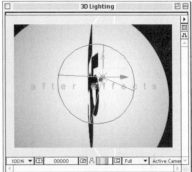

9. Drag the **Cone Feather** value and observe how the edge of the light gets softer or harder. When you're done, return the **Cone Feather** value to **50%**.

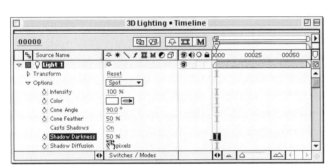

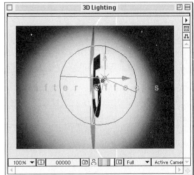

10. Set the **Shadow Darkness** value to **50%**. Observe the results in the **Composition** window.

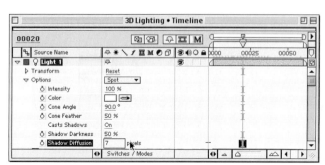

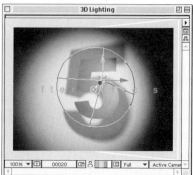

11. Move the **Time Marker** to **Frame 20** to see the effect that the lighting has on the 5 as it animates. Set the **Shadow Diffusion** property to **7** pixels. Shadow diffusion softens the edges of the shadow. Note that you haven't set any keyframes, meaning that you're making a global change to the Shadow Diffusion over the entire composition. Leave the Time Marker at Frame 20 to see the position of the 5 layer at this point in its animation. Because it is turned toward the camera view, you can see the lighting changes better.

In the following steps you will learn to position the light using the axis arrow handles.

12. Leaving the Time Marker at Frame 20, drag the red **X-axis** handle to the far left. Locate the **Point of Interest** control. (It's the round icon with the cross mark that extends from the center of the light.) Drag this control to fully illuminate the **5**.

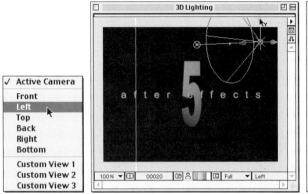

13. Select the **Left** view from the **3D View** pop-up menu in the **Composition** window. Drag the **green Y-axis** handle up to the top. Drag the **Point of Interest** control to fully illuminate the 5.

The text in the after effects *layer does not change in this view because it is a 2D layer. Only 3D layers are affected by changing views.*

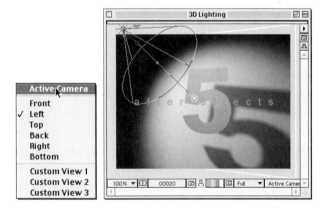

14. Select the **Active Camera** view from the **3D View** menu. This takes you back to the view that you'll see when previewing or rendering a final movie. Click **RAM Preview** in the **Time Controls** palette to play the animation.

Lights can be colors other than white. In the following steps you'll change the color of Light 1 to red. Then you'll add a green light and a blue light to your composition.

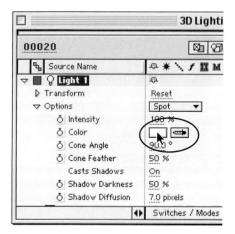

15. In the **Timeline** window, click the **Light 1** layer's **Color selector** block. Change the color to **red**.

You can have more than one light in a composition. Using multiple lights can create interesting shadows and colored effects. Next you'll learn to add extra lights.

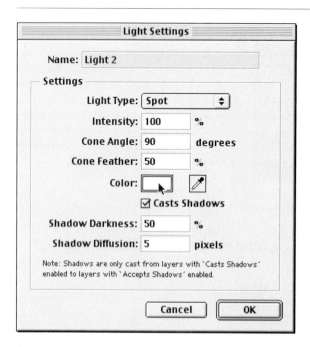

16. Choose **Layer > New > Light**. In the **Light Settings** dialog box, click the **Color selector** block. Change the color to **green**. Back in the **Light Settings** dialog box, accept the current settings by clicking **OK**.

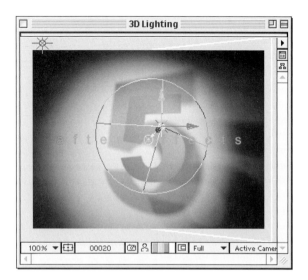

Observe the new two-color light. Its position is fine, so you don't need to adjust it.

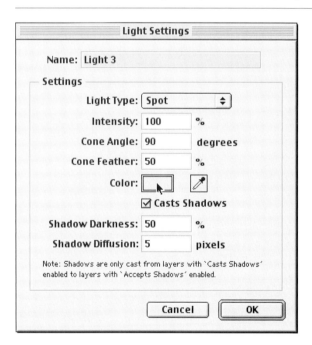

17. Select **Layer > New > Light**. In the **Light Settings** dialog box, click the **Color selector** block. Change the color to **blue**. Back in the **Light Settings** dialog box, accept the current settings by clicking **OK**.

 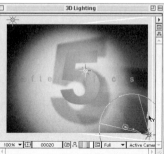 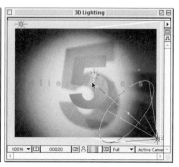

18. Drag the **red X-axis** handle to the far right. Drag the **green Y-axis** handle to the bottom. Drag the **Point of Interest** control to the center of the **5**.

---

19. Click **RAM Preview** in the **Timeline Controls** palette to view your animation. **Note:** This takes a long time to display.

In this exercise, you merely set lights in a single position and did not set keyframes for them. Notice, however, that every light has properties and every property has a Stopwatch icon. Any time you see that Stopwatch icon, it means that a property can be animated! This exercise was just a starting point that helped you begin to learn about lights. Take some time on your own to set up some lighting animation to better understand the feature.

---

20. Save your project, and leave the **3D Lighting** composition open for the next exercise.

NOTE | Using the Intensity Property with Lights

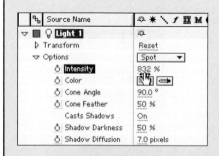 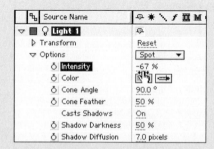

Intensity is a rather unique property. Most properties based on percentages can be adjusted from 0% to 100%. However, you can adjust the Intensity property to values higher than 100%. You can also enter negative values, which will actually take light out of your scene, something like a black hole. Used judiciously, both high values and negative values can be beneficial ways of controlling light in your scene.

5. _____Setting Material Options

Once you convert a layer into a 3D layer, it will have an extra set of properties called **Material Options**. These options are important only if a light has been added to a composition. You got a very brief preview of a Material Options property in the previous exercise when you enabled the **5** layer to cast shadows.

The Material Options properties offer a way to accurately control the effect of lights and shadows on each layer of your composition. You can have a layer that doesn't reflect a certain type of light and another layer that reflects the light in its own unique way. In this exercise you'll learn how to use each of the Material Options properties and how to control them for maximum effect.

1. Make sure your **Time Marker** is still set to **Frame 20**, in order to see the number 5 in a flat position. Select the **5** layer. Press **AA** on your keyboard to display the **Material Options** properties. Click the **Casts Shadows** option once to turn it **Off** and then again to turn it back to **On**. As you saw in the previous exercise, this option controls whether the layer will cast shadows.

2. Select the **Background** layer. Press **AA** on your keyboard to display the **Material Options** properties for the layer. Click the **Accepts Shadows** option **Off** and then back to **On**. Just as we promised, this option controls whether the layer displays any shadows.

3. On the **Background** layer, click the **Accepts Light** property **Off**, and then click it back **On**. The lights are no longer reflected, but the shadows from the lights are still displayed!

When it is Off, this option returns to the normal viewing status, which is fully lit.

In the following steps you will learn how to use the Ambient option. In order to see the Ambient option, you must have an ambient light in your composition.

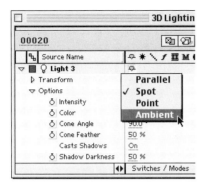

4. Click the twirlies next to display the **Options** properties for the **Light 3** layer. Set **Light 3** to the **Ambient** type.

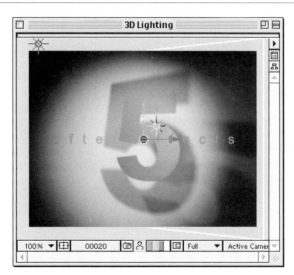

5. On the **Background** layer, set the **Ambient** property to **0%**, then to **50%**, and finally back to **100%**. Notice that the 5 layer is consistently lit by the blue ambient light while you control the ambient level for the Background layer.

6. In the **Light 3** layer, set **Light 3** back to the **Spot** type.

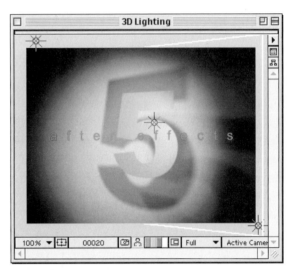

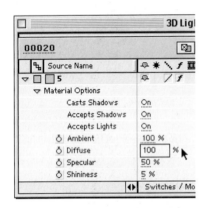

7. Select the **5** layer. Set the **Diffuse** property to **0%**, then to **100%**, and finally back to **50%**.

Diffuse light is omnidirectional, meaning that it is reflected equally in all directions. This is valuable if you are moving a camera through your 3D world and you want an object to reflect light consistently from any angle. Higher values would work better in such a case. Otherwise, the default 50% is a good setting for most uses.

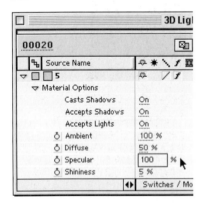

8. In the **5** layer, set the **Specular** property to **100%**. Click **RAM Preview** to see the effect of this property.

 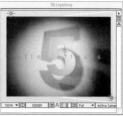  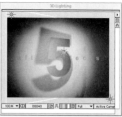

The Specular property makes the layer act like a mirror surface. The light is reflected directionally. When it is set to 100%, the mirror effect is fully reflective. When it is set to 0%, the layer is not reflective at all. Most objects look best with some mirror reflection. The default 50% value is a good place to start. If you want an object to "glint" when it reflects light, set the value higher. If you want more of a matte finish, set it lower.

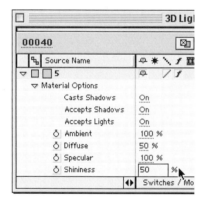

9. Set the **Shininess** property to **0%**, then to **100%**, and finally to **50%**. Scrub the **Time Marker** to see the results of each setting.

This option works only with the Specular property. It sets the size of the specular reflection. When you observe the results of each setting, notice the reflection of the red, green, and blue lights in the number 5. You should be able to see distinct points of red, green, and blue light at 100%. At 0%, the red, green and blue specular reflections are quite broad and blend together. This is because the size of the specular reflection is actually smaller at 100%. At 0%, the size of the specular reflection is quite large. In real life, a material appears shinier when the specular highlights are small, sharp, and distinct. That's why the higher values appear shinier.

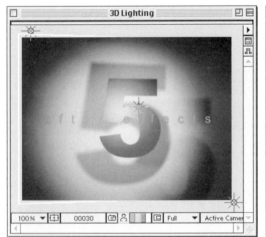

10. Click **Ram Preview** to play your finished animation.

11. Save your project, and then close the **3D Lighting** composition. Leave your project open for the next exercise.

6. _____Adding and Animating a Camera

So far in this chapter, you have been working with a camera view that was set up by After Effects, called Active Camera view. All compositions that contain 3D layers employ a single, default Active Camera view. Once you add 3D layers to your composition, this Active Camera view appears and displays 3D perspective on 2D objects, including the ability to control lights and cast shadows.

You probably didn't realize that it is possible to add a new camera to your composition. This may sound odd at first. Why would you want or need to have more than one camera?

The most common reason to add a camera is the fact that the default camera cannot be animated. This means that you *could* move the artwork or lights in 3D, but you *could not* animate the point of view of those objects with the default camera. When you add a new camera layer manually, it contains properties that can be keyframed. Setting keyframes for the camera layer makes it possible to create animations with camera views, not just by moving artwork and lights.

In the following exercise, you'll learn to add a camera, position it in your 3D world, set keyframes on its position, and animate it through your 3D world.

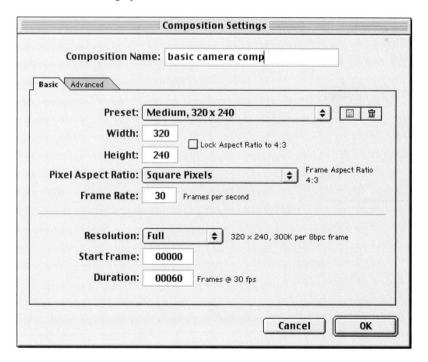

1. In the **Project** window, create a new composition. Name the composition **basic camera comp**, and use the settings that you see above.

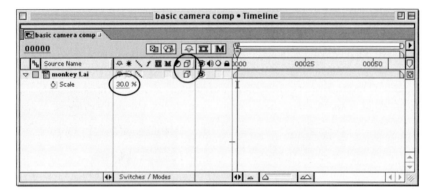

2. Add the artwork **monkey1.ai** from the Footage folder located in your Project window to the **Timeline**. Change the **Scale** property to **30%**, and click the **3D Layers** switch for the layer to set it to 3D.

3. Choose **Layer > New > Camera**. This opens the Camera Settings dialog box.

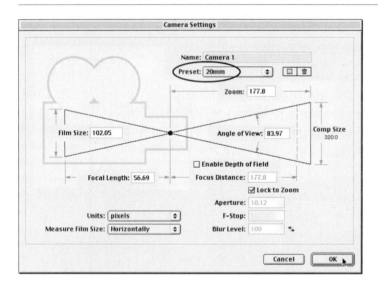

4. In the **Camera Settings** dialog box, set the **Preset** option to **20mm** and click **OK**.

The Camera Settings dialog box might seem very intimidating. It's different from most dialog boxes because of the picture and all the new terminology. A chart describing the options in this dialog box follows at the end of this exercise. The 20mm lens preset that you chose provides a very wide-angle lens view, which is going to look like a fish-eye lens, if you know what that is. Basically, setting the lens to a lower number will produce a more dramatic perspective that will be more obvious when you get close to objects. If you are not familiar with photography or cameras, that's okay. If you are, you will probably marvel at these settings, which emulate those of conventional movie cameras.

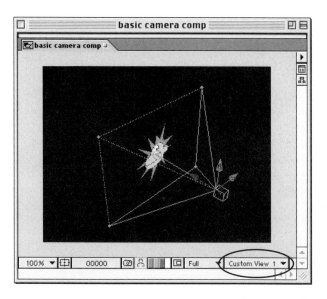

5. Select **Custom View 1** from the **3D View** menu in the **Composition** window. This view allows you to see the camera you just added. **Note:** in After Effects 5.0 the camera layer must be selected in the TImeline window in order to see the new camera. You cannot see the outline of the camera if you are in Active Camera view. That is why we suggested that you change the view to Custom View 1.

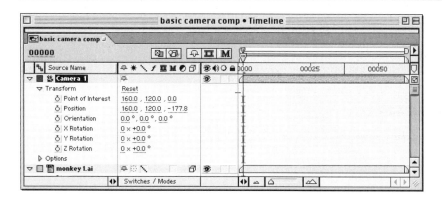

6. Click the twirly for the **Camera 1** layer, then click the twirly for **Transform** to see the camera properties. This exercise focuses on ways to move the camera while getting feedback from the view in the Composition window and the property values in the Timeline.

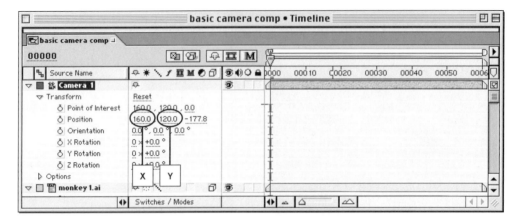

7. In the **Timeline** window, move the **Position X-axis** value back and forth and notice that the camera appears to pivot and rock from side to side in the Composition window. Move the **Position Y-axis** value back and forth and notice that the camera appears to pivot and rock up and down. It's pivoting on the point of interest, which has been set by default on the center of the Composition window.

Any time you add a new camera to a 3D composition, the new camera will place its point of interest in the center of the screen, just as it has done here. You had a little experience with the Point of Interest setting when you worked with lighting earlier. This setting tells a camera or a light where to point itself.

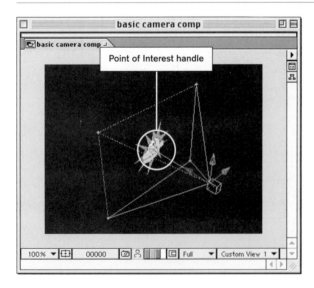

The point of interest is the origin point from which all X, Y, and Z values are based. It is what causes the camera to pivot.

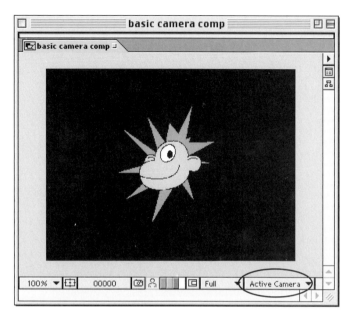

8. Change from **Custom View 1** to **Active Camera** view and move the **X** and **Y** values again to see how the pivot effect looks from this view. You won't see the outline of the camera any longer, because After Effects doesn't show you the camera in Active Camera view. What you will see, which is almost more important, is how this movement will appear in the final rendering or preview of this composition.

The custom view lets you see the camera, while Active Camera view shows you what the camera is seeing. It's extremely important to be aware of this distinction so that you can not only position the camera properly but also accurately gauge what the camera is going to see. For this reason, you will change views often when staging camera animations.

NOTE | Active Camera vs. New Cameras

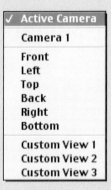

In this exercise, you have added a new camera, called Camera 1. When you choose Active Camera view you are seeing what Camera 1 sees. If you added more than one camera to this composition, Active Camera view would show the results of whatever camera was selected in the Timeline. Because you have only one camera in this Timeline, whenever you choose Active Camera view you see the point of view of Camera 1.

9. Make sure that you are in **Active Camera** view and that the **Time Marker** is set to **Frame 0**. Set the **Stopwatch** for the **Position** property. Move the **X** position to **0.0**, and move the **Y** position to **277.0** for the **Camera 1** layer. Lock the **monkey.ai** layer so you don't accidentally move it.

10. Move the **Time Marker** to **Frame 59**. Change the **X** position to **272.0** and the **Y** position to **0.0**. Preview the animation by pressing the **spacebar** or clicking **Ram Preview**.

11. Save the project and close this composition. You won't be using it again in this chapter.

You could have made the animation you just created by using a camera or by moving the object. This exercise was not intended to show you how to create an interesting animation but instead was geared to point out some issues of moving the camera. In particular, you should now be aware of the impact that the Point of Interest, Active Camera view, and Position settings have on camera animations. The next exercise kicks your awareness of moving and animating cameras up another notch.

7. ——————Animating the Point of Interest

The last exercise contained only a single 3D object. However, you would rarely create a camera animation to view a single object. Camera animations are much better suited for flying by multiple 3D objects, as the camera creates a sense of space and depth that can't be achieved simply by moving the objects themselves. This exercise builds on the previous one, adding complexity as it deals with handling multiple objects and animating the point of interest. The first part of the exercise shows you how to set up a composition that contains multiple objects set at different depths along the Z axis of the 3D environment. The second part deals with getting your camera to fly by the objects along a path that you control.

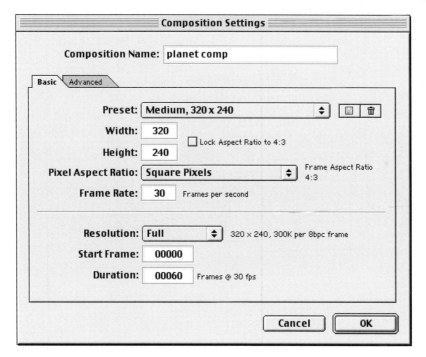

1. Create a new composition and name it **planet comp**. Use the settings that you see here.

2. Import **redplanet.psd**, **cyanplanet.psd**, **blueplanet.psd**, and **yellowplanet.psd** into the **Project** window from the **chap_13** folder. Choose to **Merge Layers** when prompted.

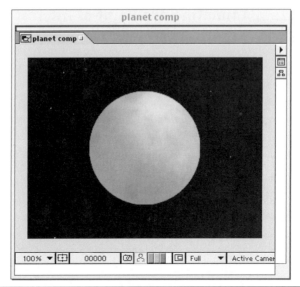

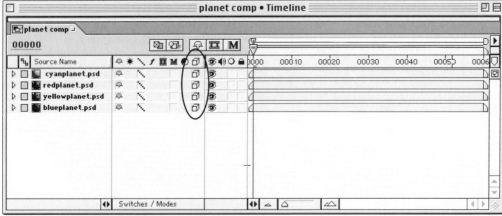

3. Drag **redplanet.psd**, **cyanplanet.psd**, **blueplanet.psd**, and **yellowplanet.psd** from the **Project** window into the **Timeline**, and arrange them in the order you see here. When you drag these images into the Timeline, each image is automatically centered in the Composition window. It will look as though only one image is in the Composition window, because all the planets are the same size and they are stacked right on top of one another, obscuring all layers but the top one. You'll soon fix this by moving them in 3D space. Click the **3D Layers** switch for each layer to turn it into a 3D object.

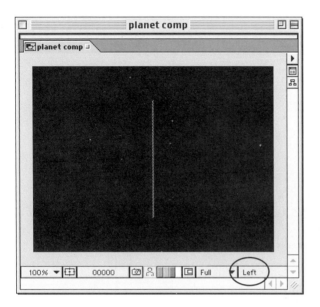

4. Change the view from **Active Camera** to **Left**. This shows the artwork from the left side. Again, this shows the four layers stacked right on top of one another, which causes them to look like a single line.

You'll be moving the layers next to position them farther apart on the Z axis. The Z axis represents depth. By moving the objects on their Z axis, you will be spreading them apart in 3D space, as you might see planets in a telescope, or better yet from a spaceship!

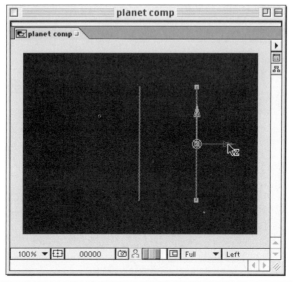

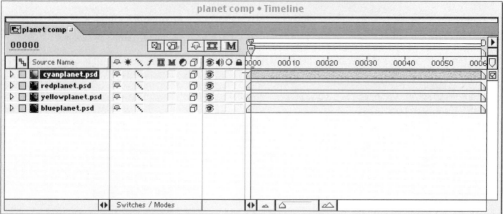

5. Select **cyanplanet.psd** in the **Timeline**. You'll see the layer's axis handles appear in the Composition window. Click the **blue handle** (your cursor arrow will show a small **z**, indicating that this is the Z axis), and drag the artwork to the right in the **Composition** window. Your screen should look like the one above.

Note: Selecting the image in the Timeline first causes its selection handles to appear, making it easier to isolate in the composition. This is a great technique for positioning artwork in 3D space, since by default all artwork is on the same Z axis until you move it. You will often encounter overlapping artwork, and this technique helps you isolate it in order to move it.

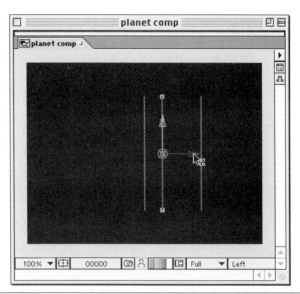

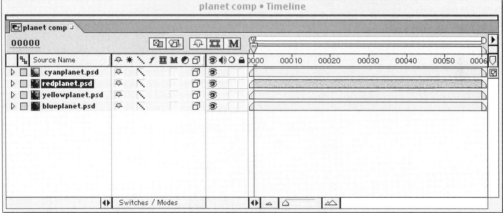

6. Select **redplanet.psd** in the **Timeline** window. This causes its selection handles to appear in the **Composition** window. Move it to the right, as you see here.

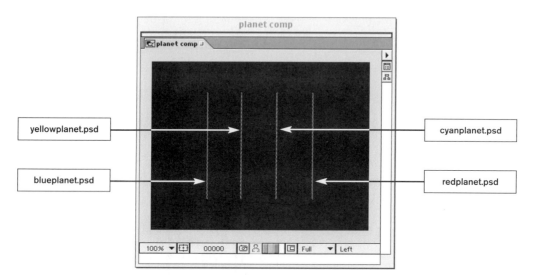

7. Repeat this process with **yellowplanet.psd** and **blueplanet.psd** until your Composition window looks like this one.

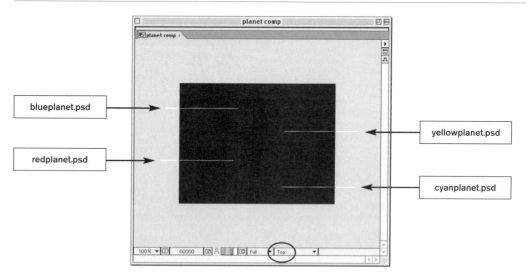

8. Change the view from **Left** to **Top**. This allows you to view the artwork from above. You are going to move the artwork from this view next. Drag the **Composition** window to make it larger so you can see the gray work area around the screen. Drag your artwork into the positions you see above.

Your artwork is now positioned so that a camera can fly around the objects and look at them. That's what you'll learn to do next.

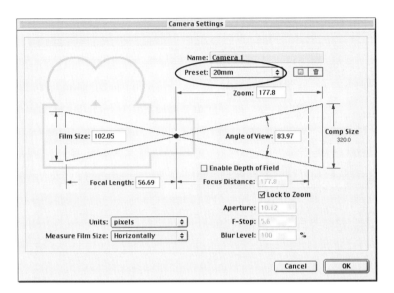

9. Choose **Layer > New > Camera**. This opens the Camera Settings dialog box. We explain the settings in this dialog box in a chart at the end of this exercise. For now, make sure the **Preset** option is set to **20mm**, as shown above, and click **OK**.

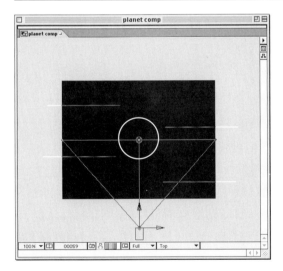

10. Camera 1 appears in your Timeline and also in the Composition window. Adding a camera to your composition is the only way to animate a camera. As you can see, the camera has handles similar to the ones 3D objects have. However, it also has a triangular shape attached to it that simulates the field of view from the lens. The Point of Interest is circled in the screen above. It indicates which way the camera is pointed—currently straight ahead.

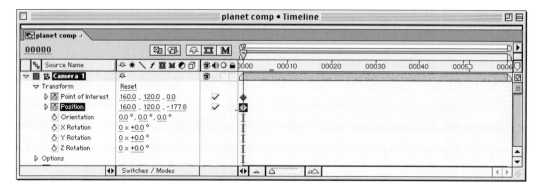

11. In the **Timeline**, click the twirly for **Camera 1**. Click the **Transform** twirly, and then click the **Stopwatch** icon for the **Point of Interest** and **Position** properties.

You have now set the keyframes to be active. Next you'll move the camera to set it for this first keyframe.

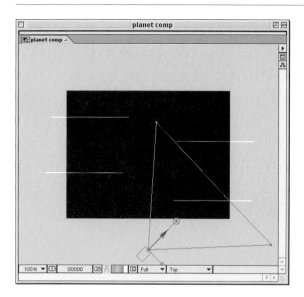

12. Move the **Point of Interest** handle to match what you see here. You have moved the camera to face the **cyanplanet.psd** object.

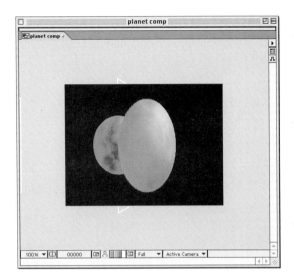

13. Change the view to **Active Camera** to see what the camera sees.

Notice the distortion in the closest planet—it doesn't look circular. That's because the camera is basically looking at a piece of flat artwork from an oblique angle, causing it to distort. You'll fix this later, after getting the camera animation set up.

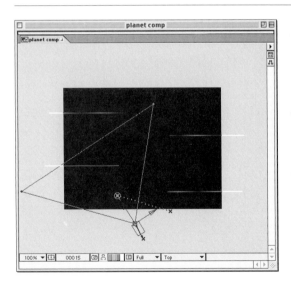

14. Return the view to **Top**. Move the **Time Marker** to **Frame 15** and change the **point of interest** to match what you see above. Move the camera's position as well by moving the **rectangle** icon closer to the **Point of Interest** handle.

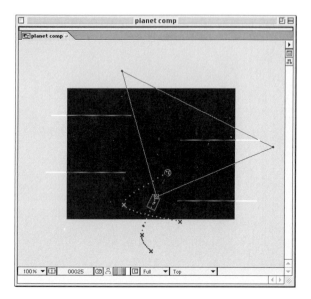

15. Move the **Time Marker** to **Frame 30**. Move the camera to match what you see here by moving the **point of interest** and **camera** position.

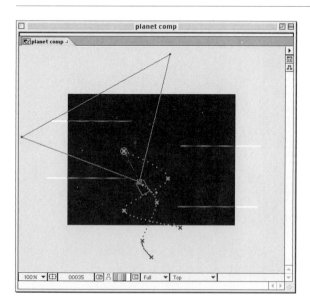

16. Move the **Time Marker** to **Frame 45**, and move the **point of interest** and **camera** to match what you see above.

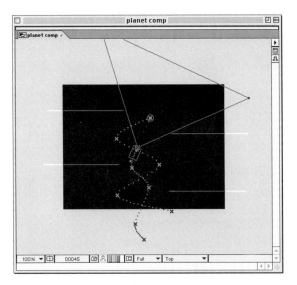

17. Move the **Time Marker** to **Frame 59**. Move the **point of interest** and **camera** to match what you see above.

18. Change the view to **Active Camera**, move the **Time Marker** to the **first frame**, and press the **spacebar**. Your camera should fly through the path of planets! The only problem is that the planets all look like cardboard cutouts, rather than being round! You'll fix this next.

19. In the **Timeline**, select **cyanplanet.psd**, **redplanet.psd**, **yellowplanet.psd**, and **blueplanet.psd** by holding down the **Shift** key and clicking each layer.

20. Choose **Layer > Transform > Auto-Orient**. The Auto-Orientation dialog box opens. Choose **Orient Towards Camera** and click **OK**. This tells each object to face the camera as it moves by. Test your movie again by pressing the **spacebar**. Voila—all the planets are now circles! Change the view to **Top** and scrub the **Time Marker** to see what After Effects is doing behind the scenes. It's causing each planet to rotate as the camera flies past. Pretty amazing!

21. Save the project and close this composition. You won't be using it again in this chapter.

NOTE | Camera Settings Dialog Box

In the last exercise, you had a chance to add a camera to your composition, and you briefly saw the dialog box for the camera. As promised, here's a handy chart that describes the numerous features found in this dialog box.

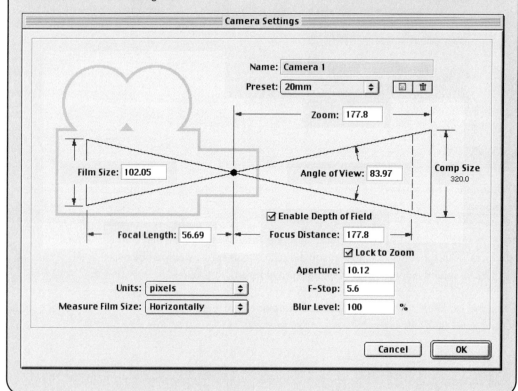

Camera Settings Dialog Box	
Setting	**Description**
Name	After Effects will automatically name your camera for you, or you can give your camera a name. This name will appear in the Timeline layer that represents the camera object.
Preset	The camera ships with a menu of different presets. These presets emulate different 35mm lens settings with different focal lengths. The angle of view, zoom, focus, distance, focal length, and aperture are all stored with each preset. You can create your own custom camera presets by changing the settings and clicking the Disk icon to save them.
Angle of View	The focal length, film size, and zoom settings all determine the angle of view. You can create wide-angle lens settings or more narrow lens settings, depending on what value is entered.
Enable Depth of Field	Affects the distance range in which the image is in focus. Images outside of the distance range are blurred. This setting is used to create realistic camera-focusing effects.
Focus Distance	Specifies the distance from the camera's position at which objects appear in focus.
Aperture	Increases or decreases the size of the lens. This setting affects depth-of-field blur as well as f-stop positions.
F-Stop	Indicates the ratio of focal length to aperture. Analog cameras specify aperture size using the f-stop measurement. If you specify a new value for this setting, the value for Aperture changes dynamically to match it.
Blur Level	Indicates the amount of depth-of-field blur in an image. A setting of 100% creates a natural blur as dictated by the camera settings. Lower values reduce the blur.
Film Size	Relates directly to the composition size. When you specify a new value for film size, the zoom changes to match the perspective of a real camera.
Focal Length	The distance from the film plane to the camera lens. The camera's position represents the center of the lens. When you specify a new value for the focal length, the zoom changes to match the perspective.
Units	The units of measurement in which the camera setting values are expressed.
Measure Film Size	The dimensions used to depict the film size.
Zoom	The distance from the position of the camera to the image plane.

8. _____Camera Options and Settings

You might have noticed that—besides the Transform properties—there is another set of camera properties, named Options.

The **Options properties** are based on physical camera options. In everyday life, actual cameras have lenses, apertures, shutters, and other components that work together to allow cameras to take photographs. Each camera you create in After Effects can have its own lens settings, aperture settings, and other features that allow you to adjust the way your 3D world is "photographed."

If you've done a bit of photography in the past, these camera terms are probably familiar to you. If you've never studied photography, these terms are probably a bit of a mystery. That's okay; you don't have to know photography. In this exercise, you'll learn the function of each option by adjusting the settings and observing the results.

1. Open the **Planets** composition and make sure that **Active Camera** view is set in the **Composition** window. Use **RAM Preview** to watch the animation. A camera move using Transform settings is already programmed for you, and all the planets were set up in 3D space ahead of time. You'll be changing the animation using features in the Options menu.

2. In the **Timeline** window, display the properties for the **Camera 1** layer, and then display the **Options** properties by clicking the corresponding twirlies. Observe the following options: Zoom, Depth of Field, Focus Distance, Aperture, and Blur Level.

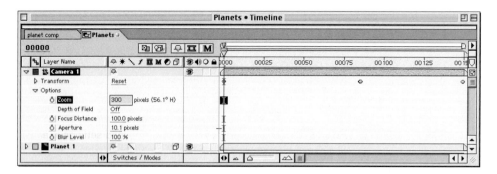

3. Change the **Zoom** setting to **300**. Click **RAM Preview** again and notice how much more dramatic the perspective is. The neat thing about changing the zoom is that it is a lot easier than animating the Transform properties of the camera, and it often has more impact on the overall perspective.

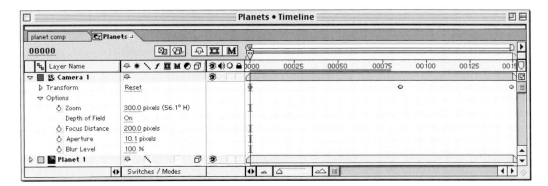

4. Toggle the **Depth of Field** setting **On** and **Off**, and notice that the planets get blurry and come back into focus. Make sure the setting is **On** before continuing. Change the **Focus Distance** from **100** to **200**. Observe the planets come more into focus, but notice that planets that are far away are less focused.

The Focus Distance property can be controlled only when the Depth of Field option is enabled. In real life, all camera lenses have depth of field. This means that not everything is in focus at the same time. A real lens can focus only within a certain range of depth. This range where everything is in focus is called the depth of field. In computer graphics, a virtual lens does not have depth of field—everything can be in focus at the same time. The Depth of Field property in After Effects provides more realistic camera focusing effects for your projects.

5. Drag the **Blur Level** value left and right to see the range of blur level setting. When you're done, return it to **100%**.

Blur Level allows you to control how much focus blur is applied to the objects in your scene. This is not related to a real camera setting. A real camera's focus blur is determined by the physical characteristics of the lens and cannot be changed. The Blur Level option in After Effects is a computer graphics setting that gives you another means of controlling the focus blur. Blur Level values can be set greater than 100%.

6. Click **RAM Preview** to see the Depth of Field property and its associated settings in action.

7. Save your project and leave the **Planets** composition open for the next exercise.

9. _____Previewing Draft 3D and Wireframe Interactions

Your computer has to work hard to create 3D images. Previewing an image or rendering a final movie will take longer whenever 3D layers are involved. Lights, shadows, and depth-of-field options take longer to process and slow down previews. You can speed up previews in After Effects 3D by using two buttons.

The Draft 3D button (in the Timeline window) disables lights, shadows, and depth of field. Clicking on this button allows you to work in Draft mode, which is After Effects' low-quality setting. You'll still see your objects in 3D, and your previews will be faster.

The **Wireframe Interactions button** (in the Timeline window) allows you to move your objects in the Composition window as wireframe objects, which won't render color, texture, fills, gradients, etc. This setting enables much quicker interactivity while dragging objects. Wireframe preview is suitable for many positioning purposes and will speed your workflow.

In this exercise you'll learn to use the Draft 3D button and the Wireframe Interactions buttons to speed up previews of your 3D work.

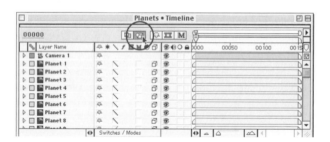

1. The **Planets** composition should be open from the preceding exercise. In the **Timeline** window, locate and click the **Draft 3D** button. Notice that the Depth of Field effect becomes disabled in the Composition window.

The Draft 3D button disables lights, shadows, and depth of field.

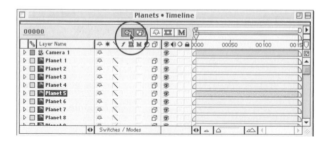

2. Click the **Wireframe Interactions** button. Select the **Planet 5** layer.

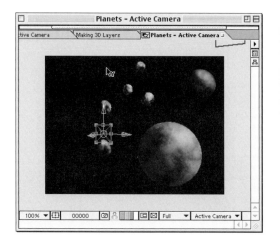 

3. In the **Composition** window, drag the **green Y-axis** handle up to a position similar to that seen in the first image above. Drag the **red X-axis** handle to the right as seen above. Notice that the Planet 5 object is displayed as a simple wireframe while it is being the moved.

If you turn the Wireframe Interactions button off and move the artwork again, you'll see that the object looks solid and maintains its color, texture, gradient, etc. The Wireframe Interactions button is useful for when you are positioning objects in 3D and you want to go a little faster.

4. Click **RAM Preview** and observe that the preview renders relatively quickly. As After Effects is building the RAM preview, the motion might appear jerky, but it will build the preview faster and play it back smoothly once it's finished.

5. Save your project and close After Effects.

NOTE | Zaxwerks 3D Invigorator

Of particular interest to After Effects users is a third-party plug-in called 3D Invigorator. Unlike After Effects' 3D objects, which never have true depth, objects built with this plug-in are true 3D models created within After Effects from vector artwork . Check out the plug-in at http://www.zaxwerks.com.

If this was a hard chapter for you, don't think badly of yourself (or us!). Honestly, there's a very big learning curve to this subject, and the more you practice the easier it will become. Take a break and get ready for one of the most advanced aspects of After Effect 5.0/5.5—expressions.

I4.

Expressions

Adding Expressions	Creating Property Relationships
Multiplying Expression Values |Arrays	Effects and Expressions
Disabling Expressions	Deleting Expressions
Expressions Library	Converting Expressions to Keyframes

chap_14

After Effects 5.0 / 5.5
H•O•T CD-ROM

Expressions are new to After Effects 5.0/5.5. The word **expression** is a mathematical and programming term that creates a new value from an old value. What this might mean to you as an After Effects user, is that you can use expressions to take the value from one property and apply it to another property.

Expressions are written in JavaScript, but the beauty is that you don't have to know how to write any code at all to use them because After Effects will automatically write them for you. However, to make expressions more than minimally useful, you will want to know how to modify the expressions that After Effects creates, which is fairly easy once you learn a few rules. This chapter will show you some practical examples of using expressions and will also teach you how to make modifications to them.

I. ——————Adding Expressions and Creating Relationships

Chapter 9, "*Parenting*," introduced you to the Pick Whip tool for creating parent-child relationships. The Pick Whip is also used to create expression relationships. In this exercise you'll learn how to add an expression to a layer's Scale property and create a one-to-one relationship with another layer's property.

1. Copy the **chap_14** folder from the **H•O•T CD-ROM** to your hard drive.

2. Open **Expressions Project.aep** from the **chap_14** folder.

3. Choose **File > Save As**, navigate to your **HOT_AE_Projects** folder, and click **Save**.

4. Double-click on the file **Creating Expressions Comp** to open it. This composition contains two layers with identical artwork and no keyframes. You are going to animate one layer and learn to apply an expression to the other layer.

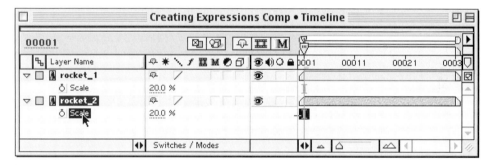

5. In the **Timeline** window, display the **Scale** property for both layers. You can do this by selecting both layers with the **Shift** key and then pressing **S** on your keyboard. Select the **Scale** property for **rocket_2**.

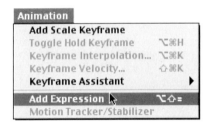

6. Choose **Animation > Add Expression**. Alternatively, press **Option+Shift+=** (Mac) or **Alt+Shift+=** (Windows) and click the **Stopwatch** icon. This will not set a keyframe; instead, it will set an expression. A new icon appears in the Switches panel of the Timeline that includes a Pick Whip icon In the middle. The icon to the left is called the Graph Overlay button, which turns on a value graph for the expression (not demonstrated in this chapter, but useful to see the velocity of changes to the property), and to the right is the Expressions Language menu, which you will learn about later in the chapter.

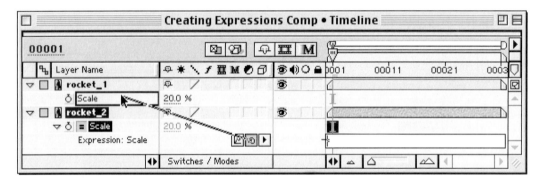

7. Click the **Pick Whip** icon for the **rocket_2 Scale** property and drag it to the **rocket_1 Scale** property.

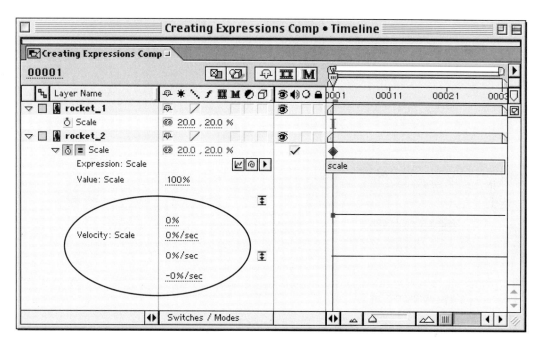

Note: After Effects 5.5 has new properties for expressions. This exercise will work identically in both applications, but readers who have 5.5 instead of 5.0 will see more attributes under the Scale property.

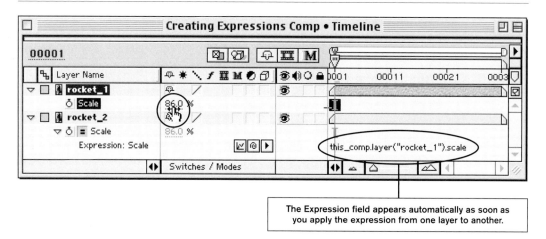

The Expression field appears automatically as soon as you apply the expression from one layer to another.

8. Notice that a JavaScript expression is automatically written in the rocket_2 Expression field.

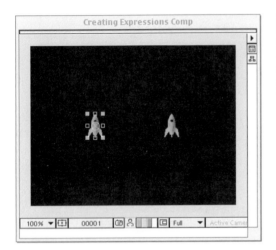 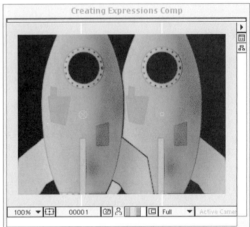

9. Drag the **rocket_1 Scale** value back and forth to change it. Observe that both rockets now scale equally when the rocket_1 value is changed because the rocket_2 value is tied to the value rocket_1 via the expression.

This is pretty neat, but couldn't you do the same thing with parenting? Yes! This is a very simple example of creating an expression that doesn't really reveal the power of expressions yet. In following exercises, things will get more exciting—we promise!

10. Set the **rocket_1 Scale** property back to **20%**. Save your project and leave this composition open for the next exercise.

WARNING | Unique Layer Names

Expressions use a layer's name to refer to layer objects. You should give layers unique names before using expressions. Without unique layer names, expressions can refer to the wrong layer object. Rename layers, if necessary, to ensure that all layers have unique names. To rename a layer, simply select the layer name and press Return (Mac) or Enter (Windows).

2. _____ Creating Property Relationships

In this exercise, you'll continue to work with the same layers and composition to build on what you've learned so far. The first expression that you created borrowed the Scale property from one layer and applied it to another. Since this same result could also have been achieved with parenting, you may not be too impressed at this point. Now, however, you are going to tell After Effects to take the value of the Scale property for one layer and apply it to the Rotation property of another layer. If you move the scale from one layer to 30 percent, the other layer will rotate 30 degrees. That is something that you cannot do with parenting!

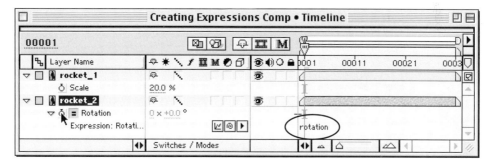

1. The file **Creating Expressions Comp** should be open from the last exercise. Select the **rocket_2** layer and press **R** on your keyboard to display the **Rotation** property.

Option+Click (Mac) or **Alt+Click** (Windows) on the **Rotation Stopwatch** icon. Notice that an expression is enabled for the Rotation property on the rocket_2 layer. You can tell that the expression is active because the word "rotation" appears within the Expression field on the layer.

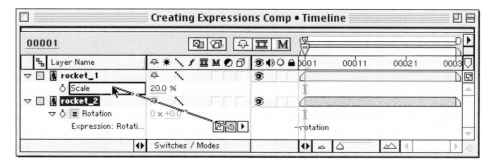

2. Click the **Pick Whip** icon for the **rocket_2 Rotation** property and drag it to the **rocket_1 Scale** property.

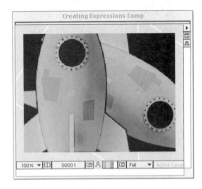

3. Drag back and forth over the **rocket_1 Scale** value. Notice that the rocket_2 layer scales and rotates, and the rocket_1 layer just scales.

Making a rocket rotate based on the scale of another rocket is not a very practical example of when to use expressions, but it illustrates their power. Future exercises in this chapter offer more practical uses, now that you've learned the basic principle!

4. Save your project, and leave the composition open for the next exercise.

3. ————————Multiplying Expression Values

As you've seen, once you use the Pick Whip to create property relationships, JavaScript code is automatically written in the Expression field. If you wish, you can edit and modify this code. This allows you to create fairly sophisticated relationships between properties.

In this exercise you will learn a simple way of modifying an expression by multiplying its values. You can use this same method to add, subtract, multiply, or divide the value of an expression. Although it might sound intimidating to write your own code, you'll soon see that this method is quite straightforward.

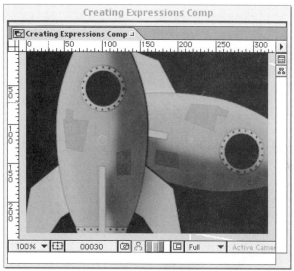

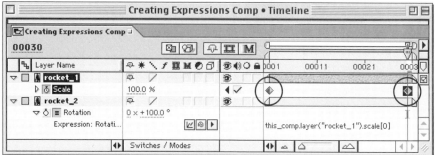

1. Make sure the **Time Marker** is at **Frame 1**, and that the **Scale Property** is showing for the **rocket_1** layer. Click the **Stopwatch** icon for **Scale** to set a beginning keyframe. Move the **Time Marker** to **Frame 30**, and set a keyframe for the **Scale** property. Change the **Scale** to **100%**. You are doing this so you can see how the expressions you've created interact with keyframes and with properties that change over time. Once you set the second keyframe, you'll see both rockets grow in size. The expression is doing its job!

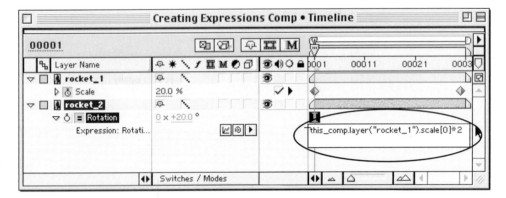

2. Move the **Time Marker** back to **Frame 1**, click in the **rocket_2 Rotation** Expression field, and place your cursor at the end of the line of code. Type ***2** and then either press **Enter** on your numeric keypad or click outside the Expression field to activate the expression.

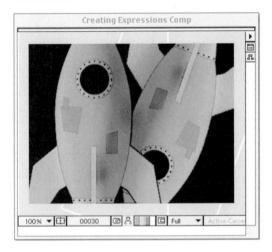

3. Scrub the **Time Marker** and notice that the rotation of rocket_2 is doubled.

4. Save your project and close **Creating Expressions Comp**. Leave your project open for the next exercise.

NOTE | Math Operations Using Expressions

In the last exercise, you added an asterisk and a value at the end of the line of JavaScript code to multiply the value for the Rotation property by 2. This method allows you to easily modify the automatically generated JavaScript code. The following chart lists the symbols to use for other simple math operations in JavaScript expressions. As you can see, they are just standard math symbols.

Simple Math Operations	
Symbol	**Operation**
+	Add
-	Subtract
*	Multiply
/	Divide

Use these symbols to perform simple math operations on expression values. You can change an action to its opposite—for example, clockwise to counterclockwise rotation—by using ***-1 (or any other value)**.

What Are Arrays?

In the previous exercise, you changed the value of the expression by multiplying it by 2. You did this simply by adding the appropriate code to the end of the expression, and it worked perfectly. Some properties have more than one value, however. For example, the Position property has an X value and a Y value. If a 3D layer is in use, the Position property has three values: X, Y, and Z.

When you use expressions, you often need to refer to individual values of a single property. For example, if you need to multiply the Position property, you must add the multiplication code to both of its property values—X and Y. If you don't do this correctly, After Effects will disable your expression. When you get into programming expressions for the Position property of a 3D layer, you need to create math for all three values—X, Y, and Z!

To refer to individual values within a property (like X and Y) using expressions, you must write the code in a specific way. This specific format you use is a JavaScript concept called an **array**.

In After Effects, an array holds property values inside an expression. Again, you don't need to learn JavaScript to refer to individual property values. You only need to learn how to identify an array. The format is very simple, and it actually is already familiar to you.

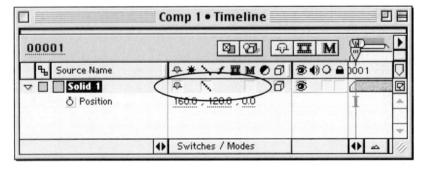

You've seen X, Y, and Z values in the Timeline, as shown above. Notice that the values are separated by commas:

`160, 120, 0`

The array format is identical, with the addition of an opening left bracket and a closing right bracket that surround the values. The brackets define the array, and the commas delineate property values within the array:

`[160, 120, 0]`

As you can see, an array is a simple means of defining property values within an expression. In the following exercise, you will learn to use a simple value array within an expression.

4. _____**Using Arrays with After Effects 5.0**

If you have After Effects 5.5, skip this exercise. Arrays are much more easily understood by version 5.5, and you don't need to build them yourself. In the previous exercise, you multiplied the Rotation value by 2. This method won't work with some expressions in After Effects 5.0, because there are multiple values, such as X and Y, within a single property. In this exercise you'll learn to use arrays, identify each property value, and access values inside an expression.

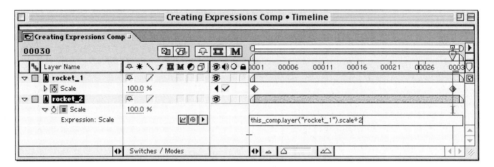

1. Open **Creating Expressions Comp**. Make sure the **rocket_2 Scale** property and expression are displayed. Click in the **Expression** field and place the cursor at the end of the code line. Type ***2** and click outside the Expression field to enable the expression. As an alternate method, press **Enter** on your numeric keypad to enable the expression.

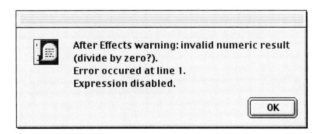

2. If you are using After Effects 5.0, you'll get a warning that you have an invalid numeric result and the expression has been disabled. Click **OK** to dismiss the warning. **Note:** Users with version 5.5 will not get this warning.

Although After Effect reports a possible "divide by zero" error, the program is unable to be sure of the error and places a question mark after the divide by zero report. In actuality, the error is due to the fact that each value of the property must be accessed individually. Because of many possible contexts, After Effects can only make an educated guess about scripting errors.

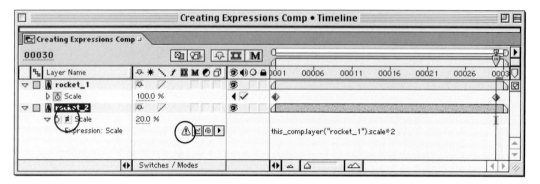

3. Look at the Timeline to observe the disabled Expression icon and the Warning icon.

4. Make sure the **rocket_2 Scale** property is selected. Choose **Animation > Remove Expression**. Alternatively, press **Option+Shift+=** (Mac) or **Alt+Shift+=** (Windows).

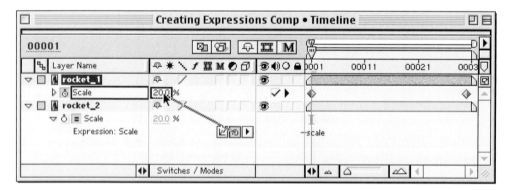

5. Option+Click (Mac) or **Alt+Click** (Windows) on the **Stopwatch** icon for the **rocket_2 Scale** property to add an expression. Drag the **rocket_2 Pick Whip** to the **rocket_1 Scale** value.

Important: Drag directly to the value, as shown above, rather than to the property name, as you were instructed to do in Exercise 1. The code that is written for your expression can differ depending on whether you drag to a property name or to a property value.

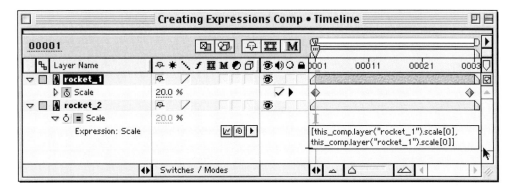

6. Click in the **Expression** field to see the new code. You'll see an array consisting of two values: X and Y.

```
[this_comp.layer("rocket_1").scale[0],
this_comp.layer("rocket_1").scale[0]]
```

This is the X value in the expression.

```
[this_comp.layer("rocket_1").scale[0],
this_comp.layer("rocket_1").scale[0]]
```

This is the Y value in the expression.

```
[this_comp.layer("rocket_1").scale[0],
this_comp.layer("rocket_1").scale[0]]
```

These are the opening left bracket, comma, and closing right bracket. Take your time here to clearly identify the X value, Y value, comma, and brackets.

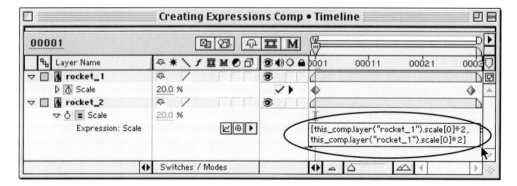

7. Place your cursor at the end of the **X** value (before the comma) and type ***2**. Next, place your cursor at the end of the **Y** value (before the closing right bracket) and type ***2**. Click outside the Expression field, or press **Enter** on your numeric keypad to activate the expression.

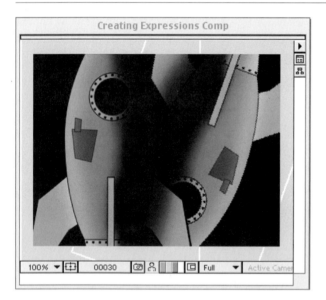

8. Scrub the **Time Marker** and notice that rocket_2 is scaled to twice the size.

9. Save your project and close **Creating Expressions Comp**.

TIP | Which Properties Require Arrays?

In the Expression field, properties with one value are displayed as expressions of single-value items. Properties with two or more values are displayed as an array. When using the Pick Whip, try to create a relationship to a property value rather than a property name. That way you'll know exactly which value is being used as the basis for your expression. The following chart lists some common properties and the number of values for each.

Properties and Values	
Property	Number of Values
Rotation	1
Opacity	1
Scale 2D	2
Position 2D	2
Anchor Point 2D	2
Scale 3D	3
Position 3D	3
Anchor Point 3D	3
Color (red, green, blue, alpha)	4

NOTE | Confused?

In Exercise 1, you were able to use the Pick Whip to create an expression involving the Scale property, long before you knew about arrays and the fact that the Scale property has two values (X and Y). Why did the exercise work? When you use the Pick Whip and point to the name of the layer, it lets you modify the expression without needing to program the math for each independent value. When you use the Pick Whip and point to the value of the property, you must use an array. The moral of the story? Always point to the value—that way you'll see the array, if one exists, and you'll always program your values correctly.

5. ———————————Text, Effects, and Expressions

Expressions can be used to control the options or parameters of Effects properties, as well as those of Transform properties. In this exercise, you will see an example of using the Basic Text effect in relation to the Fast Blur effect.

1. Create a new composition and name it **Blur Comp**.

2. Create a new solid layer by choosing **Layer > New > Solid**. For now, the color of the solid does not matter.

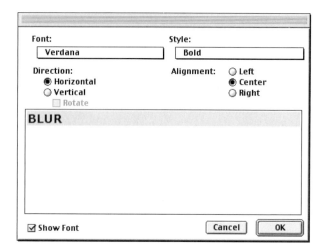

3. Choose **Effect > Text > Basic Text**. The **Basic Text** dialog box opens. Type the word **BLUR** in all caps, and choose a bold font.

4. Click **OK**. The word "BLUR" appears inside the Composition window.

Recall from Chapter 10, "Effects," that, by default, the solid layer disappears, showing the background color specified in the Composition Settings dialog box. The Basic Text effect produces red text by default, and it is set to Draft quality, meaning that the edges will not be crisp. You have learned to adjust all these settings in past chapters. In the interest of concentrating on using expressions with effects in this exercise, we will not review these settings here. Please revisit the chapters about layers, compositions, and effects if you wish to review ways to change these settings.

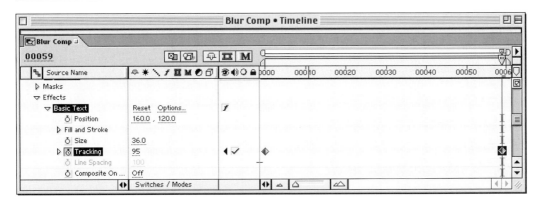

5. In the **Timeline**, twirl down the properties for the **solid** layer, and then twirl down **Effects** and **Basic Text**. Click the **Stopwatch** for **Tracking** to set a keyframe. Move the **Time Marker** to **Frame 59** (or the last frame of your composition), and change the **Tracking** value to **95**. This should set two keyframes for tracking. Scrub the **Timeline** to see the animation, and then set the **Time Marker** back to **Frame 1**.

6. Choose **Effect > Blur & Sharpen > Fast Blur**. This adds the Fast Blur effect to the Basic Text effect, though it won't look any different yet. That's because you haven't applied any settings to the Fast Blur effect. That will come in a later step.

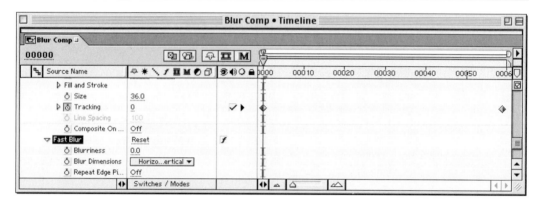

7. Move the **Time Marker** back to **Frame 0**. In the **Timeline**, scroll down to locate the **Fast Blur** effect. Click on its twirly to reveal its settings. Next, you'll create an expression.

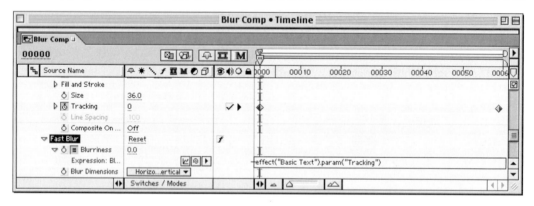

8. Option+Click (Mac) or **Alt+Click** (Windows) on the **Blurriness Stopwatch** icon to add an expression. Drag the **Blurriness Pick Whip** to the **Tracking** value. You'll see JavaScript code appear immediately for the Blurriness value.

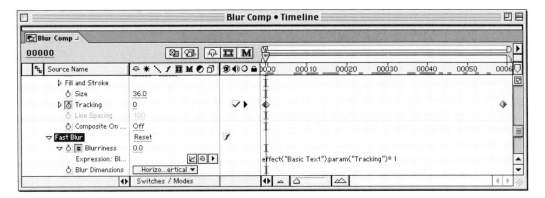

9. At the end of the Javascript code, type ***1**. This multiplies the Tracking value by 1 and applies the resulting blur to the Blurriness property. You won't see any change at first, because the value inside the first keyframe of the Tracking value is 0. Scrub the **Timeline**, and you'll see that the amount of tracking directly affects the amount of blur. Try changing the Tracking value to **0.5** or higher and scrubbing. You'll be able to pick a value that is pleasing to you this way.

You can use expressions to control all types of Effects properties and values; this is just a taste of the sort of results this kind of programming achieves.

10. Close **Blur Comp**. Leave your project open for the next exercise.

6.──────────Disabling an Expression

You've seen that After Effects can disable an expression if it contains an error. You can also choose to disable an expression manually. You may want to disable a complex expression to speed up your previews. Or you may have several expressions chained together and want to debug the chains. Or you may simply be unsure as to whether you want to use an expression or not, and choose to disable it until you decide.

In this exercise you'll learn how to disable an expression. Enabling an expression is equally easy.

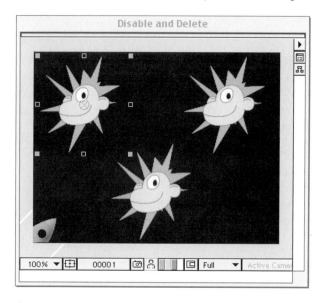

1. Double-click on the **Disable and Delete** composition to open it.

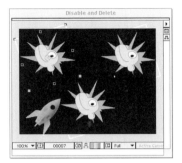 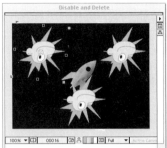 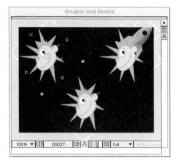

2. Scrub the **Time Marker** and notice that the monkeys rotate as the rocket position animates.

All of the monkey layers have expressions that chain to the first monkey's Rotation value. In the following step you will disable the first expression in the chain. This will disable all rotations of the monkey layer.

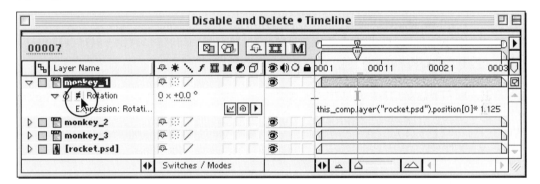

3. Click the **Expression On/Off** switch next to the **monkey_1 Rotation** property. This switch looks like an equal symbol. Notice that it changes to an equal symbol with a slash through the center when switched off.

4. Observe, in the **Composition** window, that the monkey images no longer rotate when you scrub the **Time Marker**. The chain of expressions are disabled.

5. Save your project, and leave the composition open for the next exercise.

Tip: To reenable an expression, click the Expression On/Off switch so that it appears as an equal symbol.

——————————**Deleting Expressions**

Deleting an expression is very simple; for those of you who followed Exercise 4, "Using Arrays with After Effects 5.0," you already deleted an expression. This exercise quickly reviews how to delete an expression, and covers it for the first time for those of you who didn't need to do Exercise 4.

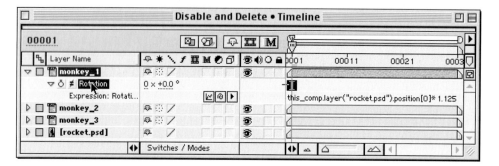

1. The **Disable and Delete** composition should be open from the last exercise. Select the **Rotation** property for the **monkey_1** layer.

2. Choose **Animation > Remove Expression**.

There are two alternative means to remove or delete a selected expression:

> **Option + Click** on the = sign (Mac) or **Alt + Click** on the = sign (Windows)

> **Option+click** on the **Stopwatch** icon (Mac) or **Alt+click** on the **Stopwatch** icon (Windows)

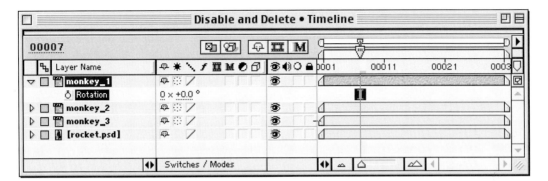

3. In the **Timeline** window, notice that the **Rotation** expression has been deleted.

4. Save your project, and close the **Disable and Delete** composition. Leave your project open for the next exercise.

JavaScript's Expressions Library

If you know JavaScript, you can use the Expressions library to write your own JavaScript expressions.

To access the library menu, click the JavaScript Library icon for an expression.

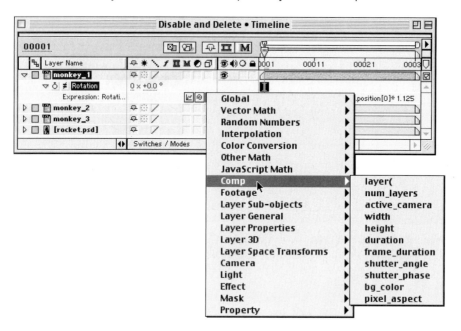

You can select from the entire library of JavaScript language elements used by After Effects. An experienced JavaScript programmer could have a blast with all these options. If you don't know JavaScript, you can ignore these options or decide to learn what they mean by reading a JavaScript book!

8. ————————Converting Expressions to Keyframes

After Effects obtains the values for an expression frame by frame during the rendering process. In essence, expressions are calculated "live." If you have a particularly complex expression, this can slow down rendering time. You can convert expressions to keyframes to speed up rendering or for other purposes. In this exercise you'll select a property that already has an expression, and you'll learn to use the **Convert Expression to Keyframes** option.

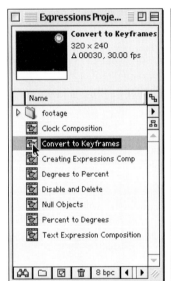
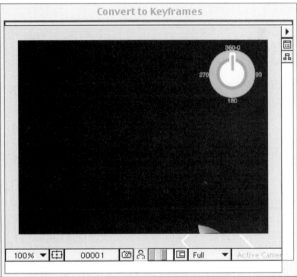

1. Open the **Convert to Keyframes** composition.

2. Click **RAM Preview** in the **Time Controls** palette, and notice that the rocket moves through the Composition window as the dial makes a complete rotation.

The rocket layer has an expression that references the dial layer. In the following steps you will convert the rocket expression to keyframes.

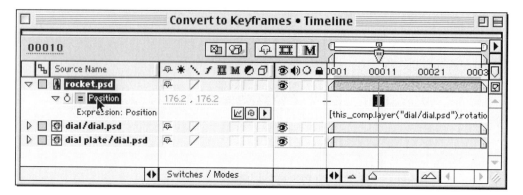

3. Select the **rocket.psd** layer **Position** property. It doesn't matter where your Time Marker is in the Timeline.

4. Choose **Animation > Keyframe Assistant > Convert Expression to Keyframes**.

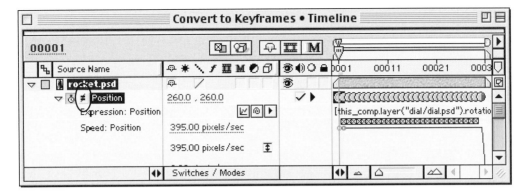

5. Observe the keyframes created from the expression. Also notice that the expression is now disabled, as demonstrated by the Expression On/Off icon with the slash through it.

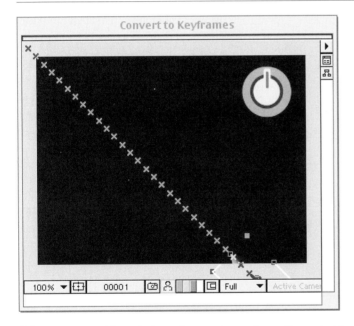

6. In the Composition window, observe the motion path created by the keyframes.

7. Save and close your project. You're finished!

That's it for this chapter. You've gotten a sampling of the power of expressions. If you like working with expressions, the sky's the limit. They are truly boundless tools that can be combined in infinite new ways.

15.

Audio

| Adding Audio to Your Compositions |

| Previewing Audio | Adding Markers and Comments |

| Audio Palette | Adjusting Volume Levels |

| Audio Effects |

chap_15

After Effects 5.0 / 5.5
H•O•T CD-ROM

Most professional animation and motion graphics work contains music, narration, sound effects, or all of these at once. After Effects is primarily a tool for motion graphics and animation, but it would not be complete if it didn't offer the opportunity to include audio. Audio files can be used simply as a "guide track" to help you choreograph moving images, or they can be used to create the final audio track for your movie.

It's important to understand that After Effects is not designed to be an audio authoring tool. Other programs are better equipped to record and process a finished music track.

However, if you want to combine a finished music track with sound effects, narration, and animation, After Effects is a great tool for the job. You can import a prerecorded track, fit it to your image, make volume adjustments, and output the final audio track with your movie. The audio capabilities of After Effects shine as a finishing tool.

Overview of Audio in After Effects

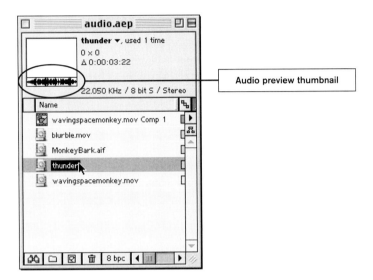

Audio preview thumbnail

You import audio files into the Project window just as you import any other file—by choosing File > Import. When you select audio footage in the Project window, rather than seeing the little image preview, you see a waveform indicating that the footage is audio only.

Audio file formats supported by After Effects include QuickTime movies, AIFF (a popular Mac audio file format), and WAV (a popular Windows audio file format). These and other audio files supported by QuickTime, including AU and Mac Sound (Mac OS only), can be imported directly into After Effects. Once imported, audio footage can be used as layers in your compositions.

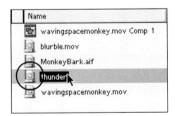

The QuickTime movie icon looks the same for images or for audio. Please refer to the section on importing QuickTime movies in Chapter 3, "*Projects*," if you need more information.

You can preview audio footage from the Project window by double-clicking on the audio items. This opens a little audio player and allows you to hear the audio track before you place it in your composition.

I. ——————————Adding Audio to Your Compositions

In this exercise you will learn to use the **Audio switch** and to view audio **waveforms** in the Timeline window.

1. Copy the **chap_15** folder from the **H•O•T CD-ROM** to your hard drive.

2. Open the **audio.aep** project file from the **chap_15** folder.

3. Double-click on **wavingspacemonkey.mov Comp 1** to open it.

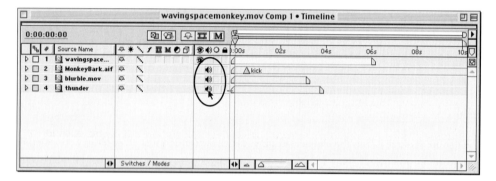

4. In the **Timeline** window, click the **Audio** switch for the **MonkeyBark.aif, blurble.mov**, and **thunder** layers.

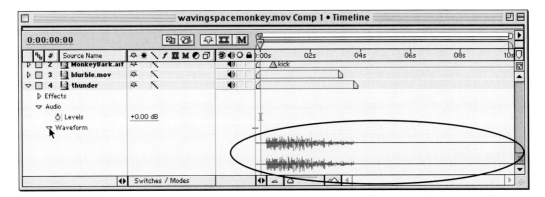

5. Click on the twirly for the **thunder** layer to display the **Audio** properties. Then click on the **Audio >** **Waveform** twirly to reveal the **Waveform** graph.

The waveform is a graphical representation of recorded sound. In the image above, the two squiggly lines represent the left and right stereo tracks. Each squiggly line represents the frequency and volume of the audio track. ***Tip:*** *The Audio switch must be on to see the waveform.*

6. Save the project in your **HOT_AE_Projects** folder, and leave the composition open for the next exercise.

2. _____Previewing Audio

One of the least intuitive parts of After Effects, strangely enough, is previewing sound. In this exercise, you will learn how to preview audio using the **Time Controls** palette and the **Audio Preview** command. You will also learn to preview sound in the **Timeline** by dragging the **Time Marker**. It sounds simple, and it is. It's just easier to figure out when someone shows you how to do it.

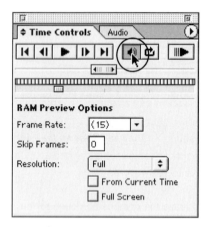

1. In the **Time Controls** palette, make sure the **Audio** button is on, and then click **RAM Preview**. The first few seconds of your audio is previewed along with the animation. Notice that the audio and image must be rendered first, which causes a slight delay. When you are done previewing, click anywhere or press any key on your keyboard to stop the preview.

Warning: If you have turned sound down on your computer, you may not hear the audio. If this is the case, locate the Sound control panel for your operating system and check the sound levels.

2. Move the **Time Marker** to the middle of the composition. Choose **Composition > Preview > Audio Preview (Here Forward)**. When you want to stop the preview, click anywhere or press any key.

Notice that the audio plays immediately from the current Time Marker position forward. No prerendering is necessary using this preview method. The image does not move using this method, so you cannot use it to check synchronization, but it's the quickest way to hear all of your audio tracks.

3. Press the **period** key on the **numeric keypad**. This is the keyboard shortcut to the Audio Preview (Here Forward) command. Click anywhere or press any key to stop the preview.

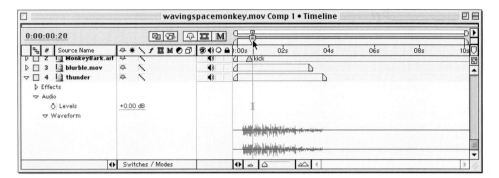

4. In the **Timeline** window, scrub the **Time Marker** while holding down the **Command** (Mac) or **Control** (Windows) key. Notice that the audio previews. Stop scrubbing the Time Marker to stop the preview.

Note: Scrubbing audio can result in jerky playback. It's best to use RAM Preview with the Audio button turned on for smooth movement and sound. If you stop moving the Time Marker while keeping the mouse button depressed, a short section of audio will loop.

5. Leave the composition open for the next exercise.

TIP | Setting the Audio Preview Duration

You can set the **audio preview duration** in the Preferences window. You might want to limit the duration if you have a long piece and you want to concentrate on how a small part of it is sounding and synchronizing with your live action or animation.

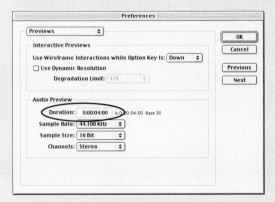

Choose Edit > Preferences > Previews (After Effects > Preferences > Previews in OS X). In the Preferences dialog box, set the Duration option to the desired time and click OK. This will cause the audio preview to last for a specified length of time. The audio preview will be cut short if the audio footage is longer than the amount of time entered in this setting.

3. ─────────────────**Adding Markers and Comments**

When working with audio layers, it's often helpful to add **markers** as references to emphasize beats in the music or passages of narration. These markers help to visualize where beats in the music occur and can be used to synchronize sound with motion events.

After Effects offers an easy way to add markers while listening to audio. In this exercise you will learn to add markers while listening to an audio layer. We've already added one marker with a comment to the layer used in this exercise. You will add more.

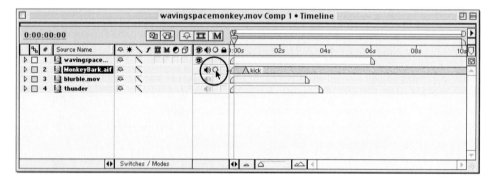

1. In the **Timeline** window, hide the **thunder** layer properties. Click the **Solo** switch for the **MonkeyBark.aif** layer to solo the layer. You learned about the Solo switch in Chapter 8, "*Layers*."

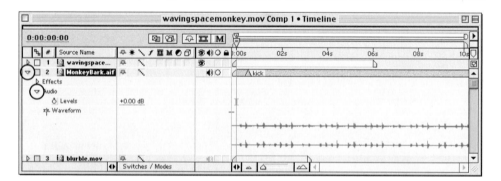

2. Select the **MonkeyBark.aif** layer. Display the **Audio** and **Waveform** properties by clicking those twirlies.

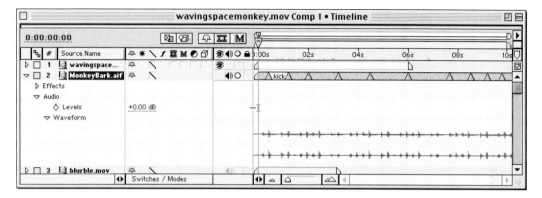

3. Press the **period** key on your **numeric keypad** to preview the **MonkeyBark** audio track. While listening to the audio track, press the **asterisk** key on the **numeric keypad** each time you hear a major beat. Click anywhere or press any other key to stop the preview.

Notice that a marker has been added at each press of the asterisk key. They look like small pyramids in the Timeline. These markers provide a helpful guide when you are setting animation keyframes that you want to match up perfectly with audio beats. **Warning:** *The markers may not appear as quickly as you would like. This has to do with the processor speed of your computer and the fact that After Effects just doesn't seem to do this task very quickly. If this technique doesn't work, there could be different causes. One is that the layer must be selected for this process to work. Also, if Num Lock is pressed on your keyboard, the feature will not work. If you work on a laptop and don't have a numeric keypad, you can add a marker manually. Do this by choosing Layer > Add Marker. Here too, a layer must be selected to access this feature. In addition, this process is not useful for timing to the beats of the audio, because it is too slow. You can move a marker once it's created.*

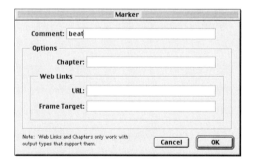

4. Double-click on any one of the markers you just added, to create a comment. This opens the **Marker** dialog box. Anything you enter in the **Comment** field will show up on the **Timeline** as a comment. Other features of this dialog box are listed in a chart at the end of this exercise.

5. Save your project, and leave this composition open for the next exercise.

The Marker Dialog Box

The Marker dialog box allows you to do more than simply enter a comment for the purpose of adding sound notations. You can access the Marker dialog box by double-clicking on any marker you've created. Here's a chart that explains the features of this dialog box.

The Marker Dialog Box	
Setting	**Description**
Comment	Adds a comment to the marker, allowing you to write notes to yourself inside the Timeline.
Chapter	A chapter marker is a QuickTime-only feature that offers the ability to jump to a certain part of a QuickTime movie. You can add the Chapter name easily to After Effects by filling in this field. To program the chapter, please visit http://developer.apple.com/quicktime/ to learn about advanced programming and development for QuickTime.
Web Links	If you create a Web link, your user can click on the part of the movie that contains the link and be transported to its destination. This is a QuickTime-only feature.
URL	Indicates the Web site that you want users to be taken to when they click the Web link. This is a QuickTime-only feature.
Frame Target	Allows you to set up the destination Web page in a separate window from the QuickTime movie containing the Web link. The target naming conventions are part of standard HTML targeting. You can learn more about this and other advanced features of QuickTime at the Apple Web site. This is a QuickTime-only feature.

The Audio Palette

Occasionally, you will need to fix a sound that you've chosen to work with in your After Effects project. You can use the **Audio** palette to make changes to your audio files. Again, we want to reiterate that After Effects is not a good sound-editing tool. The Audio palette is reserved for small, simple audio needs.

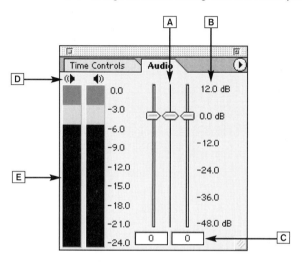

The Audio Palette	
Setting	**Description**
A. Volume Level controls	The *Volume Level* controls are used to adjust the volume.
B. Level units	The *Level units* indicate the change of volume in decibels.
C. Level values	The *Level values* indicate the exact value of each Volume Level control.
D. Audio Clipping Warning icons	The *Audio Clipping Warning* icons indicate when the audio is being "clipped"; when these icons are red, the audio level is loud enough to cause loss of audio data.
E. VU meter	The *VU (Volume Unit)* meter offers feedback about the volume of your audio; it displays the volume range as the audio plays.

To access the Audio palette, choose **Window > Audio**. The Audio palette has several tools that allow you to work with volume levels. The following chart describes these tools.

While you're previewing audio, the VU meter will display green, yellow, and red volume levels. Green audio levels during playback indicate that your volume level is perfectly safe. Yellow peaks indicate caution, but your levels are still safe. Red peaks during playback indicate that your audio levels may be in danger of being clipped. If your audio is clipped, the Audio Clipping Warning icons will turn red.

When audio is clipped, some of the audio frequency data is lost. However, if you are very familiar with digital recording techniques, you may be comfortable with some audio clipping. The safe rule of thumb is to keep the levels high enough that your audio bounces into the red zone occasionally, but never so high that audio data is clipped. If you follow this guideline, your audio will be safe while maintaining maximum fidelity, clarity, and richness of tone.

If you intend to use After Effects to finish the audio for your final movie, we recommend that you learn more about digital audio and work with other tools besides After Effects. A list of audio-related resources is at the end of this book in the Resource appendix.

4. ——————Adjusting Volume Levels

In this exercise you will learn to adjust the **Master Volume Control** slider and the **Left and Right channel** sliders.

1. In the **Timeline** window, make sure the **MonkeyBark.aif** layer is selected.

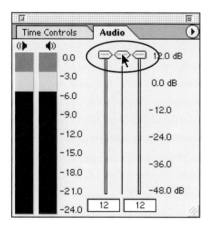

2. If the **Audio** palette is not already open, choose **Window > Audio**. Drag the **Master Volume** control (the center slider) up to 12.0 dB.

The center slider is the Master Volume control. It moves both the left and right channels equally from their current position.

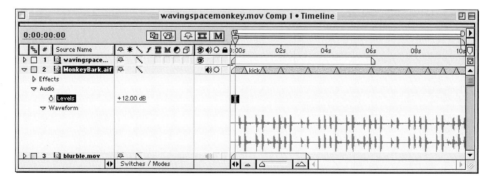

3. In the **Timeline** window, notice that the waveforms grow larger when you increase the volume.

4. Press the **period** key on your **numeric keypad** to preview the audio.

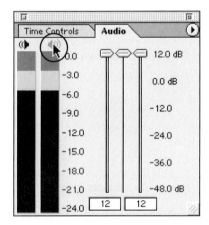

5. In the **Audio** palette, watch the **VU** meter while the audio previews. Both the left and right channels are too loud, which has caused the **Audio Clipping Warning** icons to turn red.

Click on each **Audio Clipping Warning** icon to reset it to black.

Note: Previewing audio does not alter your original audio footage data. Volume settings affect only the preview and output of audio data. It is perfectly safe to preview your audio files with clipping. You will learn how to output a final audio file in the upcoming Chapter 16, "Rendering Final Movies."

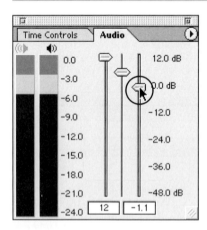

6. Drag the **right channel** slider to approximately −1.0 dB. **Note:** The audio layer must be selected, or you cannot adjust the channel slider.

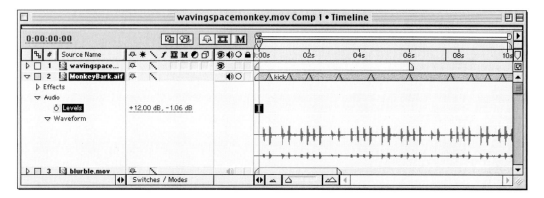

7. Notice that the **right channel** waveform shrinks as the volume decreases.

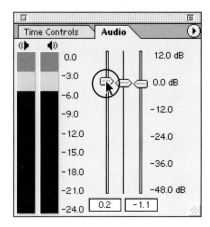

8. Drag the **left channel** slider to approximately 0.0 dB.

9. Press the **period** key on your **numeric keypad** to preview the audio. Both channels are set about as loud as possible without clipping.

TIP | Setting Volume Level Keyframes

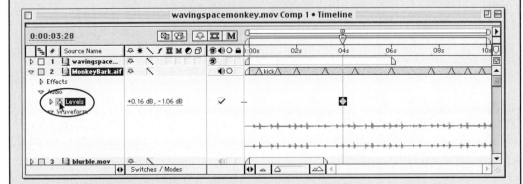

You can set keyframes for Volume Level control settings. Click on the Audio Levels Stopwatch icon to enable keyframes for the Volume Level controls. This ability is useful if you want to fade sound in or out or animate a sound effect by increasing or decreasing its levels on separate keyframes.

TIP | Production Bundle Audio Effects

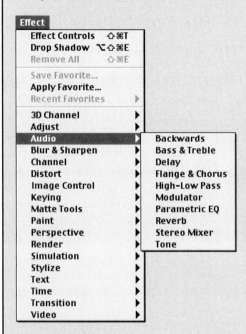

In the Production Bundle, there are audio effects that you can add to audio layers. Choose Effects > Audio and choose an audio effect from the menu. Listen to the results, practicing the previewing techniques that you learned in this chapter. As we stated previously, by using keyframes, you can animate these audio effects as well.

10. Save your project and close it.

___

You're all done with a short and sweet chapter on audio. Rock on.... Next you'll learn how to render your final movies.

___

16.

Rendering Final Movies

Render Queue	Render Settings	Output Module Settings
Rendering Audio	Saving an Alpha Channel or Motion Mask
Rendering for the Web	Saving RAM Previews
Creating and Using Rendering Templates
Collecting Files	Creating Macromedia Flash Output

chap_16

After Effects 5.0 / 5.5
H•O•T CD-ROM

Throughout this book, we've shown you how to preview movies for your own viewing. This chapter focuses on making movies that are the final product of your work. In After Effects, you can create many types of movie output from a single composition. For example, you can output a single composition to video, motion picture film, CD-ROM, streaming video on the Web, GIF animation, HDTV, and many other output types. The choices available are one of the great strengths of After Effects.

The process of outputting your project is called **rendering**. Just as an artist renders a painting, After Effects follows your instructions and renders the final movie. Each pixel of your image and each audio signal is determined and rendered to the output type of your choice.

We saved this chapter for late in the book because it's a complicated subject. While all the output choices After Effects offers are wonderful, they also require careful explanation. Don't be intimidated, though; this is a necessary step in your After Effects education, and we'll walk you through it slowly. You will always have this chapter available to refer to if you get stuck on a future project.

QuickTime Versus AVI/Video For Windows

If you use a Mac, you have likely heard of QuickTime, and if you use Windows, you've likely heard of AVI/Video For Windows. When rendering movies, After Effects defaults to producing QuickTime in its Mac version and AVI/Video For Windows in its Windows version.

In our opinion (and it is shared by the majority of video professionals), QuickTime is the superior format because of its versatility. QuickTime is used on projects ranging from low-end Web and multimedia presentations to feature-film formats that are shown in movie theaters. AVI/Video For Windows is best suited for the low end of the publishing spectrum, as it is ideal for Web movies. One of the benefits of the AVI/Video For Windows format is the fact that so many more consumers own PCs than Macs. If you surf the Web much, you will find that the low-end video formats of AVI/Video For Windows, Real Video, and QuickTime all vie for market share. Since the majority of end users have PCs, the majority of people can view AVI/Windows without installing other players such as Real Video or QuickTime. For this reason, many Web publishers prefer to render in AVI/Video for Windows format instead of QuickTime or Real Video.

It is possible to create movies in any of these formats through After Effects. In the first few exercises of this chapter, we will suggest that you create movies in your default file type—either QuickTime (Mac) or AVI/Video For Windows (Windows). After that, we'll show that you can create movies using any file type. You'll find helpful charts throughout this chapter that will assist you in your decisions about which file formats and settings to use for various types of projects.

The Render Queue Window

In this chapter, you'll work with a new interface component—the **Render Queue** (the term "queue" means to wait your turn, and is pronounced like the letter Q). This is the window that offers feedback about how you are rendering your final movies. It's possible to render a single composition or to add multiple compositions to the Render Queue and have After Effects render each composition in the order you specify.

The settings in the Render Queue window do not affect your composition, but rather how that composition is published for use outside of After Effects (for video, digital video, Web, etc.) or how it is imported back into an After Effects project.

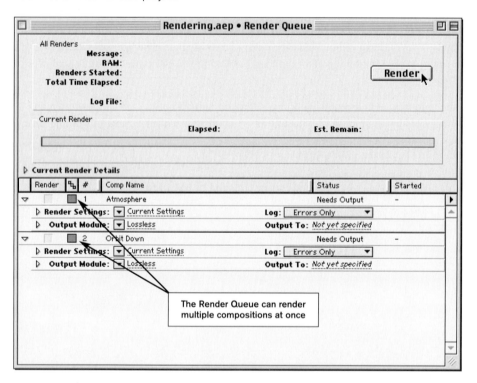

The Render Queue can render
multiple compositions at once

Each item in the Render Queue can be set to the type of output you want. Because there are many output types available, and each output type has its own set of options, rendering is a fairly substantial subject for those with no previous experience in producing digital animation. Sometimes, the best way to learn is by doing, so we'll provide exercises to help you through the learning curve. To begin, we'll show you how to render a single composition. Later we'll show you how to render multiple compositions at once.

I. ⎯⎯⎯⎯⎯⎯⎯⎯**Using the Render Queue Default Settings**

Macintosh versions of After Effects default to producing a QuickTime movie, while Windows versions default to producing an AVI movie. This exercise will walk you through the basics of rendering a movie, using the program's default settings to output a movie. Later in this chapter, you'll learn to change these settings, but for now this exercise will give you the satisfaction of learning the basic rendering steps.

1. Copy the **chap_16** folder from the **H•O•T CD-ROM** to your hard drive.

2. Open the **Rendering.aep** project from the **chap_16** folder.

3. Choose **File > Save As**. Navigate to your **HOT_AE_Projects** folder and click **Save**.

4. Double-click the **Popcorn Planets** composition to open it. Preview this movie to see what it contains.

5. Choose **Composition > Make Movie**, or use the shortcut keys **Command+M** (Mac) or **Control+M** (Windows). You will be prompted to save the movie. On a Mac, After Effects will prompt you to save this as **Popcorn Planets.mov**, and on Windows it will prompt you to save as **Popcorn Planets.avi**. Navigate to your desktop to save it there, and click **OK** (**Save** in OS X). **Note:** After Effects 5.5 users may not be asked where to save the file. In this event, the file is saved automatically to the same folder as the project.

You can save the movie anywhere on your hard drive. We're just suggesting where to save it, so you can find the movie easily once it's rendered.

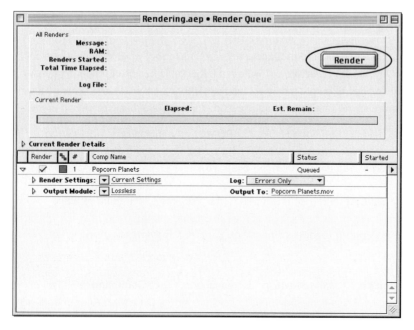

6. The **Render Queue** window opens. Observe that there are all kinds of settings in this window. For now, you'll leave these settings as they are. Simply click the **Render** button.

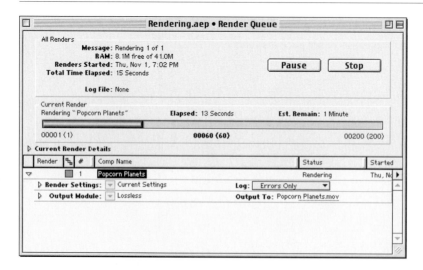

7. Notice that the **Current Render** status bar becomes active, along with messages showing the elapsed time, the estimated time remaining, and other information about the rendering process. This feedback shows you that the movie is being rendered!

8. When the movie has finished rendering, you'll hear a sound byte of a bell ringing, if your sound is turned on. After hearing the sound, locate your **Popcorn Planets.mov** or **Popcorn Planets.avi** movie on the desktop (if that's where you saved it), and double-click it to open the QuickTime or AVI/Video For Windows player. Click the **Play** button and view the movie. **Note to some Windows users:** This file might have to be played in Windows Media Player. If necessary, right-click on the movie icon to choose **Open With > Windows Media Player**.

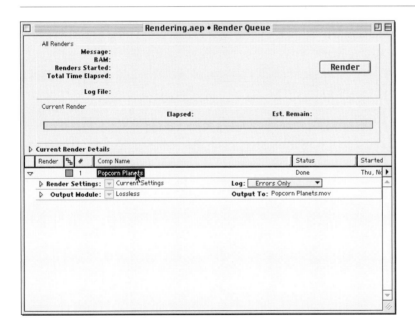

9. When you're finished watching the movie, return to After Effects. In the **Render Queue** window, select the **Popcorn Planets** composition name and press **Delete** (Mac) or **Backspace** (Windows) on your keyboard to delete the rendered composition from the Render Queue. Alternatively, choose **Edit > Clear**. Close the **Render Queue** window.

10. Save the project to your **HOT_AE_Projects** folder and close the **Popcorn Planets** composition. Leave the project open for the next exercise.

NOTE | Deleting Compositions from the Render Queue

It's not necessary to delete the composition from the Render Queue. We make this suggestion only because After Effects does not automatically delete compositions for you. It leaves rendered compositions displayed in the queue in the event that you need to check the settings or statistics for that render. It's up to you to delete rendered compositions when you no longer need to refer to them. You may choose to delete rendered compositions simply to clean out your Render Queue, as it can be confusing to see rendered and unrendered compositions in the same window. Rendered compositions will not be rendered again, even if they are left in the queue.

TIP | Close the Composition Window

Although you can view the results in the Composition window while rendering is in progress, this slows down the rendering. Before starting your render, close the Composition window to make the rendering go as fast as possible. Select the movie you want to render from the Projects window and then press Command+M (Mac) or Control+M (Windows). Everything from step 5 onward in the previous exercise will stay the same, but the process will go faster.

2. ———————————**Changing the Render Settings**

The settings in the Render Queue window are at the heart of outputting final movies. In this exercise, you'll learn to change some of these settings. The focus of this exercise is to teach you how to make a low-resolution test movie. Many After Effects professionals render movies at small sizes to test their work before outputting a final movie at high-resolution settings. At the end of this exercise is a chart that outlines the scope of all the render options and indicates when you would use each one.

1. In the **Project** window, select the **Atmosphere** composition, and then choose **Composition > Make Movie** or use the shortcut **Command+M** (Mac) or **Control+M** (Windows). Save this movie to your **HOT_AE_Projects** folder. **Note:** After Effects 5.5 users may not be asked where to save the file. In this event, the file is saved automatically to the same folder as the project.

Feel free to open and preview the Atmosphere composition before you render it. Remember to close the composition before you render it, however, because it takes longer to render a composition that is open.

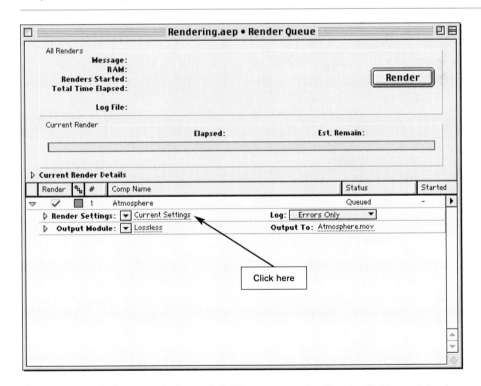

2. Click the underlined words **Current Settings** to open the **Render Settings** dialog box.

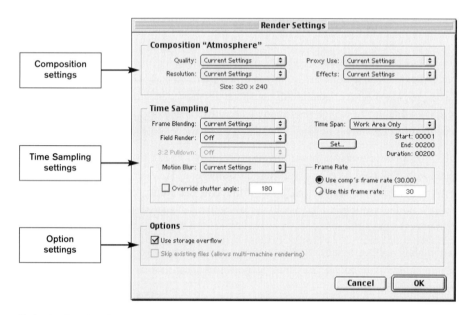

3. In the **Render Settings** dialog box, notice that there are three groups of settings: **Composition**, **Time Sampling**, and **Options**. To read about these choices, check out the chart at the end of this exercise. Meanwhile, we'll walk you through changing some of the settings.

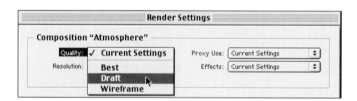

4. In the **Composition** section, click the **Quality** pop-up menu. Select **Draft** quality.

Best quality is generally used for final output. Draft quality is generally used when you need to do a test movie and you don't want to wait for Best quality to render. Wireframe quality will render wireframe outlines of each layer; it is extremely quick but lacks detail. These are the same settings available in the Quality switch in the composition's Timeline. The default is Current Settings, which pulls the setting used in your composition. Therefore, if your composition's Quality switch is set to Best, Current Settings will use that setting and you don't have to make a change here.

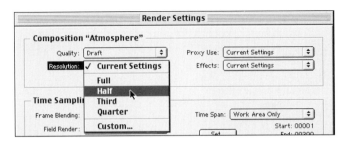

5. Click the **Resolution** pop-up menu and select **Half** resolution. After you make this change, notice that the **Size** indicates the composition size, with the half size in parentheses.

The Resolution default is Current Settings, which uses the resolution that you set for your composition. You would generally choose a smaller size for your resolution when you are making test movies, in order to speed up the rendering time and to get a quick sense of what your movie will look like.

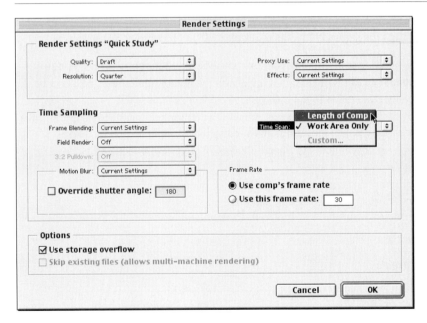

6. In the **Time Sampling** options, click the **Time Span** option and select **Length of Comp**. Click **OK** to close the Render Settings dialog box.

The Time Span setting is an important option. The default is Work Area Only. You learned to set the work area in Chapter 7, "Previewing Movies." However, in most cases you'll probably want to output the entire composition. For this reason, you should make it a habit to check this option each time you set up a composition to be rendered. The chart at the end of this exercise explains all of the settings in the Render Settings dialog box.

7. In the **Render Queue** window, click **Render**.

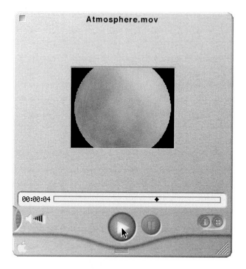

8. When your render completes, locate the **Atmosphere.mov** (Mac) or **Atmosphere.avi** (Windows) movie and double-click to open it. Click the **Play** button to view the results. This should be a smaller movie because of the changes you made to the settings.

9. In the **Render Queue** window, select the **Atmosphere** composition name and press **Delete**, or **Backspace** on Windows, to remove it from the Render Queue. Alternatively, select **Edit > Clear**. Close the Render Queue window.

10. Save your project and leave it open for the next exercise.

The Render Settings Dialog Box

Options	Settings	Description
COMPOSITION SETTINGS		
Quality	Current Settings Best Draft Wireframe	Best quality takes longest to render; use it for final output. Use Draft quality for rendering test movies, when speed of rendering is more important than quality. Wireframe quality renders only wireframe outlines of each layer. It is extremely quick but lacks detail. Current Settings, the default, uses the Quality setting in your composition.
Resolution	Current Settings Full Half Third Quarter Custom	These terms relate to the original size setting in the composition that is being rendered. When you choose one of the sizes, the Size field displays the dimensions in pixels. The Custom setting allows you to enter your own settings. After Effects artists generally pick smaller resolution settings when they want the movie to render faster, since it takes less time to render a lower-resolution movie.
Proxy Use	Current Settings Use All Proxies Use Comp Proxies Only Use No Proxies	Proxies are an advanced feature that allow you to set up dummy footage that can later be swapped with real footage. They are often used as a faster method of working by professionals who are creating high-resolution movies. The idea is that you make a low-resolution "proxy" of your footage, and once you're happy with how everything looks, you replace the proxy footage with the final footage. To learn more about proxies, refer to the After Effects manual.
Effects	Current Settings All On All Off	Current Settings uses the effects that you have active in your composition. You can also choose to render with all effects on or with all effects off (overriding the composition setting). Movies render more quickly with effects off, so consider using All Off if you need to speed up rendering.

continues on next page

Options	Settings	Description
The Render Settings Dialog Box *continued*		
TIME SAMPLING SETTINGS		
Frame Blending	Current Settings On For Checked Layers Off For All Layers	Frame blending can be used only on moving footage and is set in the Switches area of the Timeline. It creates an effect of a cross dissolve (one image fading out while another image fades in) and is usually used in footage that has been time-stretched. To learn more about frame blending and time stretching, refer to the After Effects user manual.
Field Rendering	Off Upper Field First Lower Field First	Field rendering is used only in video projects, not for film or the Web, because it deals with video fields that are present only in video footage and output. Use this option if you are outputting to NTSC or PAL video, for example. Before you can accurately set this option, you will need to know whether your video hardware (camera and recording deck) uses *upper field first* or *lower field first*. If you are not outputting to video, leave this option set to Off.
Time Span	Length of Comp Work Area Only Custom	The default time span is Work Area Only. You learned to set the work area in Chapter 7, "*Previewing Movies*". You will usually want to set this to Length of Comp to output the entire composition. The Custom setting allows you to specify time spans that aren't tied to the length of the composition or the work area.
Motion Blur	Current Settings On For Checked Layers Off For All Layers	The Motion Blur setting defines how you want to treat motion blur in the rendered output. Motion Blur must be activated in the Switches panel of the Timeline. You learned about this panel in Chapter 8, "*Layers*."
Frame Rate	Use comp's frame rate Use this frame rate	You can choose to use the composition's frame rate or set a different frame rate. Sometimes you'll choose to raise or lower the frame rate of your movie to save rendering time or disk space.
OPTIONS SETTINGS		
Use storage overflow		If your hard disk fills up before the render is complete, this option, when selected, will use another hard disk that you specify as the overflow volume. To specify overflow volumes, choose Edit > Preferences > Output.

3. ——————————**Working with the Output Module**

In the last exercise, you worked with the Render settings in the Render Queue This time, you'll learn to work with the **Output Module** that's also located in the Render Queue. Here you'll learn to choose a format and set format options. **Note to After Effects 5.0 users:** Most of the screen shots in this exercise were taken with After Effects 5.5. There are slight variations in the layout, but the content is the same for both versions.

> **1.** In the **Project** window, select the **3D Text** composition.

> **2.** Choose **Composition > Make Movie**, or press **Command+M** (Mac) or **Control+M** (Windows.) Save your movie to the **HOT_AE_Projects** folder. **Note:** After Effects 5.5 users are not asked where to save the file. It is saved automatically to the save folder as the project.

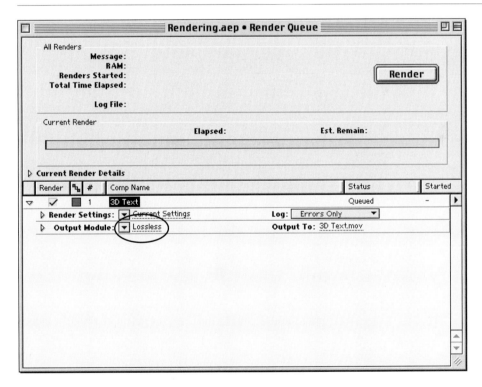

> **3.** In the **Render Queue** window, click on the underlined word **Lossless**. This opens the **Output Module Settings** dialog box. At the end of this exercise, you will find a chart that lists most of the features found inside this dialog box. For now, you'll learn to change the settings appropriate to this exercise.

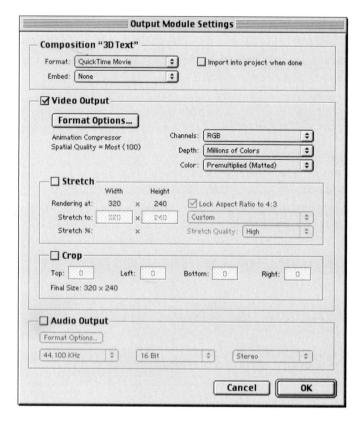

The Output Module Settings dialog box will open.

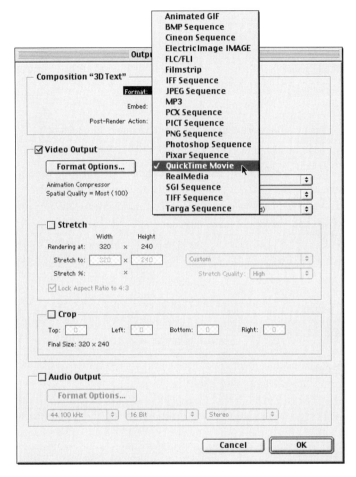

4. In the **Composition** settings, click the arrow to the right of the **Format** option, and observe the different output formats available. Make sure **QuickTime Movie** is selected. QuickTime Movie is the default format on a Mac; AVI/Video For Windows is the default format on Windows. **Note to Windows users using After Effects 5.5:** The Compression Settings dialog box will pop up automatically when you choose this setting. If this is the case, skip to step 7.

The "Output Format Types" chart at the end of this exercise explains all the format types and their uses.

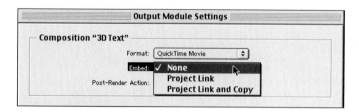

5. Click the **Embed** option and observe the options available. For this exercise, leave the selection to **None**.

If you are working with other Adobe products, like Premiere you can use the Embed option to create a link to the original After Effects project. The Project Link option will embed a link only. The Project Link and Copy option will embed a link and a copy of the project in the output file. When you use an embedded output file in Premiere, you can use the Edit Original command to easily reopen the project in After Effects.

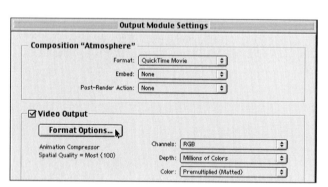

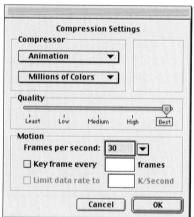

6. In the **Video Output** settings, click the **Format Options** button. The **Compression Settings** dialog box opens.

If a format other than QuickTime is selected, other sets of options are displayed. After Effects does a great job of providing the appropriate options for all supported formats.

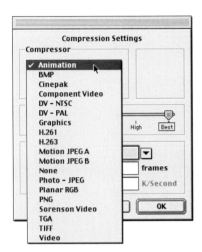

7. In the **Compression Settings** dialog box, click the **Compressor** pop-up menu that says **Animation**. Observe all the compressor types available. For this exercise, leave the compressor type set to **Animation**.

The Animation setting represents the Animation compressor. The Animation compressor is used to preserve high-quality visuals, but it can also result in large files, which aren't suitable for certain kinds of output, such as the Web. The "QuickTime Compressors" chart at the end of this exercise explains all of the compressor types and their uses.

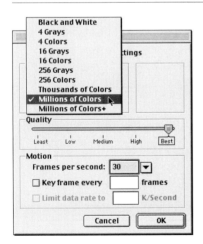

8. Click the **Color Depth** option that says **Millions of Colors**. For now, leave the setting at **Millions of Colors**.

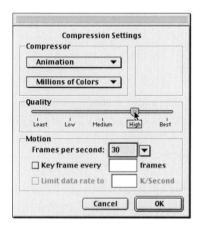

9. Set the **Quality** slider to **High**.

The Animation compressor offers a full range of quality. Best quality will result in lossless output, which means that there will be no loss of image quality. Least quality will probably show image degradation due to compression. Other compressors may or may not offer a range of quality settings as an option.

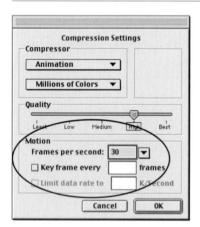

10. Observe the **Motion** section in the Compression Settings dialog box. These options allow you to set the number of frames per second, add a QuickTime key frame (not the same as an After Effects keyframe), and, for streaming video, limit the data rate. For this exercise, leave these settings as they are and click **OK**.

A key frame in QuickTime sets a reference for the compressor. Reference frames are not highly compressed. The more QuickTime key frames you set, the larger your output file. Keyframes in After Effects are different from key frames in QuickTime. A longer description of QuickTime key frames can be found in the chart at the end of this exercise.

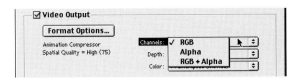

11. Back in the **Video Output** options of the **Output Module Settings** dialog box, click the **Channels** option and notice that you can select RGB only, Alpha only, or RGB + Alpha as for your output. For this exercise, make sure that **RGB** is selected. This is the most common setting. If you wanted to export a mask or a movie with a mask, you would choose one of the other settings. You'll get a chance to do this at the end of this chapter.

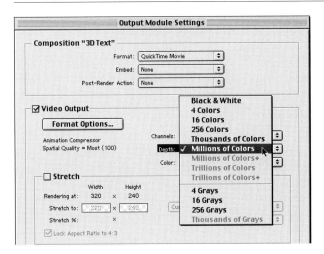

12. Click the **Depth** option and notice that the color bit depth is set to **Millions of Colors**. This option is redundant with the Colors option under Format Options. If you change the setting in either place, they both change. Again, leave it set to **Millions of Colors**.

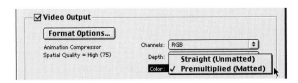

13. Click the **Color** option and notice the choices of **Straight (Unmatted)** and **Premultiplied (Matted)**. For this exercise, leave the setting at **Premultiplied (Matted)**.

Straight means that the alpha channel is straight alpha (not premultiplied with color values). Premultiplied means that the alpha channel is multiplied with color values. For most purposes, the Premultiplied option is used.

14. Observe the **Stretch** options. If you needed to stretch your output to a larger size, you would do it here by clicking the Stretch check box and typing in the size you want. For this exercise, leave the Stretch options untouched.

Stretching in After Effects will scale the movie to be larger or smaller, depending on the values you enter. We do not recommend that you stretch your final output because the image quality will be severely degraded. If you have to provide a larger output than anticipated for your project and you must use the Stretch options, be sure to set the Stretch Quality to High. In general, avoid using the Stretch options, if at all possible.

15. Observe the **Crop** options. If you needed to crop pixels off of any side of your composition, you would do it here by clicking the Crop check box and typing in the number of pixels that you wish to crop. For example, typing 10 in each box would remove 10 pixels on each side of the output. For this exercise, leave the Crop options untouched.

16. Observe the **Audio Output** options. If you needed to output audio in your QuickTime movie, you would specify it here by clicking the Audio Output check box and selecting appropriate options. In this exercise, leave the Audio options untouched. Click **OK** to complete the Output Module settings for your render.

You will learn how to use the Audio Output options in the next exercise.

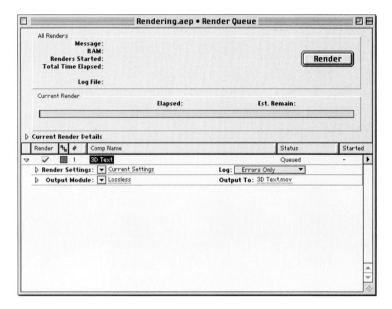

17. In the **Render Queue** window, click **Render**.

This composition is fairly complex and will take a few minutes to render. Watch the estimated time remaining, and take a short break if you like while the rendering completes.

18. When the rendering completes, double-click the QuickTime movie to play it in the QuickTime Player.

19. In the **Render Queue** window, select the **3D Text** comp name and press **Delete** on your keyboard to delete the rendered composition from the Render Queue. Alternatively, select **Edit > Clear**.

20. Save your project and leave it open for the next exercise.

The Output Module Settings Dialog Box

You got to work with the Output Module in the previous exercise. This module is a very important part of After Effects. It is where you choose exactly the type of format you wish to output and the options for the format type. For example, you can choose to output a sequence of TIFF images, a QuickTime movie, or an animated GIF file, to name just a few of the format choices available.

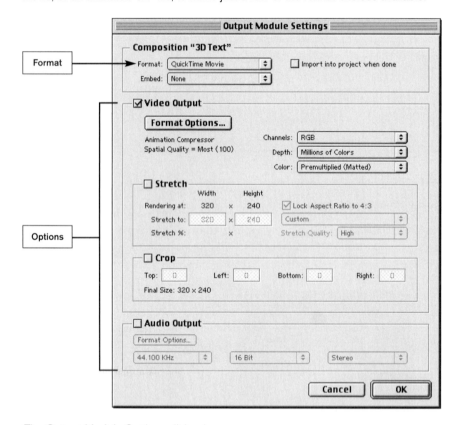

The Output Module Settings dialog box.

Here is a chart that describes the numerous features in this important dialog box.

Output Module Settings Dialog Box	
Setting	**Description**
COMPOSITION SETTINGS	
Format	Allows you to choose the format for your movie. See the "Output Format Types" chart that follows this one for a description of the available formats.
Embed	Allows you to set your movie so that it can be opened using Edit Original in programs that support this feature, such as Adobe Premiere. This allows you to launch an After Effects movie from within Premiere by double-clicking on the movie file. Any changes made to the movie in After Effects will appear in the Premiere project.
Post-Render Action	Import into Project When Done causes the finished movie to be imported into the current project when it's finished rendering.
VIDEO OUTPUT SETTINGS	
Format Options	Opens another dialog box that lets you specify format-specific options. For example, QuickTime will have different options than TIFF.
Channels	Allows you to set how many channels your movie will have. Most movies are rendered in RGB, although you can also render in RGB+Alpha, which stores the movie and an alpha channel.
Depth	Sets the bit depth of the movie. This option controls whether the movie is in grayscale, in color, or in color with an alpha channel.
Color	Specifies how colors are treated in the alpha channel. The options are Straight (Unmatted) and Premultiplied (Matted). The Premultiplied option is used for most purposes. These options are discussed in Chapter 9, "*Parenting*."
Stretch	This group of options specifies the dimensions of your final movie. If you enter dimensions that differ from the composition settings, you can choose to do so at a Low or High quality.

The following chart describes the format choices that appear on the Format pop-up menu.

Output Format Types	
Format	**Use**
Amiga IFF Sequence	A format designed for the Amiga computer.
Animated GIF	A very popular Web file format, often used for Web banners, cartoons, buttons, and simple animated graphics. GIF stands for Graphics Interchange Format.
BMP Sequence	Microsoft Windows Bitmap format.
Cineon Sequence	The Cineon file format was developed by Kodak. It is the standard file format used for professional motion picture visual effects.
Electric Image IMAGE	Electric Image is a 3D animation package. IMAGE files can be used as texture maps or cards within Electric Image.
FLC/FLI	Autodesk's "Flic" animation format was designed for Autodesk Animator and Animator Pro.
Filmstrip	The Photoshop filmstrip format was developed to contain a series of animating images that can be brought into Photoshop. This is a single file that can contain many images.
JPEG Sequence	JPEG is the popular Web file format used for continuous-tone images such as photographs. Use this format if you need to output a single image or group of images to the Web.
MP3	MP3 is an audio file format used extensively on the Web and in personal audio players.
PCX Sequence	PC Paintbrush format. You might choose this format if you needed to get a sequence of images from After Effects into another program that supports PCX.
PICT Sequence	PICT is a Macintosh image file format. You might choose this format if you needed to get a sequence of images from After Effects into another program that supports PICT.
	continues on next page

Output Format Types *continued*	
Format	**Use**
PNG Sequence	PNG is a cross-platform image file format utilizing lossless compression. Images can include an alpha channel. It is a public domain format that can be used to transport images between computers or to store images with very good compression. You might choose this format if you needed to get a sequence of images from After Effects into another program that supports PNG.
Photoshop Sequence	Use this format to output a single file or a sequence of images to Photoshop.
Pixar Sequence	Pixar format is sometimes used in professional motion picture and television work with proprietary software applications. You might choose this format if you needed to get a sequence of images from After Effects into another program that supports Pixar.
QuickTime Movie	The Apple QuickTime format is a cross-platform standard for distributing movies. QuickTime is a container file that will hold various types of audio, moving pictures, Web links, and other data. This is probably the most useful format for most digital artists working in After Effects.
SGI Sequence	This file format is used by SGI computer workstations. It is usually used only by scientific or visual effects facilities.
TIFF Sequence	Tag Image File Format is a cross-platform image file format used for lossless compression. Images can include an alpha channel. Use this format to transport images between computers or to store images with fairly good compression.
Targa Sequence	Targa is an image file format used on PCs that have Targa hardware. It has also been widely used for scanners and imaging software.

The following chart describes the compressor types available in the Compression Settings dialog box.

QuickTime Compressors	
Compressor	**Use**
Animation	Use this compressor when you have large areas of solid color, such as cartoons or motion graphics. The size will be large, and it is best for film or video projects, not the Web or CD-ROM.
BMP	BMP is a Windows image file format with medium-quality compression. Use this compressor to transport images between computers.
Cinepak	Use this option to compress 24-bit movies intended for CD-ROMs.
Component Video	This compressor can be used to output through an analog video card, if your computer has one.
DV-NTSC	Use this codec to transfer digital video to an external digital video recorder. NTSC is the standard used in North America.
DV-PAL	Use this codec to transfer digital video to an external digital video recorder. PAL is the standard used in most of Europe.
Graphics	The Graphics compressor creates 8-bit images and is intended primarily for still images.
H.261 & H.263	These codecs were developed for video conferencing. H.263 can be used for streaming Web video as well.
Motion J-PEG A Motion J-PEG B	These compressors are useful for creating video files that work with Motion J-PEG hardware such as capture and playback cards.
None	This selection means that no compression will be applied. Selecting this results in very large, lossless files.
Photo–JPEG	This compression scheme is intended for images that contain gradual color changes. It offers a range of quality settings.
Planar RGB	A lossless compression scheme intended for large areas of solid color. Use as an alternative to the Animation compressor.
PNG	PNG is a cross-platform image file format utilizing lossless compression. Images can include an alpha channel. Use this compressor to transport images between computers.

continues on next page

QuickTime Compressors *continued*	
Compressor	**Use**
Sorenson Video	Useful for compressing 24-bit movies to be used as streaming video on the Web. It can also be used to compress movies for CD-ROMs. It produces better picture quality and smaller files than Cinepak.
TGA	TGA is for use with Targa hardware.
TIFF	TIFF is a cross-platform image file format used for lossless compression. Images can include an alpha channel. Use this compressor to transport images between computers.
Video	This compressor is useful for capturing analog video. It supports both spatial and temporal compression of 16-bit movies with fairly high quality. Use it as an alternative to the Component Video compressor.

4. —————————**Rendering Audio**

Just as you can use various image compression schemes, you can also use audio compression to output audio files. In this exercise you will learn to select audio compression and render audio.

1. In the **Project** window, select the **Orbit Down** composition.

2. Choose **Composition > Add To Render Queue**. Alternatively, press **Command+Shift+/** (Mac) or **Control+Shift+/** (Windows). **Note:** The Add to Render Queue command is another way to begin the process of making a movie. It is used often because you can add multiple compositions to the queue at once this way. In this example, however, we are simply showing this as an alternative method to the Make Movie command you've used in earlier exercises.

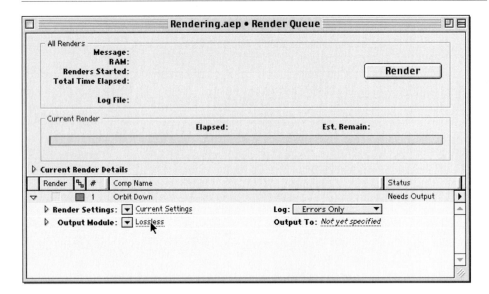

3. In the **Render Queue** window, click on the underlined word **Lossless**.

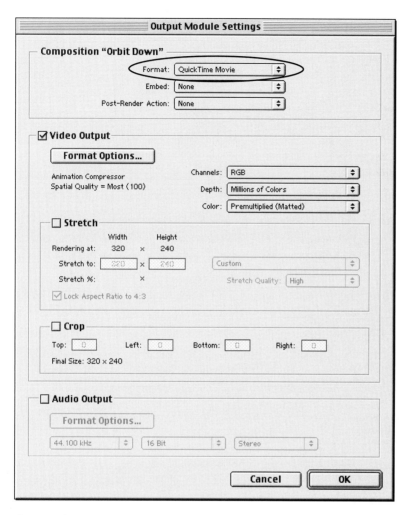

4. In the **Output Module Settings** dialog box, make sure the **Format** is set to **QuickTime Movie**. QuickTime is one of the only formats that can include audio.

5. Click the **Audio Output** check box, and then click the **Format Options** button in this option group.

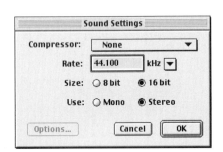
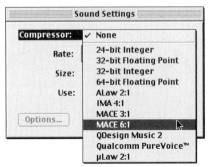

6. In the **Sound Settings** dialog box, click the **Compressor** option, select **MACE6:1, and then click** OK.

See the "QuickTime Audio Compressors" chart at the end of this exercise for information on each audio compressor type. We have chosen MACE 6:1 here, because it is a good all-purpose audio compression choice.

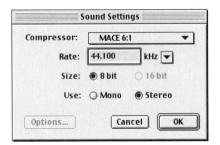

7. Accept the default **Rate, Size**, and **Use** options and click **OK**.

Rate specifies the audio sample rate in kilohertz; the higher the sample rate, the better the quality. High-quality settings are generally selected if you're going to put the movie on broadcast video. Lower audio sample rates are used when the file size is a concern, such as for Web, multimedia, or DVD output. A variety of standard sample rates can be selected from the small drop-down menu. The Size option refers to the bit depth. Just as images can have 8 bits or 16 bits per channel, audio channels are also in sizes of 8 bits and 16 bits. A high bit rate will sound better but will result in a larger file size. The Use option allows you to specify Mono for one audio channel or Stereo for two audio channels.

8. In the **Output Module Settings** dialog box, click **OK**. In After Effects 5.0 the **Output Movie** dialog box opens. In After Effects 5.5 you will be returned to the **Render Queue** window.

9. In the **Output Movie** dialog box, navigate to the desktop and click **Save**. Click the **Render** button in the **Render Queue** window.

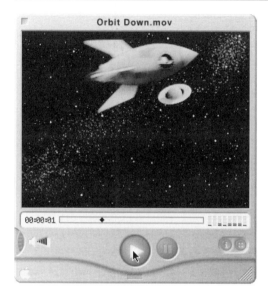

10. When your movie finishes rendering, play the movie in the QuickTime Player. You should hear audio with it!

11. In the **Render Queue** window, select the **Orbit Down** composition name and press **Delete**, or **Backspace** in Windows, on your keyboard to delete the rendered composition from the Render Queue. Alternatively, choose **Edit > Clear**.

12. Save your project and leave it open for the next exercise.

The following chart will help you sort out the various audio compressors available in the Sound Settings dialog box.

QuickTime Audio Compressors	
Compressor	**Use**
24-bit Integer and 32-bit Integer	These compressors are useful when preparing micro-processor-specific audio. If you are a hardware or software engineer, they can be useful, but they are generally not employed in animation or video editing.
32-bit Floating Point and 64-bit Floating Point	These compressors are useful when preparing micro-processor-specific audio but are not generally employed in animation or video editing.
ALaw 2:1	Used primarily for digital telephony in Europe.
IMA 4:1	Useful for cross-platform multimedia audio.
MACE 3:1 MACE 6:1	The Macintosh Audio Compression and Expansion codec (MACE) is a general-purpose audio codec available on both Macintosh and Windows platforms with QuickTime version 3.0 or greater. If you don't know which audio compression format to choose, this is a good all-purpose choice.
Qdesign Music 2	Useful for compressing high-quality music for Internet distribution. This compressor allows CD-quality sound to be delivered over a 28.8 modem connection.
Qualcomm PureVoice	This compressor is intended for speech only and is based on cellular phone technology. If you have a movie with narration, choose this option!
μ-Law 2:1	μ-Law is a standard audio format on many Unix workstations.

5.————————**Saving Alpha Channels or Motion Masks**

Sometimes it's useful to output only the alpha channel for a composition. Perhaps you want to bring some type that you designed in After Effects into another program, such as Apple's Final Cut Pro or Adobe's Premiere. Those programs will honor the alpha channel output by After Effects. In addition, many 3D programs use alpha channel information from QuickTime movies to create interesting texture effects. You can even bring the finished movie back into After Effects itself, and it will honor the alpha channel.

In this exercise you will learn to output only the alpha channel of a composition.

1. In the **Project** window, double-click the **Alpha Mask** composition to open it.

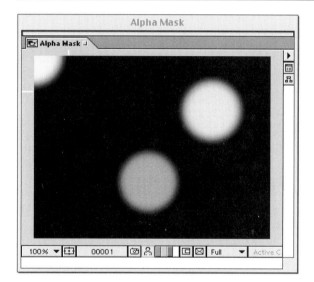

2. Click **RAM Preview** to preview the animation in color. Notice that the color circles have feathered edges. The circles and edges were all created in After Effects as solid layers, and we used mask settings with feathering to create the shapes. Whenever you create masks in this way in After Effects, the program creates an alpha channel for the composition. When you're done, close the Composition window.

Tip: *Remember, rendering is faster with the Composition window closed.*

3. Choose **Composition > Make Movie**, or press **Command+M** (Mac) or **Control+M** (Windows). Navigate to the **HOT_AE_Projects** folder where you've been saving your work. Name the file **Alpha Mask.mov** and click **OK**. **Note:** After Effects 5.5 users are not asked where to save the file. It is saved automatically to the same folder as the project.

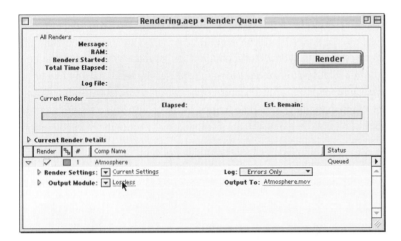

4. In the **Render Queue** window, click the underlined word **Lossless** after **Output Module**.

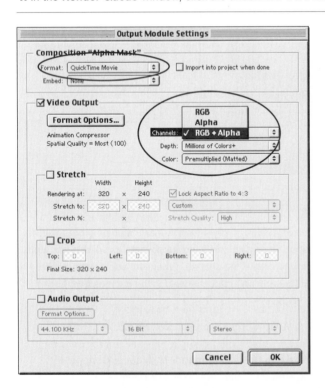

5. In the **Output Module Settings** dialog box, make sure that **QuickTime Movie** is selected as the **Format**. Click the **Channels** option and select **RGB+Alpha**. This tells After Effects that you want to make a movie that includes an alpha channel. Accept all other default settings and click **OK**.

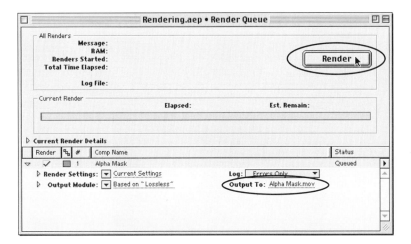

6. In the **Render Queue** window, click **Render**.

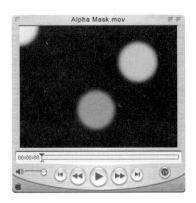

7. When the movie has been rendered, open the **HOT_AE_Projects** folder on your hard drive to locate and play the movie in the QuickTime Player. After Effects 5.5 users should go to the **HOT_AE_Projects** folder to locate their movie.

It looks like a normal movie, identical to what you saw in the Composition window. The difference occurs when you combine this movie with another movie by bringing it back into an After Effects composition or into another program, such as Apple Final Cut Pro or Premiere. When you do that, all the black areas will become transparent and the three colored circles will float on top of other content. You'll get to bring this movie file back into After Effects soon to see what we mean.

8. Return to After Effects. In the **Render Queue** window, select the **Alpha Mask** composition name and press **Delete**, or **Backspace** in Windows, on your keyboard to delete the rendered composition from the render queue. Alternatively, choose **Edit > Clear**.

9. Double-click inside the **Project** window to access the **Import File** dialog box. Navigate to the **HOT_AE_Projects** folder, and open the **Alpha Mask.mov** movie that you just rendered.

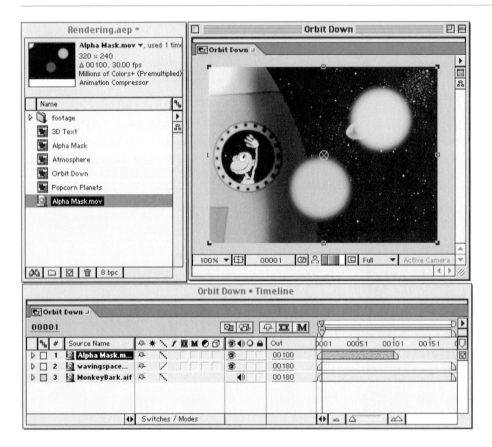

10. Open the **Orbit Down** composition from the **Project** window. Drag **Alpha Mask.mov** into the **Orbit Down** Composition window. Make sure it is positioned above the other layers—it should be listed first, as shown above.

Notice that the circles appear to float over the rest of the layers. That's because you rendered the movie with its alpha channel, and the circles are masked as a result. During the course of this book, you've worked with lots of movie files in various compositions that we created for you. This is how we did it—by rendering the alpha channel. Sometimes you want to render a movie for a layer element instead of for a final output element, as you did in this exercise. Doing so makes sense when you have a lot of layers and your composition is getting bogged down trying to render everything at once.

11. Save the project and close the **Orbit Down** composition. You won't be needing it again.

How Can You See the Alpha Channel of a Composition?

When you want to render a movie with an alpha channel, you first have to know whether the composition contains an alpha channel. As we described in previous chapters, it's easy to bring artwork into After Effects from Photoshop or Illustrator and have it preserve the transparency. When you render a composition, however, you are rendering all the layers inside your composition, and some layers might have transparency while others don't. For this reason, it becomes important to know what the alpha channel of the composition looks like before you choose to render a composition with it.

When you open the Alpha Mask composition from the Render.aep project that you just worked with, you can't tell right away that the composition contains an alpha channel. You might be wondering, as you progress to creating your own projects, how you'll know whether a composition contains an alpha channel.

Show Alpha Channel button

Every Composition window has a row of red, green, blue, and white colored buttons at the bottom. To see the alpha channel, click the white button, as shown above. This is the **Show Alpha Channel button**. The other buttons let you view the R, G, or B channels. You might want to open some of the other compositions in this project and click on those buttons to check them out. The majority of the compositions in the Render.aep project that you are working with in this chapter will show a solid white alpha channel if you click on the Show Alpha Channel button. That's because they use images as backgrounds that take up the entire screen, so the alpha channels for the composition look completely white. Try turning off background layers, and you'll see shapes emerge in the alpha channel.

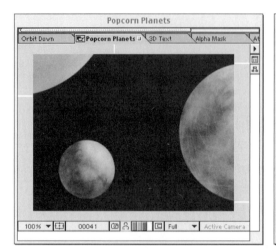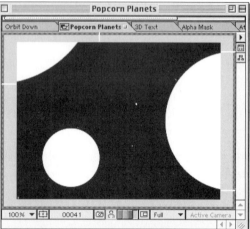

For example, try opening the Popcorn Planet composition and clicking the Show Alpha Channel button. The entire composition will turn white. If you turn off the last layer in this composition (space_backdrop.psd) and click the Show Alpha Channel button again, you'll see the shapes of the planets appear in white. Before you turned off the last layer, it was showing the alpha channel for the background layer. If you wanted to put these planets over some live action, you would need to turn the background layer off and render the composition with its alpha channel, as you learned to do in the last exercise. You could then bring the movie back into After Effects, where the planets would composite perfectly over the other layers you put into the composition. Likewise, you could take this move to Premiere or Final Cut Pro and the planets would mask over other footage.

In general, the white areas of the alpha channel are used to reveal the image in the document, while the black areas mask that image.

After Effects for the Web

We're assuming that once you get into After Effects you might want to put a portfolio of your work on the Web. This isn't a hands-on exercise, but we'll cover some of the important issues related to Web delivery in this section.

When creating for the Web, we recommend that you work with the QuickTime format. In the Output Module Settings dialog box, make sure that the Format is QuickTime Movie. Click the Format Options button.

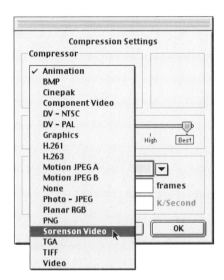

In the Compression Settings dialog box, for the Compressor type select Sorenson Video, which is the best choice for compressing 24-bit movies as streaming video.

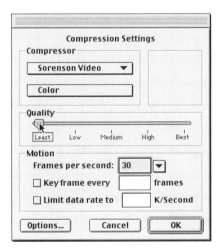

Next, experiment with the Quality setting. The lower the quality, the smaller the file will be. When publishing for the Web, always lower the frames per second to 15 or less. You can also change the key frame rate to make smaller Web movies. Recall that key frames in QuickTime are different from keyframes in After Effects. Adobe recommends a 3:1 formula to come up with a key frame rate. For example, if you choose a frame rate of 15, multiply it by 3, for a value of 45. To enter 45 as the key frame rate, check the "Key frame every" check box, and enter 45 for the value. The data rate varies depending on the speed of your end user's system. Sample data rates are: 28k modem = 2.5K per second, 56k modem = 4.0K per second, ISDN = 12K per second, and T1 = 20K per second. It's better to set your data rates for slower modems so that everyone can see your work, not just those with high-speed Internet access.

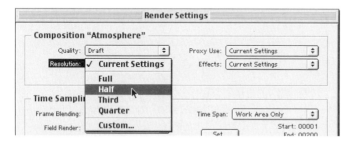

You might also want to set your resolution to Half, Third, or Quarter. Every bit of savings you can eke out of the file will save your end users downloading time.

TIP | HTML Needed for QuickTime Movies

After Effects doesn't write HTML, as some other Adobe products do. Therefore, it's up to you to write this code yourself. This is the HTML code we use to put QuickTime movies on our Web site. Feel free to use it, if you need to! If you don't know how to write HTML at all, see the resources listed in the back of this book in the Resource Appendix.

```
<embed src="chap2/01_using_the_mixer.mov" width="640" height="496" autoplay="true"
loop="true" controller="true" playeveryframe="false" cache="false" bgcolor="#FFFFFF"
kioskmode="false" targetcache="false" pluginspage="http://www.apple.com/quicktime/"
align="middle">

</embed>
```

TIP | Adding Output Modules

You can add additional Output Modules to any item in the Render Queue. This will allow you to output more than one version from the same item, using the same Render settings.

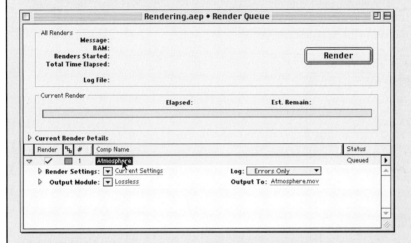

To add an Output Module, select the composition name in the Render Queue window.

Choose Composition > Add Output Module.

Another Output Module is added to the item, and you can create different output settings by clicking on its settings and changing them. When you click Render, After Effects will actually create multiple movies with different settings.

6.————————**Saving RAM Previews**

RAM previews can be saved as movie files. This allows you to save a permanent movie file quickly and easily, without making a visit to the Render Queue window. (Although the Render Queue will open quickly, you can't make any changes to settings there.) Most After Effects artists save RAM previews to be able to view them again and again, show one to a client as a quick rough, or to import them back into a project as source footage for compositions.

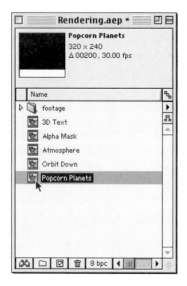

1. In the **Project** window, double-click the **Popcorn Planets** composition to open it.

Note: The composition must be open to save a RAM preview.

2. Choose **Composition > Save RAM Preview**. Once you choose this menu setting, After Effects appears to play the composition for you. While it is playing, it is rendering the composition, and it will prompt you when it is finished.

3. When the RAM preview ends, in the **Output Module Settings** dialog box, navigate to your **HOT_AE_Projects** folder to save the movie. Notice that the Render Queue pops up, and your movie renders as if you had selected Make Movie.

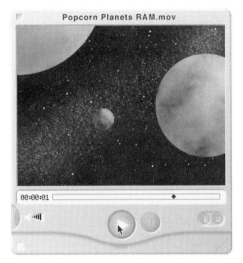

4. After your movie renders, open and view it in the QuickTime or AVI player.

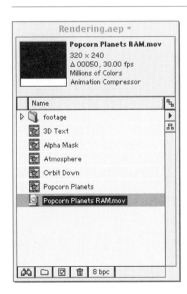

5. In the **Project** window, notice that the rendered RAM movie is automatically imported as footage. You might want to keep it there, or you might want to drag it to the Trashcan icon at the bottom of the Project window if you don't need to use it.

6. Save your project and leave it open for the next exercise.

7. ───────────Creating and Using Rendering Templates

As you've seen, the Render settings can get quite complex. Wouldn't it be neat if you could come up with your favorite settings and save them so you could access them when you needed them? You can! **Rendering templates** store predefined settings, and they're easy to make. Both the Render settings and the Output Module settings have a few default templates that you can choose from a drop-down menu. These templates have specific settings for rendering and output. Better yet, you can create your own templates with exactly the settings you need. This means that you can store the settings that you use often and have them appear via a drop-down menu. When you create a template, you can give it a name that is meaningful to your work style. In this exercise, you'll learn how to create rendering templates and choose rendering templates at output.

1. In the **Project** window, select the **Popcorn Planets** composition.

2. Choose **Composition > Make Movie**. Alternatively, press **Command+M** (Mac) or **Control+M** (Windows). Navigate to your **HOT_AE_Projects** folder and save it there. **Note:** After Effects 5.5 users are not asked where to save the file. It is saved automatically to the same folder as the project.

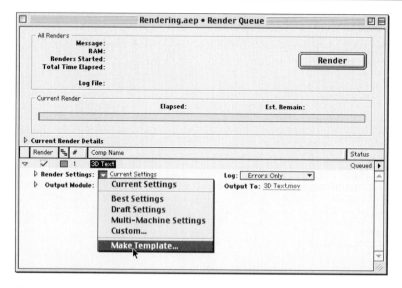

3. In the **Render Queue** window, click the arrow next to the **Render Settings** option and select **Make Template** from the drop-down menu.

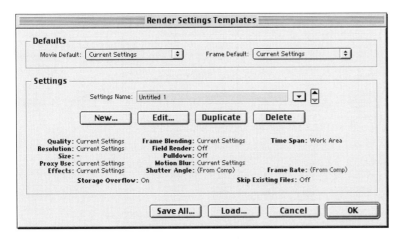

4. In the **Render Settings Templates** dialog box, locate the **Settings Name** entry box and type **Quick Study** as the name for the template. Click **Edit**. The **Render Settings** dialog box opens.

Note: This is an After Effects 5.0 screen shot. The After Effects 5.5 screen will look slightly different but will have the same functionality. To see how the After Effects 5.5 screen looks, check out step 9.

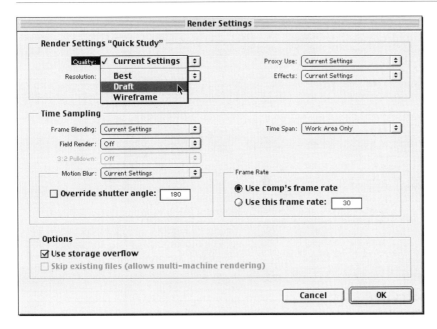

5. In the **Render Settings** dialog box, click to see the **Quality** menu and select **Draft**. In this the next few steps, you are going to create settings for a low-quality, quick-rendering, rough draft movie.

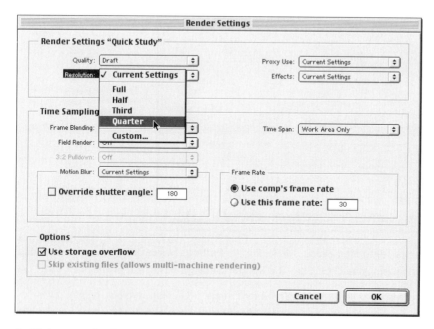

6. Click to see the **Resolution** menu and select **Quarter**.

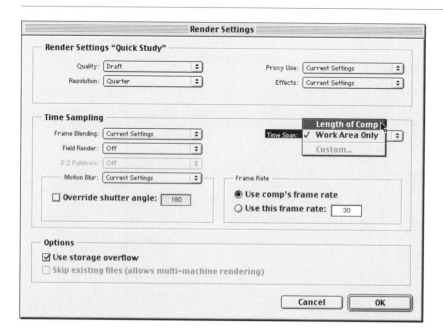

7. Click to see the **Time Span** menu and select **Length of Comp**.

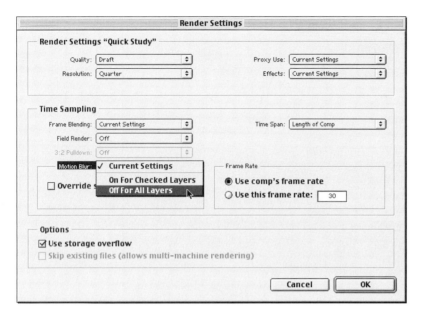

8. For the **Motion Blur** option, select **Off For All Layers**. Click **OK** to return to the Render Settings Templates dialog box.

In the following steps you will create a second template to be used for when rendering high-end movies.

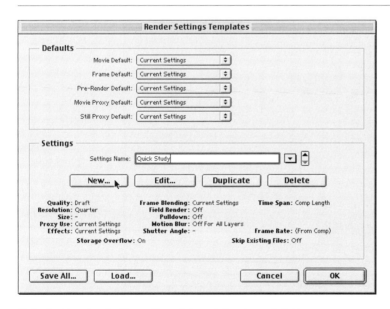

9. In the **Render Settings Templates** dialog box, click **New**.

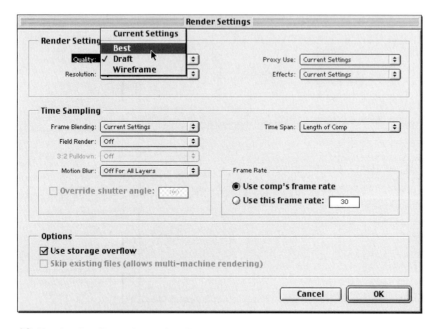

10. For the **Quality** option, select **Best**.

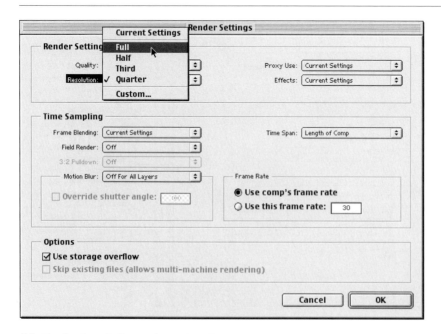

11. For the **Resolution** option, select **Full**.

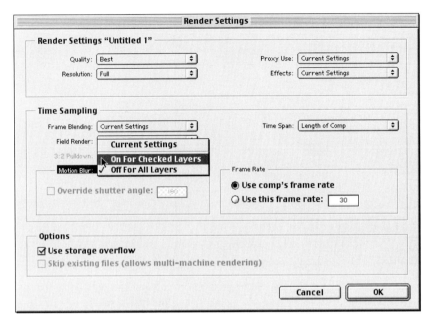

12. For the **Motion Blur** option, select **On For Checked Layers**. Click **OK**.

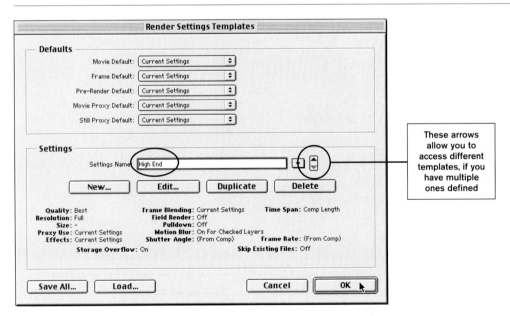

These arrows allow you to access different templates, if you have multiple ones defined

13. In the **Settings Name** entry box, type **High End** for the name of the new template. Click **OK**.

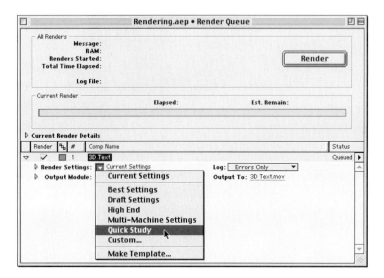

14. In the **Render Queue** window, click the **Render Settings** drop-down menu and notice that the High End and Quick Study templates have been added to menu. Select the **Quick Study** template and then click the **Render** button.

15. When the movie is rendered, locate the output file and view it in your movie player. Go back and see if you can add another movie to the Render Queue, but this time use the **High End** template you just created. Reread the steps if you can't figure this out—but we know you can! Most After Effects artists love this template feature, because it allows them to easily set up the exact render they want for their specific needs.

16. Save your project and leave it open for the next exercise.

TIP | Output Module Templates

You create Output Module templates using the same process you use to create Render Settings templates.

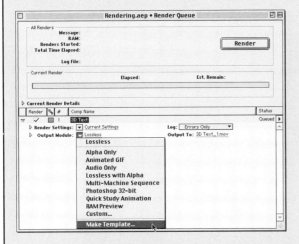

You must first add a composition to the Render Queue by choosing Composition > Make Movie. Before rendering a movie, click the Output Module drop-down menu and select Make Template.

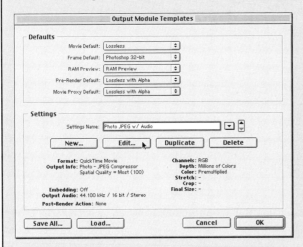

In the Output Module Templates dialog box, give your new template a name and click Edit. Select the settings you want in the Output Module Settings dialog box. Once you've selected the options, click OK to close the Output Module Settings dialog box, and then click OK again to close the Output Module Templates dialog box. Your new Output Module template will now show up in the Render Queue window in the drop-down menu for the Output Module option.

8. —————————Collecting Files

A very important automated command is available in After Effects that you will undoubtedly use frequently to help organize your work. The command is called **Collect Files**. It allows you to automatically create a copy of all the footage used for a project, along with a copy of the project file itself, and place the copies in a single folder at the location of your choice. We cannot overstate the usefulness of this command. It makes it very easy to collect all of the files for a project in the form of a copy that you can use to archive, render, or transport the project. In this exercise, you will learn to use the Collect Files command. Note that this feature can be applied to an entire project or to an individual composition.

1. Choose **File > Save**. Alternatively, press **Command+S** (Mac) or **Control+S** (Windows). This saves your project.

Note: You must save your project before using the Collect Files command. Otherwise, you'll see a prompt window notifying you that your project must be saved before collecting files and giving you the option to save the project.

2. Choose **File > Collect Files**.

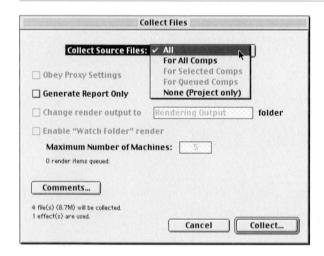

3. In the **Collect Files** dialog box, click the **Collect Source Files** option, make sure **All** is selected, and then click **Collect**.

The All option will collect the project file and all the footage items used in the project. It will also generate a report.

4. In the **Collect Files into a Folder** dialog box, navigate to the **HOT_AE_Projects** folder and click **Save**.

5. Once the collection process is complete, locate the folder and open it to see the project file and footage file copies inside.

Writing Macromedia Flash Files

One of the new features of After Effects 5.0/5.5 is its ability to write Macromedia Flash files. It's pretty easy to output After Effects movies to the Macromedia Flash file format (SWF). The question is, why would you want to use After Effects for this purpose?

Macromedia Flash supports sound, graphics, motion, and interactivity. For this reason, the scope of what you can create in Macromedia Flash is different from what you can create in After Effects. You can create an entire Web site in Macromedia Flash, with working buttons and forms for visitors to fill out.

Adobe After Effects has different capabilities and strengths. It is a stronger tool for creating bitmap motion graphics, due to its superior blending, blurring, masking, and keyframing features.

The advantage to outputting After Effects movies in the Macromedia Flash format is that you may not know how to create motion in Macromedia Flash, while you know how to do so easily in After Effects. For this reason, After Effects is attractive because you are more skilled at producing animation in it than you might be in Macromedia Flash. As well, After Effects has much more sophisticated motion control capabilities than Macromedia Flash, through the presence of keyframable effects and the independent Transform and Mask properties in the Timeline. For this reason, you might want to use After Effects because you are able to achieve a different kind of animated image than you are in Macromedia Flash.

In addition, many After Effects production companies use Macromedia Flash to create their Web sites because the format is so much more visually liberating than HTML. This is because you can produce full-screen animation and use any font you want in Macromedia Flash, which is untrue of HTML.

It's important to understand that After Effects outputs pixels, while the Macromedia SWF format for Macromedia Flash distinguishes between vectors and pixels. If you use only vectors in your Macromedia Flash work, your file sizes will be quite small and will download more quickly than if you use pixel-based artwork. Anything that includes live action, an effect, or blur in After Effects is treated as pixel-based artwork in Macromedia Flash. This almost ensures that the download will be larger if you choose to incorporate After Effects work in your Macromedia Flash work.

It is possible to output vectors only from After Effects. The key is to use vector-based artwork from Illustrator or to use solid layers and nonfeathered masks. You should also avoid effects, blurs, and live action. The truth is, however, that After Effects is best suited for pixel-based animation, and most people will want to use live action, effects, masks, and blurs freely in their After Effects work.

After Effects offers you a choice to ignore pixel-based artwork when you output in Macromedia Flash format. You can also choose to rasterize frames that contain unsupported features and add them to the SWF file as JPEG-compressed bitmaps. If you add bitmaps for each frame, however, the file size of the Flash movie will be larger, making it less efficient and less appropriate for the Web. This following exercise will walk you through some of the issues firsthand.

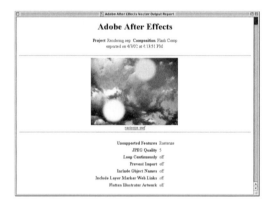

As you will learn in the upcoming exercise, you can choose to ignore unsupported SWF features. This will result in the removal of all effects as well as feathered edges from masks. This entire 300-frame animation was 24K once it was output in Macromedia SWF format.

If, instead, you chose to rasterize, the unsupported features of the Macromedia SWF format would be included (feathered masks and effects). This entire 300-frame animation was 744K once it was output in Macromedia SWF format.

Once you output in the Macromedia Flash format, you can import the resulting file into Macromedia Flash. The program accepts both SWF and QuickTlme, so you could also elect to output QuickTime format from After Effects for Macromedia Flash work. You might choose to experiment with your specific content to see whether it's better to output your After Effects work as SWF or QuickTime.

9. _____Outputting the Macromedia Flash Format

This exercise walks you through the steps to create Macromedia Flash SWF output as your final movie format. You'll see that it's quite easy, and that you are given a choice of ignoring pixel-based effects in order to write pure vectors for a smaller file size.

1. Open and play the **Flash Comp** from the **Project** window to see what it looks like. This composition includes a solid layer with feathered masks. This example was chosen because it is a good candidate for trying different settings when outputting to the Macromedia Flash (SWF) file format. Close the **Flash Comp**, but leave it selected in the Project window.

2. Choose **File > Export > Macromedia Flash (SWF)**. Unlike the other movies you have made in this chapter, the Macromedia Flash (SWF) format is supported only through Export menu, not through the Render Queue.

3. Navigate to your **HOT_AE_Projects** folder and click **Save**.

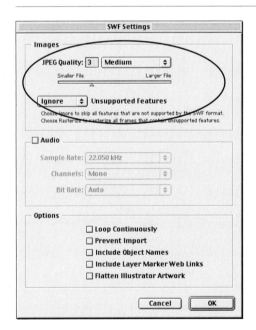

4. In the **SWF Settings** dialog box, notice the **Images** group of options. For this exercise, leave the **JPEG Quality** at the default settings.

This setting affects any pixel-based content, such as a photograph or live action footage. Choosing higher quality results in larger files.

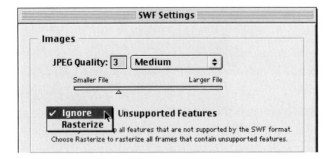

5. Click to see the **Unsupported Features** menu, and notice that you can choose to ignore unsupported features or to rasterize them. For this exercise, keep the **Ignore** setting.

The Rasterize option will convert any unsupported features as JPEG images and will increase the file size.

6. Notice the **Audio** section. In this exercise there is no audio, so leave the option off.

Audio is encoded in Flash files using MP3 compression. If you use audio in your Web project and you want to create the smallest files possible, keep the Sample Rate low (11.025 or 22.050 kHz) while still maintaining acceptable quality. Mono audio will create less data than stereo. A lower Bit Rate will also reduce file size.

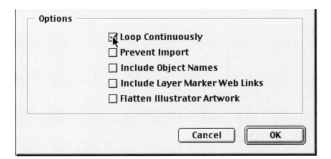

7. Click the **Loop Continuously** check box.

This option causes your movie to play over and over.

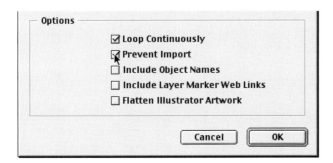

8. Click the **Prevent Import** check box.

Checking this option prevents the output SWF file from being accessed by someone else, who could then modify your content.

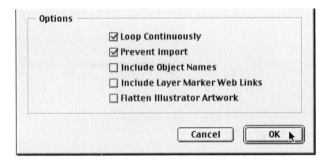

9. Take note of the remaining options, and then click **OK**.

The Include Object Names option will include the names of any layers, masks, and effects that exist in your Composition. This will increase the file size. The Include Layer Marker Web Links option allows any layers that have markers with Web links to be included and active in the Macromedia Flash output file. The Flatten Illustrator Artwork option merges Illustrator artwork. See the tip at the end of this exercise for more information about this option.

TIP | Illustrator Files

Adobe Illustrator files are vector files and are supported as an export item. However, be aware that After Effects supports only stroked paths and filled paths in CMYK or RGB color spaces.

---

10. When the export is finished, an SWF file and an HTML file will be created. Open the **HTML** file in a Web browser.

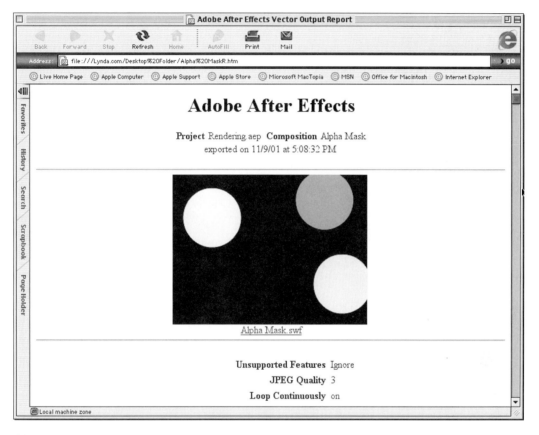

11. If you have the Flash plug-in installed in your Web browser, you will see the output playing in the HTML page. Scroll down the page and notice the report created regarding your Flash output. When you are done viewing the animation, close the browser. This HTML file is created to help you preview the final SWF file and its settings only. It is likely that you would want to bring the SWF file into Macromedia Flash or Adobe Live Motion, and thus would discard the HTML.

12. Save and close your After Effects project. You're finished with this chapter!

This was a big chapter with a lot of technical information. You can always refer to it again as you begin outputting your own projects. By completing this chapter, you have covered all the rendering basics, and you are prepared to discover each detail necessary for the type of output your projects require. As usual, the more you use the rendering tools, the more you will learn.

We hope you enjoyed working through this book, and that it turned you on to the tremendous possibilities that After Effects holds. All we can say is the more you create, the more confidence you'll build. Be sure to check out the Resource Appendix for other training and reference resources. Enjoy!

Resource Appendix

H·O·T
_____
After Effects 5.0 / 5.5

This appendix offers helpful information and resources related to After Effects, video, audio, and motion graphics.

You might be surprised to see us recommend training resources other than ours. The beauty of After Effects is that this program is so deep and vast that you will always be hungry to learn something new. Like most deep programs, there are many ways to accomplish the same tasks, many different approaches to creating content, and many experts in the field who can teach you new techniques. Dive in!

Books About After Effects

Creating Motion Graphics with After Effects
Authors: Chris and Trish Meyer
Publisher: CMP Books
ISBN: 0879306068

A great reference book for After Effects professionals, written by two of the industry's most respected experts. Especially useful if you want to learn about high-end video and film projects.

After Effects in Production
Authors: Chris and Trish Meyer
Publisher: CMP Books
ISBN: 1578200776

A project-based book with intermediate to advanced projects contributed by top After Effects luminaries.

Creative After Effects 5.0
Author: Angie Taylor
Publisher: Butterworth-Heinemann
ISBN: 0240516222

A project-based book with all exercises developed by one or two authors (offers good continuity). Covers lots of interesting techniques.

Adobe After Effects Classroom in a Book
Author: Belief
Publisher: Adobe Press
ISBN: 0201741318

Renowned motion graphics firm, Belief, takes you through a single project that lasts the entire book, culminating in an extremely complicated and advanced finale.

After Effects 5.5 Magic
Authors: Nathan Moody and Mark Christiansen
Publisher: New Riders
ISBN: 0735711445

A project-based book that features advanced techniques; especially strong on the subject of After Effects expressions.

CD-ROMs About After Effects

Learning After Effects
Authors: Bruce Heavin and Calvin Wood
Publisher: lynda.com
Time: 12 hours
http://www.lynda.com/products/videos/ae5cd/

If you liked the QuickTime movies in this book, try this CD-ROM: It has 12 hours' worth of movies to watch! It covers all the same topics as this book, in more depth in some cases.

After Effects Five-Volume Set
Author: MacAcademy
Time: 12 hours

After Effects 5.0 Six-Volume Set
Author: e-trainingdirect
http://www.e-trainingdirect.com/cdeffects.html

Videos About After Effects

What's New in After Effects 5?
Author: Brian Maffit
Publisher: Total Training
http://www.totaltraining.com
16 hours

VideoSyncrasies: The Motion Graphics Problem Solver
Authors: Chris and Trish Meyer
Publisher: Desktop Images Publishers
http://www.desktopimages.com/

After Effects Boot Camp
Author: Taz Goldstein
Publisher: Desktop Images
http://www.desktopimages.com/

Online Communities and Resources

http://www.designinmotion.com/
Design in Motion: The Art, Technology, and Business of Motion Design

http://www.creativecow.net
Professional forums

http://www.dv.com
DV magazine and DV Expo site

http://www.adobe.com
In-depth education for Web, print, and DV professionals

http://www.digitalproducer.com/aHTM/HomeSet.htm
News, tools, and techniques for content creation

http://www.wwug.com/forums/adobe_after-effects/
Adobe discussion forum for After Effects users

http://www.mgla.org/
Motion Graphics Los Angeles Users Group

http://www.2-pop.com
The Digital Filmmaker's Resource Guide

http://www.fido.se/Pages/maillist.html
After Effects discussion group

Online Resources for Audio and Video Formats

http://cit.duke.edu/resource-guides/tutorial-web-multimedia/06-audio-formats.html
Center for Instructional Technology at Duke University

http://audacity.sourceforge.net/help/tutorial_audio.htm
Guide to digital audio

http://www.kendavies.net/resources/webaudio.html
Ken Davies Music Publications

http://www.apple.com/quicktime/
QuickTime reference guide

http://www.sorenson.com/
Sorenson compression site

http://www.columbia.edu/itc/itc/webdev/design/av-intro.html
Common audio and video terminology

HTML and QuickTime Links

http://www.apple.com/quicktime/authoring/embed.html
QuickTime authoring/developer site

http://www.faculty.de.gcsu.edu/~flowney/quicktime/TS/QT4Ed/
QuickTime for educators

http://www.nd.edu/PageCreation/TipsAndHints.html
University of Notre Dame tips on WWW authoring

B

Troubleshooting Appendix

H•O•T

After Effects 5.0 / 5.5

This appendix is the first place to check if you're having a problem with any of the exercises in this book. You might also want to check the book's Web site (http://www.lynda.com/books/hot/ae5) to see if any errata have been posted. As a last resort, e-mail us with your problems— **aehot@lynda.com**. Please realize that, due to the huge amount of e-mail we receive, we cannot help you with your own After Effects projects; our support covers only issues related to the exercises in this book. Please allow 72 hours for us to get back to you with an answer (longer over holidays or weekends). For tech support on general After Effects questions, please contact Adobe or join one of the discussion groups listed in the "Online Communities and Resources" section of the Resource Appendix.

Why Don't My Timeline Frame Numbers Match the Book's?

If our steps and screen images in this book don't match the numbering system in your Timeline, here is how to change your settings.

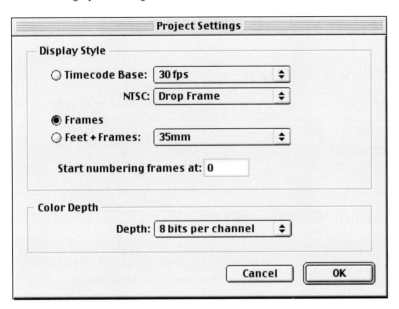

Choose **File > Project Settings** and make sure that the **Frames** option is selected and that the **Start numbering frames at** option is set to **0**.

Note: This setting was chosen for the book's exercises because they are being saved as files to your computer hard drive. If you are creating a project that will go to video, change this setting to **Timecode Base: 30fps.** If you are creating a project that will go to film, choose **Feet + Frames**. For more information on video and film settings, refer to Chapter 16, "*Rendering Final Movies*," and to the Resource Appendix.

Why Do I Get a Gray Frame at the End of a Composition?

The After Effects Timeline often shows a gray frame if you move the Time Marker to the end. This is because the Timeline often extends one frame beyond the true end of the composition. Move to the last frame by pressing the End key on the keyboard or by clicking the Last Frame button on the Time Controls palette.

Why Does My RAM Preview Stop Short?

For RAM preview to work properly, you must have enough RAM in your computer. The amount of RAM you need varies depending on how complex and large your After Effects project is. If you are on a Windows system, you may need to install more RAM. The good news is that RAM is a lot cheaper now than it's been in the past! If you are on a Macintosh using System 9 or earlier, you may also need to install more RAM.

QuickTime Isn't Working; What Should I Do?

Try going to the Apple Web site and downloading the latest QuickTime plug-in. Make sure that After Effects is not open while you do this. If you are using Windows XP, make sure you have installed the latest updates. This is accomplished by choosing **Start > All Programs > Windows Update**. There have definitely been some updates that affected QuickTime compatibility, so don't neglect to try this!

What Can I Do When the "Missing Footage" Error Message Appears?

If you double-click on the name of the missing footage inside your Project window, After Effects will let you navigate to your hard drive to locate the missing footage.

Why Is My Movie Playback Jerky?

When you play a QuickTime movie on your hard drive, it will be jerky if you don't have a fast enough processor or enough RAM. If this is a movie you created from After Effects, you might want to render it again using a higher compression method. **Tip:** Try using the Sorenson or Graphics compression types and a lower frame rate with fewer keyframes.

Why Do I Get an "Untitled" Warning?

When you open a project file created in After Effects 5.0 (which is the case for all of the project files for this book), you will encounter the following warning.

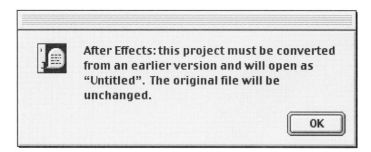

Click OK, and the project will open as originally intended, except that it will appear as an untitled project until you save it. We chose to leave all the projects in After Effects 5.0 so that readers who had either After Effects 5.0 or 5.5 could use this book.

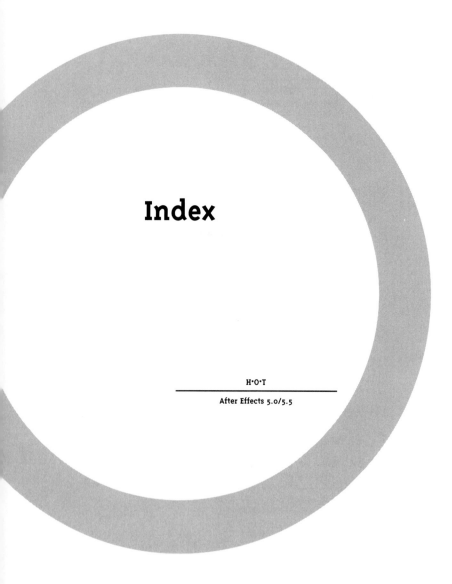

Index

H•O•T

After Effects 5.0/5.5

Symbols

A

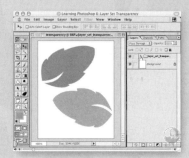

CD-ROM LICENSE AGREEMENT

THIS SOFTWARE LICENSE AGREEMENT CONSTITUTES AN AGREEMENT BETWEEN YOU AND, LYNDA.COM, LLC. . YOU SHOULD CAREFULLY READ THE FOLLOWING TERMS AND CONDITIONS BEFORE OPENING THIS ENVELOPE. COPYING THIS SOFTWARE TO YOUR MACHINE, BREAKING THE SEAL, OR OTHERWISE RE-MOVING OR USING THE SOFTWARE INDICATES YOUR ACCEPTANCE OF THESE TERMS AND CONDITIONS. IF YOU DO NOT AGREE TO BE BOUND BY THE PROVISIONS OF THIS LICENSE AGREEMENT, YOU SHOULD PROMPTLY DELETE THE SOFTWARE FROM YOUR MACHINE.

TERMS AND CONDITIONS:

1. GRANT OF LICENSE. In consideration of payment of the License Fee, which was a part of the price you paid for this product, LICENSOR grants to you (the "Licensee") a non-exclusive right to use and display this copy of a Software program, along with any updates or upgrade releases of the Software for which you have paid (all parts and elements of the Software as well as the Software as a whole are hereinafter referred to as the "Software") on a single computer only (i.e., with a single CPU) at a single location, all as more particularly set forth and limited below. LICENSOR reserves all rights not expressly granted to you as Licensee in this License Agreement.

2. OWNERSHIP OF SOFTWARE. The license granted herein is not a sale of the original Software or of any copy of the Software. As Licensee, you own only the rights to use the Software as described herein and the magnetic or other physical media on which the Software is originally or subsequently recorded or fixed. LICENSOR retains title and owner-ship of the Software recorded on the original disk(s), as well as title and ownership of any subsequent copies of the Software irrespective of the form of media on or in which the Software is recorded or fixed. This license does not grant you any intellectual or other propri-etary or other rights of any nature what-soever in the Software.

3. USE RESTRICTIONS. As Licensee, you may use the Software only as expressly author-ized in this License Agreement under the terms of paragraph 4. You may phy-sically transfer the Software from one computer to another provided that the Software is used on only a single computer at any one time. You may not: (i) electronically transfer the Software from one computer to another over a network; (ii) make the Software available through a time-sharing service, network of computers, or other multiple user arrangement; (iii) distribute copies of the Software or related written materials to any third party, whether for sale or otherwise; (iv) modify, adapt, translate, reverse engineer, decompile, disassemble, or prepare any deriva-tive work based on the Software or any element thereof; (v) make or distribute, whether for sale or otherwise, any hard copy or printed version of any of the Software nor any portion thereof nor any work of yours containing the Software or any component thereof; (vi) use any of the Software nor any of its components in any other work.

8. THIS IS WHAT YOU CAN AND CANNOT DO WITH THE SOFTWARE. Even though in the preceding paragraph and elsewhere LICENSOR has restricted your use of the Software, the following is the only thing you can do with the Software and the various elements of the Software:DUCKS IN A ROW ARTWORK: THE ARTWORK CONTAINED ON THIS CD-ROM MAY NOT BE USED IN ANY MANNER WHATSOEVER OTHER THAN TO VIEW THE SAME ON YOUR COMPUTER, OR POST TO YOUR PERSONAL, NON-COMMER-CIAL WEB SITE FOR EDUCATIONAL PURPOSES ONLY. THIS MATERIAL IS SUBJECT TO ALL OF THE RESTRICTION PROVISIONS OF THIS SOFTWARE LICENSE. SPECIFI-CALLY BUT NOT IN LIMITATION OF THESE RESTRICTIONS, YOU MAY NOT DISTRIB-UTE, RESELL OR TRANSFER THIS PART OF THE SOFTWARE DESIGNATED AS "CLUTS" NOR ANY OF YOUR DESIGN OR OTHER WORK CONTAINING ANY OF THE SOFTWARE DESIGNATED AS "DUCKS IN A ROW ARTWORK" NOR ANY OF YOUR DESIGN OR OTHER WORK CONTAINING ANY SUCH "DUCKS IN A ROW ARTWORK," ALL AS MORE PARTICULARLY RESTRICTED IN THE WITHIN SOFTWARE LICENSE.

5. COPY RESTRICTIONS. The Software and accompanying written materials are protected under United States copyright laws. Unauthorized copying and/or distribution of the Software and/or the related written materials is expressly forbidden. You may be held legally responsi-ble for any copyright infringement that is caused, directly or indirectly, by your failure to abide by the terms of this License Agreement and if the software is not otherwise copy protected, you may make one copy of the Software for backup purposes only. The copyright notice and any other proprietary notices which were included in the original Software must be reproduced and included on any such backup copy.

6. TRANSFER RESTRICTIONS. The license herein granted is personal to you, the Licensee. You may not transfer the Software nor any of its components or elements to anyone else, nor may you sell, resell, lease, loan, sublicense, assign, or otherwise dispose of the Software nor any of its components or elements without the express written consent of LICENSOR, which con-sent may be granted or withheld at LICENSOR's sole discretion.

7. TERMINATION. The license herein granted hereby will remain in effect until terminated. This license will terminate automatically without further notice from LICENSOR in the event of the violation of any of the provisions hereof. As Licensee, you agree that upon such termina-tion you will promptly destroy any and all copies of the Software which remain in your posses-sion and, upon request, will certify to such destruction in writing to LICENSOR.

8. LIMITATION AND DISCLAIMER OF WARRANTIES. a) THE SOFTWARE AND RELATED WRITTEN MATERIALS, INCLUDING ANY INSTRUCTIONS FOR USE, ARE PROVIDED ON AN "AS IS" BASIS, WITHOUT WARRANTY OF ANY KIND, EXPRESS OR IMPLIED. THIS DISCLAIMER OF WARRANTY EXPRESSLY IN-CLUDES, BUT IS NOT LIMITED TO, ANY IMPLIED WARRANTIES OF MERCHANTABILITY AND/OR OF FIT-NESS FOR A PARTICULAR PURPOSE. NO WARRANTY OF ANY KIND IS MADE AS TO WHETHER OR NOT THIS SOFT-WARE INFRINGES UPON ANY RIGHTS OF ANY OTHER THIRD PARTIES. NO ORAL OR WRITTEN INFORMATION GIVEN BY LICEN-SOR, ITS SUPPLIERS, DISTRIBUTORS, DEALERS, EMPLOYEES, OR AGENTS, SHALL CREATE OR OTHERWISE ENLARGE THE SCOPE OF ANY WARRANTY HEREUNDER. LICENSEE ASSUMES THE ENTIRE RISK AS TO THE QUALITY AND THE PERFOR-MANCE OF SUCH SOFTWARE. SHOULD THE SOFTWARE PROVE DEFECTIVE, YOU, AS LICENSEE (AND NOT LICENSOR, ITS SUPPLIERS, DISTRIBU-TORS, DEALERS OR AGENTS), ASSUME THE ENTIRE COST OF ALL NECESSARY CORRECTION, SERVIC-ING, OR REPAIR. b) LICENSOR warrants the disk(s) on which this copy of the Software is recorded or fixed to be free from defects in materials and workmanship, under normal use and service, for a period of ninety (90) days from the date of delivery as evidenced by a copy of the applicable receipt. LICENSOR hereby limits the duration of any implied warranties with respect to the disk(s) to the duration of the express warranty. This limited warranty shall not apply if the disk(s) have been damaged by unreasonable use, accident, negligence, or by any other causes unrelated to defective materials or workmanship. c) LICENSOR does not war-rant that the functions contained in the Software will be uninterrupted or error free and Licensee is encouraged to test the Software for Licensee's intended use prior to placing any reliance thereon. All risk of the use of the Software will be on you, as Licensee. d) THE LIM-ITED WARRANTY SET FORTH ABOVE GIVES YOU SPECIFIC LEGAL RIGHTS AND YOU MAY ALSO HAVE OTHER RIGHTS WHICH VARY FROM STATE TO STATE. SOME STATES DO NOT ALLOW THE LIMITATION OR EXCLUSION OF IMPLIED WARRANTIES OR OF INCIDENTAL OR CONSEQUENTIAL DAMAGES, SO THE LIMITATIONS AND EXCLUSIONS CONCERNING THE SOFTWARE AND RELATED WRITTEN MATERIALS SET FORTH ABOVE MAY NOT APPLY TO YOU.

9. LIMITATION OF REMEDIES. LICENSOR's entire liability and Licensee's exclusive remedy shall be the replacement of any disk(s) not meeting the limited warranty set forth in Section 8 above which is returned to LICENSOR with a copy of the applic-able receipt within the war-ranty period. Any replacement disk(s)will be warranted for the remainder of the original war-ranty period or thirty (30) days, whichever is longer.

10. LIMITATION OF LIABILITY. IN NO EVENT WILL LICENSOR, OR ANYONE ELSE INVOLVED IN THE CREATION, PRODUCTION, AND/OR DELIVERY OF THIS SOFTWARE PRODUCT BE LIABLE TO LICENSEE OR ANY OTHER PER-SON OR ENTITY FOR ANY DIRECT, INDIRECT, OR OTHER DAMAGES, INCLUDING, WITHOUT LIMITATION, ANY INTERRUPTION OF SERVICES, LOST PROFITS, LOST SAVINGS, LOSS OF DATA, OR ANY OTHER CONSEQUENTIAL, INCIDEN-TAL, SPECIAL, OR PUNITIVE DAMAGES, ARISING OUT OF THE PURCHASE, USE, INABILITY TO USE, OR OPERATION OF THE SOFTWARE, EVEN IF LICENSOR OR ANY AUTHORIZED LICENSOR DEALER HAS BEEN ADVISED OF THE POSSIBILITY OF SUCH DAMAGES. BY YOUR USE OF THE SOFTWARE, YOU ACKNOWLEDGE THAT THE LIMITATION OF LIABILITY SET FORTH IN THIS LICENSE WAS THE BASIS UPON WHICH THE SOFTWARE WAS OFFERED BY LICENSOR AND YOU ACKNOWLEDGE THAT THE PRICE OF THE SOFTWARE LICENSE WOULD BE HIGHER IN THE ABSENCE OF SUCH LIMITATION. SOME STATES DO NOT ALLOW THE LIMITATION OR EXCLUSION OF LIABILITY FOR INCIDENTAL OR CONSEQUENTIAL DAMAGES SO THE ABOVE LIMITATIONS AND EXCLUSIONS MAY NOT APPLY TO YOU.

11. UPDATES. LICENSOR, at its sole discretion, may periodically issue updates of the Software which you may receive upon request and payment of the applicable update fee in effect from time to time and in such event, all of the provisions of the within License Agreement shall apply to such updates.

12. EXPORT RESTRICTIONS. Licensee agrees not to export or re-export the Soft-ware and accompanying documentation (or any copies thereof) in violation of any applicable U.S. laws or regulations.

13. ENTIRE AGREEMENT. YOU, AS LICENSEE, ACKNOWLEDGE THAT: (i) YOU HAVE READ THIS ENTIRE AGREEMENT AND AGREE TO BE BOUND BY ITS TERMS AND CONDITIONS; (ii) THIS AGREEMENT IS THE COMPLETE AND EXCLUSIVE STATEMENT OF THE UNDERSTANDING BETWEEN THE PARTIES AND SUPERSEDES ANY AND ALL PRIOR ORAL OR WRITTEN COMMUNICATIONS RELATING TO THE SUBJECT MATTER HEREOF; AND (iii) THIS AGREEMENT MAY NOT BE MODIFIED, AMENDED, OR IN ANY WAY ALTERED EXCEPT BY A WRITING SIGNED BY BOTH YOURSELF AND AN OFFICER OR AUTHORIZED REPRESENTATIVE OF LICENSOR.

14. SEVERABILITY. In the event that any provision of this License Agreement is held to be illegal or otherwise unenforceable, such provision shall be deemed to have been deleted from this License Agreement while the remaining provisions of this License Agreement shall be unaffected and shall continue in full force and effect.

15. GOVERNING LAW. This License Agreement shall be governed by the laws of the State of California applicable to agreements wholly to be performed therein and of the United States of America, excluding that body of the law related to conflicts of law. This License Agreement shall not be governed by the United Nations Convention on Contracts for the International Sale of Goods, the application of which is expressly excluded. No waiver of any breach of the provisions of this License Agreement shall be deemed a waiver of any other breach of this License Agreement.

16. RESTRICTED RIGHTS LEGEND. Use, duplication, or disclosure by the Government is subject to restrictions as set forth in subparagraph (c)(1)(ii) of the Rights in Technical Data and Computer Software clause at 48 CFR § 252.227-7013 and DFARS § 252.227-7013 or subparagraphs (c) (1) and (c)(2) of the Commercial Computer Software-Restricted Rights at 48 CFR § 52.227.19, as applicable. Contractor/manufacturer: LICENSOR: LYNDA.COM, LLC, c/o PEACHPIT PRESS, 1249 Eighth Street, Berkeley, CA 94710.